AMERICAN WOMEN PLAYWRIGHTS
1964–1989
A Research Guide
and Annotated Bibliography

Christy Gavin

GARLAND PUBLISHING, INC. • NEW YORK & LONDON
1993

Library of Congress Cataloging-in-Publication Data

Gavin, Christy, 1952–
    American women playwrights, 1964–1989 : a research guide and
annotated bibliography / Christy Gavin.
        p.   cm. — (Garland reference library of the humanities ; vol.
879)
    Includes indexes.
    ISBN 0-8240-3046-X (alk. paper)
    1. American drama—Women authors—History and criticism—
Bibliography. 2. Women and literature—United States—History—20th
century—Bibliography. 3. American drama—20th century—History
and criticism—Bibliography. 4. American drama—Women authors—
Bibliography. 5. American drama—20th century—Bibliography.
I. Title. II. Series.
Z1231.D7G38   1993
[PS338.W6]
016.812'54099287—dc20   92–42768
                                                                CIP

Printed on acid-free, 250-year-life paper
Manufactured in the United States of America

Contents

Preface   iii

Contemporary American Women Playwrights 1964-1989:
    A Bibliographical Essay   3

Contemporary Women Playwrights and Feminist Theatre:
    General Discussions   24

Individual Playwrights   74

Indices
    Author Index   481
    List of Multicultural Playwrights   492

Preface

In its January 1990 "Best of the Decade" issue, *Time Magazine* identified its choices for the most "outstanding" theatrical plays of the 1980s. Ten plays were selected. With the lone exception of August Wilson, an African American, all were written by white males. Interestingly, *Time* ignored three plays by women that won Pulitzer Prizes for drama during the 1980s: Beth Henley's *Crimes of the Heart* (1981), Marsha Norman's *'night Mother* (1983), and Wendy Wasserstein's *The Heidi Chronicles* (1989). *Time's* lack of recognition of the contributions of women dramatists underscores the fact that women playwrights continue to write and produce in relative obscurity.

Because of the invisibility of these women, the theatrical community, academia, and the general public remain ignorant of the extent of the achievements of female dramatists over the past thirty years. It is hoped that this book, the first of its kind to document the work and critical reception of women writing drama since the early 1960s, will enlighten scholars, instructors, critics, students, and the theatrical community as to the accomplishments of contemporary American women dramatists and encourage systematic study of their achievements.*

This book focuses on American women writers of full-length plays who have demonstrated a sustained record of achievement and who have produced at least one play on Broadway, Off Broadway, or Off-Off Broadway from the early 1960s through 1989. For the purposes of this book, an American playwright is defined as one residing in the United States over an extended period of years.

Arrangement and Form

The book is arranged in three sections. Section one is a bibliographical essay assessing the key studies related to contemporary women playwrights and feminist theatre. The essay concludes with suggestions for new areas of critical and historical investigation. Section two provides an annotated list of general discussions of contemporary American women dramatists and feminist theatre. The third section, arranged alphabetically by individual playwright, lists selected plays, playscripts, profiles, interviews, press reviews, preview articles, and critical studies. The dates of production for plays listed generally are for the earliest Broadway or Off Broadway staging. If there was no New York production, I have listed the earliest staging I could verify. Plays a playwright directed but did not write have been excluded. An index lists authors of annotated entries, including authors discussed in the bibliographical essay.

Live theatre presents unique challenges to the researcher. Other disciplines have sophisticated access tools that allow the researcher to gain easy access to the primary and secondary literature. However, the bibliographic control of information in theatre arts is chaotic. Theatre arts lacks a comprehensive access tool that indexes production reviews, critical studies, interviews, biographies in performing arts and allied magazines and journals. Thus deprived of a systematic research approach, the researcher must employ a variety of tools and methods to acquire information about individual plays and playwrights.

To gather the material for this book, pertinent retrospective bibliographies were consulted as well as several on-line public access catalogs including OCLC, ORION, and MELVYL. Because so much of the information on these playwrights is concentrated in popular and scholarly periodical literature, several periodical indexes and computerized databases were searched. These include: *MLA Bibliography, Humanities Index, Reader's Guide to Periodical Literature, Access: The Supplementary Index to Periodicals, Alternative Press Index, Arts & Humanities Citation Index, California Periodicals Index, Chicano Periodicals Index, Hispanic American Periodicals Index, Index to Periodicals By and About Blacks,* and *Magazine Index.* To obtain reviews of plays produced in major cities, general newspaper indexes such as the *National Newspaper Index, Newsearch, Newspaper Abstracts,* and *Black Newspapers Index* were consulted as well as the indexes to individual newspapers: *New York Times, Christian Science Monitor, Los Angeles Times, Washington Post, Wall Street Journal, Times-Picayune, San Francisco Chronicle, Chicago Tribune, Boston Globe,* and *Philadelphia Inquirer.*

Preface

I am deeply indebted to the encouragement and the editorial assistance given to me by Camille Gavin and for the valuable comments from Anita Dupratt, theatre director at California State University, Bakersfield. I am also grateful to Lorna Frost, who performed miracles in procuring items from other libraries. The following theatre organizations contributed a great deal of information to this book: New Dramatists, Women's Project of the American Place Theatre, Actors Theatre of Louisville, Omaha Magic Theatre, South Coast Repertory, Los Angeles Theater Center, Los Angeles Theatre Works, Alternate Roots, and the Association of Hispanic Arts Inc. Finally, I owe thanks to the librarians and staffs at the University of California, Los Angeles, University of California, Berkeley, and the University of Southern California.

*Brenda Coven's bibliography *American Women Dramatists of the 20th Century* (1982), however, does include some of the earlier dramatists such as Maria Irene Fornes, Roslyn Drexler, and Megan Terry.

American Women Playwrights
1964–1989

Contemporary American Women Playwrights 1964-1989

A Bibliographical Essay

Canon of Contemporary Women's Drama

A viable canon of the primary and secondary works of female playwrights depends on the availability of the texts and productions of their plays. Scholars and theatre critics cannot assess the work of any playwright unless they have access to published texts of their plays. The publication of playscripts by women is crucial to building a canon of women's plays not only for critical purposes but also to establish a dramatic tradition for the playwrights themselves. As theatre scholar Margaret Lamb points out, "research should be done because . . . artistic work comes out of a tradition, and women may need models to know it's possible" (Lamb, 48, see item 57). Unlike their male counterparts, women have no two-thousand-year dramatic tradition. They lack a body of material that contains dramas written about women's experiences from a woman's vantage point. Marsha Norman once commented, "I did not know that writers for the theater were from Kentucky or were women, except of course for Lillian Hellman. Lillian Hellman was it . . . she was my only indication that this kind of life was possible" (Betsko, 341, see item 9).

But the women's liberation movement of the 1960s gave women the impetus to push beyond their expected roles in society. In raising the consciousness of women, the message from the movement was that experiences of women are valid. Consequently, many women chose to "go public" on stage, using theatre as a forum to express their feelings of anger, joy, oppression, and freedom. Women recognized the theatre's twofold potential of making others aware of the oppression of women and as a catalyst for change. As Patti Gillespie states, "In theatre, women found an instrument for symbolic protest which permits the simultaneous display of the personal and the political" (Gillespie, 5, see item 39).

The first generation of women dramatists working in the experimental theatre during the 1960s and to a certain extent those of the early to mid-1970s were nearly invisible to most critics and producers who looked upon them as angry feminists. And because the plays were unnoticed, they failed to attract large audiences and, in turn, were ignored by the publishing houses, which traditionally choose plays based on their potential sales and their appeal to professional, amateur, and summer stock companies.

A break for women playwrights came in the mid-1960s in the form of new playwrights' programs or festivals organized by a small number of theatre groups. The purpose of these festivals was to discover new talent and to assist novice playwrights in the mounting of their plays. These theatre groups have excellent reputations. As a result, their productions attract major New York critics whose reviews generate additional visibility for women playwrights, many of whom have seen their plays move to even more prominent houses on or off Broadway.

The Women's Project at the American Place Theater, created in 1978 by Julia Miles, has had tremendous impact. Miles organized the project because "approximately 7% of non-profit plays produced were written by women." By 1989, the Women's Project had produced 38 new plays by female dramatists, including Lavonne Mueller, Maria Irene Fornes, Marlene Meyer, Kathleen Collins, and Joan Schenkar. Equally important, it has published many of their plays, including four anthologies.

The festivals of other theatre groups also have been instrumental in staging plays by previously unknown women dramatists. Jon Jory's program at Actors Theatre of Louisville introduced Marsha Norman, whose 'night Mother premiered at Louisville, ultimately moved to Broadway's Golden Theatre, and won the Pulitzer Prize, as well as Beth Henley, Jane Martin, Jane Chambers, and Megan Terry. Other major regional theatres that have produced plays by women are the O'Neill Theater Centers National Playwrights Conference, Tyrone Guthrie Theatre, Yale Repertory Theatre, Mark Taper Forum, and Long Wharf.

Close scrutiny of the majority of scholarly surveys of American theatre and play anthologies published since the 1960s reveals that women writers continue to be underrepresented. Theatre history surveys and textbooks written in the 1970s and 1980s devote little or no space to the achievements of individual contemporary women playwrights or to the phenomenon of the feminist theatre movement. Brockett's well-

known textbook on theatre, representative of many such historical
treatments of the theatre, provides very little discussion of individual
women dramatists and/or feminist theatre (Brockett, 1982).
Women playwrights are equally invisible in the majority of
anthologies of contemporary plays. A glaring example is theatre critic
Ross Wetzsteon's *The Obie Winners; The Best of Off Broadway*, an
anthology of ten plays, all recipients of the *Village Voice's* Obie
award. Each of the ten was written by a white male. Wetzsteon's
exclusion of female dramatists is striking given the fact that in his
introductory remarks he recognizes the contributions of several female
playwrights to the avant-garde theatre movement. He fails to provide a
rationale for inclusion of the selected plays, but one thing is certain: he
did not exclude women on the basis of their not having won Obies—
between 1958 and 1979, playwrights Gretchen Cryer, Roslyn Drexler,
Adrienne Kennedy, Rochelle Owens, Susan Miller, Megan Terry, and
Maria Irene Fornes were Obie winners.

Gaps left by these anthologizers gradually are being filled by the
publication of collections devoted solely to plays by women. The first
to appear was Sullivan and Hatch's *Plays by and About Women*
(1973). It includes plays by Megan Terry and Alice Childress. Other
anthologies soon followed: Harriet Kriegel's *Women in Drama: An
Anthology* (1975), Honor Moore's *The New Women's Theatre: Ten
Plays by Women* (1979), Susan La Tempa's *New Plays by Women*
(1979), Rachel France's *A Century of Plays by American Women*
(1979), Julia Miles' *Womenswork: Five New Plays from the Women's
Project* (1989), Michelle Wander's *Plays By Women* (1982), Margaret
Wilkerson's *9 Plays by Black Women* (1986), Francoise Kourilsky's
Plays by Women (1988), Sandra Eagleton's *Women in Literature: Life
Stages Through Stories, Poems and Plays* (1987). In the future more
anthologists should seek a better balance of plays written by men and
women.

Response to the Canon: The Press and the Scholars

Paralleling the increased accessibility of women's plays through
publication of playscripts is the slow but steady accumulation of
criticism of the work of contemporary women dramatists. These
critical assessments emanate from two sectors: theatre critics who
review staged productions of plays and scholars who analyze the plays
as literary texts.

Critical Response from the Press

One of the first indications that the New York theatrical community was taking notice of women playwrights as a viable force came in 1973, when the *New York Times,* piqued that so few women were writing for the theatre, asked "Where Are the Women Playwrights?" (see item 103). The *Times* invited several successful women dramatists, including Gretchen Cryer, Adrienne Kennedy, Rochelle Owens, among others, to reflect upon the question.

Six years later, theatre critic Mel Gussow wrote a series of three articles for the *New York Times* (see item 48) on what he perceived as a "proliferation" of women playwrights. Gussow's choice of playwrights implies that he favors those who adhere to the tenets of mainstream theatre. He views these particular playwrights as moving beyond "women's subjects [and] indulg[ing] in the politics of feminism to writing about adolescence and adulthood, sex, and psychological and sociological problems . . . and unlikely areas as polar expeditions, the prison systems and men in battle." Clearly, Gussow's preference for female dramatists who deal in realism reflects his and other critics' discomfort with the themes being tackled in the experimental theatre of the sixties and seventies. As many women in contemporary theatre have pointed out, drama critics, most of whom are male, have contributed greatly to the repression and suppression of women's creative efforts. Playwright Kathleen Betsko observes, "It is the critics who police the stage for unacceptable behavior under the guise of aesthetic judgment. Since women are still more restricted and less valuable than men in the theater—as in society at large—the possibilities and actuality of stepping out of line are higher and the consequences more cruel than for men" (Betsko, 461, see item 9). Unfortunately, the critics, who tend to represent the values of a patriarchal society, have in many instances ignored, misinterpreted, and ridiculed the work of women playwrights. By allowing themselves to become more receptive to feminist perspectives, it is hoped that such critics will begin to view plays by women in a new light and to find "women's subjects" as stageworthy as those topics that inspire male writers.

Although Gussow's articles thrust women dramatists into the arena, they provoked strong reactions among women theatre artists. Using *Performing Arts Journal* as their platform, several artists responded to Gussow's 1983 article, which was the last in the series mentioned above. Julia Miles, director of the Women's Project, believes that Gussow exaggerates the "proliferation" of women playwrights. Collette Brooks voices the concern of many that Gussow concentrated on mainstream dramatists who write plays grounded in realism and virtually ignored the contributions of experimental theatre artists such as Megan Terry, Rochelle Owens, Rosalyn Drexler, Julie Bovasso, Adrienne Kennedy, Maria Irene Fornes, and Alice Childress. Roberta Sklar, writer and director, expressed disappointment at Gussow's omission of women's contributions to collaborative theatre, which she sees as a significant innovation and a major departure from traditional male-oriented theatre.

Response from Academia: Feminist Theatre Scholars

As mentioned earlier, critical assessment of the works of individual female playwrights and feminist theatre has been slow in developing, lagging behind the research in other areas, especially in literature and the visual arts. As Tracy C. Davis states in her historiographical essay on the theatre, "[w]hether because of political conviction, coincidence, or lethargy, feminist theatre historians have yet seriously to attempt an all-embracing manifesto or methodological design to research" (Davis, 59). Others outside of feminist scholarship have also commented on the relative inactivity. Walter Meserve, in his 1987 bibliographic essay for *American Literary Scholarship*, comments "[p]erhaps the time has come for serious investigation as scholars become more aware of the neglect and begin to show a concern for women's work on the stage."

The reasons why feminist theatre scholarship has been slow in assuming critical responsibility for the canon of women's plays are complex. Meserve finds that "the prejudice against drama in general combined with past attitudes toward women writers has proved to be a substantial barrier to scholarship." Nancy S. Reinhardt maintains that conservatism in the theatre inhibits critical response to contemporary female dramatists: "Theatre . . . is the most traditional and conservative member of the consortium of dramatic and related media arts. Aware, perhaps, of this strongly conservative tradition, theatre historians and critics have been slow to react to the latest critical trends." Observing that theatre scholars have lagged far behind film scholars in the examination of women's role in theatre, Reinhardt cites three reasons. First, the cinematic arts, a new art form, do not "carry around centuries of critical baggage" and tend to be more receptive to new critical viewpoints and methodologies. Second, sexism in the theatre is more overt making its creators more vulnerable to criticism from feminist scholars. And third, theatre is a much more communal art form than film and thus more dependent on the male-dominated public and social arena for its creation and production (Reinhardt, see item 85).

Despite the comparatively slow development of feminist dramatic
theory and methodology, significant works in the past fifteen years
reflect a growing canon that will advance the analysis and interpretation
of plays written by women. In developing critical and methodological
contructs, theatre scholars have not been reticent in borrowing from
others. They have appropriated the works of such notable feminist
writers as Kate Millet and Betty Friedan, key British and French authors
including Michelle Wandor and Helene Cixous, theorists of the
cinematic arts, especially the writings of Teresa de Lauretis, and major
feminist scholars who have contributed to revisionist theories and
interpretations for the literary arts, the most prominent being Elaine
Showalter and Susan Gubar. Furthermore, like their literary
counterparts, feminist theatre writers are incorporating the tenets of
deconstruction, semiotics, and postmodernism in addition to relevant
discourses in other disciplines including anthropology, sociology, and
political science.

Scholars began grappling with the problems of defining and
categorizing feminist theatre in the mid-'70s. One of the first
discussions on feminist theatre was by Linda Killian, who defines it "as
theater written by women which tries to explore the female psyche,
women's place in society and women's potential." Her definition was
subsequently expanded with a political perspective by Patti Gillespie.
In her article in the *Quarterly Journal of Speech* (see item 39) Gillespie
argues that all feminist theatre is political, describing such expositions
as "rhetorical enterprises . . . their primary aim is action, not art."
Moreover, underlying all feminist dramas, Gillespie asserts, is the
assumption that women are the oppressed and that theatre can provide a
vehicle to pierce the oppression and serve to change the status quo.

Janet Brown also approaches the subject from a rhetorical
perspective in her book *Feminist Theatre* (see item 12), the first book-
length examination of drama grounded in feminism. Brown offers a
definition of feminist drama and develops a critical methodology which
she applies to five plays, including *The Bed Was Full* (Roslyn
Drexler), *In the Boom Boom Room* (David Rabe), *Wine in the
Wilderness* (Alice Childress), *Birth and After Birth* (Tina Howe), and
*for colored girls who have considered suicide/ when the rainbow is
enuf* (Ntozake Shange). Brown's exploration hinges on the "feminine
impulse," which she defines as "a woman's struggle for autonomy
against an oppressive, sexist society." In her analysis of these plays
and collaborations of selected theatre groups, Brown develops a
theoretical construct based on Kenneth Burke's literary theory in which
he argues that all fictive works have a "rhetorical or persuasive motive."

For a play to qualify as feminist Brown contends, it must have as its "central rhetorical motive" a woman grappling for independence within the patriarchal society. Rosemary Curb holds that Brown's construct "seems more a limitation than an illuminating tool of critical analysis. Choosing a formalistic approach rather than a feminist one, Brown treats her material with the same chilly academic patriarchal objectivity as medical students witnessing the dissection of a corpse." (Curb, 104). Curb also questions Brown's choice of plays, noting that they seem to ignore the myriad of "admittedly feminist plays" such as those by playwrights Megan Terry, Maria Irene Fornes, Adrienne Kennedy, Myrna Lamb, and others. Curb also finds it perplexing that Brown fails to discuss the criteria used in selecting the five dramas assessed in *Feminist Theatre.*

Like Janet Brown, Dinah Leavitt, in her 1980 examination of feminist theatre, *Feminist Theatre Groups,* also attempts to clarify the genre but does not attempt to formulate a theoretical construct. Rather than restricting a definition of feminist theatre with simplistic labels, Leavitt points out that feminist theatre is more than merely a reaction to male-constructed theatre, its nature being far more complex. She extrapolates some common elements of feminist groups, identifying four Minneapolis-based theatre groups for her examination. Leavitt concludes that although these groups are highly individual in their feminist ideologies, nearly all "agree that all art is politics." Gladys Crane comments in her review of the book that Leavitt's "methodology and the research materials are strong and competently handled," but the study is limited because its assumptions are primarily based on four theatre groups operating in the same geographical area (Crane, 274).

Closely following the books by Janet Brown and Dinah Leavitt is Judith Olauson's *The American Woman Playwright: A View of Criticism and Characterization* (see item 78). Olauson focuses on women playwrights who were active over a forty-year period (1930-1970) and who have created roles that deviated from the conventional one-dimensional, submissive women characters traditionally portrayed in the past. Unfortunately, Olauson's work fails to deepen one's understanding of individual women playwrights and the feminist influence upon their works or theatre in general. Olauson contends that her book will "explore the problem of the apparent lack of both women-centered material and theory." But as Janet Brown, author of *Feminist Theatre* argues, Olauson "scarcely addresse[s]" her stated purpose and the book's utility extends only to "its useful summary of commercially successful plays by women." (Brown, 324). Further, Olauson's insubstantial analysis is directly linked to her failure to incorporate major studies on her subjects. In short, Olauson's work did little to enhance or advance an understanding of contemporary women playwrights. Fortunately, this is not the case with the book-length studies published in the mid to late 1980s, which continued to expand upon the work pioneered by Brown and Leavitt. Two such works are Helen Keyssar's *Feminist Theatre* (see item 54) and Elizabeth Natalle's *Feminist Theatre: A Study in Persuasion* (see item 76). Although both explore feminist theatre and its intimate relationship with the feminist movement, they differ in approach and methodology. Natalle asserts "some of the artistic differences can be minimized and a definition offered" by approaching the problem from a "rhetorical perspective," a concept she borrows from Gillespie and Brown. Natalle's rhetorical analysis of twenty plays shows how feminist theatre collectives use dramatic strategies to persuade the spectators to reconsider their roles in relationship to the patriarchal system, the family, and other institutions. The major purpose, concludes Natalle, of these collectives is to reinforce the beliefs of the respective organization and its audience. In other words, these theatre groups are primarily interested in "strengthening and supporting" beliefs rather than persuading audiences to change their beliefs. Natalle says her analyses are based on Aristotle's *Rhetoric* and are not meant to "delineate a feminist dramatic aesthetic." However, employing Aristotle's model, Natalle reasons, is appropriate when examining works from a rhetorical rather than a theatrical perspective. Although Karen Laughlin finds Natalle's examination of individual plays illuminating, she feels the author's application of the Aristotelian model "seems rather mechanical and is not always as central to the discussions of the plays as her methodological statements suggest" (Laughlin, 123).

Whereas Natalle bases her arguments and conclusions on the examination of theatre collectives and their relationship to the feminist movement, Helen Keyssar bases her conclusions on the analysis of the works of individual feminist dramatists. Keyssar attempts to establish a definition of a feminist aesthetic based upon the dramatic strategy of "transformations." She contends feminist drama has shifted away from the traditional "recognition scene," where the protagonist comes to know himself or herself and reveal the knowledge to others. Instead, feminist theatre artists are moving away from conventional ego-centered drama and toward the "recognition of others and a concomitant transformation of the self and the world" through transformational drama. According to Keyssar, feminist playwrights have rejected the recognition scene because it is identified with the traditional, male-oriented theatre and regard it as subverting possibilities for a true metamorphosis of self and society. Laughlin, however, criticizes Keyssar for her generalization "that *all* traditional theatre utilizes the recognition structure" which, she says, is "in keeping with the other sweeping generalizations that occasionally mar her otherwise sound commentary" (Laughlin, 120). Although Keyssar's and Natalle's books contribute to the small but growing canon of feminist theatre criticism, it is unfortunate that neither incorporates the ideas of leading feminist theater writers such as Michelle Wandor, Gillian Hanna, Helene Cixous, and feminist theorists working in the literary and visual arts.

However, theatre writers Sue-Ellen Case and Jill Dolan cannot be accused of writing in a vacuum. Both Case's *Feminism and Theatre* (see item 19) and Dolan's *The Feminist Spectator as Critic* (see item 28) reflect the influence of feminist theorists. Moreover, both monographs signal the increased attention with which feminists are applying deconstruction and semiotics to their critical, theoretical, and methodological constructs. Dolan states that feminist theatre scholars are "deconstructing performance from a feminist perspective [which] entails uncovering the ideological determinants within which performance works."

Readers without a basic understanding of feminist and deconstructionist theories should start with Case's work rather than Dolan's. Her book examines the position of women in the theatre and its relationship to the feminist movement. Case chose not to employ a single theoretical construct but rather to provide a "sampler of feminist critical techniques, theories, political positions, issues, explorations and theatre practices." The book has generated a good deal of debate among theatre scholars. Rosette C. Lamont describes the book as a "personal and passionate study" (Lamont, 161). Lynda Hart hails Case's work as "the most intellectually ambitious, politically radical, and theoretically sophisticated book in the field to date" (Hart, 261). Not everyone has welcomed Case's monograph with such wholehearted enthusiasm, however. Several scholars, such as Gabrielle Cody, Joyce Van Dyke and J.W. Lafler, believe Case undertakes too much material in such a short book. More specifically, these scholars have criticized Case for her rather myopic approach in examining the role of women in the classical Greek and Renaissance theatre. Most, however, who have commented on Case's work seem to agree with Cody's observation that she "demonstrates greater authority in chapters which focus on modern female-constructed representation" (Cody, 118). Here Case delineates and articulates different feminisms, which she considers particular ways of approaching a feminist critique of dramatic texts and representation.

Jill Dolan's *The Feminist Critic as Spectator,* like Case's study, provides an insightful discourse on the major feminisms: liberal, radical, and materialist, in feminist dramatic theory. Although her ideological sympathies are clearly with the materialist feminists, she analyzes specific dramatic performances representing these feminisms. Dolan views her book "as an introduction to feminist critical and theoretical ideas relevant to theatre and performance." The majority of critics who have commented on Dolan's monograph would agree with Lynda Hart's contention that it is "daring in its theoretical applications, exciting in its choice of subjects, and radical in its conclusions" (Hart, 161). The parts of the book that have stimulated the most attention are Dolan's discussion of feminism and its relationship to the performance and representation of lesbian desire. Helen Keyssar, for instance, commends Dolan's explanation of the three major feminisms—liberal, cultural/radical, and materialist—as being "cogent and illuminating" and the way she avoids being "simplistic" and "reductive." But, Keyssar argues, the position of culture within the feminisms is problematic in Dolan's discourse as with other such discourses. In Keyssar's opinion, Dolan's "heavy reliance on a relatively small circle of critical resources tends to obscure the key problem of the relationship of culture to production and representation" (Keyssar, 432). Keyssar suggests that Dolan and other "compatible voices . . . would be enriched if placed in dialogue with someone like Raymond Williams or M.M. Bakhtin . . . whose discussions [have] enriched understanding of materialist or socialist feminism."

Her chapter on lesbian desire in performance has inspired the most intense reactions among the critics. Walter Meserve for one, criticizes Dolan's overemphasis on lesbian theatre practice. In his bibliographic essay in *American Literary Scholarship* (see item 69), he states that "Dolan's thesis appears admirable, but the book marches quickly off in a slightly oblique direction" by dismissing the other feminisms "to wave a banner in support of materialist feminism" and to defend lesbianism and lesbian theatre. Meserve considers Dolan's chapter an excuse to describe and justify lesbian performance as a legitimate part of modern theatre and lesbian sexuality as a legitimate perspective for the "feminist spectator as critic" as well as an appropriate alternative to the "white middle class, heterosexual male spectator " (Meserve, 395).

Yet others disagree with Meserve. Chaudhuri, for example, claims that Dolan's discourse on lesbian performance is the book's "best chapter" (Chaudhuri, 164). And Elinor Fuchs finds Dolan's argument "compelling" and "requir[ing] thorough discussion in the field" (Fuchs, 138).

Complementing as well as supplementing the theoretical works of Dolan and Case are two sociological works on women and the theatre. The earliest of these is Helen Krich Chinoy's and Linda Walsh Jenkins' sourcebook *Women in Theatre*, first published in 1981 and revised in 1987 (see item 21). The co-authors' purpose is "to gain new insights into the larger untold 'herstory' of the American theatre." The book is the first to document the full range of contributions of women to the theatre, historical as well as contemporary. Several chapters highlight the achievements of female playwrights writing for the stage in the last thirty years.

Betsko's and Koenig's *Interviews with Contemporary Women Playwrights* (see item 9) should be considered a companion volume to *Women in Theatre*. A landmark volume, it contains thirty interviews of internationally prominent women dramatists. Van Dyke hails the collection as providing "unusually good interviews—energetic, lithe, funny, vivid voices that spring off the page and have . . . the presence of good stage dialogue" (Van Dyke, 1). The interview subjects explain how their femaleness affects their work in the theatre. Several identify completely with the feminist label; while others see themselves as "writers who happen to be women" and believe that "true art is genderless." Some of the playwrights contend that being labelled a "woman writer" hinders creativity, isolates them, or ghettoizes them within the theatre community. Still others are more cautious in their feminism, arguing that the dramatization of women's issues and experiences must be gradually introduced and that women writers must gain a reputation before pursuing women's issues. But as Van Dyke observes, regardless of these playwrights' opinions about a femininst aesthetic, they display an "unwillingness to 'talk back'—on stage or off—exclusively in the vocabulary and timbre of a feminist" (Van Dyke, 3).

Women Playwrights of Multicultural Backgrounds

Female dramatists from multicultural backgrounds have been writing and producing for the theatre at an increasing rate over the past twenty years, yet critical comment has not reflected the extent of these accomplishments. Most theatre surveys and histories as well as feminist theatre discussions have excluded expositions on the contributions and influence of playwrights from culturally diverse backgrounds. Sue-Ellen Case provides the first extensive overview of this kind in *Feminism and Theatre*, emphasizing the accomplishments of female African-Americans and Hispanic-Americans, primarily Chicanas. Few would disagree with Case's contention that the research on female playwrights of multi-ethnic backgrounds is difficult to conduct: "The companies concerned are relatively poor and often short-lived, requiring the critic either to have access to their productions, press releases and reviews . . . or to interview artists in the field."

African-American Women Playwrights

Of the scant material on multiculturally diverse female playwrights, most has been on African-Americans, and the majority focuses on Ntozake Shange. Exclusion of the contributions of African-American women dramatists from the canon is evident in anthologies, books and articles devoted to African-American drama. An examination of anthologies of black plays published in the last twenty-five years reveals that plays written by males form the major portion of the contents. Only two of the eleven plays in Ed Bullins' *New Plays from the Black Theatre* (1969) are by females. And William Couch's *New Black Playwrights* and *The New Lafayette Theatre Presents* each contain one play by a woman among the six included.

However, a turnaround might be in the offing. In 1986, Margaret Wilkerson's *9 Plays by Black Women* (see item 77) was published. And three years later appeared *New Plays for the Black Theatre*, which according to the editor Woodie King, "represents the best of the new breed of Black playwrights." Although male writers dominate the volume, one third of the plays are by black women, a marked improvement over King's earlier *Black Drama Anthology* (1972) in which two plays out of the twenty-two are by black women.

African-American female playwrights have not fared much better with the press and the scholars, and in terms of critical consideration of their contributions to modern theatre, continue to be overshadowed by their male counterparts. C.W.E. Bigsby observes in his critical survey of twentieth-century drama that "[d]espite the initial success of Lorraine Hansberry, black drama has been dominated by male writers" (Bigsby, 409). Many of the studies and surveys on contemporary black drama—Fabre's *Drumbeats, Masks and Metaphor: Contemporary Afro-American Theatre* (see item 592), Errol Hill's *The Theater of Black Americans*, Leslie Catharine Sanders' *The Development of Black Theater; From Shadows to Selves* (1988)—exclude or briefly mention the contributions of individual black female playwrights active since the 1960s. Bigsby's three-volume work on twentieth-century drama is the only major survey to devote a modicum of critical attention to female writers active in the post-Hansberry era.

It took Shange's smash hit *for colored girls who have considered suicide/when the rainbow is enuf* to jolt mainstream theatre critics and academicians into an awareness of the work of the black female dramatist. Considered by many in the theatrical and academic communities to be the "breakthrough" play for black female theatre artists, the play won several awards and inspired dozens of articles in the popular and scholarly press.

Unfortunately, the blaze of attention was not sustained; the momentum gained in the seventies has slowed. As Betsko points out "the black female voice is heard less and less frequently in the theater these days, as raw vitality and defiance in women, on and off the stage, grows increasingly less fashionable" (Betsko 460). Betsko also surmises that "Critics feel that they have heard enough 'black' problems and 'women' problems and 'poverty' problems; they are bored by 'victims'."

Ignored by the critics, black women theatre artists feel they are equally disregarded by white women playwrights. In 1981, Elizabeth Hadley Freydberg charged, in her article covering the American Theater Association's National Conference for All Women in Theatre (see item 37), that the program was elitist, primarily promoting the work of white women theatre artists and that this group was "mak[ing] the same mistake of excluding blacks and other traditionally ignored groups."

Elizabeth Brown-Guillory is a major contributor to the critical canon of African-American female dramatists. Her abundant articles on black theatre artists demonstrate her commitment to increasing the awareness and understanding of the achievements of black women playwrights. In *Their Place on the Stage, Black Women Playwrights in America* (see item 13), the first book-length critical analysis of contemporary black female playwrights, Brown-Guillory examines selected playwrights such as Alice Childress and Ntozake Shange according to the similarities and differences of their dramas to those of their male counterparts. Unfortunately, Brown-Guillory omits several key playwrights. Assessing the response of the scholars to Brown-Guillory's book is difficult, since at least through 1990, no reviews appeared in major theatre journals.

Hispanic-American Women Playwrights

Critical attention to the work of Hispanic-American women dramatists, including Mexican-Americans, Puerto-Ricans, and Cuban-

Americans, has lagged far behind the critical canon of African-American women dramatists. Case declares "[Chicanas] do not enjoy a stable of playwrights . . . they have not won national prizes or attained national prominence as directors." Chicana theatre artists, observes Case, are hindered by additional obstacles unknown to black playwrights. Latinas are circumscribed by family traditions that are influenced greatly by the Catholic Church.

Many articles dealing with Hispanic playwrights and theatre exclude women writers. For example, in his recent survey of Hispanic theatre Anselmo Conde mentions several Hispanic dramatists who are "gaining recognition," none of whom are women (Conde, 11-13). Moreover, Nicolas Kanellos has consistently omitted the work of women writers from his writings on Hispanic playwrights. This lack of recognition of Latinas' dramatic achievements is also reflected in *Hispanic Theatre in the United States* (1984), a collection of essays edited by Kanellos. For example, in her essay assessing the work of Cuban-American playwrights, Maida Watson-Espener fails to mention Maria Irene Fornes, a multi-Obie winner and a pioneer in the experimental theatre movement.

What little exposure female Hispanic theatre artists have gained has come mainly through an occasional play published in anthologies devoted to Latino theatre. Huerta's anthology *Necessary Fictions* (see item 3195) includes two plays by women but both have male co-authors. And in *Contemporary Chicano Theatre* (see item 3079), Garza offers only one play out of eight by a woman (Estela Portillo-Trambley's *The Day of the Swallows*). Encouraging for women playwrights, however, is Elizabeth Osborn's *On New Ground: Contemporary Hispanic-American Plays* (see item 1035). Half of its six plays are by women (Lynn Alvarez, Maria Irene Fornes, and Milcha Sanchez-Scott). In addition to anthologies, Hispanic women playwrights have also gained exposure though published reviews and critical interpretations of their plays, expecially those by Fornes, Sanchez-Scott, and Portillo-Trambley.

The first survey of Chicana theatre artists appears in Sue-Ellen Case's *Feminism and Theatre*. Yarbro-Bejarano is another significant writer of the Chicana theatre. Needless to say, before much critical work can be done on Hispanic women playwrights, their work needs to be produced and thus become readily accessible to the spectator, critic, and scholar.

Asian-American Women Playwrights

Little information exists on the activity of Asian-American women playwrights. And what little there is is the result of the relatively recent efforts of playwrights Velina Houston, Jessica Hagedorn, Momoko Iko, and Wakako Yamauchi. Stephanie Arnold's essay "Dissolving the Half Shadows: Japanese American Women Playwrights," in Hart's critical anthology *Making a Spectacle: Feminist Essays on Contemporary Women's Theatre* (see item 64), is the first scholarly attempt to assess the critical canon of Asian-American female dramatists, although she emphasizes the efforts of Japanese-Americans, who "have made the primary contributions as playwrights thus far." Arnold cites the Asian-American theatre movement as a primary force for creating an atmosphere conducive to encouraging those of a similiar ethnicity.

Another encouraging sign of interest in Asian-American playwrights is Misha Berson's anthology *Between Worlds: Contemporary Asian-American Plays* (see item 8), which includes Jessica Hagedorn's *Tenement Lover: no palm trees/in new york city,* and Wakako Yamauchi's *And the Soul Shall Dance.*

Lesbian Playwrights

There are very few anthologies of gay plays and even fewer which focus solely on the lesbian playwright. As its title states, Kate McDermott's *Places Please! The First Anthology of Lesbian Plays* (1985) was the first of its kind.

Most critical analyses devoted to the work of a lesbian playwright support particular points relative to discussions on lesbian representation and performance. One of the earliest articles to attempt a definition and to identify the parameters of lesbian theatre is Emily L. Sisley's "Notes on Lesbian Theatre," in *Drama Review* (see item 95). Sisley adapts William Hoffman's concept of gay theatre, which he views as a "production that implicitly or explictly acknowledges that there are [gays] on both sides of the footlights."

Since Sisley's article, there has been a spate of articles on lesbian theatre, representation and performance, many of which are concerned with defining the parameters and lesbian theatre's relationship to feminism. Jill Dolan and Sue-Ellen Case have been major contributors to the lesbian-feminist critical canon; both writers have been especially concerned with the position of the female subject. Dolan, Case, and Elinor Fuchs, as well as other feminist theatre writers, recognize lesbian feminist theory as being in the forefront of feminist theory, because the lesbian position "resists [the] ideology of gender" (Fuchs,

1990). Case, for example, in her essay "Toward a Butch-Femme Aesthetic" (see item 20), agrees with Teresa de Lauretis's assertion that to undergo ideological change, the female subject must be viewed in terms of her relationship with other women; otherwise to be continued to be perceived in relation to men perpetuates her "entrapment." Thus entrapped, the female subject is incapable of finding her identity. The female subject, suggests de Lauretis, needs to disencumber herself from the cultural prescriptions of the patriarchal state and position herself outside the ideology of gender to "find self-determination . . . change." Case suggests that to instigate change for the female subject "it would appear that the lesbian roles of butch and femme, as a dynamic duo, offer precisely the strong subject position the movement requires." Case also discusses the lesbian position in performance.

Jill Dolan's recent book, *The Feminist Critic As Spectator* (see item 28), expands upon her articles on lesbian theory. Dolan disagrees with the cultural feminists who assert the female subject must "disarm desire." For Dolan, this is an ineffective approach to freeing the female subject from the dictates of the male-oriented representational system; she is still trapped in the net of male desire. Elinor Fuchs observes that Dolan "seems to suggest the female sexual identity must tend either towards lesbian resistance or risk being trapped in the representational system of pornography." Fuchs finds this a provocative argument and suggests that it serve as a catalyst for further discussion.

Future Directions in the Research on Contemporary Women Playwrights

The scholarship on women playwrights and feminist theatre has gained momentum in the last few years and will accelerate in the 1990s. Another indication of the growing interest in women in theatre is the publication of *Women & Performance: The Journal of Feminist Theory*, the first journal devoted to women in the performing arts. Articles range from critical examination of the work of individual playwrights to discussions of feminist aesthetics and theory. In addition, several major theatre periodicals have devoted special issues to women in theatre, including *Modern Drama* (March 1989), *Southern Quarterly* (Spring 1987), *Themes in Drama* (1989), and *Studies in American Drama 1945-Present* (1989). Gaps continue to exist in the scholarship, however. Especially needed is a historical examination of contemporary American women playwrights who began writing in the early 1960s. Such a study should evaluate the canon of these dramatists from a socio-historical perspective in order to establish relationships between the works as aesthetic objects and their impact on the theatrical world as well as the general milieu at the time of their creation. This exploration should determine whether their contributions provide a "sociological key" to contemporary social meanings and values. Furthermore, a socio-historical study should expand upon the work of Janet Brown and Elizabeth Natalle which sought to explore how the feminist and civil rights movements of the sixties influenced women's approaches to and strategies for drama and theatre.

Closely connected to feminism and its relationship to the theatre is the role of women playwrights in the development of the experimental theatre in the 1960s. As Leavitt and others have observed, the women's liberation movement along with the experimental and radical theatre movements were vital forces, giving women theatre artists the freedom to challenge patriarchal values and to focus on the experiences of women previously unseen on the stage. Most of these female dramatists—Megan Terry, Roberta Sklar, Maria Irene Fornes, Rochelle Owens, and Myrna Lamb, among others—recognized that the traditional dramatic forms were inadequate in expressing the experience of femaleness from a woman's perspective. The conventional forms of realism in theatre were ill-suited for conveying meaningful statements because the stories of women have been filtered by the so-called "male gaze." Feminist critics need to rigorously examine the canon of these early women dramatists in terms of their efforts to subvert the cultural meanings embedded in the realistic theatre. In other words, they must examine how these unique playwrights twisted traditional dramatic forms and manipulated language to shape the kind of texts and subtexts that enabled them to express woman's experience as defined by the consciousness of woman.

In addition to the texts, feminists need to study the reactions of the audiences, especially the theatre critics, whose shock and disgust at some of their plays affected the reviews, which in turn influenced the spectator. Consider, for example, Myrna Lamb's *Mod Donna*, a play about "the obsession with sexuality. . . that dominates every woman's life." Vivian Gornick, whose review of the play appeared in the *Village Voice* (see item 2157), is correct in her observation that the New York critics misinterpreted the play because the issues threatened their male values, thus blinding them to the feminist statements Lamb was attempting to convey.

Assessing the canon of these women experimentalists will also provide scholars with a better understanding of how these avant-garde dramatists influenced later playwrights. Also needed is a fresh look at the feminist dramatists' key role in the development of collaborative theatre. As Leavitt and others have pointed out, collaborative theatre is a phenomenon that evolved out of many women's disillusionment with the experimental theatre community.

Feminist theatre scholars must continue the work Jill Dolan and others have pioneered in formalizing a feminist theatre aesthetic and constructing theoretical models to evaluate dramatic texts and productions. However, not all would agree that a formal dramatic aesthetic is necessary. Some fear that a formalized feminist aesthetic will ghettoize women writers, that its canon will become excluded from the mainstream. Eve Merriam claims she "would never identify herself as a woman playwright," fearing her work would be "done in a woman's theatre exclusively." And Corinne Jacker declares women shy away from a feminist tag because "they don't want the bull-dyke, aggressive feminist-separatist label" (Betsko, 302, 240).

But others believe feminist critical models are crucial to the canon of women playwrights as well as to drama in general. Otherwise plays, especially those written by women, will continue to be misinterpreted by scholars and theatre critics. As Betsko points out, "the concerns, the irony, the innovations, and intentions of women playwrights are, for the most part, woefully lost on the majority of critics" (Betsko, 57).

Feminist constructs may possibly eliminate another problem voiced by many women playwrights over the last thirty years. Women dramatists believe the subjects they choose to write about are judged according to a different standard than those of male dramatists. Critics, according to these playwrights, view their themes and subjects as being less important and universal than male themes, thus implying that universality cannot be drawn from the experiences of women. Beth Henley comments "when *Firecracker* was done out here, in California, they called it a petty play about a beauty contest. They wouldn't look for any of the deeper meanings or the spiritual levels in the play. Whereas if a man wrote a play about a baseball game, critics might be more inclined to find deep meanings about the Lost American Dream" (Betsko, 219).

To establish a viable critical reputation, closer scrutiny needs to be directed toward the canon of individual female playwrights according to prevailing critical standards such as feminist theory, deconstruction, semiotics, and postmodernism. To date, when compared to their male counterparts, few critical studies have been conducted on contemporary women playwrights.

To gain a critical as well as sociological perspective, full-length critical biographies are needed for the major women playwrights, especially Childress, Fornes, Norman, Henley, Wasserstein, Terry,

Kennedy, and Shange. Scholars need to examine how these playwrights' earlier works have affected their later works, how their themes and dramatic strategies have evolved, and the extent to which both theatrical and societal forces have shaped their arts and aesthetics.

Thus, as feminist theory becomes more prominent in theatre criticism, the plays written by female dramatists will be better understood and will prevent pressure on women playwrights to "write like a man," that is, to conform to the dramatic conventions traditionally developed by male models.

References

Bigsby, C.W. E. 1982. *A Critical Introduction to Twentieth-Century American Drama*. Volume 3. Cambridge: Cambridge University Press.

Brockett, Oscar G. 1982. *History of the Theatre*. 4th ed. Boston: Allyn and Bacon, Inc.

Brown, Janet. 1982. Review of the *American Woman Playwright: A View of Criticism and Characterization, Modern Drama*, 25: 324-327.

Chaudhuri, Una. 1990. Review of *The Feminist Spectator as Critic*, by Jill Dolan. *Performing Arts Journal*, 12: 163-165.

Cody, Gabrielle. 1988. Review of *Feminism and Theatre*, by Sue-Ellen Case. *Performing Arts Journal*, 32: 116-118.

Crane, Gladys. 1982. Review of *Feminist Theatre Groups*, by Dinah Leavitt. *Theatre Journal*, 34: 273-275.

Curb, Rosemary. 1981. Review of *Feminist Theatre*, by Janet Brown. *Modern Drama*, 24: 102-104.

Davis, Tracy C. *Interpreting the Theatrical Past: Essays in the Historiography of Performance*. Edited by Thomas Postlewait, 58-81. Iowa City: University of Iowa Press, 1989.

Fuchs, Elinor. 1990. Review of *The Feminist Spectator as Critic*, by Jill Dolan. *Applause Book Catalog*, Spring: 136-137.

Hart, Lynda. 1989. Review of *Feminism and Theatre*, by Sue-Ellen Case. *Theatre Journal*, 41: 61-263.

_____. 1989. Review of *The Feminist Spectator as Critic*, by Jill Dolan. *Modern Drama*, 32: 161-163.

Keyssar, Helene. 1989. Review of *The Feminist Spectator As Critic*, by Jill Dolan. *Theatre Journal*, 41: 431-433.

Killian, Linda. 1974. "Feminist Theatre." *Feminist Art Journal*, Spring: 23.

Lafler, J.W. 1988. Review of *Feminism and Theatre*, by Sue-Ellen Case. *Choice*, 26: 657.

Lamont, Rosette C. 1989. Review of *Feminism and Theatre*, by Sue-Ellen Case. *Modern Drama*, 32: 159-161.

Laughlin, Karen. 1987. Review of *Feminist Theatre: An Introduction to Plays of Contemporary British and American Women*, by Helen Keyssar. Modern Drama, 30: 119-22.

Meserve, Walter J. 1987. "Drama." *American Literary Scholarship: An Annual*, 367-391.

Van Dyke, Joyce. 1989. Review of *Feminism and Theatre*, by Sue-Ellen Case. *Women's Review of Books*, 6: 1-3.

_____. 1989. Review of *Interviews With Contemporary Women Playwrights*, by Kathleen Betsko and Rachel Koenig. *Women's Review of Books*, 6: 1-3.

Contemporary Women Playwrights and Feminist Theatre
General Discussions

1. Arnold, Stephanie. "Dissolving the Half Shadows: Japanese
American Women Playwrights." In *Making a
Spectacle: Feminist Essays on Contemporary
Women's Theatre*. Edited by Lynda Hart, 181-194.
Ann Arbor: University of Michigan Press, 1989.
Encouraged by the Asian-American theatre
movement, Arnold maintains that the visibility of
Asian-American women playwrights is increasing.
Furthermore, she claims "Japanese American
women have made the primary contribution as
playwrights so far." Arnold focuses on the work of
three female Japanese American theatre artists—
Momoko Iko, Wakako Yamauchi, and Velina
Houston. Arnold's essay is also useful for its
survey of the evolution of the Asian-American
theatre movement.

2. "American Experimental Theatre: Then and Now."
Performing Arts Journal, 2, ii (Fall 1977): 13-24.
A number of theatre artists, including playwrights
Megan Terry and Rochelle Owens, articulate their
perceptions about the changes that shook the
American theatre in the 1960s and how they have
affected the experimental theatre of the 1970s.

3. Austin, Gayle. "The 'Woman' Playwright Issue."
Performing Arts Journal, 7, iii (1983): 87-102.
Several women theatre artists react to Mel
Gussow's 1983 article on contemporary women

playwrights (see item 48). Julia Miles, director of the Women's Project in New York, believes Gussow's estimation of the "proliferation" of women dramatists is somewhat exaggerated. Collette Brooks, former associate director of Interart Theatre, voices the concern of many that Gussow virtually ignored the contributions of experimental theatre artists such as Megan Terry, Rochelle Owens, Rosalyn Drexler, Julie Bovasso, Adrienne Kennedy, Maria Irene Fornes, and Alice Childress. Roberta Sklar, writer and director, expressed disappointment with Gussow's omission of women's contributions to collaborative theatre, which she sees as a significant innovation and a major departure from traditional male-oriented theatre. The article also includes comments from playwrights Karen Malpede, Maria Irene Fornes, and Joan Schenkar.

4. _____. Women/Text/Theatre. *Performing Arts Journal,* 9, ii & iii (1985): 185-190.
Austin argues that the majority of contemporary women playwrights adhere to traditional theatrical forms—"they usually begin by writing an 'Arthur Miller play'"—and are reluctant to pursue the experimentations of Megan Terry and Maria Irene Fornes in dramatizing the female experience. Austin contends that more roles for women should be developed, that a broader range of themes of women's experiences should be explored, and that there should be a "rethinking of the forms theatre takes." One way, Austin suggests, for women dramatists to "break out" out of the practice of writing in conventional modes or "looking to male models" is to work with a feminist theatre group that creates plays as a collaborative effort. Many such groups "do not assume [traditional] forms and simply fill them in with women's content [but] they question everything and then develop or adopt structures which will express their concerns." Austin advocates a deeper concern for the fusion of theatre and feminist theory. She concludes her

article with several thought-provoking questions
such as, "What can women do with the 'essence of
drama in conflict' idea—work with it, ignore it,
change it?"

5. Barranger, Milly. "Southern Playwrights: A Perspective On
Women Writers." *Southern Quarterly*, 25, iii
(Spring 1987): 5-9.
Barranger's essay introduces *Southern Quarterly's*
special issue on Southern women dramatists, which
includes critical studies on Lillian Hellman, Carson
McCullers, Beth Henley, Alice Childress, Marsha
Norman, and Sandra Deer. Although these
playwrights closely identify with the Southern
literary tradition, according to Barranger, they add a
new dimension by interpreting the characters'
experiences through women's eyes. Thus, the new
"heroine's individualism is asserted in violating
taboos, rejecting dependency, committing suicide,
maiming the male, casting out social, racial, and
gender stereotypes in favor of a creative,
autonomous individualism."

6. "Behind the Scenes: Outreach '87, This Year's Women's
Committee Event, Was an Ambitious Three-Day
Gathering." *Dramatists Guild Quarterly*, 24, ii
(Summer 1987): 60-68.
This article highlights the major sessions of
Outreach '87, the Dramatists Guild Committee for
Women's eighth annual event, which was held in
New York City, in June of 1987. One session
focused on two theatre groups, Second Stage and
Theater for a New City; the panelists included
several playwrights: Brenda Currin, Deborah
Eisenberg, Corinne Jacker, Susan Miller, Rosalyn
Drexler, and Joan Schenkar. In another session, a
group of women playwrights and directors
participated in a discussion on contemporary
regional theatre and its relevance to women theatre
artists. And finally, the ubiquitous question "What
Is a Feminist?" was addressed in a panel discussion

by playwrights Kathleen Betsko, Eve Merriam,
Sally Ordway, and others.

7. Bennetts, Leslie. "Is the Road To a Theater Career Rockier
for Women?" *New York Times* (Nov. 23, 1986):
72.
Bennetts reports on a program, "Women On
Broadway: Do They Make a Difference?," sponsored
by the Outer Critics Circle. Relevant issues that
continue to concern women theatre artists were
addressed by a panel made up of producers,
actresses, directors, and playwright Wendy
Wasserstein. Of special concern was the ongoing
problem of women theatre artists being ignored.
Actress and director Elizabeth McCann, for
example, pointed out that there is a "subtle
prejudice in the old-boy network . . . there is not
one theatre that can be booked in the ladies' room."
McCann emphasizes that women need to be part of
that network in order to compete equally with their
male counterparts. Wasserstein voiced the concern
of many playwrights when she noted that women's
experiences seemed to be viewed less "stageworthy"
than the themes male playwrights write about.

8. Berson, Misha. "Between Worlds." *American Theatre*, 6
(Mar. 1990): 21-25.
Berson's article is one of the few published sources
that discusses the evolution of the Asian-American
theatre movement in the United States from its
beginnings. A theme inherent in many of the
plays of contemporary Asian-American
playwrights, she comments, is that "they have
created characters who hover between worlds,
suspended between countries of origin and adopted
homelands, between marriage and divorce, between
life and death, between war and peace." Although
the article does not focus on women playwrights, it
does elicit comments from Asian-American
playwrights Wakako Yamauchi and Jessica
Hagedorn.

9. Betsko, Kathleen and Rachel Koenig. *Interviews with Contemporary Women Playwrights*. New York: Beach Tree Books, 1987.
    Betsko and Koenig's volume contains thirty interviews of contemporary British, American, Chinese, Argentine, and French women dramatists who have been successful in the commerial theatre. The interviews reflect the diversity and dynamism of these playwrights as they converse on their experience in writing for a theatre traditionally the preserve of their male counterparts. Questions posed by the interviewers (some of whom are also interviewees, e.g., Megan Terry and Corinne Jacker) pursue the dramatists' attitudes toward the presence of a "female aesthetic," their associations with directors and members of the theatre community, and the forces that have influenced their writing. Of the thirty interviews, twenty-one are American playwrights, including: Kathleen Betsko, Alice Childress, Anne Commire, Gretchen Cryer, Diane DeMatteo, Roslyn Drexler, Maria Irene Fornes, Mary Gallagher, Beth Henley, Tina Howe, Corinne Jacker, Adrienne Kennedy, Karen Malpede, Emily Mann, Eve Merriam, Marsha Norman, Rochelle Owens, Ntozake Shange, Megan Terry, Wendy Wasserstein, and Susan Yankowitz.

10. Billman, Carol. "Women and the Family in American Drama." *Arizona Quarterly*, 36, i (1980): 35-48.
    Billman asserts that, with few exceptions, major American dramatists traditionally have portrayed women characters who accepted the "unbreakable ties between woman and her place in the home." These "ties" began to be challenged in the late 1960s and early 1970s when dramatists began exploring a diversity of images of women, exploring *femaleness* beyond hearth and home. Billman outlines three areas of concern now being addressed by playwrights: 1) women's sense of powerlessness in their domesticity; 2) women establishing an identity outside the family; and 3) women who confront moral and political issues

unrelated to gender. In discussing how these three areas are reflected in contemporary plays, Billman examines the plays of Corinne Jacker, Myrna Lamb, Ursule Molinaro, Megan Terry, Ruth Wolff, and others.

11. Brater, Enoch. *Feminine Focus: The New Women Playwrights*. Cambridge: Oxford University Press, 1989.

Brater's collection of eighteen essays "draw[s] our attention to a new dramatic moment." She remarks in her introduction to the essays that for many years no one challenged the "sexist implications" of the character of Regina ("one of the primal spoilers, a Southern . . . patriarchal figure in drag,") in Hellman's *Little Foxes,* nor did they go beyond the superficial reality of Regina, her daughter Zan, or the sister-in-law, Birdie. Brater states that even in contemporary productions, these characters are still being seen in terms of the male standard, and questions of sexism, feminism, and racism still are being ignored. However, Brater's introductory essay reflects the achievements of female playwrights who are committed to portraying realistic views of women and women's experiences. Although the essays reflect an international cross-section of women playwrights, several essays represent the work of contemporary American women dramatists such as Maria Irene Fornes, Rochelle Owens, Ntozake Shange, Adrienne Kennedy, Sonia Sanchez, Tina Howe, and Marsha Norman.

12. Brown, Janet. *Feminist Drama: Definition and Critical Analysis*. Metuchen, New Jersey: Scarecrow Press, 1979.

Brown's work is one of the earliest in-depth studies of feminist theatre criticism. She addresses the question, "What is feminist about a play?" Brown's exploration hinges on her idea of feminism or the "feminine impulse," which she defines as "a woman's struggle for autonomy against an

oppressive, sexist society." In addition, the author
employs Kenneth Burke's literary theory that all
fictive works have a "rhetorical or persuasive
motive." Brown argues that for a play to qualify as
feminist, it must have as its "central rhetorical
motive" a woman grappling for independence in the
dominant patriarchal society. To illustrate her
methodological approach, Brown analyzes six
plays: Rosyln Drexler's *The Bed Was Full,* David
Rabe's *In the Boom Boom Room,* Alice Childress's
Wine in the Wilderness, Tina Howe's *Birth and
After Birth,* and Ntozake Shange's *for colored girls
who have considered suicide /when the rainbow is
enuf* as well as several feminist theatre groups (for
example, Westbeth Playwrights Feminist
Collective, B & O Theatre, Circle of the Witch).
Although dated, *Feminist Drama* includes a
selected bibliography of primary and secondary
materials.

13. Brown-Guillory, Elizabeth. *Their Place On the Stage:
Black Women Playwrights in America.* Westport,
Connecticut: Greenwood Press, 1988.
Until Brown-Guillory's book, there had been no
comprehensive study of black women dramatists.
The author, whose articles on black women
dramatists have contributed to this book, provides
an in-depth analysis of the works of Lorraine
Hansberry, Alice Childress, and Ntozake Shange,
playwrights whose works "are crucial links in the
development of black playwriting in America from
the 1950's to the 1980's." In her examination of
these playwrights, Brown-Guillory demonstrates
the similarities and differences of their plays to the
dramas of their male counterparts. She begins,
however, by presenting a historical overview of the
"long and vibrant" theatrical tradition from which
black female playwrights evolved, and also devotes
a chapter to the works of women dramatists
identified with the Harlem Renaissance, for
example, May Miller, Georgia Douglas Johnson,
Angelina Weld Grimke.

14. _____. "Black Women Playwrights: Exorcising Myths."
Phylon, 68, iii (Fall1987): 230-238.
Brown-Guillory focuses on Alice Childress,
Lorraine Hansberry, and Ntozake Shange, who
"present a vital slice of [black] life." They offer
realistic images of the black experience that differ
markedly from the perceptions of black males and
white writers. In effect, the images of the these
female dramatists smash the misconceptions of 'the
contented slave', 'the tragic mulatto', 'the comic
Negro', 'the exotic primitive', and 'the spiritual
singing, toe-tapping faithful servant'. According to
the author, Childress, Hansberry, and Shange use
three images repeatedly in their work: "the black
male in search of his manhood"; the black male as
"the walking wounded"; and, "the evolving black
woman." For example, Childress dramatizes the
image of the black man's quest for manhood one of
two ways—a man whose quest leads him to a
responsible, productive life or a man who is too
frozen in his own insecurities to endure such a
quest. Brown-Guillory also demonstrates how
Shange and Childress employ the image of the
evolving black woman: both show women as
victims, disappointed and abused by their men;
however, ultimately the women transcend their
victim-ness by becoming independent and rely upon
themselves for fulfillment.

15. _____. "Contemporary Black Women Plawrights: A View
From the Other Half." *Helicon Nine,* 14 & 15
(Summer 1986):120-127.
Brown-Guillory asserts that Hansberry, Childress,
and Shange consciously avoid the stereotypical
images of black women that are found in the plays
of black males and white playwrights. Brown-
Guillory observes the "[o]ne image which
dominates their plays is 'the evolving black
woman,' a phrase which embodies the multiplicity
of emotions of ordinary black women for whom the
act of living is sheer heroism." And the "evolving

woman" image in Childress's *Wine in the Wilderness* and Shange's *for colored girls* are "preoccupied with themselves" because their expectations about the men in their lives have been shattered. But rather than wallowing in self-pity or in man-hating and considering themselves perpetual victims, the women in these plays emerge as independent selves so as to avoid being trapped in abusive relationships.

16. Byers-Pevitts, Beverly. "Feminist Thematic Trends in Plays Written by Women for the American Theatre: 1970-1979," Ph.D. diss., Southern Illinois University of Carbondale, 1980.
Byers-Pevitts observes that women dramatists are exploring five distinct themes, which focus on feminist concerns. These themes include: social oppression; family oppression; mother and daughter relationships; women's struggle for autonomy; and friendship among women. In addition, Byers-Pevitts notes women are diverging from tradition and experimenting with new dramatic forms to convey meaning. The following is a list of the plays that Byers-Pevitts analyzes: Myrna Lamb's *But What Have You Done For Me Lately?* and *Apple Pie,* Eve Merriam's *The Club,* Ntozake Shange's *for colored girls who have considered suicide/when the rainbow is enuf,* Marsha Norman's *Getting Out,* Anne Commire's *Shay,* Tina Howe's *Birth and After Birth* and *Museum,* Megan Terry's *Hothouse,* Roma Greth's *Windfall Apples,* Honor Moore's *Mourning Pictures,* Corinnne Jacker's *Later* and *Bits and Pieces,* Gretchen Cryer's *I'm Getting My Act Together and Taking It On the Road,* Susan Griffin's *Voices,* Wendy Wasserstein's *Uncommon Women and Others,* and Maria Irene Fornes's *Fefu and Her Friends.*

17. _____. "Imaging Women in Theatre: Departures from Dramatic Tradition." *Theatre Annual,* 40 (1985): 1-6.

Byers-Pevitts, who is the co-editor of this special issue on women in theatre, provides a brief overview of the feminist scholarship in theatre studies. Following the overview, she summarizes the articles included in the issue. These articles, according to the editor, "reflect women experiencing theatre. No single ideology, no single methodology emerges; there are a variety of critical voices and subjects as there are a variety of critical approaches."

18.   Carlson, Susan. "Women in Comedy: Problems, Promises, Paradoxes." *Themes in Drama,* 7 (1985): 159-171. Carlson argues that "in the upheaval of comedy's role reversals, women acquire a dominance they normally do not possess." But the subversive nature of comedy is undermined by the "happy ending," which serves to sustain the status quo; thus, "the female freedom and power that comedy celebrates are circumscribed." Carlson illustrates her case in two ways: by analyzing W. Somerset Maugham's play *The Constant Wife* and by discussing several contemporary women playwrights, Megan Terry and Marsha Norman, whose plays depart from traditional forms of comedy.

19.   Case, Sue-Ellen. *Feminism and Theatre.* New York: Methuen, 1988.
A basic, easy-to-understand introduction to feminist theatre. The first chapter discusses feminism and theatre within a historical context, in which Case introduces the reader to "a deconstruction of the classics [which is] only one of the many ways for feminists to think their way out of its patriarchal prescription." In the second chapter, "Women Pioneers," Case's historical examination of women playwrights ranges from the ancient maker of plays to those female mimes working in Greece and Rome, to Hroswitha, Aphra Behn, Sor Juana, and Mercy Warren. The next several chapters describe major feminist positions and their effect on theatre

practice. For example, Case suggests that feminist theatre evolved out of the radical feminist consciousness-raising groups. Case also covers the development of several feminist theatre groups and individual dramatists representing diverse racial and sexual backgrounds (e.g., Wendy Wasserstein, Jane Chambers, Ntozake Shange) in relation to their various feminist positions, such as radical feminism and materialist feminism. The final chapter focuses on the application of deconstruction, semiotics, poststructuralism, and other theoretical constructs to feminist positions in the theatre. *Feminism and Theatre* also includes a substantial bibliography of source material.

20. _____. "Toward a Butch-Femme Aesthetic." In *Making a Spectacle: Feminist Essays on Contemporary Women's Theatre*. Edited by Lynda Hart, 282-299. Ann Arbor: University of Michigan Press, 1989. Case agrees with Teresa de Lauretis's opinion that to undergo ideological change, the female subject must be viewed in terms of her relationship with other women; otherwise, to be continued to be perceived in relation to men perpetuates her "entrapment." Case suggests that to instigate change "outside the ideology of sexual difference . . . it would appear that the lesbian roles of butch and femme, as a dynamic duo, offer precisely the strong subject position the movement requires."

21. Chinoy, Helen Krich and Linda Walsh Jenkins. *Women in American Theatre:* Revised Edition. New York: Theatre Communications Group, 1987. Chinoy's earlier edition, published in 1981, was one of the first books to document the achievements of women working in the theatre. Like its predecessor, the revised edition is made up of essays, illustrations, and interviews that serve to give the reader a prismatic view of the involvement of women in the theatre: major women playwrights and other theatre artists, women's theatre groups, feminist theatre, and the issues surrounding the

image of women on stage. The 1987 edition also includes two new sections, "Theatre Artists Working Today," and "New Problems, Practices and Perspectives." Jenkins updates the "Sourcebook" section, which contains a compendium of information on plays, awards, and feminist theatres.

22. Cohn, Ruby. *New American Dramatists, 1960-1980.* New York: Grove Press, 1982.
    In terms of treatment of women dramatists, Cohn's book is a disappointment; although she includes sections on gay and black playwrights, she fails to include one assessing the contributions of women in the theatre. Nevertheless, she does discuss the work of several dramatists throughout the book. For example, in chapter four, Cohn examines the work of Megan Terry and Maria Irene Fornes along with Jack Gelber, Israel Horovitz, and Jean-Claude Van Itallie, dramatists who she identifies as "working closely with performance." In the sixth chapter Cohn includes Adrienne Kennedy, Ed Bullins, and Amiri Baraka as writers "for whom Blackness is an obsessive theme." Rochelle Owens's plays are analyzed along with the works of Robert Lowell and Michael McClure in chapter eight.

23. Curb, Rosemary K. "Re/cognition, Re/presentation, Re/creation in Woman-Conscious Drama: The Seer, The Seen, The Scene, The Obscene." *Theater Journal,* 37, iii (Oct. 1985): 302-316.
    Curb defines "woman conscious" drama as being "by and about women that is characterized by multiple interior reflections of women' s lives and perceptions." She draws upon the ideas of authors N. O. Keohane and Barbara C. Gelpi, who "distinguish three lives of women's self-consciousness: feminine, female, and feminist. The feminine consciousness is defined by male desire, that is, woman as sex object. The female consciousness, although "less inert and passive"

but still deeply rooted in the male tradition, is the
"age-old experience of women in giving and
preserving life, that is, woman as earth mother."
And, the feminist consciousness focuses on
women's experience within the patriarchal system,
yet "envisions alternative levels of consciousness
that operate in drama." Curb examines the
following plays: Adrienne Kennedy's *Funnyhouse
of a Negro*, Joan Schenkar's *Signs of Life*, Wendy
Kesselman's *My Sister in This House*, Megan
Terry's *Babes in the Bighouse*, Ntozake Shange's
*for colored girls who have considered
suicide/when the rainbow is enuf*, Karen Malpede's
Aphrodite, and *Daughters* by Clare Coss, Sondra
Segal, and Roberta Sklar.

24. Diamond, Elin. "Brechtian Theory/Feminist Theory:
Toward a Gestic Feminist Criticism." *Drama
Review*, 32, i (Spring 1988): 82-94.
Diamond develops a form of feminist theatre
criticism called "gestic criticism." Gestic criticism
stems from intertextual readings of feminist theory
and Brechtian theory, which involves "demystifying
representation . . . releasing the spectator from
imaginary and illusory identifications." Although
Diamond concedes that feminist dramatic theory has
been influenced substantially by cinematic theory,
semiotics, and psychoanalysis, she believes the
Brechtian theory can be a major contributor because
its tenets enable the representation of the female
body to "resist fetishization" and help reposition
the female spectator. For example,
Verfremdungseffect, central to Brechtian theory, can
be used to "alienat[e] . . . iconicity, by
foregrounding the expectation of resemblance,
[thus] the ideology of gender is exposed and thrown
back to the spectator." See also Diamond's article
"Mimesis, Mimicry, and the 'True-Real'." *Modern
Drama*, 32, i (Mar. 1989): 58-72.

25. Dickerson, Glenda. "The Cult of True Womanhood: Toward
A Womanist Attitude in African-American

Theatre." *Theatre Journal,* 40, ii (May 1988): 178-187.

Dickerson, adapter and director, describes how her "miracle plays," which she calls dramatic "tapestries" rich in archetypal and mythic images and language, bring forth the voices of women who have been oppressed by the "two-headed serpent—racism and sexism."

26. Dolan, Jill. "Bending Gender to Fit the Canon: The Politics of Production." In *Making a Spectacle: Feminist Essays on Contemporary Women's Theatre.* Edited by Lynda Hart, 318-344. Ann Arbor: University of Michigan Press, 1989.

Dolan contends that while the number of women playwrights is increasing, the "mainstream critical response to plays written by women continues to reveal deep-seated gender biases." She uses Norman's *'night Mother* as a basis for an analysis of the process of the inclusion and exclusion of plays by women playwrights in the traditional dramatic canon, which reflects the critical standards set by males. In her case study of the play, Dolan addresses the following questions: "If Marsha Norman's play is allowed into the traditional canon, will it establish a precedent for women playwrights to follow? Or, is *'night Mother* read as a contender for membership in the canon because it so closely follows the male precedent the canon has already set?"

27. _____. "Feminists, Lesbians, and Other Women in Theatre: Thought on the Politics of Performance." *Themes in Drama,* 11 (1989): 199-207.

In Dolan's opinion throughout theatre history women have not been realistically represented on stage. Instead they are simply creatures created through the "male gaze." Furthermore, the women theatre artists who are redefining theatre from a feminist perspective are being undermined "by categorizing the diverse movement only in terms of its difference from the mostly male standard." Still

Dolan believes politics is at the root of the issue. She blames the conservative atmosphere of the last few years for discouraging many theatre groups from identifying with a particular ideology because of the fear they will be refused funding: "[i]t's dangerous these days to be branded a feminist." Acknowledging that feminism is a sensitive issue, Dolan argues that no single feminist ideology exists to the "strains of feminist rhetoric" For related article, see Dolan's "Breaking the Code: Musings on Lesbian Sexuality and the Performer." *Modern Drama*, 32, i (Mar. 1989): 146-158.

28. _____. *The Feminist Spectator as Critic.* Ann Arbor, Michigan: UMI Research Press, 1988. Dolan approaches this feminist theatre criticism from a materialist feminist position. Yet her intention is not to provide a "definitive study" but "a historical accounting of the different methodological and ideological pathways this criticism has taken over the last twenty-odd years." To illustrate her points, she analyzes the work of several female playwrights (e.g., Marsha Norman), performance artists (e.g., Rachel Rosenthal), and feminist theatre groups (e.g., Split Britches, Spiderwoman, and WOW Cafe). Dolan assumes the reader has a basic knowledge of feminist theatre, semiotics, poststructuralism, and deconstruction. For the beginner, readers should consult Sue-Ellen Case's *Feminism and Theatre* (see item 19). For an additional discussion of *The Feminist Spectator as Critic,* see pages 8-9 of this research guide.

29. _____. "In Defense of the Discourse: Materialist Feminism, Postmodernism, Post-structuralism Theory." *Drama Review,* 33, iii (Fall 1989): 58-71. Dolan, a self-described "materialist feminist performance theorist," defends feminist postmodernist criticism. She expresses concern about "feminism's general backlash against theory." For instance, Dolan takes issue with the reviewers

of Sue-Ellen Case's book, *Feminism and Theatre*
(see item 19). She contends, for example, that
Gabrielle Cody, whose review of Case's book
appeared in *Performing Arts Journal* (1988) "get[s]
uneasy when the canon is attacked," and that
feminist critics, such as Joyce Van Dyke, "refuse to
take responsiblity for their own positions as critics,
since they regard criticism and theory as male-like."
See also: Janelle Reinelt. "Feminist Theory and
the Problem of Performance." *Modern Drama*, 32, i
(Mar. 1989): 47-57.

30. _____. "Women's Theatre Program [of] ATA: Creating a
Feminist Forum." *Women and Performance*, 1, ii
(1984): 5-13.
Dolan contends that the American Theatre
Association's (ATA) Women's Theatre Program
(WTP) needs to exert additional effort in involving
feminists and lesbians by developing a political
perspective. Heretofore, the WTP, according to
Dolan, emphasizes "examining women's exclusions
from and hopes for entry into mainstream,
professional theatre." She believes that WTP
should foster the development of a critical feminist
perspective from which to evaluate plays written by
women because it is the only organization that can
communicate on a national level. Dolan concedes
that at the 1983 ATA Conference the WTP
attempted to address issues of concern to feminists
and lesbians, but the attempt failed because the
programs lacked a critical focus. However,
questions about a feminist theatre arose indirectly
during the critiques of the plays that were
performed. She discusses some of these works,
including: Martha Boesing's *Antigone Too*,
Monique Wittig's *The Constant Journey*, Patricia
Montley's *Sisters*, and Jane Chambers's
Quintessential Image.

31. Ellenberger, Harriet. "The Dream Is the Bridge: In Search of
Lesbian Theatre." *Trivia*, 5 (Fall 1984):17-59.

In this essay Ellenberger explores the relationship
between lesbians and theatre—"[w]e make our lives
the way theatre is made. And this synchronicity,
attraction, connection, between lesbians and theatre
fascinates me."

32. Feral, Josette. "Writing and Displacement: Women in
Theatre." *Modern Drama*, 27, iv (Dec.1984): 549-
63.
Feral argues that although women writers of the
avant-garde are experimenting with new dramatic
forms they "still are confined to the masculine
mode unless they shatter traditional discourse."
Feral bases her discussion on Luce Irigaray's
feminist position "in which the feminine element
would be seen no longer as the Other, as non-
identity, non-entity or non-unity . . . but as
difference." According to Irigaray, features of a
"feminist voice" would include simultaneity and
continuity. The former "rejects fixed . . . meaning
. . . and would transform meaning into a
continuous flow within the text." And the latter
occurs when "words always touch one another,
touch a woman's body . . . and trace the outline of
her truest self." To illustrate these features, Feral
examines five plays, one of which is *The Daughter
Cycle*, by Clare Coss, Roberta Sklar, Sondra
Segal.

33. "Five Important Playwrights Talk About Theatre."
Mademoiselle, 75 (Aug. 1972): 288-289.
Mademoiselle interviews five of the six members
of the non-profit Women's Theatre Council (WTC):
Roslyn Drexler, Irene Maria Fornes, Julie Bovasso,
Megan Terry, Rochelle Owens. Adrienne Kennedy
was not available. The interview focuses on the
purpose of the WTC, which is to "nurture the
works of innovative playwrights" and "to develop
women directors and other theatre artists as well as
make a place for women playwrights." Council
members say they want the opportunity to produce
plays that express their mutual social and aesthetic

concerns; these dramatists feel the commercial theatre fails to "understand where we're at because we are in the vanguard of our art." Each Council member describes her experience as a woman writing and/or directing in the theatre, and the sexism that affects them as playwrights. For example, Megan Terry comments, "I was living like a gorilla in this society, hiding behind men, trying to work through men." For additional information on the Women's Theatre Council see: *New York Times* (Feb. 22, 1972): 44.

34. Fisher, Berenice. "Learning to Act: Women's Experience With 'Theater of the Oppressed'." *Off Our Backs* (1986): 14-15.
Fisher describes the use of Theater of the Oppressed, developed by the Brazilian director Agosto Boal as a medium to raise consciousness of feminist issues and concerns.

35. Forte, Jeanie. "Realism, Narrative, and the Feminist Playwright—A Problem of Reception." *Modern Drama*, 32, i (Mar. 1989): 115-127.
Forte's article reflects the ongoing debate concerning the relationship of classic realist dramatic texts and feminism. Forte asserts that if a playwright subverts the dominant ideology, which realism embraces, then "strategies must be found within the realm of discourse, particularly *vis a vis* narrative, which can operate to deconstruct the imbedded ideology." To illustrate her points, Forte analyzes the texts of Marsha Norman's *'night Mother*, Terry Baum's and Carolyn Meyer's *Dos Lesbos*, and Adrienne Kennedy's *The Owl Answers*.

36. Freedman, Samuel G. "Enter Success, Followed by Problems." *New York Times* (July 28, 1985), sect. 2: H1, H4.
Several playwrights, among them Marsha Norman and Wendy Wasserstein, talk about their "collision with fame," which is a "mixed blessing, something both sought-after and distrusted."

37. Freydberg, Elizabeth Hadley. "Black Women and Feminism:
     One More Time." *Theatre News,* 22 (Fall 1981):
     22.
     Freydberg reports on her participation in the
     American Theatre Association's National
     Conference for All Women in Theatre, held in San
     Diego in 1981. The purpose of the conference was
     to explore ways of promoting the work of women
     theatre artists. The majority of the group was
     white, according to Freydberg. In her view, the
     participants appeared to focus on furthering the
     work of white theatre artists. She expresses her
     dismay that this group "would make the same
     mistakes of excluding blacks and other traditionally
     ignored groups."

38. Gillespie, Patti. "American Women Dramatists, 1960-
     1980." In *Essays on Contemporary American
     Drama.* Edited by Bock Hedwig and Albert
     Wertheim, 111. Munich: M. Hueber, 1981.
     This collection of essays introduces the reader to
     the contemporary American theatrical scene.
     Gillespie's straightforward essay surveys the work
     of women playwrights writing and producing plays
     from the late 1950s through the 1970s. Gillespie
     briefly examines the work of Megan Terry, Myrna
     Lamb, Adrienne Kennedy, and Ntozake Shange.
     Following her essay, Gillespie provides a list of
     the women dramatists discussed, their major works,
     and a list of anthologies and collections of plays.

39. _____. "Feminist Theatre: A Rhetorical Phenomenon."
     Quarterly Journal of Speech, 64 (Oct. 1978): 284-
     294. Reprinted in 21.
     Gillespie's article is one of the earliest scholarly
     treatments of the feminist theatre phenomenon. She
     addresses the question, Why have feminist theatre
     groups proliferated at such a rapid rate, and why do
     many of them extend beyond the traditional to
     experimental dramatic forms? To answer these
     questions, Gillespie argues that one must accept
     "that all feminist theatres are rhetorical enterprises;

their primary aim is action, not art." These diverse groups wish to promote awareness of women and the concerns and the issues connected with women. Furthermore, Gillespie says, "[the] groups. . . appear to share two convictions: that women in this society have been subjected to unfair discrimination based on their gender, and that theatre can provide at least a partial solution to certain problems arising from such discrimination." See also: Killian, Linda. "Feminist Theatre." *Feminist Art Journal* (Spring 1974): 23 (see page 6).

40. _____. "Feminist Theatre of the 1970's." *Theatre News,* 10 (Nov. 1977): 5, 19.
Gillespie provides an overview on the nature of feminist theatre groups, a medium in which "women found an instrument for symbolic protest." The common goal of feminist theatre groups, Gillespie contends, is to raise the consciousness of women, to make them aware of the fact that they live in a society that discriminates against them because they are female. The author identifies two major groups within the feminist theatre movement. One group emphasizes the artistic contributions to women's theatre, that is, "showcasing the works of talented women and for providing employment for women trained in the arts." These theatre groups are organized according to the traditional structure associated with theatre groups. The other group of feminist theatres views theatre as a way to force the audience to re-evaluate their attitudes and beliefs about women and their role in society, to "jolt the audience into new ways of looking at the world." These feminist theatre organizations depart from the conventonal theatre structure; they are organized as collectives, emphasizing collaborative creations.

41. Ginsberg, Elaine. "Playwrights, Poets, and Novelists: Sisters Under the Skin." *Toward the Second*

Decade, Edited by Betty Justice and Renate Pore, New York: Greenwood Press, 1981.
Ginsberg discusses common problems women writers share, despite the diversity of forms and styles they pursue. For example, Ginsberg observes that women writers have had to liberate themselves from the "power men exert over their lack of confidence, and sense of inadequacy from which women suffer in their relationships with male agents, editors, publishers, directors, and others. Furthermore, women writers, especially playwrights, do not have an extensive field of female role models to draw upon. Yet another area of concern is handling male characters. Many women simply avoid the problem by not emphasizing male characters, which, Ginsberg warns, might lead to "creating a literature for women alone." For another discussion on the problem of male characters, see Corinne Jacker's essay (see item 52).

42.   Goetz, Ruth. "Is There a Feminine Sensibility in the House?" *Dramatists Guild Quarterly*, 16, iv (Winter 1980): 7-9.
This article focuses on Goetz's reactions to a program sponsored by the Women's Committee of the Dramatists Guild and the Society of Stage Directors and Choreographers, which addressed the issue of whether a female sensibility exists in drama.

43.   Gonzalez, Yolanda Broyles. "Toward a Re-Vision of Chicano Theatre History: The Women of El Teatro Campesino." In *Making a Spectacle: Feminist Essays on Contemporary Women's Theatre*. Edited by Lynda Hart, 209-238. Ann Arbor: University of Michigan Press, 1989.
Although she focuses on woman as actress rather than playwright, Gonzalez provides penetrating insights into Chicana theatre artists working with Luis Valdez and El Teatro Campesino. The author asserts that women as depicted in the plays

produced by the company are women seen as "one-dimensional stereotypes." Because the plays are developed according to standards of the Chicano male, women are restricted to roles closely identified with the family: daughter, mother, sister, grandmother, wife, or girlfriend. And the role of each of these is protrayed as either being a whore or a virgin. As a result of the male-dominated theatre, Chicanas' experiences are not represented on stage nor are their experiences allowed to be interpreted through the eyes of Chicanas.

44. Goodman, Dean. "Women, Minorities and Occasionals." In *San Francisco Stages: A Concise History, 1849-1986.* San Francisco: Micro Pro Litera Press, 1986.
Unfortunately, Goodman provides only a brief sketch of the women's theatre groups that have produced in San Francisco.

45. Goulianos, A. "Women and the Avant-garde Theatre; Interviews with Rochelle Owens, Crystal Field, Roslyn Drexler." *Massachusetts Review,* 13 (Winter 1972):257-261.
The interviewees, playwrights Roslyn Drexler and Rochelle Owens and actress and director Crystal Field, were chosen to be interviewed because of their significant achievements in the avant-garde theatre. These theatre artists describe how they got their start in the theatre, their experiences as women working in the industry, and their attitudes toward the feminist movement and its affect on their work.

46. Gray, Amlin. "The Big If." *American Theatre,* 6 (June 1989): 18-21, 56.
Several playwrights, including Megan Terry, Tina Howe, Maria Irene Fornes, and Emily Mann, respond to Gray's question, What do you think about when you are creating a play? These dramatists talk about the conditions and obstacles they must consider when creating a play. Fornes,

for instance, remarks, "it may be that I limit my
plays unconsciously because I know that if I
demand too much in sets. . . the theatre may not be
able to do them."

47.   Greene, Alexis. "Revolutionary Off-Off Broadway: A
Critical Study of Developments In Form,
Character, Language, and Theme." Ph.D. diss.
City University of New York, 1987.
Greene analyzes the plays of several avant-garde
playwrights of the sixties to determine what made
them "revolutionary" in comparison to their
counterparts of the fifties. With respect to women
playwrights, Greene examines the works of Roslyn
Drexler, Maria Irene Fornes, Rochelle Owens, and
Megan Terry.

48.   Gussow, Mel. Three articles from the *New York Times:*
"Women Write New Chapter." *New York Times*
(June 8, 1979): C3; "Women Playwrights Show
New Strength," *New York Times* (Feb. 15, 1981),
sect. 2: 4, 24; "Women Playwrights: New Voices
in the Theater." *New York Times Magazine* (May
1, 1983): 22-27.
Gussow's trio of articles is one of the earliest
attempts by a drama critic from a major newspaper
to survey and assess the work of contemporary
women playwrights. Gussow focuses on the
"proliferation" of female playwrights, which he
claims was foreshadowed by Ntozake Shange's *for
colored girls.* He cites several reasons for the
upsurge of plays written by women, such as the
women's movement, the increase in grants
encouraging women to write, and the Actors
Theatre of Louisville. Gussow also discusses
individual achievements in theatrical forms and
innovations in language and subject matter, and a
movement away from "militancy" to examining a
broader spectrum of issues and concerns. The critic
highlights the work of Beth Henley, Tina Howe,
Ntozake Shange, Corinne Jacker, Mary Gallagher,
Kathleen Tolan, J.E. Franklin, and others;

however, Gussow focuses on Marsha Norman in
his May, 1983 article. Gussow's choice of
playwrights has been criticized by feminist theatre
artists for his exclusion of experimentalists such as
Megan Terry, Rochelle Owens, and Adrienne
Kennedy, among others.

49. Grossman, Samuel Larry. "Trends in the Avant-Garde
Theatre of the United States During the 1960's."
Ph.D. diss. University of Minnesota, 1974.
Grossman examines the historical, social, and
political forces that engendered the experimental
theatre movement of the 1960s. Following a
general anaysis of the avant-garde theatre and its
aesthetic principles, Grossman analyzes the canon
of five experimental playwrights of the period,
three of whom are women: Adrienne Kennedy,
Maria Irene Fornes, and Roslyn Drexler.

50. Herman, William. *Understanding Contemporary Drama*.
Columbia, South Carolina: University of South
Carolina Press, 1987.
Herman introduces the reader to the personalities,
forces, and trends that have pushed the American
theatre to innovative heights since the early 1960s.
Unfortunately, Herman fails to devote much space
to a discussion of the contributions of women
dramatists; however, he does provide general critical
remarks on the work of Adrienne Kennedy and
Marsha Norman.

51. Honigberg, Nadine. "Women's Project: An Interview with
Julia Miles." *Theater*, 18, i (Winter 1985): 57-62.
An informative interview with Julia Miles,
Associate Director of the American Place Theatre,
who founded the organization's Women's Project in
1978. She formed the Women's Project to prompt
women to write, direct, and design—roles which
women have not been heretofore encouraged to
pursue. She discusses issues that concern female
theatre artists, including publishing women's plays,
developing a feminist aesthetic, funding future

projects. During the course of the interview, Miles
mentions some of the dramatists whose works have
been produced by the Women's Project: Lavonne
Mueller, Rose Leiman Goldemberg, and Paula
Cizmar.

52. Jacker, Corinne. "Better Than A Shriveled Husk: New
Forms for the Theater." *Toward the Second Decade:
Impact of the Women's Movement on American
Institutions.* Edited by Betty Justice and Renate
Pore, 25-34. New York: Greenwood Press, 1981.
Jacker, a successful playwright, surveys the
progress women theatre artists have made in terms
of being members of that "exclusive club," the
theatre. But, Jacker wistfully asks,"Why do we
still have a nagging feeling of incompletion?" The
problem, says Jacker, is that women dramatists feel
producers and other powers that be do not consider
their plays as stageworthy. Some of the reasons
Jacker cites are: (1) the lack of role models among
women playwrights; (2) the notion that a woman's
particular sensibilites are inappropriate for a career
as a playwright; (3) many women are
uncomfortable writing male roles; and (4) the
confusion among critics and audiences when
women playwrights create plays that diverge from
traditional dramatic forms. Jacker draws upon her
own experience in writing plays throughout the
essay; for example, she describes how she
confronted and worked through her fear of writing
about the "male psyche."

53. Jenkins, Linda Walsh. "Locating the Language of Gender
Experience." *Women & Performance*, 2, i (1984):
5-20.
Jenkins discusses what she refers to as "the
language of gender experience." That is, she asserts
that although men and women use the same
language, they "tend to image and enact [words] in
different ways." In short, females speak the
"mother tongue" and males speak the "father
tongue." Drawing upon her investigations in

women's studies and gender research, Jenkins
concludes that the reason both sexes name and
perceive in distinct ways is not primarily biological
but because the social roles are prescribed to each
sex. Consequently, the individual "grows up with
the engendered language" of that social role. The
author illustrates her assertions with excerpts from
several playwrights, including Marsha Norman,
Beth Henley, Irene Maria Fornes, and Adrienne
Kennedy.

54. Keyssar, Helen. *Feminist Theatre: An Introduction to Plays
    of Contemporary British and American Women.*
    Basingstoke: Macmillan, 1984.
    Keyssar's book pivots around her contention that
    feminist drama has shifted away from the
    "recognition scene," in which the protagonist
    comes to know herself and reveal the knowledge to
    others; instead, "the impetus is not towards self-
    recognition and revelation of a 'true self' but
    towards recognition of others and a concomitant
    transfromation of the self and the world." In other
    words, the protagonists must not only know who
    they are but they must also become aware of and
    transcend the constrictive roles to which they have
    been relegated. And to do this, Keyssar contends,
    feminist theatre is replacing the traditional
    "recognition scene" with experimental
    "transformational" drama, which "inspires and
    asserts the possiblity of change." Thus,
    tranformational drama focuses on the
    metamorphosis of self and society instead of solely
    on revelation of self. Following a historical
    overview of feminist theatre, Keyssar analyzes the
    works of over thirty British and American women
    dramatists (e.g., Megan Terry, Ntozake Shange,
    Wendy Wasserstein, Beth Henley, Myrna Lamb,
    and Wendy Kesselman) and several women's theatre
    collectives. Keyssar also includes an impressive
    bibliography of secondary sources.

55. _____. "Rites and Responsibilities: The Drama of Black American Women." *Feminine Focus; The New Women Playwrights*. Edited by Enoch Brater, 226-240. Cambridge: Oxford University Press, 1989.
Keyssar maintains there is "potential power" in the plays of black women playwrights because of their duality of perception. They "see the world as an American *woman* and as a black *woman*." Thus the duality of perceptions results in viewing experiences prismatically. Consequently, to express their mulitplicity of views, "in which diverse voices and world views collide," many black playwrights have used a variety of dramatic strategies, often incorporating song, dance, music and visual imagery. Keyssar assesses the works of earlier twentieth-century playwrights as well as contemporary dramatists including, Shange's *Boogie Woogie Landscapes*, Adrienne Kennedy's *The Owl Answers*, and Sonia Sanchez's *Sister Son/ji*.

56. Kingsbury, Marty. "Way Off Broadway: A Feminist Reponse to Theatre." *The Second Wave*, 5 (Summer/Fall 1979): 32-38.
Kingsbury's article, based on personal interviews, profiles four women's theatre companies: Rhode Island Feminist Theatre (RIFT), Circle of the Witch, Spiderwoman, The Muse Conceptions, Inc.

57. Lamb, Margaret. "Feminist Criticism." *Drama Review*, 18, iii, (Sep. 1974): 46-50.
Lamb asserts that viable critical approaches need to be formulated in three areas: 1) Research on the role of women in the theatre. Women need a theatrical tradition to encourage them in creating dramatic works. Historical research is also important in discovering "wrongly assessed" women playwrights. 2) The use of valid critical constructs in analyzing the creative work of contemporary women playwrights. 3) Examination of women's theatre and its relationship to feminism. In addition, Lamb suggests avenues feminist theatre

critics might pursue, for example, analysis of
critics of plays by women, criticism which
examines the "woman question," study of
international feminist theatres, exploration of the
"unconscious attitudes and values" inherent in
commerical theatre, and "sustained visionary work
by a critic who believes that feminist theatre has a
. . . great future as a revolutionary but undogmatic
approach to the art."

58. Leavitt, Dinah. *Feminist Theatre Groups*. Jefferson, South
Carolina: McFarland, 1980.
Leavitt attempts to clarify the nature of the
feminist theatre by extrapolating common elements
of feminist groups from four Minneapolis-based
theatre groups. Leavitt argues that feminist theatre
is more than merely a reaction to male-constructed
theatre, its nature being far more complex. For
further discussion about this book, see the
bibliographical essay.

59. Lewis, Barbara. "What's $80,000 Split 35 Ways?" *Ms.*, 7
(May 1979): 71.
A profile of the American Place Theatre's Women's
Project and its contributions to women's theater.

60. Lowell, Sondra. "Widening Goals of Feminist Theater." *Los
Angeles Times* (Sep. 29, 1974), Calendar sect: 36.
Lowell briefly discusses the diversity of women's
theatre, performance, dance, and lesbian theatre in
the Los Angeles area. She also covers the various
philosophies of the feminist aesthetic, ranging
from the highly personal to the highly political
that these women's theatre groups use in
approaching their productions.

61. Lutenbacher, Cindy "'So Much More Than Just Myself':
Women Theatre Artists in the South." *Themes in
Drama*, 11 (1989): 253-263.
The author surveys the work of several women
theatre artists who are working in the South. Most
are members of ROOTS (Regional Organization of

Theatres South), which, Lutenbacher believes is "integral in the continuity and potential of [the] theatrical movement in the South; its goals represent some of the most important common bonds between the women I have observed and interviewed."

62. MacDonald, Erik L. "Theatre Rhinoceros; A Gay Company." *Drama Review,* 33, i (Spring 1989): 77-93.
    MacDonald profiles Allan Estes, founder of Theatre Rhinoceros in San Francisco. Theatre Rhinoceros, which has had, according to the author, a tremendous impact on the gay-lesbian theatre, was created to dramatize "gay sensibilites and attitudes." Although the majority of the plays produced by the theatre are written by men, it has mounted several by female playwrights such as Jane Chambers's *My Blue Heaven,* the play that "underscored the issue of lesbian participation in a formerly all-male theatre company."

63. Mael, Phyllis. "Feminism and Theatre: A Drama of Our Own." *Chrysalis,* 10 (1980): 51-62.
    Mael takes a cursory look at the trends in feminist theatre. Although many women playwrights such as Marsha Norman dislike being labeled "feminist," Mael maintains that feminist theory has had a tremendous impact on the content and form of women's plays since the1960s. Female playwrights have found in the theatre a medium that allows them to express their experiences, feelings, and thoughts on a myriad of topics, including re-examining women's history, challenging tradtitional male-female roles, exposing the emotional trauma of rape and abortion, and exploring relatively uncharted areas such as the relationships between women. An annotated bibliography of plays written by women follows Mael's article.

64. *Making a Spectacle: Feminist Essays On Contemporary Women's Theatre.* Edited by Lynda Hart. Ann Arbor, Michigan: University of Michigan Press, 1989.
The first of its kind, Hart's collection of essays by scholars, "celebrates the intersection of feminism and theatre." International in scope, the collection grapples with a number of subjects and issues. Some of the essays evaluate the work of individual playwrights, including Joan Schenkar (see item 3248), Tina Howe (see item 1780), Maria Irene Fornes (see item 1115), Ntozake Shange (see item 3365), Beth Henley (see item 1606), Wendy Kesselman, (see item 2092) and Marsha Norman (see item 2888). Other essays related to American women's theatre concentrate on specific minorities, such as Japanese-American dramatists (see item 1), Chicana theatre artists affiliated with El Teatro Campesino and lesbian-feminist theatre groups.

65. Malpede, Karen. *Women in Theatre: Compassion & Hope.* New York: Drama Book Publishers, 1983.
Part of the first wave of books on feminist theatre writings, Malpede's work includes the writings of female actors, playwrights, directors and other theatrical figures, past and present who "had created or envisioned entire theatres, which . . . existed outside a commercial mainstream." In the last section of the book, "Feminist Plays and Performance: Ending the Violence We Have Known, " Clare Coss, Sondra Segal, and Roberta Sklar talk about the Women's Experimental Theatre they founded and a trilogy of plays they developed, *The Daughters Cycle* (see item 696). Following this discussion are Malpede's program notes for three of her plays, *The End of War, A Lament for Three Women,* and *Making Peace: A Fantasy.*

66. Malnig, Julie "The Women's Project: A Profile." *Women & Performance,* 1, i (1983): 71-73.
Malnig reports that Julia Miles organized the Women's Project at the American Place theatre in

1978 after discovering that "only 7% of the playwrights and 6% of the directors during 1969-1975 were women." According to Malnig, the Women's Project "has served as a 'home' where women theatre artists share their work in a supportive, non-competitive atmosphere." The Women's Project is credited with the mounting of several well-known plays including Katherine Collins's *The Brothers,* Paula Cizmar's *Death of a Miner,* Lavonne Mueller's *Little Victories,* and Rose Leiman Goldemberg's *Letters Home.*

67.   Marranca, Bonnie and Gautam Dasgupta. *American Playwrights: A Critical Survey.* Volume 1. New York: Drama Book Specialists, 1981.
The authors provide introductory surveys to the major plays of seventeen dramatists, four of whom are women: Maria Irene Fornes, Rochelle Owens, Rosalyn Drexler and Megan Terry. According to Marranca and Dasgupta the major critierion for inclusion in their book is that the playwrights had to have had a play produced on Off or Off-Off Broadway before 1967.

68.   Mason, Louise Cheryl. "The Fight To Be an American Woman and a Playwright: A Critical History from 1773 to the Present." Ph.D. diss., University of California, Berkeley, 1983.
Mason's thesis presents a historical analysis of American women playwrights from the late eighteenth century to the present. The analysis reveals that female playwrights have focused on issues and concerns close to the experiences of women. Many of these dramatists have created roles that portray realistically the sterotypic roles of mother, spinster, "fallen" woman, and older women. Mason further asserts that women playwrights have been in the forefront of much of the innovation and experimentation in the American theatre. "They have written some of the most radical dramatic experiments in form ever staged in America." Mason includes the following

playwrights as being representative of women
writing for the theatre since the early 1960s: Maria
Irene Fornes, Corinne Jacker, Ntozake Shange,
Megan Terry, Rochelle Owens, Rosalyn Drexler,
Alice Childress, Adrienne Kennedy, Barbara
Garson, Julie Bovasso, and Myrna Lamb.

69. Meserve, Walter J. "Women Playwrights." *American
Literary Scholarship: An Annual, 1989,* 377-380.
Durham: Duke University Press, 1990.
In his bibliographic essay on the year's work in
drama, Meserve acknowledges the neglect of
scholars in assessing the work of women
playwrights; he sees "the prejudice against drama in
general combined with past attitudes toward women
writers has proved to be a substantial barrier to
scholarship."

70. Michaelson, Judith. "Women Playwrights and Their Stony
Road." *Los Angeles Times* (Nov. 6, 1988): 47,
54-55.
Michaelson reports on the First International
Women's Playwrights Conference held at the
Buffalo-Amherst campus of State University of
New York. She summarizes some of the key
issues that were addressed at the conference. Women
theatre artists, for example, are still agonizing over
whether a feminist aesthetic exists or "is true art
genderless?" And women playwrights continue to
deal with the problem of the male attitude toward
the stageworthiness of plays written by women.
Among the American women playwrights
Michelson quotes are Kathleen Betsko and Alice
Childress. For another report on the International
Women's Playwrights Conference see item 92.

71. Miles, Julia. "Introduction." *Women's Project 2.* New
York: PAJ Publications, 1984.
In her introduction to the second volume of a
collection of contemporary plays written by
women, Julia Miles gives a brief overview of the
purpose of the Women's Project.

72. Miller, Jeanne-Marie. "Black Women Playwrights from
    Grimke to Shange: Selected Synopses of Their
    Works." In *But Some of Us Are Brave: Black
    Women's Studies*. Edited by Gloria T. Hull, P.B.
    Scott, and Barbara Smith, 280-290. Old Westbury,
    New York: Feminist Press, 1982.
    Miller succinctly surveys the work of several
    contemporary African-American women whose
    plays "offer a unique insight into the Black
    experience," including Alice Childress, Ntozake
    Shange, Adrienne Kennedy, Sonia Sanchez, and
    Martie Charles.

73. Moore, Honor. "Introduction." *The New Women's Theatre:
    Ten Plays by Contemporary American Women.*
    New York: Vintage Books, 1977.
    Moore's introduction to the texts of ten plays
    briefly examines the position of women dramatists
    in Western theatre history. In highlighting the
    work of several early playwrights (e.g., Hroswitha,
    Aphra Behn, Anna Cora Mowat, Lillian Hellman,
    and others) she discusses the difficulties that
    women faced when writing for theatre dominated by
    men. Moore then focuses on the playwrights
    included in her anthology. These playwrights
    represent a movement in the late 1960s and early
    1970s of "women [who] have begun to write their
    own experience." Moore states that she has selected
    plays that represent the various ways in which
    these experiences can be dramatized. These dramas
    illustrate the trend of women playwrights in
    experimenting with different theatrical forms and
    styles. Of the ten plays Moore includes, eight are
    by playwrights included in this bibliography: *Bits
    and Pieces* (Corinne Jacker), *Breakfast Past Noon*
    (Ursule Molinaro), *Birth and After Birth* (Tina
    Howe), *Mourning Pictures* (Honor Moore),
    Wedding Band (Alice Childress), *The Abdication*
    (Ruth Wolff), *I Lost A Pair of Gloves Yesterday*
    (Myrna Lamb), and *Out of Our Father's House*
    (Eve Merriam).

74. _____."Theatre Will Never Be the Same." *Ms.*, 6 (1977): 36-39, 74-75.

Moore reports on the aesthetic and political positions of women in the theatre, focusing on dramatists and directors. She points out that female playwrights are a "vulnerable minority." That is, their plays are often "judged against men's plays or against everyone's ideal of a play about female experience." However, women playwrights continue their exploration of modes for dramatizing the inner experiences of being woman. For example, Moore observes that many female dramatists use collaborative and choral forms, both of which she sees as a reaction against the "male-invented leading lady isolated in her predicament." And those playwrights employing the single protagonist depart from the stereotypical leading ladies. Ruth Wolff, for instance, dramatizes the fragmentation of self by using several actors to represent one fragment of self. Moore touches upon the political reality of women working in the theatre. She states that women playwrights and directors have difficulty in obtaining jobs and receiving grants in the theatre. Moore quotes one woman director, "When producers think in mainstream terms, they see playwrights and directors as men."

75. Morrow, Lee Alan and Frank Pike. *Creating Theater: The Professionals' Approach to New Plays.* New York: Vintage Books, 1986.

Distinguished dramatists, actors, directors, designers and critics meet, in what resembles a "mock round table discussion," to answer questions pertaining to their respective roles in the theatre. The arrangement of interviews of these theatrical notables offer the reader a prismatic view of the intricacies of creating and producing a new play. For example, one can learn how playwright Beth Henley and director Marshall M. Mason feel about the relevance of staged readings. Chapter one is

devoted to several playwrights' responses to
pertinent questions covering career beginings in the
theatre, major role models, approaches to writing
plays, among others. The authors also provide
brief biographical data on each of the interviewees.
Women playwrights interviewed are Beth Henley,
Marsha Norman, Maria Irene Fornes, Corinne
Jacker, Tina Howe, Emily Mann, and Wendy
Wasserstein.

76.   Natalle, Elizabeth. *Feminist Theatre: A Study in
         Persuasion*. Metuchen, N.J.: Scarecrow Press,
         1985.
         Natalle explores feminist theatre and its intimate
         relationship with the feminist movement. Natalle
         approaches her analysis from a rhetorical stance,
         which attempts to show how feminist theatre
         collectives use dramatic strategies to persuade the
         spectators to reconsider their roles in relationship to
         the patriarchal system, the family, and other
         institutions. See also Natalle's "Function of
         Feminist Theatre as a Rhetorical Medium within
         the Women's Movement." Ph.D diss., Florida State
         University, 1983.

77.   *9 Plays by Black Women*. Edited by Margaret Wilkerson.
         New York: New American Library, 1986.
         In this anthology of plays, Wilkerson includes an
         introductory essay and a profile of each of the
         playwrights that accompanies their plays, which
         include: Alice Childress's *Wedding Band*, Alexis
         DeVeaux's *The Tapestry*, Aishah Rahman's
         *Unfinished Women Cry in No Man's Land While a
         Bird Dies in a Gilded Cage*, Ntozake Shange's *Spell
         #7*, Kathleen Collins's *The Brothers*, Elaine
         Jackson's *Paper Dolls*, and P.J. Gibson's *Brown
         Silk and Magenta Sunsets*.

78.   Olauson, Judith. *The American Woman Playwright: A
         View of Criticism and Characterization*. Troy, New
         York: Whitson, 1981.

Olauson's general examination focuses on women playwrights, active over a forty year period (1930-1970), who have created roles that deviate from the conventional one-dimensional, submissive women characters traditionally portrayed in the past. According to Olauson, these female dramatists are significant contributors to "women-centered material and theory." Mirroring the changes of the American woman in society, the plays of these women dramatists reflect their exploration of the uncharted areas of women's experience, "their themes encompass identification with domestic difficulties, social ills, personal frustrations and psychic confusion." Chapter five surveys the major work of five contemporary female playwrights: Adrienne Kennedy, Rosalyn Drexler, Megan Terry, Rochelle Owens and Myrna Lamb. Olauson apparently chose these playwrights to represent the 1960s and early 1970s because they are identified with the "new" or "vanguard" theatre; these playwrights experimented with mixed media on stage to "produce purely theatrical rather than verbal effects."

79. O'Rourke, Joyce Williams. "New Female Playwrights in the American Theatre, 1973-1983; A Critical Analysis of Thought in Selected Plays," Ph.D. diss., Louisiana State University and Agricultural and Mechanical College, 1988.
O'Rourke contends that the women writing in the last two decades have "produced an extra-ordinary body of work, signifying a new thrust in the American theatre." In her examiniation of the work done during this period, O'Rourke has chosen ten dramatists: Tina Howe, Rosalyn Drexler, Rose Leiman Goldemberg, Mary Gallagher, Adele Eddling Shank, Lavonne Mueller, Wendy Wasserstein, Ntozake Shange, Beth Henley and Marsha Norman. These dramatists, according to the author, "represent the creative impulse of the '80s" and have "invigorated the American stage and

influenced their contemporaries, both male and
female."

80. Patraka, Vivian. "Staging Memory: Contemporary Plays by
Women." *Michigan Quarterly Review*, 26 (Winter
1987): 285-292.
Patraka critiques plays, representing experimental
as well as realistic styles, whose themes revolve
around memory, "linking women's memory to
women's history." The plays include: Megan
Terry's *Mollie Bailey's Traveling Family Circus:
Featuring Scenes from the Life of Mother Jones*,
Joan Schenkar's *Signs of Life*, Marsha Norman's
'night Mother, Joanna Glass's *Play Memory*, and
Ntozake Shange's *for colored who have considered
suicide/when the rainbow is enuf.*

81. Primus, Francesca. "Hyphenates: Performers Who Wear
Several Hats." *Back Stage* (Oct. 23, 1987), sect. 2:
24-26, 28.
Primus interviews Austin Pendelton, Geraldine
Fitzgerald, and Gretchen Cryer, whom she sees as
"hyphenates," theatre artists who wear more than
one hat. Gretchen Cryer, in particular, responds to
questions that explore her roles as playwright,
actress, and director, and how they inform each
other.

82. _____. "Women's Theatres Around Town: Feminist or
Contemporary?" *Back Stage* (Dec. 6, 1985), sect.
2:1A, 22, 24-29.
Primus addresses the question, "Is feminist theatre
dead?" In light of the fact that feminist theatres,
which "sprouted like weeds in the 1970s," have
diminished in numbers in the 1980s, these
remaining theatres represent "new directions and
forces" in theatre. Women's theatre companies
have evolved from the "didactic" to a more
"pragmatic approach"; in other words, they have
"incorporat[ed] the polemics and philosophy of
feminism—sans comment—into the theatre
companies." Primus asserts that many such theatre

groups avoid the label "feminist" because of its ideological and political overtones, and artistic directors feel the label restricts their artistic vision. Although noting there has been an influx of women playwrights and directors, they continue to remain in the shadows of the theatre world. Since the 1960s and 1970s, the topics chosen by women dramatists have expanded from "yesterday's rhetoric of sexual politics . . . to a wider range of concerns." The remainder of the article is devoted to lengthy descriptions of the major women's theatres in New York City such as The Women's Project, Women's Interart Center, Eccentric Circles, and others.

83. "The Public Forum." *Women and Performance*, 3, i (1986): 126-132.
    This article comprises two excerpts relating to women's theatre. The first excerpt is taken from a panel discussion, "Writing About Women in Performance," held at the Eastern Central Theatre Conference of the American Theatre Association, February 1985. The panelists, including playwright Karen Malpede, discussed how they incorporate a feminine aesthetic into their work. The second excerpt is from playwright Peggy Gold's address delivered at the National Women's Political Caucus in Atlanta, 1985. Gold addresses the implication of sexual discrimination in the theatre.

84. Rea, Charlotte. "Women for Women." *Drama Review*, 18, iv (1974):77-87.
    Rea examines the development of feminist theatre by surveying six theatre groups operated by women, ranging from the establishment-oriented groups such as The New York Feminist Theatre to experimental groups or "performing collectives" such as It's All Right To Be Woman, Women's Guerrilla Theatre, Westbeth Feminist Collective and Vancouver Women's Caucus. The philosophy, artistic objectives, and major dramatic techniques

employed by these theatre groups are discussed.
Underlying Rea's article is the assumption that
those theatre groups who experiment with
alternative dramatic forms that reflect "their
consciousness" affect spectators to a much greater
degree than those who do not challenge
conventional dramatic forms.

85.   Reinhardt, Nancy S. "New Directions For Feminist
          Criticism in Theatre and the Related Arts."
          Soundings, 64, iv (Winter 1981): 361-387.
          In the first part of her essay, which is one of very
          few that deals with the problems of scholarship in
          feminist drama, Reinhardt presents three probable
          reasons why theatre arts scholarship lags behind
          film and television studies in applying feminist
          theories to the examination of works in classical
          drama. First, cinema and television studies are new
          art forms and do not "carry around centuries of
          critical baggage." Thus unencumbered, film and
          television scholarship is more receptive to "new
          perspectives and challenges in its search for a
          pertinent critical vocabulary." Secondly, sexism is
          much more overt on celluloid; therefore, such sex
          exploitation make the media vulnerable to criticism
          from feminist scholars. And thirdly, theatre is
          more dependent on the male-dominated public and
          social arena for its creation and production. The
          remainder of Reinhardt's essay focuses on ways of
          approaching classical tragedy from a feminist
          perspective and how it can "stimulate new
          directions in theatre scholarship." The author also
          analyzes gender differences in the visual imagery
          used in the acting space.

86.   Roberts, Vera Mowry. "Bright Lights and Backstage;
          Women Playwrights in the Theatre." *Furman
          Studies*, 34 (Dec. 1988):26-35.
          Roberts traces the history of female playwrights.
          She observes that for centuries women were

excluded from active participation in the theatre because "essentially only three life roles [were] open to women . . . wife/mother, virgin/nun, and whore/outcast." But, despite the fact that these restrictive roles discouraged the expression of creativity, some women, like the tenth-century playwright Hrotswitha, were "pushed and pulled somehow into the male-approved framework." Although Roberts mainly highlights the work of female playwrights in previous eras, she concludes her essay with a discussion of the playwrights who contributed to the formation of the femnist theatre, which got its impetus from the women's liberation movement of the 1960s. Noting that dramatists such as Corinne Jacker, Megan Terry, Ntozake Shange, and Roberta Sklar collectively represent a myriad of styles and forms, the author concludes "that about the only statement possible at this time is that many women are unselfconsciously exploring what it means to be a woman in today's world."

87. Robinson, Alice M., Vera Mowry Roberts, and Milly S. Barranger. *Notable Women in the American Theatre: A Biographical Dictionary.* New York: Greenwood, 1989.
The first of its kind, this handbook focuses solely on the contributions of women in the theatre. Represented here are playwrights, producers, actresses, directors, designers, critics, and managers. For playwrights, each signed entry includes a biographical sketch as well as a cursory discussion of selected plays. Includes a selected list of primary and secondary sources.

88. Rose, Phyllis Jane. "A Harvest of Voices; Women in Theatre Fest Flourishing in Boston." *American Theatre*, 6 (July/Aug., 1989): 52-53.
Rose reports on the fifth annual Women in Theatre Festival in Boston.

89. Roth, Martha. "Notes Toward a Feminist Performance
    Aesthetic." *Women and Performance*, 1, i
    (Spring/Summer 1983):5-14.
    Roth calls for "women in performance to take off
    the masks of the male imagination." The roles
    women portray on stage are based on patriarchal
    models and reinforces the culture's "political
    economy of sex." Roth would like to see a theatre
    in which "women lift women and women lift
    men." She wants woman to act and not simply to
    react according to their sexual relations to men as
    she has done for hundreds of years. Roth
    recognizes that new images of women must be
    performed and that the spectators must "examine
    [their] preconceptions. If we are made
    uncomfortable by the spectacle of woman behaving
    in unpatterned ways, we need to look at this
    discomfort."

90. Rothstein, Mervyn. "Women Playwrights: Themes and
    Variations. *New York Times* (May 7, 1989): H1.
    Rothstein moderates a stimulating discussion
    among four prominent women playwrights—Tina
    Howe, Ntozake Shange, Wendy Wasserstein, and
    Cindy Lou Johnson—who respond to several
    questions focusing on "women's voices in today's
    theater." The views of these playwrights are
    penetrating and at times disparate. Tina Howe, for
    example, feels that "we're playwrights and that we
    may be women, that may be our gender, but I don't
    think there's such a thing as a woman's voice. I
    think there are women's voices that . . . are very
    distinct from each other." But Shange believes that
    "I am not a generic playwright, I am a woman
    playwright. I don't have anything that I can add to
    the masculine perception of the world. What I can
    add has to be from what I've experienced." The
    playwrights respond to other questions such as,
    Should playwrights ignore gender? What is the
    present situation for women in the theatre and has
    it changed over time? What can encourage more
    women to become theatre artists?

91. Savran, David. *In Their Own Words: Contemporary
     American Playwrights.* New York: Theater
     Communications Group, 1988.
     Savran conducted the interviews for this book to
     determine what the leading playwrights in America
     felt was the "relationship between aesthetic and
     moral mission." In short, should theatre be a
     "vehicle for social change." To prepare the reader
     for each of the interviews, Savran provides a
     biographical profile of the individual and a general
     assessment of his or her method of making plays.
     What emerges from the interviews is a
     kaleidoscopic view of the American theatre
     situation, reflecting a myriad of impressions,
     opinions, and reflections on dramatic strategies,
     critics, and other playwrights. Complementing the
     interviewees' responses to general issues, they also
     respond to specific questions pertaining to their
     own work and situation in the theatrical world.
     Among the playwrights, five women are included:
     Maria Irene Fornes, Emily Mann, Marsha Norman,
     Megan Terry and Joan Holden.

92. Shepard, Richard F. "Women Plan Playwrights'
     Conference." *New York Times* (July 14, 1988):
     C13.
     Shepard reports on the First International Women
     Playwrights Conference sponsored by State
     University at Buffalo, which was held in October,
     1988 at Buffalo. Accoring to Shepard, participants
     included playwrights and directors representing
     several countries, including the United States,
     England, Mexico, South Africa, Greece, among
     others. Comprised of a series of panel discussions,
     staged readings, and theatrical productions, the
     participants were to address a myriad of issues—
     feminist aesthetics, censorship, lesbian theatre,
     minority theatre artists—confronting women
     writing, directing, and producing for the theatre.
     For another report on the outcome of the
     conference, see item 70.

93. Shewey, Don. "Gay Theatre Grows Up." *American Theatre*,
    5 (May 1988): 11-17, 52-53.
    Shewey affirms the perception that, until recently,
    gays, like women and minorities, have been the
    victims of misrepresentation on stage—"[gays] had
    the choice of being frivolous fairies, psychotic
    bull-dykes or suicidal queens." The article, which
    is devoted to a survey of plays that treat
    thematically homosexuality, is set against a
    historical background that discusses the traditional
    view of the images of homosexuality on stage.
    Shewey touches upon the contributions of female
    dramatists such as Emily Mann, Jane Chambers,
    Alexis Deveaux, and Kathleen Tolan.

94. Siegel, June. "Behind the Scenes: Women's Activities:
    Onstage Drama." *Dramatists Guild Quarterly*, 18, ii
    (Summer 1987): 65-66.
    Siegel briefly notes the formation of the Women In
    Theatre Network, Inc., a non-profit organization
    founded in 1981. She also describes the fifth
    annual anniversary of the Dramatist's Guild
    Committee for Women.

95. Sisley, Emily L. "Notes on Lesbian Theater." *Drama
    Review*, 25, i (1981): 47-56.
    William Hoffman, who wrote *Gay Plays: The First
    Collection*, defines gay theatre as "a production that
    implicitly or explicitly acknowledges that there are
    [lesbians] on both sides of the footlights." Sisley
    adapts Hoffman's definition to clarify the
    parameters of lesbian theatre. She begins by
    stating that lesbian theatre evolved out of the
    feminist movement of the 1960s and early 1970s.
    Sisley proceeds to compare lesbian theatre with
    feminist theatre and "just plain theatre." Lesbian
    and feminist theatres, the author maintains, create
    productions or collectives and they "draw from the
    experiences of women as *women* experience them
    not as men think they do." Sisley also addresses
    the chronic problem of the low visibility of lesbian
    theatre and its difficulty in obtaining quality

scripts. She suggests that greater exposure could
be created by developing a master list of lesbian
plays and organizing more theatre festivals. Sisley
also summarizes the work of several lesbian theatre
troupes including: The Lavender Cellar,
Minneapolis Lesbian Resource Center, and It's All
Right To Be Woman Theatre.

96.   Steadman, Susan M. Flierl. "Feminist Dramatic Criticism:
Where We Are Now." *Women and Performance*, 4,
ii (1989): 118-148.
Steadman provides a fairly extensive bibliography
of books and articles devoted to evaluating women's
theatre and to studies on single women
playwrights, historical as well as contemporary.
American theater is emphasized; British and
Canadian theatre is treated to a limited extent.
Steadman includes a cursory essay evaluating
feminist theatre research.

97.   Suntree, Susan. "Women's Theatre: Creating the Dream
Now." In *Women's Culture; Renaissance of the
Seventies*. Edited by Gayle Kimball. Metuchen,
New Jersey: Scarecrow Press, 1981.
Suntree contends that many women's theatre groups
are challenging traditional images and roles of
women through the manipulation of alternative
dramatic forms and styles. The author states that
"contributing to this discovery of women's roots
and expanding the definitions of modern theatre
practice is the increasing use of ritual by women's
groups." She illustrates her comments by focusing
on her involvement with the Berkeley Stage
Company during the winter of 1975-1976. This
theatre group used the Antigone myth to dramatize
the nature of women. Suntree describes the various
theatrical methods the group used to create their
dramatic piece *Antigone Prism.*

98.   Tate, Claudia. *Black Women Writers at Work*. New York:
Continuum, 1983.

The purpose of Tate's collection of interviews,
which include writers who have written for the
stage (Maya Angelou, Alexis DeVeaux, Toni
Morrison, Sonia Sanchez, and Ntozake Shange), is
to transport the reader "into the heart of the creative
process." Her questions focus on general areas of
modes of writing, such as these writers' perceptions
of the author/reader relationship and specific queries
geared toward their works. For instance, individual
approaches and techniques to writing.
Unfortunately, little is revealed about the writers'
dramatic works, with the exception of Shange's
interview, as Tate concentrates on their fiction and
poetry. Tate does achieve a dialog of sorts,
however, when she asks Alexis DeVeaux and others
about their reactions to Shange's controversial
choreopoem, *for colored girls who have considered
suicide/when the rainbow is enuf.*

99.   Temple, Joanne. "Women's Theatre Finds a Stage of Its
       Own." *Village Voice* (Oct. 27, 1975): 84.
       Temple acknowledges the tendency to censor plays
       written by women because of content, pointing out
       that producers consider them to be "soap operas" or
       "antimale." Nevertheless, Temple accuses women's
       theatre of conducting the "worst from of
       censorship." Granted women theatre artists have
       been bold in pushing the boundaries of dramatic
       form but they have "shied away from the most
       difficult content—the whole category of 'afterward'
       has been missing." What happened to Ibsen's
       Nora, Temple asks, after she left Torgvald?
       Temple's discussion contains brief comments about
       playwright Myrna Lamb.

100. Thrall, Judy. "Women Playwright Upsurge; Gain
       Stronghold on Stage. *Back Stage* (Feb. 12, 1982):
       1, 48, 50, 52, 56.
       A lively article based on interviews with
       playwrights Wendy Kesselman, Barbara
       Schottenfeld, E. Katherine Kerr, Casey Kelly, Tina
       Howe, Wendy Wasserstein, Marsha Norman, and

Jane Stanton Hitchcock. These playwrights
respond to questions dealing with their early days in
the theatre, whether they perceive an increase in the
number of women playwrights, their opinions on
how gender affects playwriting, and their encounters
with sexual discrimination.

101. Turner, S.H. Regina."Images of Black Women in the Plays
of Black Female Playwrights, 1950-1975," Ph.D.
diss., Bowling Green State University, 1982.
In addition to considering the images of black
women in the dramatic works by black women,
Turner also studies these images as they appear in
the literature of the social sciences. The
contemporary playwrights included in her study are:
Alice Childress, Sonia Sanchez, Adrienne Kennedy,
and Marti Charles.

102. Weales, Gerald. *The Jumping-Off Place: American Drama
in the 1960's.* New York: Macmillan Company,
1969.
In Weales's examination of the Off-Off Broadway
scene, he includes brief assessments of several
women playwrights such as Megan Terry, Maria
Irene Fornes, and Barbara Garson.

103. "Where Are the Women Playwrights?" *New York Times*
(May 20, 1973), sect. 2: 1,3.
In 1973, the *Times'* curiosity was piqued by the
fact that so few women were writing for the theatre,
so the newspaper asked several prominent female
playwrights to discuss the issue of the scarcity of
women dramatists. For Gretchen Cryer, the
problem is guilt, "[who] knows how many
potential playwrights there may be out there fixing
bag lunches for their children who would be
attempting to write their plays, and get them on,
were it not for the fact that they would guiltily
consider their efforts self-indulgent folly."
Adrienne Kennedy adds that women are not
encouraged by society to pursue the solitary course
of creative endeavor, "a woman listens to several

voices . . . women are taught to answer the voices
and needs of others, to surrender to the desires of
those we love." And Rochelle Owens declares that
there are many "latent playwrights [women who]
deplete their creative force and inspiration in the
aeons-old traditional habit of overnurturing and
pampering their 'genius' husbands who are driven to
kvetching out 'The Novel'." Other playwrights
included in the article are Rosalyn Drexler, Lillian
Hellman, Renee Taylor, Clare Boothe Luce, and
Jean Kerr.

104.   Wilkerson, Margaret B. "Music as Metaphor: New Plays of
        Black Women." In *Making a Spectacle: Feminist
        Essays On Contemporary Women's Theatre*. Edited
        by Lynda Hart, 61-75. Ann Arbor, Michigan:
        University of Michigan Press, 1989.
        Wilkerson, who has published several articles on
        black women playwrights, maintains that
        contemporary black women dramatists are re-
        defining how music is used in drama. They have
        refused to conform to the conventions of the
        American musical because it fails to express the
        "deepest, unspoken . . . feelings and experiences of
        human existence." Wilkerson examines the plays
        of Shange, DeVeaux, Childress, Gibson, and
        Rahman in terms of how the music used as subtext
        for their dramas serves as "a second language that
        gives profound anguish and joy of their vision and
        experience."

105.   Wilson, Edwin. "Separate and Subversive: Female
        Playwrights." *Wall Street Journal* (Sep. 23,
        1987): 32.
        Wilson reports on the tenth annual conference of
        the Susan Smith Blackburn Prize held in Houston.
        The conference focused on the progress of women's
        theatre since the 1970s. He mentions Francine du
        Plessix Gray, a speaker at the 1982 conference,
        who presciently observed that the earlier women's
        voices in the theatre were "militant," often
        "confrontational" and made "a very frontal attack on

the male as exploiter and tyrant" but the emphasis has shifted in the last few years; female playwrights have redirected their focus from "anti-male" to "pro-female drama." Speakers at the conference noted that despite the increased recognition of women dramatists, they continue to lag far behind their male counterparts in terms of the number of plays produced. Furthermore, according to speaker Gretchen Cryer, the double standard still operates. Themes covered by male playwrights continue to be treated more seriously by producers and directors than those focused upon by female dramatists. The consensus of many of the participants is that until this situation is rectified, male and female playwrights will "reside in separate worlds: the acceptable group—the men, and the subversives—the women."

106. "Women Playwrights Set Up Four Committees at the [Dramatists] Guild; Offer Workshop Stagings at the American Place." *Dramatists Guild Quarterly*, 16, ii (Summer, 1979).
This article includes brief news notes on the activities of the Dramatists Guild.

107. Yarbro-Bejarano, Yvonne. "Chicanas' Experience in Collective Theatre: Ideology and Form." *Women and Performance*, 2, ii (1985): 45-58.
Yarbro-Bejarano points out that theatre collectives offer Chicana theater artists more opportunities for involvement. Unlike commercial theatres, these collectives allow Hispanic women "to share responsibility for decisions, to have input into the entire process, to spearhead projects and assume leadership positions." But, however democratic the collective is, Yarbro-Bejarano asserts that Chicana women continue to encounter sexist attitudes and practices in many of the collectives, which in turn restricts their involvement and creative input. The author also examines several theatre groups, including the San Francisco Mime Troupe, the Teatro de la Esperanza, and the Teatro Campesino.

The two former collectives are receptive to the involvement of Chicanas and the latter the author claims is grounded in the male tradition. Although Chicana theatre artists recognize the benefits of being affiliated with a collective, they also realize advantages of the commercial theatre such as increased salary and working with a diverse group of actors and directors.

108. _____. " The Image of Chicana in Teatro." *Theaterwork* (May-June, 1982): 19-21. Reprinted in *Rivista Literaria del Tecolote*, 11, i (Dec. 1981): 3-4. The author evaluates the roles women play in Chicano theatre by examining four plays produced by El Teatro de la Esperanza. These dramas demonstrate that this particular theatre collective recognizes the importance of dramatizing the social issues confronting the Chicano community from the perspective of women's experiences as well as men's.

109. _____. "The Role of Women in Chicano Theater Organizations." *El Tecolote Literary Magazine*, 12 (December,1981): 7, 10. The author briefly discusses the formation and contributions of W.I.T. (Women in Teatro), an organization devoted to developing Chicana Theatre artists, founded by Chicanas who felt that Teatros Nacionales de Aztlan (TENAZ) failed to respond to their needs and concerns. Yarbro-Bejarano also describes a seminar, held at the eleventh annual International Chicano/Latino Teatro Festival, which focused on women's issues in the theatre. The participants of the seminar drafted a resolution which addressed the problem of sexism and homophobia, which was strongly opposed by many male participants. According to the author, these men were opposed to the resolution on "ideological" grounds that homosexuality is an aberration against the natural order; the female participants interpreted this to mean "that the

natural order they are defending includes sexist
definitions of the roles of men and women."

110. Zivanovic, Judith. "The Rhetorical and Political
Foundations of Women's Collaborative Theatre."
Themes in Drama (1989): 209-219.
Zivanovic affirms Patti Gillespie's observation (see
item 39) that political ideology and rhetoric is
fundamental to feminist theatre. "Their primary aim
is action, not art." The author points out that
female theatre artists long have recognized the
power of working collectively to communicate a
higher awareness of feminist concerns and the
experiences of women. Accoring to Zivanovic,
there are two modes of collaboration: "among the
artists and between the artists and the audience prior
to a performance or during a performance." She
examines both processes, drawing upon several
collaborative theatre groups such as Omaha Magic
Theatre, At the Foot of the Mountain, and
Spiderwoman, to prove her contention that "these
processes of collaboration reveal most strongly the
foundation of feminist rhetoric and politics within
such companies."

Individual Playwrights

Akalaitis, JoAnne

Selected Plays

111. *Dead End Kids: A History of Nuclear Power* (New York Shakespeare Festival, Public Theatre, 1980)
112. *Dressed Like an Egg* (based on the works of Colette, Mabou Mines, Public Theatre, 1977)
    Playscript: *Wordplays 4: An Anthology of New American Drama*. New York: PAJ Publications, 1984.
113. *Green Card* (Joyce Theater, 1988)
114. *Southern Exposure* (New York Shakespeare Festival, Public Theatre, 1979)

Profiles and Interviews

115. Bell-Metereau, Rebecca. "JoAnne Akalaitis." In *Critical Survey of Drama: Supplement*. Edited by Frank McGill, 1-7. Pasadena, California: Salem Press, 1986.
    Bell-Metereau provides a biographical sketch of Akalaitis's life and achievements as well as a cursory analysis of her major plays.

116. *Contemporary Theatre, Film and Television*. Volume 5. Edited by Monica M. O'Donnell, 5. Detroit: Gale Research Company, 1988.
    The entry contains a brief biography, including a list of Akalaitis's plays.

117. Drake, Sylvie. "A Three Mile Island Spinoff." *Los Angeles Times* (Feb. 9, 1984), sect. 6: 1, 6.
     Written shortly before Akalaitis's *Dead End Kids* was performed at the Mark Taper Forum, this article highlights the theatrical career of Akalaitis, especially her role as a founding member of the experimental group Mabou Mines.

118. Kalb, Jonathan. "JoAnne Akalaitis." *Theater*, 15, ii (Spring 1984): 7-13.
     Akalaitis describes her debut as a director with Mabou Mines and how its collaborative style has affected her development as a writer and director. She discusses some of her significant productions (e.g., *Dead End Kids, Request Concert* and *The Photographer*) in terms of their conception, development, and the directorial techniques she employed. She also touches upon her experiences as a woman working in the theatre, "women . . . have to watch themselves and behave better than men." Kalb asks her about works-in-progress and future projects.

Reviews

Dead End Kids

119. Bergart, Catherine and Clark Candy. *Drama Review*, 25, iii (Fall 1981): 92-94.

120. Brustein, Robert. *New Republic*, 183 (Dec. 27, 1980): 26.

121. Chaillet, Ned. *Times* (London) (Jan. 13, 1981): 9d.
     Chaillet reports on the New York production of *Dead End Kids*.

122. Collins, William B. *Philadelphia Inquirer* (Feb. 25, 1983), sect. C: 4.
     See also letters to the editor commenting on the performance in *Philadelphia Inquirer* (Mar. 10, 1983): A14.

123. Drake, Sylvie "Stage Watch." *Los Angeles Times* (Feb. 14,
      1984), sect. 6: 1, 6.
      Akalaitis briefly discusses the conception of *Dead
      End Kids*.

124. Fuchs, Elinor. "Staging the Obscene Body." *Drama Review,*
      33, i (Spring 1989): 33-58.
      Briefly discusses the staging of *Dead End Kids* and
      the reactions of the audience to the production.

125. _____. *SoHo News* (Nov. 19, 1980): n.p.

126. Gerard, Jeremy. "Mabou Mines Revivals in a Brief Chelsea
      Run." *New York Times* (Mar. 20, 1987): C3.
      Gerard briefly mentions *Dead End Kids* in his
      survey of recent productions of the Mabou Mines.

127. Harris, William. "Through the Lens." *Village Voice* (Mar.
      26, 1985): 104.
      This item discusses the film version of *Dead End
      Kids*.

128. Hoberman, J. *Village Voice*, 31 (Nov. 11, 1986): 51.
129. Novick, Julius. *Nation*, 231 (Dec. 20, 1980): 683-684.
130. Rich, Frank. *New York Times* (Nov. 19, 1980), sect. 3:
      C34.
131. _____. *New York Times* (Nov. 28, 1980), sect. 3: C1,
      C16.
132. _____. *New York Times* (Dec. 26, 1980), sect. 3: C3.
133. _____. *New York Times* (May 31, 1981), sect. 2: D1,
      D4.
134. Sanello, Frank. *After Dark*, 13 (Mar. 1981): 68.

135. Shewey, Don. "A Revue for the Nuclear Age Moves From
      Stage to Film." *New York Times* (Nov. 9, 1986):
      H15.
      Akalaitis discusses the film version of her play
      Dead End Kids.

136. Sterritt, David. *Christian Science Monitor* (Jan. 6, 1981):
      18.

Sterritt interviews Akalaitis backstage during a
performance of *Dead End Kids* at the Public
Theatre. Akalaitis touches several topics: the
"scientific theme" of her plays ("I've been
increasingly dissatisfied with the subject matter of
the arts. It's just neurotic . . . narcissistic, and
decadent."); her views on the state of the theatre
("It's hard to analyze . . . because it's sort of
floundering and falling apart."); and her intentions
for theatre "to talk about the unthinkable. And also
to give people information!"

137. _____. *Christian Science Monitor* (Dec. 3, 1980): 23.

Dressed Like An Egg

138. *American Theatre Annual 1976-1977,* 127. Detroit: Gale
Research Company, 1978.

139. Copland, Roger. "Where Theatrical and Conceptual Art Are
Blended." *New York Times* (May 1, 1977), sect.
2: 12, 20.
Copland previews the Mabou Mines production,
Dressed Like An Egg, conceived and directed by
Akalaitis. Very little of the article, however, is on
Akalaitis; Copland devotes most of the article
discussing the Mabou Mines theatre troupe: its
development and artistic goals, its utilization of
various theatrical forms and styles, and its
achievements.

140. Fox, Terry Curtis. *Village Voice* (May 23, 1977): 77, 79.
141. Gussow, Mel. *New York Times* (May 17 1977): 27.
142. _____. *New York Times* (Sep. 30, 1977), sect. C: 5.
143. _____. *New York Times* (Mar. 18, 1984): H1, H18.
144. Hoffman, Ted. *The Villager* (May 19, 1977): 13.
145. Munk, Erica. *Village Voice* (May 30, 1977): 87.
146. Ochiva, Dan. *Show Business* (May 19, 1977): 26.
147. Wetzsteon, Ross. *Village Voice* (June 6, 1977): 91-93.

Green Card

148. Arkatov, Janice. "*Green Card* Drawing Ethnic Parallels."
      Los Angeles Times (May 21, 1986), sect. 6: 1, 8.
      In this preview article, written shortly before the
      opening of *Green Card* at the Mark Taper Forum
      in May of 1986, multi-talented Akalaitis discusses
      the play, which confronts "issues of immigration
      and immersion into American society." Akalaitis
      wrote the play as a result of a commission from the
      Taper, which had requested a play from her "about
      all the different people in L.A." The latter part of
      the article focuses on Akalaitis's theatrical career as
      a director, writer, and actress. Akalaitis sees herself
      primarily as a director and claims her "artistic
      identity" is not "tied up" in writing—"[i]f I write
      something, it's because the script *has* to be written
      as opposed to a burning need to write."

149. Goodman, Walter. *New York Times* (June 20, 1988): C14.
150. Kim, Sophia Kyung. *Los Angeles Times* (June 29, 1986),
      Calendar sect: 3-4.
151. Kramer, Mimi. *New Yorker,* 64 (July 18, 1988): 66.
152. Lochte, David. *Los Angeles,* 31 (July 1986): 42-44.
153. Morris, Steven. *Drama Quarterly,* 162 (4th quarter 1986):
      43-44.
154. Munk, Erica. *Village Voice* (June 28, 1986): 121-122.
155. Ricky, Carrie. *Philadelphia Inquirer* (Sep. 19, 1987): D4.
156. Sharbutt, Jay. *Los Angeles Times,* (June 18, 1988), sect. 6:
      1.

157. Shirley, Don. "*Green Card* to Move East for N.Y.
      Festival." *Los Angeles Times* (Apr. 27, 1988),
      sect. 6: 6.
      Shirley announces that *Green Card,* which
      premiered at the Mark Taper Forum, will move to
      New York's Joyce Theater for the first annual New
      York Festival of the Arts in June, 1988.

158. Sullivan, Dan. *Los Angeles Times* (May 30, 1986), sect.
      6: 1, 23.
159. _____. *Los Angeles Times* (June 29, 1986), Calendar sect.:
      3-4.

160. Valle, Victor. *Los Angeles Times* (June 29, 1986),
     Calendar sect.: 3-4.
161. Wurm, Mark. *Los Angeles Times* (June 29, 1986),
     Calendar sect.: 3-4.

Southern Exposure

162. Curtis, Terry Fox. *Village Voice* (Mar. 5, 1979): 77-78.
163. Gussow, Mel. *New York Times* (Feb. 28, 1979): C19.
164. Mehta, Xerxes. *Theater Journal*, 36, ii (May 1984): 173-
     181.

Alvarez, Lynn

Selected Plays

165. *Don Juan of Seville* (translation of Tirso de Molina's work,
     INTAR and CSC Repertory, 1989)
166. *The Guitarron* (St. Clements, 1983)
     Playscript: *On New Ground: Contemporary
     Hispanic-American Plays.* Edited by Elizabeth M.
     Osborn, 1-43. New York: Theatre Communications
     Group, 1987.
167. *Hidden Parts* (New Dramatists, 1983-1984)
168. *Latinos* (with Manuel Martin and Omar Torres, INTAR,
     1978-1979)
169. *Mundo* (INTAR, 1982)
170. *The Red Madonna or a Damsel for a Gorilla* (by Fernando
     Arrabal and translated by Alvarez, INTAR, 1986)
171. *The Reincarnation of Jamie Brown* (staged reading Women's
     Project, 1987-1988)
172. *Thin Air: Tales From a Revolution* (San Diego Repertory
     Theatre, 1989)
173. *The Wonderful World of Humbert Lavoignet* (New
     Dramatists, 1984-1985)

Profiles and Interviews

See page 18.

174. Alvarez, Lynn. "Introduction to *The Guitarron*." In *On New
     Ground; Contemporary Hispanic-American Plays.*

Edited by Elizabeth M. Osborn. New York:
Theatre Communications Group, 1987.
In a preface to the text of Alvarez's play *The
Guitarron*, Alvarez profiles herself. She describes
her early years in journalism, how her playwriting
evolved from her poetry writing, and her confusion
over her cultural identity.

Reviews

Don Juan of Seville

175. *American Theatre,* 6 (May 1989): 11.
176. *Drama-Logue* (Apr. 20-26, 1989): 24.
177. Solomon, Alisa. *Village Voice* (Apr. 18, 1989): 98.

The Guitarron

178. Stone, Laurie. *Village Voice* (June 28, 1983): 102.

Mundo

179. Massa, Robert. *Village Voice* (Sep. 14, 1982): 77-78.

Thin Air: Tales From a Revolution

180. Churnin, Nancy. *Los Angeles Times* (Aug. 12, 1989), sect.
     5: 1, 5.

181. "Drama League Awards to Go to 7 Playwrights." *New York
     Times* (Dec. 14, 1987): C22.
     The *Times* notes that Alvarez received a Drama
     League Playwright's Assistance Award for *Thin
     Air*.

182. *Drama-Logue* (Aug. 24-30, 1989): 10.

Angelou, Maya

Selected Plays

183. *Ajax* (adaptation of Sophocles' play, Mark Taper Forum, 1973-1974)
184. *And Still I Rise* (AMAS Repertory Theater, 1979)
185. *On a Southern Journey* (Spirit Square Theatre, Charlotte North Carolina, 1983)

Profiles and Interviews

See items 87, 98.

186. *Black Writers: A Selection of Sketches from Contemporary Authors.* Edited by Linda Metzger, 13-15. Detroit: Gale Research Inc., 1989.
     The entry provides a biographical sketch of Angelou's achievements.

187. Bloom, Lynn Z. *Dictionary of Literary Biography.* Volume 38. *Afro-American Writers After 1955: Dramatists and Prose Writers.* Edited by Trudier Harris, 3-12. Detroit: Gale Research Company, 1985.
     This introductory article contains an extensive biographical and critical survey of Angelou's work. A primary and secondary bibliography of her works is included.

188. *Contemporary Authors: A Bio-Bibliographical Guide.* Volume 19. New Revised Series. Edited by Linda Metzger, 21-24. Detroit: Gale Research Inc., 1987.
     The entry includes a biographical sketch and general comments about Angelou.

189. Peterson, Bernard. *Contemporary Black American Playwrights and Their Plays: A Biographical Directory and Dramatic Index,* 16-19. New York: Greenwood Press, 1988.
     Peterson provides a biographical sketch and a brief staging history of Angelou's works.

Reviews

And Still I Rise

190. Halpert, Susanna. *Village Voice* (Nov. 12, 1979): 109-110.
191. *New York Times* (Oct. 15, 1979), sect. C: C19.
　　　　The *Times* briefly notes the opening of Angelou's musical *And Still I Rise* at the Amas Repertory Theatre.
192. Redmond, Eugene. *Black Scholar*, 8 (Sep. 1976): 50-51.
193. Stone, Judy. *San Francisco Chronicle* (Aug. 9, 1976): 37.

A Southern Journey

194. *Jet* (Dec. 9, 1983): 61.

Baizley, Doris

Selected Plays

195. *Bugs/Guns* (Mark Taper Forum, Los Angeles, 1977)
196. *Catholic Girls* (Mark Taper Forum, Los Angeles, 1979)
　　　　Playscript: *West Coast Plays*, 11/12 (Winter/Spring, 1982): 229-284.
197. *A Christmas Carol* (adaptor, Cleveland Playhouse, Cleveland, 1982-1983)
198. *Concrete Dreams* (Mark Taper Forum, Los Angeles, 1980)
199. *Daniel in Babylon* (L.A. Stage Company, Los Angeles, 1982)
　　　　Playscript: *West Coast Plays*, 19/20 (Spring/Summer, 1986): 187-222.
200. *In Darkest Africa: A Ladies' Guide to the Nile* (Workshop of the Player's Art, 1972)
201. *Mrs. California* (Mark Taper Forum, Los Angeles, 1985)
202. *My Rebel* (Lex Theatre, Hollywood, 1989)
203. *A Nightclub Miracle Play* (with Richard Weinstock, L.A. Theatre Works, Los Angeles, 1981)
204. *Tears of Rage* (Philadelphia Theatre Company, Philadelphia, 1988)

Profiles and Interviews

See item 206.

205. Arkatov, Janice. "Doris Baizley's Women in a Duty
     Contest." *Los Angeles Times* (Apr. 14, 1986),
     sect. 6:1, 9.
     Arkatov's article anticipates the opening of
     Baizley's *Mrs. California* at the Coronet Theatre in
     Los Angeles. Scattered throughout the discussion
     on the play are insights into Baizley's life and her
     career as a dramatist.

Reviews

Bugs/Guns

206. Drake, Sylvie. "No Kidding Around At the Taper." *Los
     Angeles Times* (June 5, 1977), Calendar sect: 56.
     Baizley and John Dennis, artistic director of the
     Improvisational Theater Project of the Mark Taper
     Forum, talk about the productions of *Bugs* and
     Guns.

207. Lochte, Dick. *Los Angeles*, 22 (July 1977): 201.
208. Sullivan, Dan. *Los Angeles Times* (Apr. 12, 1976), sect.
     4: 19.
209. _____. *Los Angeles Times* (June 13, 1977), sect. 4: 1,
     13.

Catholic Girls

210. Sullivan, Dan. *Los Angeles Times* (Oct. 15, 1979), sect. 4:
     1, 12.

Concrete Dreams

211. Coe, Richard L. *Los Angeles Times* (Apr. 29, 1978), sect.
     2: 11.
212. Sullivan, Dan. *Los Angeles Times* (Apr. 10, 1980), sect.
     6: 1, 4.

Mrs. California

See item 205.

213. Drake, Sylvie. *Los Angeles Times* (Apr. 22, 1986), sect. 6:
       1, 7.
214. _____. *Los Angeles Times* (Mar. 1, 1988), sect. 6: 1, 3.
215. *Drama-Logue* (Mar. 3-9, 1988): 8.
216. Lochte, Dick. *Los Angeles,* 31 (June 1986): 46-48.
217. Sullivan, Dan. *Los Angeles Times* (Oct. 30, 1985), sect. 6:
       1, 3.

My Rebel

218. Arkatov, Janice. "*My Rebel:* A Return to Vietnam Era."
       Los Angeles Times (Sep. 17, 1989), Calendar
       sect: 46.
       Arkatov previews Baizley's play, opening at the
       Lex Theatre in Hollywood. Interspersed throughout
       the article are comments by Baizley about *My
       Rebel.*

219. Drake, Sylvie. *Los Angeles Times* (Oct. 4, 1989), sect. 6:
       6.

Tears of Rage

220. Collins, William B. *Philadelphia Inquirer* (June 13, 1988):
       E4.
221. Keating, Douglas J. *Philadelphia Inquirer* (July 5, 1988):
       C5.

Barlow, Anna Marie

Selected Plays

222. *Ambassador* (with Don Ettlinger, based on the novel by
            Henry James, Lunt-Fontanne Theater, 1972)
223. *The Artists* (New Dramatists, 1964)
224. *The Bicycle Riders* (Actors Studio, 1968)
            Playscript: *The Best Short Plays 1980.* Edited by
            Stanley Richards, 190-199. Radnor, Pennsylvania:
            Chilton Book Company, 1980.

225. *Cold Christmas* (New Dramatists, 1955-1956)
226. *Cruising Speed 600 M.P.H.* (ANTA Matinee Series,
          Theater de Lys, 1970)
227. *Ferryboat*
          Playscript: *Ferryboat*. New York: Dramatists Play
          Service, 1990
228. *Glory! Hallelujah!* (New Dramatists, 1968-1969)
229. *Half-Past Wednesday* (Orpheum Theater, 1962)
230. *A Limb of Snow* (ANTA Matinee Theater, Theater de Lys,
          1967)
          Playscript: *A Limb of Snow* and *The Meeting:
          Two Short Plays*. New York: Dramatists Play
          Service, 1969.
231. *The Meeting* (ANTA Matinee Theater, Theater de Lys,
          1967)
          Playscript: see item 230.
232. *Mr. Biggs* (New Dramatists, 1959-1960)
233. *Other Voices, Other Rooms* (based on Truman Capote's
          book, Studio Arena Theater, Buffalo, 1973)
234. *A Spit in the Ocean* (New Dramatists, 1964)
235. *Windchimes* (New Dramatists, 1977)

Profiles and Interviews

See brief profile in item 224.

Reviews

Ambassador

236. Barnes, Clive. *New York Times* (Nov. 20, 1972): 46.
237. Mazo, Joseph. *Women's Wear Daily* (Nov. 21, 1972).
          Reprinted in item 238.
238. *New York Theater Critics' Reviews*, 33 (Nov. 27 1972):
          177-78.
239. *New York Times* (Nov. 28, 1972): 53.
          The Times notes the closing of *Ambassador* after
          nine performances.
240. Watt, Douglas. *New York Daily News* (Nov. 20, 1972).
          Reprinted in item 238.
241. Watts, Richard. *New York Post* (Nov. 20, 1972).
          Reprinted in item 238.

Cruising Speed 600 M.P.H.

242. *Drama-Logue* (Jan. 22-28, 1987): 23.
243. Gussow, Mel. *New York Times* (Jan. 6, 1970): 48.
244. _____. *New York Times* (Oct. 4, 1981): 77.
245. Sullivan, Dan. *New York Times* (Dec. 13, 1967): 55.

A Limb of Snow

See items 247, 248.

246. *Drama-Logue* (Jan. 22-28, 1987): 23.

The Meeting

247. Gussow, Mel. *New York Times* (Oct. 4, 1981): 77.
248. Sullivan, Dan. *New York Times* (Dec. 13, 1967): 55.

Betsko, Kathleen (Yale)

Selected Plays

249. *Beggar's Choice* (Eugene O'Neill Theater Center National
        Playwrights' Conference, Waterford, Connecticut,
        1978)
250. *Johnny Bull* (Eugene O'Neill Theater Center National
        Playwrights' Conference, Waterford, Connecticut,
        1981)
        Playscript: *Johnny Bull*. New York: Dramatists
        Play Service.
251. *Stitchers and Starlight Talkers* (Eugene O'Neill Theater
        Center National Playwrights' Conference,
        Waterford, Connecticut, 1982)

Profiles and Interviews

See items 9, 70.

252. *Contemporary Theatre, Film and Television*. Volume 2.
        Edited by Monica M. O'Donnell, 351. Detroit:
        Gale Research Company, 1986.

The entry contains a brief biography, including a
list of Betsko's plays.

Reviews

Johnny Bull

253. Brown, Joe. *Washington Post* (Apr. 18, 1986), sect N: 9.

254. Frankel, Haskel. "Playwright's Path To a New Premiere."
     New York Times (Apr. 11, 1982), sect. 23: 20.
     This preview article, written shortly before the
     premier of *Johnny Bull* at the Yale Repertory
     Company in New Haven, highlights the career of
     Kathleen Betsko. According to Betsko the play is
     second in a trilogy of plays, the first being *Beggar's
     Choice,* which she sold to National Public Radio.
     The third is *Stitchers and Starlight Talkers.*

255. Mano, Keith. *National Review*, 33 (Oct. 2, 1981): 1154.

256. Sharbutt, Jay. "Meeting of the Twain in the World of Prime
     Time." *Los Angeles Times* (May 22, 1984), sect.
     6: 1.
     Sharbutt discusses Betsko and other playwrights
     who have adapted their plays for television.

257. *Variety* (May 12, 1982).

Bingham, Sallie

Selected Plays

258. *The Awakening* (adapted from Kate Chopin, Horse Cave
     Theatre, Kentucky, 1988)
259. *Couvade* (Actors Theatre of Louisville, Kentucky, 1984)
260. *Dancing in the Dark* (staged reading, Women's Project,
     1979-1980)
261. *The Darkness and the Light* (staged reading, Women's
     Project, 1986-1987)
262. *Hopscotch* (Horse Cave Theatre, Kentucky, 1987-1988)
263. *In the Yurt* (Actors Theatre of Louisville, Kentucky, 1979)

264. *Lovers* (staged reading, Women's Project, 1984-1985)
265. *Milk of Paradise* (Women's Project, American Place Theater, 1985)
266. *Paducah* (Women's Project, American Place Theater, 1985)
267. *Piggyback* (staged reading, Women's Project, 1982-1983)
268. *Propinquity* (Actors Theatre of Louisville, Kentucky, 1980)
269. *The Wall Between* (staged reading, Women's Project, 1986-1987)

Profiles

270. *Contemporary Authors: A Bio-Bibliographical Guide.* Volume 18, New Revised Series. Edited by Linda Metzger, 140-141. Detroit: Gale Research Company, 1986.
 The entry provides a biographical sketch of Bingham's achievements.

271. *Contemporary Theatre, Film and Television.* Volume 1. Edited by Monica M. O'Donnell, 61. Detroit: Gale Research Company, 1984.
 This entry provides a brief biography.

Reviews

Couvade

272. Mootz, William. *Courier-Journal* (May 20, 1984), sect. 1: 1, 7.

Milk of Paradise

273. Clurman, Harold. *Nation*, 230 (Apr. 5, 1980): 411-412.
274. Kakutani, Michiko. *New York Times* (Mar. 4, 1980), sect. 3: 8.

Paducah

275. Blumenthal, Eileen. *Village Voice.* (Apr. 30, 1985): 106.
276. Gussow, Mel. *New York Times* (Apr. 22, 1985): C17.

Bovasso, Julie

Selected Plays

277. *Angelo's Wedding* (Circle Repertory Company, cancelled before staged, 1985)

278. *Down By the River Where Water Lilies Are Disfigured Everyday* (Circle Repertory Company, 1975)

279. *The Final Analysis* (La Mama Experimental Theatre Club, 1975)

280. *Gloria and Esperanza* (La Mama Experimental Theatre Club, 1969)
     Playscript: *Gloria and Esperanza: A Play in Two Acts.* New York: Samuel French, 1969; *The Off-Off Broadway Book; The Plays, People, Theatre.* Edited by Albert Poland, 317-351. New York: Bobbs-Merrill, 1972.

281. *Monday on the Way to Mercury Island* (La Mama Experimental Theatre Club, 1977)

282. *The Moon Dreamers* (La Mama Experimental Theatre Club, 1968, new version, Ellen Stewart Theater, 1969)
     Playscript: *The Moondreamers: A Play in Two Acts with Music.* New York: Samuel French, 1969.

283. *The Nothing Kid* (La Mama Experimental Theatre Club, 1975)

284. *Schubert's Last Serenade* (La Mama Experimental Theatre Club, 1971)
     Playscript: *Spontaneous Combustion: Eight New American Plays.* Edited by Rochelle Owens, 149-174. New York: Winter House LTD, 1972.

285. *Standard Safety*
     Playscript: *Standard Safety: A Play in One Act.* New York: Samuel French, 1976; *The Best Short Plays 1976.* Edited by Stanley Richards, 95-122. Radnor, Pennsylvania: Chilton Book Company, 1976.

286. *Super Lover* (La Mama Experimental Theatre Club, 1975)

Profiles and Interviews

See items 33, 87 and page 7.

287. Catenra, Linda Brandi. *Growing Up Italian,* 212-225. New
York: William Morrow & Company, Inc., 1987.
Catenra's volume contains the autobiographies of
twenty-four "celebrated" Americans who talk about
how their Italian-American upbringing "shaped"
their lives. Bovasso talks very little about her
playwriting, although she does discuss briefly
Angelo's Wedding. Interestingly, Bovasso remarks
that she is not a joiner of groups. She claims, for
instance, she "avoids the woman's caucus at the
Dramatists Guild. I avoid it like the plague. What
is the woman's caucus? An opportunity to push
the ladies into a corner so they can write their own
little plays."

288. *Contemporary Authors: A Bio-Bibliographical Guide.*
Volumes 25-28, First Revision. Edited by
Christine Nasso, 85-87. Detroit: Gale Research
Company, 1977.
The entry provides a concise description of
Bovasso's personal and professional life, including
excerpts of critics' commentaries. Also included is
a list of productions in which she has participated
as actress, director, or playwright; a list of awards;
and a list of secondary sources on her work.

289. *Contemporary Theatre, Film and Television.* Volume 7.
Edited by Linda S. Hubbard, 40-41. Detroit: Gale
Research Inc., 1989.
The entry provides a biographical sketch.

290. Sainer, Arthur. *Contemporary Dramatists.* 3rd edition.
Edited by James Vinson, 64-65. New York: St.
Martin's Press, 1982.
Sainer describes Bovasso as a "kind of mad
mathematician, marshaling people and events into
lunatic propositions and hallucinatory equations."
The author touches upon three of Bovasso's works:
*The Moon Dreamers, Monday on the Way to
Mercury Island,* and *Down By the River Where the
Waterlilies Are Disfigured Everyday.*

Reviews

See item 68.

Angelo's Wedding

291. Freedman, Samuel G. "Altercation May End Run At Circle
     Rep." *New York Times* (May 14, 1985): C11.
     Freedman reports Bovasso's *Angelo's Wedding*
     may close early because of disputes between the
     playwright and director Marshall W. Mason as well
     as some of the members of the cast. The
     production was later cancelled. See related articles
     in *New York Times* (May 16, 1985): C2 and (May
     21, 1985): C12.

Gloria and Esperanza

292. Barnes, Clive. *New York Times* (Apr. 5, 1969): 30.
293. Bunce, Alan. *Christian Science Monitor* (Feb. 9, 1970): 6.
294. Gill, Brendan. *The New Yorker*, 45 (Feb. 14, 1970): 57.
295. Hewes, Henry. *Saturday Review*, 52 (Apr. 19, 1969): 53-54.
296. Hughes, Catherine. *Plays and Players*, 17 (Apr. 1970): 19,
     24.
297. Kerr, Walter. *New York Times* (Feb. 15, 1970), sect. 2: 7.

Down By the River Where the Waterlilies Are Disfigured Everyday

298. Gussow, Mel. *New York Times* (Mar. 25, 1975): 23.
299. Novick, Julius. *New York Times* (Jan. 2, 1972), sect. 2: 5,
     14.
300. Oliver, Edith. *The New Yorker*, 51 (Apr. 7, 1975): 60.

The Moon Dreamers

301. Barnes, Clive. *New York Times* (Dec. 9, 1969): 68.

302. Calta, Louis. *New York Times* (Dec. 4, 1969): 68.
     Calta notes that Theater Development Fund, Inc.,
     whose purpose is to attract wider audiences to
     "serious" theatre, has bought tickets valued at

$10,000 for two shows, one of which is *The Moon Dreamers.*

303. Davis, James. *New York Daily News* (Dec. 9, 1969).
        Reprinted in item 307.

304. Di Scipio, Giuseppe Carlo. "Italian-American Playwrights
        on the Rise." *Journal of Popular Culture*, 19, iii
        (Winter 1975): 103-108.
        Di Scipio offers a cursory survey of individual
        works of several Italian-American playwrights,
        including Bovasso's *The Moon Dreamers.*

305. Gottfried, Martin. *Women's Wear Daily* (Dec. 9, 1969).
        Reprinted in item 307.
306. Kerr, Walter. *New York Times* (Dec. 21, 1969), sect. 2:
        D3, D15.
307. *New York Theatre Critics' Reviews*, 30 (Dec. 22, 1969):
        132-134.
308. O'Connor, John J. *Wall Street Journal* (Dec. 10, 1969): 22.
        Reprinted in item 307.
309. Oliver, Edith. *The New Yorker*, 45 (Dec. 20, 1969): 58.
310. Watts, Richard. *New York Post* (Dec. 9, 1969): 32.

The Nothing Kid

311. Gill, Brendan. *The New Yorker*, 50 (Jan. 13, 1975): 65-66.
312. Gussow, Mel. *New York Times* (Jan. 3, 1975): 14.

Schubert's Last Serenade

313. Baker, Rob. *After Dark*, 10 (Oct. 1977): 27.
314. Weiner, Bernard. *San Francisco Chronicle* (Mar. 8, 1978):
        52.

Standard Safety

See items 311, 312.

315. Weiner, Bernard. *San Francisco Chronicle* (Mar. 22, 1979):
        51.

Burr, Anne

Selected Plays

316. *Huui, Huui* (Public Theatre, 1968)
 Playscript: *Huui, Huui: A Play In Two Acts.* New
 York: Samuel French, 1968.
317. *Mert & Phil* (New York Shakespeare Festival, Vivian
 Beaumont, 1974)

Profiles

318. *Contemporary Authors: A Bio-Bibliographical Guide.*
 Volumes 25-28, First Revision. Edited by
 Christine Nasso, 112. Detroit: Gale Research
 Company, 1977.
 The entry provides brief biographical information
 on Burr's achievements.

Reviews

Huui, Huui

319. Barnes, Clive. *New York Times* (Nov. 25, 1968): 58.
320. Clurman, Harold. *Nation*, 207 (Dec. 16, 1968): 665.
321. *Contemporary Literary Criticism: Excerpts from Criticism
 of Today's Novelists, Poets, Playwrights and Other
 Creative Writers.* Volume 6. Edited by Carolyn
 Riley, 103-105. Detroit: Gale Research Company,
 1976.

322. Kroll, Jack. *Newsweek*, 72 (Dec. 16, 1968): 115.
 Reprinted in item 321.
323. Oliver, Edith. *The New Yorker*, 44 (Dec. 7, 1968): 142.
 Reprinted in item 321.

Mert & Phil

324. Barnes, Clive. *New York Times* (Oct. 31, 1974): 50.
 Reprinted in item 337.
325. Beaufort, John. *Christian Science Monitor* (Nov. 3, 1974).
 Reprinted in item 337.

326. Gaver, Jack. *Los Angeles Times* (Nov. 2, 1974), sect. 2: 10.
327. Gill, Brendan. *New Yorker*, 50 (Nov. 11, 1974): 105. Reprinted in item 321.
328. Gottfried, Martin. *New York Post* (Oct. 31, 1974): 53. Reprinted in item 337.
329. Greer, Edward G. *Drama: The Quarterly Theatre Review*, 115 (Winter 1974): 38-39.
330. Hatch, Robert. *Nation*, 219 (Nov. 30, 1974): 573. Reprinted in item 321.
331. Hughes, Catherine. *Plays and Players*, 22 (Feb. 1975): 34.
332. Kalem, T.E. *Time* (Nov. 18, 1974): 98. Reprinted in items 321, 337.
333. Kerr, Walter. *New York Times* (Nov. 10, 1974), sect. 2: D5.
334. Kroll, Jack. *Newsweek*, 84 (Nov. 11, 1974): 122. Reprinted in items 321, 337.
335. Lassell, Michael. *Yale/Theater*, 6, ii (Winter 1975): 73-80.
336. Hughes, Catherine. *Progressive*, 39 (April, 1975): 39-40.
337. *New York Theatre Critics Reviews*, 35 (Nov. 4, 1974): 198-200.

338. *New York Times* (Dec. 5, 1974): 54.
     The *Times* notes *Mert & Phil* will close after forty-one performances at the Vivian Beaumont Theatre.

339. Sharp, Christopher. *Women's Wear Daily* (Nov. 1, 1974). Reprinted in item 337.
340. Simon, John. *New York*, 7 (Nov. 18, 1974): 122-124. Reprinted in item 321.
341. Stasio, Marilyn. *Ms.*, 4 (Sep. 1975): 38. Reprinted in item 321.
342. Watt, Douglas. *New York Daily News* (Oct. 31, 1974). Reprinted in item 337.
343. Wilson, Edwin. *Wall Street Journal* (Nov. 1, 1974): 8. Reprinted in item 337.

Byron, Ellen

Selected Plays

344. *Asleep on the Wind* (INTAR 1987)
345. *Election '84* (Philadelphia Festival Theatre for New Plays, Philadelphia, 1987-1988)
346. *Ghost on the River* (reading, Philadelphia Theater Company, Philadelphia, 1988-1989)
347. *Graceland* (staged reading, Ensemble Studio Theatre, 1983) Playscript: *The Best Short Plays of 1985.* Edited by Ramon Delgado, 23-45. Radnor, Pennsylvania, 1985.

Profiles

See profile in item 347.

Reviews

Graceland

348. Mazer, Cary M. *Theatre Journal,* 35, iv (Dec. 1983): 557.
349. *Variety* (May 4, 1983): 534.

Carroll, Vinnette

Selected Plays

350. *The Boogie-Woogie Rumble of a Dream Deferred* (with Micki Grant, Urban Arts Theater, 1982)
351. *But Never Jam Today* (with Micki Grant, Urban Arts Corps, 1979)
352. *Don't Bother Me, I Can't Cope* (with Micki Grant, Urban Arts Corps, 1970-1971) Playscript: *Don't Bother Me, I Can't Cope: A Musical Entertainment.* New York: Samuel French, 1972.
353. *Croesus and the Witch* (with Micki Grant, Urban Arts Corps, 1971) Playscript: *Croesus and the Witch.* New York: Broadway Play Publishing, 1984.
354. *I'm Laughin' But I Ain't Tickled* (Micki Grant, Urban Arts Corps, 1976)
355. *Love Power* (Urban Arts Corps, 1974-1975)

356. *Trumpets of the Lord* (adapted from *God's Trombone* by
         James Weldon Johnson, Astor Place Playhouse,
         1963)
357. *The Ups and Downs of Theophilus Maitland* (with Micki
         Grant, Urban Arts Corps, 1974)
358. *When Hell Freezes Over, I'll Skate* (with Micki Grant,
         Urban Arts Corps, 1979)
359. *What You Gonna Name the Pretty Baby?* (Fort Lauderdale,
         Texas, 1985)
360. *Your Arms Too Short To Box with God* (with Micki
         Grant, Urban Arts Corps, Ford's Theatre, 1975)

Profiles and Interviews

See item 87.

361. "Black Women 'Star' Behind the Scenes in New York
         Drama; Talented Directors, Producers, Playwrights
         Work 'On' and 'Off' Broadway." *Ebony*, 28 (April
         1973): 106-108, 110-11.
         This article briefly profiles African-American
         women theatre artists, including Vinnette Carroll,
         J.E. Franklin, and Shaunielle Perry.

362. *Black Writers: A Selection of Sketches From
         Contemporary Authors.* Edited by Linda Metzger,
         90-92. Detroit: Gale Research Inc., 1989.
         This entry includes a biographical sketch as well as
         general comments about Carroll's plays.

363. *Contemporary Authors: A Bio-Bibliographical Guide.*
         Volume 114 . Edited by Hal May, 93-94. Detroit:
         Gale Research Company, 1985.
         This entry provides a brief biography and list of
         plays.

364. *Contemporary Theatre, Film and Television.* Volume 5.
         Edited by Monica M. O'Donnell, 47-49. Detroit:
         Gale Research Company, 1988.
         This entry provides a brief biography and list of
         plays.

365. *Current Biography Yearbook.* Edited by Charles Moritz, 54-58. New York: H.W. Wilson, 1983.
This article surveys the life and professional career of Carroll.

366. Mason, Clifford. "Vinnette Carroll Is Still In There Swinging." *New York Times* (Dec. 19, 1976), sect. 2:4.
Mason's article, based primarily on an interview with Carroll, anticipates the opening of *Your Arms Too Short To Box With God* at the Lyceum Theater on Broadway. Carroll candidly talks about her difficulties in developing and producing "straight plays." According to Carroll, "the reason that I do so many musicals is that white producers won't pick up anything intellectual by [black playwrights], no matter how good it is. They only want the singing and the dancing. It's where the quick money is." And she needs lots of money to sustain her Urban Arts Corps theatre, which she created to enable the black actor to "learn his art and not have to rely on just being black to get a job." Carroll also relates her experiences working with white producers, compares the state of black theatre today to the black theatre movement of the 1960s, and speaks on the issue of the involvement of white producers, directors, and critics with black productions. See related article: Fraser, C. Gerald. "At 10, Urban Arts Keeps Pace." *New York Times* (June 24, 1979): 30.

367. Peterson, Bernard L. *Contemporary Black American Playwrights and Their Plays: A Biographical Directory and Dramatic Index,* 99-102. New York: Greenwood Press, 1988.
Peterson provides a biographical sketch of Carroll and a staging history of her productions.

368. Smith, Karen Lynn. "Vinnette Carroll: Portrait of an Artist in Motion." Ph.D. diss., University of California, Los Angeles, 1975.

Smith assesses Carroll's contributions as an
actress, director, and as artistic director of the Urban
Arts Corps.

369. White, Miles. *Afro-American* (Sep. 22, 1979), sect. 2:11.
White announces the opening of *Your Arms Too
Short To Box With God* at the Warner Theatre and
briefly highlights the career of Carroll.

370. Williams, Mance. *Black Theatre in the 1960s and 1970s: A
Historical-Critical Analysis of the Movement.*
Westport, Connecticut: Greenwood Press, 1985.
Mance explores the contemporary Black Theatre
Movement by examining its major playwrights,
theatre companies, and producers. Included are brief
discussions on several black women dramatists:
Vinnette Carroll, Alice Childress, Ntozake Shange,
Adrienne Kennedy, Micki Grant, Judi Ann Mason,
and Sonia Sanchez.

Reviews

The Boogie-Woogie Rumble of a Dream Deferred

371. Holden, Stephen. *New York Times* (Dec. 6, 1982): C15.

But Never Jam Today

372. Gussow, Mel. *New York Times* (Aug. 1, 1979): C18.

373. Lawson, Carol. "A Carroll Revival?" *New York Times*
(Aug. 8, 1979): C17.
Lawson reports that Carroll's *But Never Jam Today*
closed at the Longacre after seven performances.
However, she claims there is "serious talk" about
reviving her *Your Arms Too Short To Box With
God.*

374. _____. "*Jam Today* on the Move." New York Times (May
9, 1979): C17.
Lawson talks about Carroll's new musical, which
is her second attempt at staging a musical version

of *Alice in Wonderland.* Her first version of *Alice,* "an expensive fiasco," closed shortly after its opening in Philadelphia.

375. *New York Theatre Critics' Reviews* (Sep. 17, 1979): 168-170.
376. O'Connor, John J. *Wall Street Journal* (May 9, 1969): 18.
377. Wilson, Edwin. *Wall Street Journal* (Aug. 7, 1979): 20.

Croesus and the Witch

378. Gussow, Mel. *New York Times* (Aug. 27, 1971): 18.
379. Oliver, Edith. *The New Yorker,* 47 (Sep. 4, 1971): 54.

Don't Bother Me, I Can't Cope

See item 592.

380. Barnes, Clive. *New York Times* (Apr. 20, 1972): 51.
381. Beaufort, John. *Christian Science Monitor* (June 9, 1980): 19.
382. Clurman, Harold. *Nation* (June 5, 1976): 701-702.
383. Kalem, T.E. *Time,* 99 (May 8, 1972): 75.
     Reprinted in item 386.
384. Kerr, Walter. *New York Times* (Apr. 30, 1972), sect. 2: 30.
385. Mazo, J. *Women's Wear Daily* (Apr. 21, 1972).
     Reprinted in item 386.
386. *New York Theatre Critics' Reviews,* 33 (May 8, 1972): 304-306.
387. Watt, Douglas. *New York Daily News* (Apr. 21, 1972).
     Reprinted in item 386.
388. Watts, Richard. *New York Post* (Apr. 20, 1972): 48.
     Reprinted in item 386.
389. Wilson, Edwin. *Wall Street Journal* (Apr. 21, 1972): 8.
     Reprinted in item 386.

Trumpets of the Lord

390. Barnes, Clive. *New York Times* (Apr. 30, 1969): 37.
391. Funke, Lewis. *New York Times* (Dec. 23, 1963): 22.

392. *New York Times* (May 1, 1969): 53.
     The *Times* announces the closing of *Trumpets of the Lord* at the Brooks Atkinson Theatre after seven performances.

The Ups and Downs of Theophilus Maitland

393. Eder, Richard. *New York Times* (Nov. 2, 1976): 24.
394. Taitte, W.L. *Texas Monthly*, 13 (Dec. 1985): 200-201.
395. Tucker, Carll. *Village Voice* (Nov. 29, 1976): 99-101.

When Hell Freezes Over, I'll Skate

396. Lask, Thomas. *New York Times* (May 3, 1979): C17.

397. *New York Times* (Nov. 8, 1979): C20.
     The *Times* reports *When Hell Freezes Over, I'll Skate* has been nominated for an Audelco award as has Micki Grant's *It's So Nice to Be Civilized*.

398. Richards, David. *Washington Post* (May 7, 1984): C1.
399. Rogers, Charles E. *N.Y. Amsterdam News* (Apr. 28, 1984): 23.
400. Shepard, Richard F. *New York Times* (Feb. 14, 1979): C18.
401. Sweeney, Louise. *Christian Science Monitor* (May 17, 1984): 27.

Your Arms Too Short To Box With God

402. *Afro-American* (May 21, 1983), sect. 5: 21.
403. *American Theatre Annual 1979-1980*, 197. Detroit: Gale Research Company, 1981.

404. Barnes, Clive. "New Face: Delores Hall, Fervent Star." *New York Times*. (Dec. 31, 1976): C3.
     This item highlights the career of Delores Hall, the singer-actress starring in the Broadway production of *Your Arms Too Short To Box With God*.

405. Barnes, Clive. *New York Times* (Dec. 23, 1976): 20.

406. Beaufort, John. *Christian Science Monitor* (June 9, 1980): 19.

407. _____. *Christian Science Monitor* (Sep. 20, 1982): 16.

408. Calloway, Earl. *Chicago Defender* (Aug. 11, 1979), Arts sect.: 2.

409. _____ "Linda's Dancing Fine." *Chicago Defender* (Oct. 3, 1981): 4-36.
Calloway focuses on Linda James, who performs in the role of Dancing Mary in *Your Arms Too Short To Box With God.*

410. _____. *Chicago Defender* (Apr. 11, 1983): 14.

411. Clurman, Harold. *Nation,* 224 (Jan. 15, 1977): 61.

412. Drake, Sylvie. *Los Angeles Times* (Nov. 9, 1979), sect. 4: 28.

413. Gill, Brendan. *The New Yorker,* 52 (Jan. 3, 1977): 60.

414. _____. *The New Yorker,* 56 (June 16, 1980): 96.

415. Gottfried, Martin. *New York Post* (Dec. 23, 1976): 11, 12.

416. Griffin, Rita. *The Michigan Chronicle* (June 3, 1979), sect. B: 6.
Griffin announces the opening of *Your Arms Too Short To Box with God* at the Music Hall in Detroit.

417. Gussow, Mel. *New York Times* (June 3, 1980): C7.

418. Hughes, Catherine. *America* (Jan. 22, 1977): 60.

419. Kalem, T.E. *Time,* 109 (Jan. 24, 1977): 55.
Reprinted in item 424.

420. Kroll, Jack. *Newsweek,* 89 (Jan. 10, 1977): 66.
Reprinted in item 424.

421. Lochte, Dick. *Los Angeles,* 25 (Jan. 1980): 210.

422. McClain, Rosa. *Atlanta Daily World* (May 2, 1982): 3.

423. *N.Y. Amsterdam News* (Jan. 8, 1977), sect. D: 8.

424. *New York Theatre Critics' Reviews,* 38 (Dec. 31, 1976): 52-55.

425. Scott, Lucille M. *Atlanta Daily World* (May 13, 1979): 2.

426. Simon, John. *New York,* 10 (Jan. 10, 1977): 63.

427. Watt, Douglas. *New York Daily News* (Dec. 23, 1976).
Reprinted in item 424.

428. Weiner, Bernard. *San Francisco Chronicle* (May 29, 1982): 34.
429. Wilson, Edwin. *Wall Street Journal* (Dec. 23, 1976): 6. Reprinted in item 424.
430. _____. *Wall Street Journal* (June 6, 1980): 17.
431. Wood, William R. *Call and Post* (Cleveland) (Jan. 27, 1983): 5A.

Chambers, Jane

Selected Plays

432. *Common Garden Variety* (Interart Theatre, 1974-1975)
433. *Kudzu* (Playwrights Horizons, 1981-1982)
434. *Last Summer at Bluefish Cove* (The Glines, Actors Playhouse, 1980)
     Playscript: *Last Summer at Bluefish Cove.* Village Station, New York: JH Press, 1982.
435. *A Late Snow* (Playwrights Horizons 1974)
     Playscript: *A Late Snow.* Village Station, New York: JH Press, 1986; *Gay Plays: The First Collection.* Edited by William M. Hoffman, 281-335. New York: Avon, 1979.
436. *Mine!* (Interart Theatre, 1974)
437. *My Blue Heaven* (Shandol Theatre, 1982)
     Playscript: *My Blue Heaven.* Village Station, New York: JH Press, 1987.
438. *The Quintessential Image* (Courtyard Playhouse, 1989)
439. *Random Violence* (Interart Theatre, 1973-1974)
440. *Tales of the Revolution and Other American Fables* (Eugene O'Neill Theatre Center National Playwrights' Conference, Connecticut, 1972)
441. *The Wife* (Interart Theatre, 1973-1974)

Profiles and Interviews

See profiles in item 87 and Hoffman's anthology (item 435), and page 5.

442. *Contemporary Authors: A Bio-Bibliographical Guide.* Volume 109. Edited by Hal May, 76. Detroit: Gale Research Company, 1983.

A brief obituary that includes a list of Chambers's
theatrical productions and awards. For a fuller
entry, see: *Contemporary Authors*. Volumes 85-
88. Edited by Frances Carol Locher, 103. Detroit:
Gale Research Company, 1980.

443. Dace, Tish. "For Whom the Bell Tolled." *New York Native*
(Oct. 24-Nov. 6, 1983): n.p.
Beth Allen, Jane Chambers's companion of
fourteen years, reminisces about Chambers's
theatrical career.

444. "Jane Chambers Dead; Won Awards for Plays." *New York
Times* (Feb. 17, 1983): D23.
A brief obituary mentioning Chambers's
contributions as a dramatist.

445. Klein, Alvin. "Play's Theme: Lesbians Without Apology."
New York Times (Feb. 8, 1981), sect. 21: 15.
Chambers talks about being a woman, a lesbian,
and a playwright. Her "biggest frustration":
wanting to be a playwright. While in college,
Chambers recalls that she and other women were
not encouraged to become playwrights but were
"steered into design and acting." Only two of
Chambers's plays deal with lesbianism, but she is
determined in her "mission of enlightening people
about the 'gay image' in theater." The lesbian
characters in Chambers's plays do not "apologize
for being lesbian"; these characters also deviate
from the stereotypical images of lesbians as
psychological aberrants or suicides.
See letters to the editor commenting on Klein's
article in: *New York Times* (Mar. 1, 1981), sect.
21: 18.

446. Landau, Penny M. "Jane Chambers: In Memoriam." *Women
& Perfomance*, 1, ii (Winter 1984): 55-57.
Landau, a theatrical press agent, reminisces about
her relationship with Jane Chambers, who died of
cancer in February, 1983.

447. "Lesbian Playwright Jane Chambers Dies." *Off Our Backs,* 13 (Apr. 1983): 13.

448. Loynd, Ray. "Where Does Gay Theater Go From Here?" *Los Angeles Times* (Jan. 7, 1990); Calendar sect.: 8, 80-81.
     Loynd discusses the situation of gay and lesbian theater in Los Angeles and briefly mentions Los Angeles's lesbian theatre and the influence of Jane Chambers's work, "which had the most impact locally of any lesbian show."

449. *Variety Obituaries, 1980-1983*, n.p. Volume 9. New York: Garland Publishing, Inc., 1988.

Reviews

See items 28, 30, 31, 62.

Kudzu

450. *New York Times* (Oct. 21, 1981), sect. C: 29.
     The *Times* describes the play and cast of *Kudzu,* which is in rehearsal at the Playwrights Horizons.

A Late Snow

451. Lardner, James. *Washington Post* (Jan. 23, 1981), sect. B: 6.
452. Mahoney, John. *Los Angeles Times* (May 28, 1982), sect. 6: 2, 4.
453. Munk, Erica. *Village Voice* (Oct. 25, 1983): 98.
454. Weiner, Bernard. *San Francisco Chronicle* (Sep. 15, 1987): E6.

Last Summer at Bluefish Cove

455. Christon, Lawrence. *Los Angeles Times* (Jan. 24, 1983), sect. 6: 2.
456. Currie, Glenne. *Los Angeles Times* (Jan. 5, 1981), sect. 6: 5.

457. Koehler, Robert. *Los Angeles Times* (Nov. 13, 1985), sect. 6: 3.
458. Lochte, Dick. *Los Angeles*, 30 (Dec. 1985): 46.
459. Moe, Christina. *Theatre Journal*, 37, iv (Dec. 1985): 499-500.
460. Rich, Frank. *New York Times* (Dec. 27, 1980): 15.
461. Sevcik, Sally. *Village Voice* (Feb. 11-17, 1981): 92.
462. Simon, John. *New York*, 13 (Aug. 4, 1980): 43-44.
463. Vanderburgh, Nancy. *Women's Press*, 13 (May-June, 1983): 17.

My Blue Heaven

See item 62.

464. Koehler, Robert. *Los Angeles Times* (May 12, 1990), sect. F: 11.
465. Massa, Robert. *Village Voice* (June 17-23, 1981): 77.
466. Stasio, Marilyn. *After Dark*, 14 (Oct. 1981): 17.

My Quintessential Image

See item 30.

467. *Drama-Logue* (Sep. 7-13, 1989): 24-25.
468. Feingold, Michael. *Village Voice* (Aug. 15, 1989): 93.

469. *New York Times* (Oct. 10, 1982), sect. 21: 3.
     This brief article describes the stage reading of Chambers's one-act play *My Quintessential Image*, which was performed in conjunction with other one-acts by Edward Albee and Arthur Laurents at Southampton College.

470. Holden, Stephen. *New York Times* (Aug. 17, 1989): C18.
     This review includes a brief discussion of *In Her Own Words*, a biographical collage based on Chambers's writings and arranged by John Glines.

471. Simon, John. *New York*, 22 (Aug. 14, 1989): 77-78.

Charles, Martie

Selected Plays

472. *African Interlude* (New Federal Theatre, 1978)
473. *Black Cycle* (Afro-American Studio, 1973)
          Playscript: *Black Drama Anthology.* Edited by
          Woodie King and Ron Milner, 25-55. New York:
          New American Library, 1972.
474. *Boochie* (Billie Holiday Theater, 1989)
475. *Jamimma* (New Federal Theater, Henry Street Settlement,
          1972)
476. *Job Security* (Black Magicians, Third World House, 1970)
          Playscript: *Black Theater, U.S.A.: Forty-Five
          Plays By Black-Americans.* Edited by James
          Vernon Hatch and Ted Shine. New York: Free
          Press, 1974.
477. *Where We At?* (Playwrights Workshop of NEC, St. Mark's
          Playhouse, 1972)
          Playscript: see item 476.

Profiles

478. Peterson, Bernard L. *Contemporary Black American
          Playwrights and Their Plays: A Biographical
          Directory and Dramatic Index,* 167-168. New York:
          Greenwood Press, 1988.
          Peterson provides a brief biography and a staging
          history of Charles's plays.

Reviews

See items 72, 101.

Black Cycle

See items 72, 1203.

Boochie

479. Boyd, Herb. *N.Y. Amsterdam News* (June 24, 1989): 25.

Jamimma

480. Kupa, Kushauri. *Black Theatre,* 6 (1972): 38-42.
481. Oliver, Edith. *New Yorker,* 48 (Mar. 25, 1972): 106-107.
482. Thompson, Howard. *New York Times* (Mar. 18, 1972): 17.

Job Security

483. Perrier, Paulette. *Black Theatre* (1971): 51-52.

Chavez, Denise

Selected Plays

484. *Language of Vision* (Albuquerque Convention Center, Albuquerque, 1987)
485. *El Mas Pequeno de Mis Hojos (The Smallest of My Children)* (Kimo Theater, Albuquerque, 1983)
486. *Novena Narrativas y Ofrendas Nuevomexicanas* (Our Lady of Guadalupe Church, Taos, New Mexico, 1986) Playscript: *Chicana Creativity and Criticism: Charting New Frontiers in American Literature.* Edited by Maria Hererra-Sobek and Helena Maria Viramontes, 85-100. Houston: Arte Publico Press, 1988.
487. *Plaza* (Kimo Theater, Albuquerque, 1984)
488. *Si, Hay Posada (Yes, There Is Shelter)* (Kimo Theater, Albuquerque, 1981)

Profiles

489. *Hispanic Writers: A Selection of Sketches from Contemporary Authors.* Edited by Bryan Ryan. Detroit: Gale Research Inc., 1991. This entry provides a biographical sketch and a list of Chavez's works.

Childress, Alice

Selected Plays

490. *The African Garden*

Playscript: *Black Scenes*, 137-146. Garden City,
New York: Zenith Books, 1971.

491. *Florence, A One-Act Drama* (American Negro Theatre,
1949)
Playscript: *Masses and Mainstream*, 3 (Oct. 1950):
34-47.

492. *Freedom Drum* (retitled *Young Martin Luther King, Jr.*,
Performing Arts Repertory Theatre, 1969)

493. *Gold Through the Trees* (Club Baron Theatre, 1952)

494. *Gullah* (revised version of *Sea Island Song*, University of
Massachusetts, Amherst,1984)

495. *Just a Little Simple* (Club Baron Theatre, 1950)

496. *Let's Hear It for the Queen*
Playscript: *Let's Hear It for the Queen: A Play.*
New York: Coward, McCann & Geoghegan, 1976.

497. *Mojo: A Black Love Story* (New Heritage Theatre, 1970)
Playscript: *Mojo and String: Two Plays.*
Dramatists Play Service, 1971; *Best Short Plays of
the World.* Edited by Stanley Richards, 126-137.
New York: Crown Publishers, 1973; *Black World,*
20 (Apr. 1971): 54-82.

498. *Moms* (Hudson Guild Theater, 1987)

499. *Sea Island Song* (see item 494) (Stage South, Charleston,
1977)

500. *String* (adapted from Guy de Maupassant's "A Piece of
String," Negro Ensemble Company, 1969)

501. *Trouble in Mind* (Greenwich Mews Theatre, 1955)
Playscript: *Black Theater: A 20th Century
Collection.* Edited by Lindsay Patterson, 135-174.
New York: Dodd, Mead and Company, 1971.

502. *Wedding Band* (New York Shakespeare Festival, Public
Theatre, 1972)
Playscript: *Wedding Band: A Love/Hate Story in
Black and White.* New York: Samuel French Inc.,
1973; see items 73,77.

503. *When the Rattlesnake Sounds*
Playscript: *When the Rattlesnake Sounds: A Play.*
New York: Coward, McCann & Geoghegan, 1975.

504. *Wine in the Wilderness* (New Dramatists, 1971-1972)
Playscript: *Wine in the Wilderness: A Comedy-
Drama.* New York: Dramatists Play Service, 1969;
Wines in the Wilderness; Plays by African

American Women. Edited by Elizabeth Brown-
Guillory, 379-421. Westport, Connecticut:
Greenwood Press, 1990; *Best Short Plays 1971*.
Edited by Stanley Richards. New York: Chilton
Book Company, 1972; *Plays By and About
Women*. Edited by Victoria Sullivan and James
Hatch. New York: Vintage, 1973.

505. *World on a Hill*
Playscript: *Plays to Remember*. New York:
Macmillan, 1968.

Profiles and Interviews

See items 9, 70, 72.

506. *Black Writers: A Selection of Sketches from Contemporary
Authors*. Edited by Linda Metzger, 100-103.
Detroit: Gale Research Inc., 1989.
This entry includes a biographical sketch as well as
general comments about Childress's work.

507. Brown-Guillory, Elizabeth. "Alice Childress: A Pioneering
Spirit." *Sage: A Scholarly Journal on Black
Women*, 4, i (Spr. 1987): 66-68.
Brown-Guillory encourages Childress to talk about
the forces that shaped her passion for reading and
writing, such as her grandmother, Eliza ("she
wasn't your typical grandmother"); the Salem
Church in Harlem ("I remember how people . . .
used to get up and tell their troubles to
everybody"); her school teacher Miss Thomas; and
her access to the library. Childress also reminisces
about her start in the theatre and articulates her
creative processes and the work she is currently
working on.

508. Childress, Alice. "But I Do My Thing." *New York Times*
(Feb. 2, 1969), sect. 2: D9.
Childress's article is part of a group of pieces by
well-known black theatre artists, each of whom
addresses the dilemma for many black artists of
whether to concentrate their creative efforts on

developing a black theatre in the black community
or to focus their energies on the Broadway and Off
Broadway theatres. Alice Childress seems to say
that black artists should not be restricted to either
realm but to "Cope! cope anyhow, anywhere you
can, to the best of your ability."

509. _____. "For a Negro Theatre." *Masses and Mainstream*, 4
(Feb. 1951): 61-64.
Childress articulates the need for a black theatre to
nurture the creative talents of black theatre artists
and to develop an aesthetic for black playwrights
and other theatre artists. Blacks working in the
theatre, Childress asserts, do not get the necessary
training or education from white schools and theatre
classes, whose curriculum is based on the cultural
heritage of the white man. As Childress remarks,
"[t]he Negro people's theatre must study and teach
not only what has been taught before but found and
establish a new approach to study of the Negro in
the theatre." See related articles by Childress in
Negro Digest (Jan. 1968): 36, 85-87, and *Black
Women Wrtiers (1950-1980): A Critical
Evaluation*. Edited by Mari Evans, 111-116. Garden
City, New York: Anchor Books, 1984.

510. *Contemporary Authors: A Bio-Bibliographical Guide.*
Volume 3, New Revision Series. Edited by Ann
Evory, 122-124. Detroit: Gale Research,1981.
The entry includes a biographical sketch and general
comments on her work by critics and by Childress
herself.

511. *Contemporary Literary Criticism: Excerpts from Criticism
of the Works of Today's Novelists, Poets,
Playwrights, and Other Creative Writers.* Volume
12. Edited by Dedria Bryfonski, 104-109. Detroit:
Gale Research Company, 1980.

512. Curb, Rosemary. "Alice Childress." *Dictionary of Literary
Biography.* Volume 7. *Twentieth Century*

American Dramatists. Edited by John MacNicholas,
118-124. Detroit: Gale Research Company, 1981.
This extensive introductory essay on the life and
work of Childress includes a primary and secondary
bibliography. See also: Harris, Trudier.
Dictionary of Literary Biography. Volume 38.
*Afro-American Writers After 1955: Dramatists and
Prose Writers.* Edited by Thadious M. Davis, 67-
79. Detroit: Gale Research Company, 1985.

513. Downey, Maureen. "Alice Childress: Blacks Must Write
About All Issues." *Atlanta Constitution* (Mar. 27,
1986), sect. C: 1-2.
Downey reports on Childress's participation in
"Black Women: Images, Styles and Substance," a
seminar sponsored by Georgia State University.
Childress reflects on her life and her work as a
novelist and playwright.

514. Holliday, Polly. "I Remember Alice Childress." *Southern
Quarterly*, 25, iii (Spring 1987): 63-65.
Polly Holliday, who played the part of Annabelle
in Childress's *Wedding Band* in Joseph Papp's
production at the Public Theatre in 1972, fondly
reminisces about working with the playwright
during the play's rehearsals.

515. "Near Broadway Playwrights." *Ebony*, 14 (Apr. 1959): 100.
This brief feature article profiles Childress among
other dramatists.

516. Peterson, Bernard L. *Contemporary Black American
Playwrights and Their Plays: A Biographical
Directory and Dramatic Index*, 106-108. Westport,
Conn.: Greenwood Press, 1988.
Peterson provides a biographical sketch and a brief
staging history of Childress's plays.

517. Turner, Darwin T. *Contemporary Dramatists.* 3rd Edition.
Edited by James Vinson, 87-88. New York: St.
Martin's Press, 1982.

Darwin's succinct entry includes a list of
Childress's plays and general comments on her
work.

Reviews and Criticism

See items 13, 14, 68, 72, 101,104, 370 and pages 5, 7, 17,
23.

Florence

See items 19, 553, 2016.

518.   Mitchell, Loften. *Black Drama; The Story of the American
Negro In the Theatre,* 146-147. New York:
Hawthorn Books, Inc., 1967.
Mitchell briefly discusses *Florence* and *Gold
Through the Trees.*

Gold Through The Trees

See items 73, 518, 592.

519.   Jefferson, Miles M. *Phylon,* 13 (3rd Quarter 1952): 205.

A Man Bearing a Pitcher

520.   Mitchell, Loften. "Three Writers and a Dream." *Crisis*
(April 1965): 219-223.
Mitchell discusses the works of William Branch,
John Oliver Killens, and Alice Childress in terms
of why the works of these successful African-
American playwrights "sit on the shelf." In terms
of Childress's *A Man Bearing a Pitcher*, Mitchell
claims that the reason the play was not produced
was because she was told "that as a Negro writer
her concern should be with the racial theme." And
as for *Wedding Band*, which apparently was bound
for Broadway, it never made it because the play
"changed hands five times." However, several years
later the play was finally produced by Joseph Papp
at the Public Theatre in 1972.

Mojo

See items 14, 553, 592.

521. Bailey, Peter. *Black Collegian*, 14 (Jan/Feb. 1984): 34.
522. _____. *Black World* (Apr. 1971): 4-7.
523. Kupa, Kushauri. *Black Theatre*, 6 (1972): 39.
524. Lowell, Sandra. *Los Angeles Times* (Oct. 13, 1978), sect. 4: 28, 29.
525. Mahoney, John C. *Los Angeles Times* (May 18, 1982), sect. 6: 3.
526. Richardson, Alice. *N.Y. Amsterdam News* (Mar. 12, 1988): 33.

Moms

527. *American Theatre*, 3 (Feb. 1987): 7-8.

528. "Author of *Moms* Sues Actress Over Copyright." *New York Times* (Oct. 22, 1987): C17.
    The *Times* announced that Childress brought suit against Clarice Taylor, who starred in *Moms*, for infringement of copyright.

529. Bennetts, Leslie. *New York Times* (Aug. 9, 1987), sect. 2: H5.
530. Boyd, Herb. *N.Y. Amsterdam News* (Sep. 5, 1987): 26.
531. _____. *Guardian* (N.Y.), 40 (Oct. 7, 1987): 17.
532. Caldwell, Ben. *Washington Post* (May 6, 1988), sect. B:1.
533. *Drama-Logue* (Mar. 5-11, 1987): 25.
534. Feingold, Michael. *Village Voice* (Feb. 17, 1987): 100.

535. Gussow, Mel. *New York Times* (Aug. 18, 1987): C13.
    Gussow reports on a dispute concerning the authorship of *Moms*. For additional information, see item 528.

536. _____. *New York Times* (Feb. 10, 1987): C16.
537. Loving-Sloan, Cecilia. *Crisis*, 94 (Dec. 1987): 8-9.
538. Oliver, Edith. *The New Yorker*, 63 (Feb. 23, 1987): 105.
539. Paige, Nathan. *Call and Post* (Cleveland) (June 2, 1988): 5.

540. Simon, John. *New York,* 20 (Feb. 23 1987):128.
541. Sinclair, Abiola. *N.Y. Amsterdam News* (Feb. 28, 1987): 32.
542. Weiner, Bernard. *San Francisco Chronicle* (Oct. 12, 1983): 62.
543. _____. *San Francisco Chronicle* (June 5, 1984): 57.

String

544. Barnes, Clive. *New York Times* (Apr. 2, 1969): 37.
     Reprinted in item 511.
545. Kerr, Walter. *New York Times* (Apr. 13, 1969), sect. 2: 1, 20.
546. Lowell, Sandra. *Los Angeles Times* (Oct. 13, 1978), sect. 4: 28, 29.
547. Oliver, Edith. *The New Yorker,* 45 (Apr. 12, 1969): 131.

Trouble in Mind

See items 14, 19, 592, 2016, 2042.

548. Abramson, Doris E. *Negro Playwrights in the American Theatre, 1925-1959,* 189-205. New York: Columbia University Press, 1969.
     Unfortunately, Abramson devotes much of her discussion on Childress to summarizing *Trouble in Mind* rather than a rigorous critical examination of the play. Although she allows that the primary significance of this play is that the majority of the roles are for blacks, nevertheless she pinpoints several problems associated with the play. First of all, Childress's characters lack individuality and depth because of her constant "assaults on racial prejudice." Secondly, Childress's manipulation of her characters is overt, the audience is "very much aware of the author pulling strings." And thirdly, although the characters and dialogue are "interesting" yet they "ring false whenever they are saturated with sermonizing."

549. Austin, Gayle. "Alice Childress: Black Woman Playwright as Feminist Critic." *Southern Quarterly,* 25, iii (Spring 1987): 53-62.
    Austin concurs with Rosemary Curb (see item 566) and others who feel that Childress has been neglected by theatre scholars. Austin attributes this neglect, in part at least, to the fact that Childress was "ahead of her times in the combination of subject and treatments." One of Childress's major contributions, according to the author, is that her plays portray realistic images of blacks and whites, they dispel several "binary oppositions so prevalent in Western society—black/white, male/female, north/south, artist/critic—with their implications that one is superior to the other." Thus Childress's ideology and aesthetics are important to modern criticism and feminist critical theory. Austin analyzes *Trouble in Mind* and *Wine in the Wilderness* within the context of what she sees as the three stages of feminist literary criticism and also how these plays employ the "concept of absence."

550. *Encore American & Worldwide News,* 8 (Feb. 5, 1979): 40-41.

551. Evans, Donald T. *Black World,* 20 (Feb. 1971): 43-45.
    Reprinted in item 511.

552. Gelb, Arthur. *New York Times* (Nov. 5, 1955): 23.
    Reprinted in item 511.

553. Hay, Samuel A. "Alice Childress's Dramatic Structure." In *Black Women Writers, (1950-1980): A Critical Evaluation.* Edited by Mari Evans, 117-128. Garden City, New York: Anchor Books, 1984.
    Hay observes that Childress is fundamentally a traditionalist in terms of dramatic structure, that is, her plays have a beginning, a middle, and an end; each episode builds upon the preceding ones; and she avoids experimental devices. However, unlike the conventional episodic frameworks used by Eugene O'Neill, Tennessee Williams, and Arthur Miller to dramatize psychological characterizations,

Childress exchanges characterization for theme. Consequently, "the substitution strains the traditional structure because Childress does not reveal the theme through characterization but through argumentation." Of Childress's seventeen plays, Hay analyzes *Florence, Trouble in Mind, Wine in the Wilderness,* and *Mojo: A Black Love Story.*

554. Killens, John O. "The Literary Genius of Alice Childress." In *Black Women Writers, (1950-1980): A Critical Evaluation.* Edited by Mari Evans, 129-133. Garden City, New York: Anchor Books, 1984.
Killens celebrates Alice Childress, whom he refers to as "a tremendously gifted artist who has consistently used her genius to effect change . . . to change the image we have of ourselves as human beings, Black and white." He briefly discusses Childress's *Trouble in Mind* and *Wedding Band.*

555. Koyama, Christine. *Chicago Tribune* (Apr. 5, 1984), sect. 5: 10.

556. Richardson, Alice. *N.Y. Amsterdam News* (June 13, 1987): 29.

557. Sinclair, Abiola. *N.Y. Amsterdam News* (June 17, 1987): 20.

558. Sommer, Sally R. *Village Voice* (Jan. 15, 1979): 91. Reprinted in item 511.

559. Turner, Darwin T. "Negro Playwrights and the Urban Negro." *CLA Journal,* 12, i (Sep. 1968): 19-25. Turner briefly discusses Childress's *Trouble in Mind.*

560. Williams, V.A. "Alice Childress: An Uncompromising Playwright." *Afro-American* (Oct. 14, 1988): 4-5. Williams reports on a press conference held by Childress prior to attending a performance of *Trouble in Mind* by Washington D.C.'s Takoma Players. Childress talks about her plays (especially *Trouble in Mind* and *Wedding Band)* as well as issues confronting the American theatre, such as

color-blind casting. Childress comments that she
has turned down many profitable projects, having
rejected them because "she refused to write
romanticized or untrue things about . . . heroines of
Black History."

Wedding Band

See items 554, 560, 2016.

561. Bailey, Peter. *Black Collegian*, 14 (Jan/Feb. 1984): 34.
562. Barnes, Clive. *New York Times* (Oct. 27, 1972): 30.
      Reprinted in item 511.

563. Childress, Alice. "Why Talk About That?" *Negro Digest*, 16
      (Apr. 1967): 17-21.
      Childress's title refers to the controversial racial
      issues raised in her play *Wedding Band.*
      Controversial because at the time of this article,
      there were very few plays produced on Broadway or
      its environs that dramatized society as perceived by
      African-Americans. Childress talks about the
      genesis of *Wedding Band* and the state of black
      theatre.

564. Christon, Lawrence. *Los Angeles Times* (June 15, 1977),
      sect. 4: 17.
565. Clurman, Harold. *Nation*, 215 (Nov. 13, 1972): 475-476.
      Reprinted in item 511.

566. Curb, Rosemary. "An Unfashionable Tragedy of American
      Racism: Alice Childress' *Wedding Band*." *Melus*,
      7, iv (Winter 1980): 57-68.
      Curb views *Wedding Band*, a play about the tragic
      consequences of miscegenation laws, as Childress's
      "finest and most serious piece of literature." The
      play dramatizes the playwright's concern for the
      racist laws as well as "anti-woman" laws that
      oppress the characters of the play. Childress's
      greatness lies in the fact that she does not portray
      them entirely as innocent victims—they too have
      their defects. And the protagonists, Julia and

Herman do not represent martyrs in the cause of
civil rights but rather "they are weak, confused,
superstitious, lonely, and impatient." However,
the integrity of the lovers shows in their
willingness to defy the laws of miscegenation to
pursue their relationship.

567.   Dillon, John. "Alice Childress' *Wedding Band* At the
Milwaukee Repertory Theater: A Photo Essay."
Studies in American Drama 1945-Present, 4
(1989): 129-141.
Accompanying Dillon's piece are nine photographs
depicting scenes from the Milwaukee Repertory
Theater's 1989 production of *Wedding Band.* He
discusses the play within a historical context.

568.   Eder, Richard. *New York Times* (Jan. 11, 1979): C17.
569.   Gottfried, Martin. *Women's Wear Daily* (Oct. 10, 1972).
Reprinted in item 577.
570.   Kauffmann, Stanley. *New Republic,* 167 (Nov. 25, 1972):
22, 26.
571.   Kerr, Walter. *New York Times* (Nov. 5, 1972), sect. 2: 5,
14.
Reprinted in item 577.
572.   Lowell, Sandra. *Los Angeles Times* (May 20, 1977), sect.
4: 22, 23.
573.   _____. *Los Angeles Times* (May 12, 1978), sect. 4: 25.
574.   Mahoney, John C. *Los Angeles Times* (Feb. 25, 1983),
sect. 6: 9.
575.   Mitchell, Loften. *Crisis* (Apr. 1965): 221-223.
Reprinted in item 511.

576.   Molette, Barbara. "They Speak: Who Listens?" *Black World,*
25 (Apr. 1976): 28-34.
Molette believes that the reason why few African-
American women playwrights get their plays
produced is because they "are at the mercy of
various media brokers," the producers and
publishers (usually white males) who "will not
present informative entertainment or the exposition
of truths that might be of some use to an oppressed
group of people in reducing their oppression."

Molette argues that whites are uncomfortable with the realistic portrayal of blacks and the issues they engender. To substantiate her accusation, the author cites the example of a few black female playwrights, such as Alice Childress. According to Molette, Childress's *Wedding Band*, a play about the romantic relationship between a black woman and white man, never fulfilled its scheduled run at the Atlanta Municipal Theatre because "white folks were not ready to deal with the issue." To rectify the situation, Molette suggests that women concentrate on moving into the administrative areas of the theatrical community and that black artists develop "regional Black theaters . . . to produce plays that are talking to Black people . . . and Black women in particular."

577. *New York Theatre Critics' Reviews*, 33 (Dec. 4, 1972): 163-164.
578. Oliver, Edith. *The New Yorker*, 48 (Nov. 4, 1972): 105.
    Reprinted in item 511.
579. Simon, John. *New York*, 5 (Nov. 13, 1972): 134.
580. *Variety* (Dec. 20, 1972): 58.
581. Watt, Douglas. *New York Daily News* (Nov. 27, 1972).
    Reprinted in item 577.
582. Watts, Richard. *New York Post* (Nov. 27, 1972).
    Reprinted in item 577.
583. Weathers, Diane. *Black Creation,* 4 (Winter 1973): 60.

When the Rattlesnake Sounds

584. Burns, Mary M. *Horn Book Magazine* (June 1976): 300-303.
    Reprinted in item 511.
585. Sutherland, Zena. *Bulletin of the Center for Children's Books* (May 1976): 139-140.
    Reprinted in item 511.

Wine in the Wilderness

See items 12, 15, 549, 553, 592, 2016.

586.   Hatch, James V. *Black Theater, U.S.A: Forty-Five Plays
       by Black Americans,* 737.
       Reprinted in item 511.

587.   Anderson, Mary Louise. "Black Matriarchy: Portrayal of
       Women in Three Plays." *Negro American
       Literature Forum,* 10 (Spring 1976): 93-95.
       Anderson examines the role of the black matriarch,
       which "white society has forced" on the black
       woman, in three plays: Lorraine Hansberry's *A
       Raisin in the Sun,* James Baldwin's *The Amen
       Corner,* and Childress's *Wine in the Wilderness.*
       Anderson describes the stereotyped black matriarch
       as religious; as one who identifies strongly with
       her role as mother, nurturer, and protector; and who
       teaches her children to accept the condemnation of
       whites. Furthermore, the black matriarch is often
       portrayed as being responsible for the black man's
       inability to exercise his masculinity. In *Wine in
       the Wilderness,* Anderson examines how a black
       man confronts the stereotype of the black maternal
       figure, and how he ultimately recognizes that "the
       beauty of the Black matriarch is long past due."

588.   Bailey, Peter. *Black Collegian,* 14 (Jan./Feb. 1984): 34.
589.   _____. *Black World* (April 1977): 4-7.

590.   Brown-Guillory, Elizabeth. "Contemporary Black Women
       Playwrights: A View from the Other Half."
       Helicon Nine, 14/15 (Summer 1986): 120-127.
       Brown-Guillory, a prolific writer on black women
       dramatists, asserts that Lorraine Hansberry, Alice
       Childress, and Ntozake Shange "are crucial links in
       the development of black women playwriting in
       America." These dramatists consciously avoid the
       stereotypical images of black women that are found
       in the plays of their black male counterparts and
       white playwrights. Brown-Guillory observes that
       one image that dominates the plays of these women
       is the "'evolving black woman,' a phrase which
       embodies the multiplicity of emotions of ordinary
       black women for whom the act of living is sheer

heroism." And for the evolving woman in
Childress's *Wine in the Wilderness* and Shange's
*for colored girls who considered suicide/when the
rainbow is enuf* the men in their lives have been
shattered. But rather than wallowing in self-pity or
engaging in man-hating, these women "become
independent because of their fear of being abused
physically and/or emotionally in subsequent
relationships."

591. Childress, Alice. "Negro Woman in Literature."
Freedomways, 6 (Winter 1966): 14-19.
Black writers have portrayed the "strong,
matriarchal" woman in their plays yet underlying
many of these portrayals is the assumption that the
strength of these women somehow diminishes their
femininity and is the "culprit[s]" in emasculating
the black male, and they are to blame for the failure
of black men in "express[ing] their manhood."
Childress defends the position of the strong black
woman and explains the historical circumstances
that demanded assertiveness and independence. The
playwright also summarizes several racist and
sexist laws that deeply affected the black woman;
for example, Childress points out that a black
woman "came out of bondage with the burden of
the white and black man's child," because a law was
passed that stipulated that children born of a black
woman during slavery "shall be known as the
legitimate children of *their mother only*." Thus,
the white and black males were released of any
responsibility. Realistic depictions of the black
woman in literature, says Childress, will happen
only when "those of us who care about truth,
justice, and a better life tell her story."

592. Fabre, Genevieve. *Drumbeats, Masks and Metaphor:
Contemporary Afro-American Theatre*. Cambridge,
Mass.: Harvard University Press, 1983.
Fabre examines contemporary black theatre writing
within a socio-cultural context. She categorizes
black theatre into two camps: militant theatre and

theatre of experience; she asserts that both are based on a quest for identity. The major purpose of militant theatre, according to the author, is to politicize the experiences of African' Americans, to reject decades of oppression and humiliation and "recover [the blacks'] voice and a form of power." Theatre of experience, unlike militant theatre, which transforms politics into art, focuses on the "rituals of daily life," dramatizing the experiences of African-Americans, both as individuals and as a community. To illustrate these two forms of theatre, Fabre examines the plays of well-known playwrights; unfortunately she reserves her extensive discussions to black male dramatists. She briefly mentions selected works of Alice Childress, Vinnette Carroll, Micki Grant, Adrienne Kennedy, Ntozake Shange, and Sonia Sanchez.

593. Kupa, Kushauri. *Black Theatre*, 6 (1972): 38-40.
594. Richardson, Alice. *N. Y. Amsterdam News* (Mar. 12, 1988): 33.
595. Weiner, Bernard. *San Francisco Chronicle* (Jan. 19, 1983): 55.

Cizmar, Paula

Selected Plays

596. *Al's Lunchette*Stationers*Drink Coca Cola* (staged reading, Women's Project, 1984-1985)
597. *Apocryphal Stories, Exceptional Friends* (staged reading, Women's Project, 1983-1984)
598. *Candy and Shelley Go to the Desert* (Women's Project, American Place Theater, 1984)
     Playscript: *Candy and Shelly Go to the Desert*. New York: Dramatists Play Service, 1988.
599. *Cupcakes* (Actors Theatre of Louisville, Kentucky, 1980-1981)
600. *Death of a Miner* (Women's Project, American Place Theater, 1982)
601. *The Girl Room*

Playscript: *Poets' Theatre: A Collection of Recent Works*. Edited by Michael Slater and Cynthia Savage, 40-49. New York: Ailanthus Press, 1981.

602. *Madonna of the Powder Room* (staged reading, Women's Project, 1982-1983)

603. *Stages* (collaborator, Actors Theatre of Louisville, Kentucky, 1981)

604. *Tough Girls* (Eugene O'Neill Theater Center National Playwrights' Conference, Waterford, Connecticut, 1984)

605. *You Always Get What You Want* (staged reading, Women's Project, 1984-1985)

Profiles

606. *Contemporary Authors: A Bio-Bibliographical Guide.* Volumes 122. Edited by Hal May, 106-107. Detroit: Gale Research Company, 1988.
The entry includes a biographical sketch and general comments on Cizmar's plays.

607. *Contemporary Theatre, Film and Television.* Volume 1. Edited by Monica M. O'Donnell, 107. Detroit: Gale Research Company, 1984.
Cizmar's entry contains a brief biography, including a list of her plays.

Reviews

Candy and Shelley Go to the Desert

608. *Drama-Logue* (Aug. 20-26, 1987): 10.

609. Loynd, Ray. *Los Angeles Times* (Aug. 20, 1987), sect. 6: 9.

610. Solomon, Alisa. *Village Voice* (April 3, 1984): 90.

Death of a Miner

611. Christon, Lawrence. *Los Angeles Times* (Nov. 11, 1983): sect. 6: 10.

612. Garson, Barbara. *Village Voice* (Apr. 13, 1982): 86.

613. Gussow, Mel. *New York Times* (Apr. 1, 1982): C19.

Tough Girls

614. Killen, Tom. *Connecticut*, 46 (Oct. 1983): 57-61.

Cloud, Darrah

Selected Plays

615. *The House Across the Street* (unproduced)
616. *O! Pioneers* (adapted from Willa Cather's novel, Women's Project, 1989)
617. *The Obscene Bird of Night* (adapted from Jose Donoso, Perseverence Theatre, Juneau, 1988-1989)
618. *The Stick Wife* (Los Angeles Theater Center, 1987)
619. *Work in Progress* (staged reading, Women's Project, 1987-1988)

Profiles and Interviews

620. Arkatov, Janice. "Cloud's New Play." *Los Angeles Times* (Jan. 14, 1987), sect. 6: 2.
     This is a preview article written prior to the opening of Cloud's *The Stick Wife* at the Los Angeles Theater Center. Although the article focuses on the playwright's comments about the play, information about her life is interspersed throughout the article.

621. O'Steen, Kathleen. "Being A Playwright In Tinseltown Is Tough Without TV-Film Work." *Variety* (Mar. 11, 1987): 103, 110.
     Cloud, along with several other playwrights, talks about writing for the movies. Cloud comments that upon receiving several calls from film producers, "It was really quite incredible ... but I don't think a lot of them would have called if they had realized what my play really was about."

Reviews

The Stick Wife

See item 620.

622. *Drama-Logue* (Jan. 22-28, 1987): 9.
623. Gussow, Mel. *New York Times* (Apr. 25, 1987): 16.
624. Sullivan, Dan. *Los Angeles Times* (Jan. 17, 1987), sect. 6: 1, 9.
625. *Variety* (Apr. 15, 1987): 218.
626. Weiner, Bernard. *San Francisco Chronicle* (Mar. 14, 1989), sect. E: 1.

Cohen, Alice Eve

Selected Plays

627. *Colette in Love* (with Lavonne Mueller, staged reading, Women's Project, 1985-1986.
    Playscript: see **Mueller, Lavonne**
628. *Lady Moonsong, Mr. Monsoon* (Practical Cats Theater Co., Westbeth Theater Center, 1987)
629. *Oklahoma Samovar* (Cubiculo, 1987)
630. *The Owl Was a Baker's Daughter* (Fools Company, Inc. Douglas Fairbanks Studio, Theatre Row, 1984)
631. *Women in Comedy* (collaborator, Manhattan Punch Line, 1989)

Reviews

Lady Moonsong, Mr. Monsoon

632. Holden, Stephen. *New York Times* (Mar. 20, 1987), sect. C: 3.

The Owl Was a Baker's Daughter

633. Knox, Alice. *Women & Performance*, 2, i (May 1984): 91-93.

Collins, Kathleen

Selected Plays

634. *The Brothers* (staged reading, Women's Project, American
     Place Theater, 1980-1981)
     Playscript: *9 Plays By Black Women.* Edited by
     Margaret B. Wilkerson, 293-347. New York: New
     American Library, 1986.
635. *In the Midnight Hour* (Richard Allen Center for Culture and
     Art, 1982)
     Playscript: *The Women's Project: Seven New
     Plays by Women.* Edited by Julia Miles, 35-82.
     New York: Performing Arts Journal Publications
     & American Place Theater, 1980.
636. *Only the Sky Is Free* (Richard Allen Center for Culture and
     Art, 1986)
637. *The Reading* (staged reading, Women's Project, 1984-1985)
638. *Remembrance* (American Place Theater, 1985)
639. *When Older Men Speak* (staged reading, Women's Project,
     1985-1986)

Profiles

See item 77.

640. *Black Arts Annual 1988-1989,* 162. New York: Garland,
     1990.
     A brief assessment of the life and career of Collins,
     who died at the age of forty-six of cancer.

641. *Contemporary Authors: A Bio-Bibliographical Guide.*
     Volume 119. Edited by Hal May, 67. Detroit:
     Gale Research Company, 1987.
     The entry includes a brief biographical sketch and a
     list of plays. See Collins's obituary in
     Contemporary Authors. Volume 126. New
     Revision Series. Edited by Susan M. Trosky, 55.
     Detroit: Gale Research Company, 1989.

642. "Kathleen Collins, A Film Maker, Dies at 46." *New York
     Times* (Sep. 24, 1988): 33.

643. Peterson, Bernard L. *Contemporary Black American
     Playwrights and Their Plays: A Biographical*

Directory and Dramatic Index, 116-118. New York: Greenwood Press, 1988.
Peterson provides a biographical sketch and a staging history of Collins's plays.

644. *Variety* (Sept. 28, 1988).
This item reports Collins's death and provides a brief biography.

Reviews

The Brothers

645. Feingold, Michael. *Village Voice* (Apr. 13, 1982): 83.
646. Mitchell, Loften. *N.Y. Amsterdam News* (Apr. 17, 1982): 28.
647. Rich, Frank. *New York Times* (Apr. 6, 1982): C13.

Commire, Anne

648. *Melody Sisters* (Eugene O'Neill Theater Center National Playwrights' Conference, Waterford, Connecticut, 1983)
649. *Put Them All Together* (WPA Theater, 1980)
650. *Starting Monday* (WPA Theater, 1990)
651. *Shay* (Playwrights Horizons, 1978)

Profiles

See item 9.

652. *Contemporary Authors: A Bio-Bibliographical Guide.*
Volume 21. New Revised Series. Edited by Deborah A. Straub, 95-96. Detroit: Gale Research Company, 1987.
The entry includes a biographical sketch and a list of plays.

653. *Contemporary Theatre, Film and Television.* Volume 1.
Edited by Monica M. O'Donnell. Detroit: Gale Research Company, 1984.
This entry provides a brief biography.

Reviews

Melody Sisters

654. Steckling, D. Larry. *Drama-Logue* (Oct. 5-11, 1989): 8.

Put Them All Together

655. Dunning, Jennifer. *New York Times* (Oct. 25, 1980): 13.
656. Frankel, Haskel. *New York Times* (Feb. 10, 1980), sect. 22: 18.
657. Gussow, Mel. *New York Times* (Jan. 30, 1979), sect. C: 7.

Shay

See item 16.

658. Christon, Lawrence. *Los Angeles Times* (June 12, 1983), Calendar sect.: 44.
659. Fox, Terry Curtis. *Village Voice* (Mar. 27, 1978): 76.
660. Gussow, Mel. *New York Times* (Mar. 8, 1978), sect. 3: 16.

Starting Monday

661. Holden, Stephen. *New York Times* (Apr. 5, 1990): C18.
662. Houppert, Karen. *Village Voice* (Apr. 24, 1990): 114.

Congdon, Constance

Selected Plays

663. *Casanova* (New Dramatists, 1989)
664. *A Conversation with Georgia O'Keeffe* (Avery Theater, Hartford, 1987)
665. *The Gilded Age* (adapted from Mark Twain's novel, Hartford Stage Company, 1986)
666. *Native American* (staged reading, Women's Project, 1982-1983)
667. *No Mercy* (Actors Theatre of Louisville, Kentucky, 1986)

668. *Raggedy Ann and Andy* (adapted from Johnny Gruelle, Children's Theatre Company, Minneapolis, 1987-1988)
669. *Rembrandt Takes a Walk* (adaptation of Mark Strand's and Red Groom's book, Children's Theatre Company, Minneapolis, 1989)
670. *Tales of the Lost Formicans* (Women's Project, Apple Corps Theater, 1990) Playscript: *Plays From Actors Theatre of Louisville*, 279-342. New York: Broadway Play Publishing Inc., 1989.
671. *Transatlantic Bridge* (staged reading, Playwrights Horizons, 1976)

Profiles and Interviews

672. *Contemporary Authors: A Bio-Bibliographical Guide.* Volume 123. Edited by Hal May, 56. Detroit: Gale Research Company, 1988.
    This entry includes a biographical sketch and a list of plays and awards.

673. Klein, Alvin. "An Artist Is Drawn on Stage." *New York Times* (Oct. 18, 1987), sect. 23: 35.
    Although Kline's article focuses on Congdon's one-woman play, *A Conversation With Georgia O'Keeffe,* he does include comments by Congdon herself concerning her life and art.

674. Klementowski, Nancy and Sonja Kuftinec. "An Interview with Constance Congdon." *Studies in American Drama 1945-Present,* 4 (1989): 203-221.
    The interviewers' questions evoke personal responses from Congdon regarding her career as a dramatist. She explains how she turned to play writing after her submission to a poetry contest was rejected. Part of the interview is devoted to the discussion of the existence of a particular feminine perspective in art. Congdon points out that few plays reveal the stories from a female consciousness, "[w]omen's lives are stories that have not been told." The dramatist also elaborates

on her belief that women continue to be misrepresented on stage, which she attributes in part to the "people who become actresses." These actresses, "pretty, petite young ingenues" do not resemble real women—"they weren't my friends, they were someone else." Many of the questions prompt Congdon to discuss several of her plays, especially *No Mercy, Tales of the Lost Formicans, Native American,* and *The Gilded Age.*

Reviews

A Conversation With Georgia O'Keeffe

See item 673.

The Gilded Age

675. Gussow, Mel. *New York Times* (Oct. 19, 1986): 75.
676. Klein, Alvin. *New York Times* (Oct. 12, 1986), sect. 23: 14.
677. Teich, Jessica. *American Theatre*, 3 (Dec. 1986): 6.

Native American

678. Billington, Michael. *Guardian* (London) (Oct. 7, 1988): 32.
679. Peter, John. *Sunday Times* (London) (Oct. 9, 1988): C8h.

No Mercy

680. Christiansen, Richard. *Chicago Tribune* (Mar. 30, 1986), sect. 13: 8-9.
681. Gussow, Mel. *New York Times* (Mar. 27, 1986): C16.
682. Liston, William T. *Theatre Journal,* 38, iv (Dec. 1986): 488-489.
683. Ransom, Rebecca. *Southern Exposure*, 14 (May-Aug., 1986).

Rembrandt Takes a Walk

684. *American Theatre*, 5 (Mar. 1989): 12-14.

Tales of the Lost Formicans

685. DeVries, Hilary. *New York Times* (Mar. 26, 1989), sect. 2: H5, H24.
686. *Drama-Logue* (Oct. 12-18, 1989): 25.
687. *Drama-Logue* (Nov. 30-Dec. 6, 1989): 8.
688. Feingold, Michael. *Village Voice* (May 8, 1990): 101.
689. Gussow, Mel. *New York Times* (Apr. 5, 1989): C9.
690. _____. *New York Times* (Apr. 29, 1990): 60.
691. Henry, William. *Time*, 133 (Apr. 17,1989): 70-71.
692. Solomon, Alisa. *Village Voice* (May 1, 1990): 116.
693. Sullivan, Dan. *Los Angeles Times* (Nov. 14, 1989), sect. F: 1.
694. Weiner, Bernard. *San Francisco Chronicle* (Sep. 22, 1989), sect. E: 12.

Coss, Clare

Selected Plays

695. *The Blessing* (American Place Theater, 1989)
696. *The Daughters Cycle Trilogy* (with Sondra Segal and Roberta Sklar)
    Playscript: see item 704.
    Daughters (Interart, 1978)
    Sister/Sister (Interart, 1978)
    Electra Speaks (Interart, 1980)
    Playscript: see item 703.
697. *The Dial Tone* (staged reading, Women's Project, 1982-1983)
698. *Growing Up Gothic* (Theater for the New City, 1983)
699. *Lillian Wald: At Home on Henry Street* (New Federal Theater, 1986)

Reviews

The Blessing

700. Gussow, Mel. *New York Times* (May 22, 1989): C12.
701. Solomon, Alisa. *Village Voice* (June 6, 1989): 92.

Daughters

See items 23, 32, 65, 3559.

702. Sainer, Arthur. *Village Voice* (Dec. 4, 1978): 126-127.

Electra Speaks

See items 23, 27, 31, 32, 6, 3559.

703. Coss, Clare, Sondra Segal and Roberta Sklar. "The
      Daughters Cycle: Electra Speaks." *Union
      Seminary Quarterly Review*, 35, iii & iv
      (Spring/Summer, 1980): 223-253.
      Prefacing the text of the play is an introduction to
      the drama explaining the dramatists' use of the
      technique of transformation in the *Daughters*
      trilogy to dramatize women's roles within the
      familial structure and women's attempts to "reclaim
      [themselves] lost within these roles."

704. _____. "Separation and Survival: Mothers, Daughters,
      Sisters—The Women's Experimental Theater." In
      The Future of Difference. Edited by Hester
      Eisenstein and Alice Jardine, 193-235. New
      Brunswick, N.J.: Rutgers University Press, 1985.
      A brief summary of a post-performance discussion
      with the spectators follows excerpts from the *The
      Daughters Cycle* trilogy.

705. Dunning, Jennifer. *New York Times* (Nov. 20, 1980):
      C22.
706. Moore, Honor. *Ms.*, 6 (Nov. 1977): 29-30.
707. Munk, Erica. *Village Voice* (July 11, 1977): 63.
708. Sommer, Sally R. *Village Voice* (Dec. 17, 1979): 117-118.

Growing Up Gothic

709. Gussow, Mel. *New York Times* (Jan. 18, 1983): C14.
710. Stone, Laurie. *Village Voice* (Jan. 25, 1983): 90.

Lillian Wald: At Home on Henry Street

711. Goodman, Walter. *New York Times* (Oct. 14, 1986): C14.

Sister/Sister

See items 23, 32, 65, 3559.

712. Sainer, Arthur. *Village Voice* (Dec. 4, 1978): 126-127.
713. Stone, Laurie. *Ms.*, 7 (Nov. 1978): 40-45.

Croswell, Anne

Selected Plays

714. *Bodo* (with Hugh Wheeler, Goodspeed Opera House, East
      Haddam, Connecticut, 1983)
715. *Chips 'n Ale* (with Jon Jory and Jerry Blatt, Actors Theatre
      of Louisville, Kentucky, 1973-1974)
716. *Conrack* (with Granville Burgess and Lee Pockriss, AMAS
      Repertory Theater, 1987)
717. *Earnest In Love* (Theater Off Park, 1980)
718. *Sidekicks; Or, A Merger of Marvelous Magnitude*
      Playscript: *Sidekicks.* New York: Workman
      Publishing, 1983.

Profiles

719. *Contemporary Theatre, Film, and Television.* Volume 1.
      Edited by Monica M. O'Donnell, 27. Detroit: Gale
      Research Company, 1984.
      The entry includes a biographical sketch and a list
      of plays.

Reviews

Bodo

720. *Variety* (Dec. 21, 1983): 71.
      This item announces the opening of *Bodo* at the
      Promenade Theater on January 8, 1984.

Conrack

721. Holden, Stephen. *New York Times* (Nov. 5, 1987): C36.

Sidekicks

722. *USA Today* (Feb. 22, 1984): 2B.
      This item announces the publication of *Sidekicks*.

Cruz, Migdalia

Selected Plays

723. *Lillian* (New Dramatists, 1987-1988)
724. *Lucy Loves Me* (New Dramatists, 1987-1988)
725. *Miriam's Flowers* (Playwrights Horizons, 1990)
726. *Not Time's Fool* (New York Shakespeare Festival, 1986)
727. *Welcome Back to Salamanca* (INTAR, 1988)

Profiles and Interviews

728. Greene, Alexis. "South Bronx Memoirs: Migdalia Cruz
      Explores Her Urban Roots." *American Theatre*, 7
      (June 1990): 58.
      Written on the occasion of the debut of her play
      Miriam's Flowers at Playwrights Horizons, this
      profile of Cruz describes her personal and
      professional background, as well as the play, which
      was based on a true incident during Cruz's girlhood
      in the South Bronx.

Reviews

Miriam's Flowers

See item 728.

Welcome Back To Salamanca

729. Hampton, Wilborn. *New York Times* (June 21, 1988):
      C16.

Cryer, Gretchen

Selected Plays

730. *Circle of Sound* (Manhattan Theatre Club, 1973)
731. *Grass Roots* (Leatherhead Theater Club, London, 1968)
732. *Hang on to the Good Times* (Manhattan Theatre Club, 1985)
733. *I'm Getting My Act Together and Taking It On the Road* (New York Shakespeare Festival, Public Theatre, 1978)
734. *The Last Sweet Days of Isaac* (East Side Playhouse, 1970)
735. *Now Is the Time For All Good Men* (Theater De Lys, 1967)
736. *Shelter* (John Golden Theater, 1973)
737. *The Wedding of Iphigenia and Iphigenia in Concert* (adapted from Euripides, with Doug Dyer and Peter Link, New York Shakespeare Festival, Public Theatre, 1971)

Profiles and Interviews

See items 9, 81, 103, 105 and page 5.

738. Berg, Beatrice. "From School Days." *New York Times* (Feb. 15, 1970), sect. 2: 1,3.
    Berg interviews Cryer and collaborator Nancy Ford during a run of *The Last Sweet Days of Isaac* Although the play is the major topic of conversation, Cryer and Ford also recollect their previous collaborations and friendship.

739. Christon, Lawrence. "No Yellow Brick Road For Cryer." *Los Angeles Times* (Nov. 4, 1980), sect. 4: 1, 6.
    Christon interviews Cryer prior to the opening of *I'm Getting My Act Together* at the Hartford Stage Company. Cryer talks about her childhood in central Indiana and her years writing musicals with Nancy Ford.

740. *Contemporary Authors: A Bio-Bibliographical Guide.* Volume 123. Edited by Hal May, 65-67. Detroit: Gale Research Company, 1988.

The entry provides a brief biography and a list of
Cryer's achievements as well as general comments
about her work.

741. *Contemporary Theatre, Film and Television.* Volume 4.
Edited by Monica M. O'Donnell, 116-117. Detroit:
Gale Research Company, 1987.
This entry includes a biographical sketch and a list
of Cryer's works.

742. Dworkin, Susan. "Hang on to the Good Times." *Ms.*, 6
(Dec. 1977): 64-65.
Dworkin's profile on Cryer and Ford focuses on
their recordings.

743. Green, Stanley. *The World of Musical Comedy*, 357-358,
373-374. New York: A.S. Barnes & Company,
1980.
Green provides overviews of the professional
careers of Gretchen Cryer and Elizabeth Swados.

744. Kleiman, Carol. "Gretchen Cryer Takes a Big Step Forward
on the Road to Salvation." *Chicago Tribune* (Apr.
10, 1980), sect. 2: 1, 4.
Kleiman focuses on Cryer's college days, her long
friendship with Nancy Ford, her marriage and
divorce, her children, and her struggle to become a
writer. In short, Cryer talks about the events in her
life that enabled her ultimately to "get her act
together," which, she says "took a long, long
time." Kleiman discusses the parallels between the
lives of Cryer and Heather Jones, the cabaret singer
in Cryer's *I'm Getting My Act Together.* Kleiman
points out "it is not Cryer's story word for word
[but] the emotions are 100 percent Cryer's." Cryer
denies that the play is intended to be a feminist
"diatribe." On the contrary, although Cryer is a
self-described feminist, she meant the play to be
"fun" and she hopes that both men and women will
see "universal truths" inherent in the play.

745. Klemesrud, Judy. "She's Got Her Act Together Again." *New York Times* (Dec. 16, 1978): 48.

    Cryer reflects on the parallels between her life and that of Heather, the protagonist in her hit musical *I'm Getting My Act Together and Taking It On the Road.* Both women find relationships difficult. Like Heather, Cryer reverted to baby talk when she wanted her husband to help with the household chores, "[I became] a baby-talking child lunatic." Similarities notwithstanding, Cryer claims she and Heather do not "see eye to eye in every aspect." For instance, Heather takes "it" all too seriously, "she is caught up in the passion." Whereas, her real-life counterpart "see[s] it all as funnier." Not so with many male members of the audience. According to Cryer, "one man told me he wanted to blow me away with a shotgun" because he believed Cryer and women in general were "trying to change things too fast."

Reviews

Circle of Sound

746. Wilson, John S. *New York Times* (Oct. 25, 1973): 53.

Grass Roots

747. Billington, Michael. *Times* (London) (Oct. 16, 1968): 16d.
748. Bryden, Ronald. *Observer* (Oct. 20, 1968): 26f.

Hang on to the Good Times

749. Gussow, Mel. *New York Times* (Feb. 24, 1985), sect. 2: H5, H24.
750. Rich, Frank. *New York Times* (Feb. 19, 1985): C18.
751. Simon, John. *New York,* 18 (Mar. 4, 1985): 111.
752. *Variety* (Feb. 27, 1985): 90.

I'm Getting My Act Together and Taking It on the Road

See item 16.

753. Christiansen, Richard. *Chicago Tribune* (Oct. 31, 1980), sect. 2: 5.
     The *Tribune's* theatre critic discusses changes in the cast of *I'm Getting My Act Together.*
754. _____. *Chicago Tribune* (May 13, 1982), sect. 3: 18.
755. Christon, Lawrence. *Los Angeles Times* (May 21, 1981), sect. 6: 2.
756. *Contemporary Literary Criticism: Excerpts from Today's Novelists, Poets, Playwrights, and Other Creative Writers.* Volume 21. Edited by Sharon R. Gunton, 77-82. Detroit: Gale Research Company, 1982.
757. Drake, Sylvie. *Los Angeles Times* (Feb. 11, 1981), sect. 6: 8.
758. _____. *Los Angeles Times* (Oct. 26, 1982), sect. 6: 1, 5.
759. Eder, Richard. *New York Times* (June 15, 1978): C17.
760. Eldenberg, T. *Show Business* (June 22, 1978): 22.

761. Hewson, David. *Times* (London) (May 19, 1981): 21b.
     Hewson reports the closing of *I'm Getting My Act Together* at the Apollo Theatre after a two-month run.

762. Kerner, Mary. *Los Angeles Times* (July 26, 1980), sect. 2: 11.
763. Kerr, Walter. *New York Times* (July 9, 1978); sect. 2: 3.
764. Kimball, R. *New York Post* (June 15, 1978): 55.
765. Kissel, Howard. *Women's Wear Daily* (June 16, 1978): 8.
766. Lochte, David. *Los Angeles,* 26 (Jan. 1981): 217.
767. Nachman, Gerald. *San Francisco Chronicle* (Jan. 2, 1981): 43.
768. Novick, Julius. *Village Voice* (June 26, 1978): 79-80.
     Reprinted in item 756.

769. Reich, Howard. "Gretchen Cryer Is On the Road Again." *Chicago Tribune* (Apr. 23, 1982), sect. 3: 1.
     Reich interviewed Cryer shortly before a revival of *I'm Getting My Act Together* at the World Playhouse in Chicago. This production presents a new challenge for Cryer because the stage is traditional, not a theater-in-the-round. Although

intimacy is lost on a proscenium stage, Cryer says
that on a proscenium stage "the show is much
more focused, and its comedic and dramatic effects
can be stronger." Cryer also mentions that she and
collaborator Nancy Ford are working on a new
musical based on Eleanor Roosevelt.

770. Rosenfeld, Megan. *Washington Post* (Jan. 26, 1981), sect.
C: 1.
771. Sheridan, Sid. *Punch*, 280 (Apr. 8, 1981): 570.
772. Simon, John. *New York* (July 3, 1978): 74.
773. Smith, Sid. *Chicago Tribune* (Sep. 29, 1987), sect. 5: 5.
774. Stern, Alan. *Denver Post* (July 26, 1984), sect. B: 1.
775. Sullivan, Dan. *Los Angeles Times* (Nov. 10, 1980), sect.
6: 1, 6, 12.

776. *Times* (London) (Feb. 6, 1981): 16d.
The *Times* notes the opening of *I'm Getting My
Act Together* at the Apollo Theatre on March 31,
1981.

777. Wardle, Irving. *Times* (London) (Apr. 1, 1981): 11c.
778. Zorn, Eric. *Chicago Tribune* (Aug. 20, 1980), sect. 3: 10.

The Last Sweet Days of Isaac

779. Barnes, Clive. *New York Times* (Jan. 27, 1970): 49.
780. _____. *New York Times* (Jan. 9, 1971): 17.

781. Berkvist, Robert. "Alice Doesn't Poach Oysters." *New York
Times* (June 28, 1970), sect. 2: 17.
Berkvist highlights the career of Alice Playten,
who plays the role of the "uptight secretary" in the
Off Broadway production of *The Last Sweet Days
of Isaac.*

782. Bunce, Alan. *Christian Science Monitor* (Mar. 16, 1970):
10.

783. Gussow, Mel. "How Austin Pendleton Uneasily Crawled to
Success." *New York Times* (Mar. 3, 1970): 34.

Gussow focuses on Austin Pendleton, star of *The Last Sweet Days of Isaac.*

784. Kerr, Walter. *New York Times* (Feb. 8, 1970), sect. 2: 1, 5.

Now Is the Time For All Good Men

785. Barnes, Clive. *New York Times* (Sep. 27, 1967): 42.

786. _____. *New York Times* (Oct. 27, 1967): 49.
Barnes reappraises his review of *Now Is The Time For All Good Men.*

787. Lewis, Theophilus. *America* (Oct. 14, 1967): 421-422.

788. *New York Times* (Dec. 29, 1967): 13.
The *Times* announces the closing of *Now Is the Time For All Good Men* at the Theater de Lys on Sunday, December 31, 1967.

789. Oliver, Edith. *New Yorker*, 63 (Oct. 7, 1967): 133-134.
Reprinted in 756.
790. Thompson, Howard. *New York Times* (May 2, 1971): 73.

Shelter

791. Barnes, Clive. *New York Times* (Feb. 7, 1973): 31.
792. Kerr, Walter. *New York Times* (Feb. 18, 1973), sect. 2: 1, 23.
Reprinted in 756.

793. "Producer of Flop Sues Over Disk." *New York Times* (Sep. 11, 1973): 25.
The *Times* reports the producer of the musical *Shelter* has filed suit against Columbia Records, blaming the company for the "early closing" of the play.

794. Wilson, Edwin. *Wall Street Journal* (Feb. 8, 1973): 12.

The Wedding Of Iphigenia and Iphigenia in Concert

795. Barnes, Clive. *New York Times* (Dec. 17, 1971): 28.

Cunningham, Laura

Selected Plays

796. *Bang!* (Steppenwolf Theatre, Chicago, 1986)
797. *Beautiful Bodies* (Whole Theater, Montclair, New Jersey, 1987)
798. *The Man At the Door* (New Dramatists, 1987)
         Playscript: *I Love You, Two* [includes: *The Man at the Door* and *Where She Went, What She Did.* New York: Samuel French Inc., 1989.
799. *Where She Went, What She Did* (Manhattan Punch Line, 1988)
         Playscript: see 798.

Profiles

800. *Contemporary Authors: A Bio-Bibliographical Guide.* Volume 23. New Revision Series. Edited by Deborah A. Straub, 110. Detroit: Gale Research Company, 1988.
         The entry includes a biographical sketch and a list of plays.

Reviews

Bang!

801. Christiansen, Richard. *Chicago Tribune* (Sep. 29, 1986), sect. 2: 6.

Where She Went, What She Did

802. Collins, William B. *Philadelphia Inquirer* (June 22, 1987): D4.
803. Gussow, Mel. *New York Times* (Feb. 17, 1988): C21.
804. Stone, Laurie. *Village Voice* (Mar. 15, 1988): 97.

Curran, Leigh

Selected Plays

805. *Alterations* (WPA Theater, 1986)
806. *Lunch Girls* (Long Wharf Theatre, New Haven, 1978)

Profiles

807. *Contemporary Theatre, Film, and Television.* Volume 5.
      Edited by Monica M. O'Donnell, 67-68. Detroit:
      Gale Research Company, 1988.
      A biographical profile is included in the entry along
      with a list of Curran's performances as an actress
      and her work as a playwright.

Reviews

Alterations

808. *Variety* (Nov. 12, 1986): 89.
809. Oliver, Edith. *The New Yorker*, 62 (Nov. 3, 1986): 46-47.
810. Rich, Frank. *New York Times* (Oct. 31, 1986): C3.

Lunch Girls

See item 10.

811. Fleckenstein, Joan S. *Educational Theatre Journal*, 30 (Oct.
      1978): 417-418.
812. Kroll, Jack. *Newsweek*, 90 (Dec. 19, 1977): 88.
813. Moore, Honor. *Ms.*, 6 (June 1978): 26.

Deer, Sandra

Selected Plays

814. *Beauty and the Beast* (Alliance Theater, Atlanta, 1988-89)
815. *Amazing Grace* (Alliance Theater, Atlanta, 1987)
816. *So Long on Lonely Street* (Jack Lawrence Theater, 1986)

Playscript: *So Long on Lonely Street*. New York:
Samuel French, Inc., 1988.

817. *Wrinkle in Time* (adapted from Madeleine L'Engle, Alliance
Theater, Atlanta, 1987-1988)

Profiles

818. Crouch, Paula. "Deer To the Hearts of Atlanta; Sisters Cast
In Major Roles." *Atlanta Journal-Constitution*
(June 24, 1984), sect. H: 1.
Crouch highlights the careers of the Deer sisters.
Playwright Sandra Deer is literary manager of the
Alliance Theatre, and her sibling Sue is director of
the High Museum's Department of
Communications.

819. _____. "New Plays By Three Atlanta Women To Open
This Week." *Atlanta Journal-Constitution* (Apr.
12, 1987),sect. J: 1, 8.
Crouch profiles the careers of three local women
playwrights on the eve of the opening of their
plays: Sandra Deer's *Amazing Grace*, Barbara
Lebow's *Cyparis* and Marsha Jackson's *Sisters*.

820. Sherbert, Linda. "Nine Atlanta Playwrights Discuss the
Importance of New York." *Atlanta Journal-
Constitution* (May 18, 1986), sect. J: 2.
Sherbert addressed the question—does a New York
run validate the success of a playwright?—to
several Atlanta-based dramatists, including Sandra
Deer and Barbara Lebow. In Lebow's opinion, a
playwright should "build a reputation elsewhere and
then go to New York." Deer, however, felt that a
successful play in Atlanta is "sufficient."

821. Trader, Beverly. "Placing the Playwrights." *Southern
Exposure,* 14, iii (1986): 83-84.
Trader briefly profiles the theatrical career of Deer.

Reviews

Amazing Grace

822. *Drama-Logue* (June 23-29, 1988): 28.
823. Futterman, Ellen. *St. Louis Post Dispatch* (Mar. 20, 1988), sect. F: 3.
824. Lochte, Dick. *Los Angeles Magazine*, 33 (Aug. 1988): 316.
825. Pollack, Joe. *St. Louis Post Dispatch* (Mar. 28, 1988), sect. E: 4.
826. Shirley, Don. *Los Angeles Times* (June 10, 1988), sect. 6: 16.
827. *Variety* (May, 20, 1987): 94-96.

So Long on Lonely Street

828. Barnes, Clive. *New York Post* (Apr. 4, 1986).
     Reprinted in item 842.
829. Beaufort, John. *Christian Science Monitor* (Apr. 9, 1986): 24.
     Reprinted in items 831, 842.
830. Cohen, Ron. *Women's Wear Daily* (Apr. 4, 1986).
     Reprinted in item 842.
831. *Contemporary Literary Criticism: Excerpts from Criticism of the Works of Today's Novelists, Poets, Playwrights, and Other Creative Writers.* Volume 45. Edited by Daniel G. Marowski and Roger Matuz, 119-121. Detroit: Gale Research Company, 1987.
832. Crouch, Paula. *Atlanta Journal-Constitution* (May 5, 1985), sect. J: 2.
833. _____. *Atlanta Journal-Constitution* (Feb. 20, 1986), sect. C: 7.
834. Dace, Tish. *Plays International*, 2 (Aug. 1986): 42.
835. Gill, Brendan. *The New Yorker*, 62 (Apr. 14, 1986): 84-85.
     Reprinted in item 831.
836. Gold, Sylviane. *Wall Street Journal* (Apr. 28, 1986): 22.
837. Henry, William A. *Time*, 127 (Apr. 14, 1986): 103.
     Reprinted in item 831, 842.

838. Hirsch, Foster. "Still Savvy After All These Years." *American Theatre*, 2 (Mar. 1986): 12-15.
     Hirsch profiles Cheryl Crawford, producer of Deer's *So Long on Lonely Street.*

839. Hubert, Linda L. "Humor and Heritage in Sandra Deer's *So
      Long on Lonely Street." Southern Quarterly*, 25
      (1987): 105-115.
      Hubert discusses *So Long on Lonely Street* in
      terms of its development, staging history, and
      reception by the New York critics, and explains
      how Deer's comic vision "has inspired audiences to
      rethink their responses to the large southern
      heritage of social and literary conventions."

840. Kelly, Kevin. *Boston Globe* (Feb. 19, 1986), sect. 3: 25.
841. Loynd, Ray. *Los Angeles Times* (May 26, 1989), sect. 6:
      13.
842. *New York Theatre Critics' Reviews* 47 (Mar. 17, 1986):
      334-337.
843. Rich, Frank. *New York Times* (Apr. 4, 1986): C5.
      Reprinted in item 831, 842.

844. Sherbert, Linda. "Sandra Deer Won't Say 'So Long' To Her
      Play." *Atlanta Journal-Constitution* (Dec. 15,
      1985), sect. 2: 1.
      Sherbert announces that producer Cheryl Crawford
      will open Deer's *So Long on Lonely Street* on
      Broadway or Off Broadway. Deer will retain artistic
      control to avoid the fate of previous Atlanta-based
      playwrights whose plays flopped in New York
      because they lost artistic control.

845. _____. *Atlanta Journal-Constitution* (May 10, 1985),
      sect. P: 3.
846. _____. *Atlanta Journal-Constitution* (Dec. 9, 1985), sect.
      B: 1.
847. _____. *Atlanta Journal-Constitution* (Apr. 5, 1986), sect.
      A: 2.
848. _____. *Atlanta Journal-Constitution* (Apr. 13, 1986),
      sect. J: 1.

849. _____. *Atlanta Journal-Constitution* (Oct. 9, 1986), sect.
      B: 1.
      Announces the London opening of *So Long on
      Lonely Street.*

850. Smith, Helen C. *Atlanta Journal-Constitution* (Sep. 5, 1985), sect. B: 1.
851. _____. *Atlanta Journal-Constitution* (Sept. 22, 1985), sect. J: 12.
852. _____. *Atlanta Journal-Constitution* (Oct.13, 1985), sect. J: 3.
853. _____. *Atlanta Journal-Constitution* (Apr. 27, 1986), sect. J: 2.
854. *Variety* (May 29, 1985): 162.
855. *Variety* (Apr. 9, 1986): 130.
856. Watt, Douglas. *New York Daily News* (Apr. 4, 1986). Reprinted in item 842.

DeMatteo, Donna

Selected Plays

857. *Barbecue Pit* (HB Studios, Theater East, 1969)
858. *Dear Mr. G* (Roundabout Theater Company, 1975)
859. *The Silver Fox* (John Drew Theatre, 1987)

Profiles

See item 9.

860. *Contemporary Authors: A Bio-Bibliographical Guide.* Volumes 25-28. First Revision. Edited by Christine Nasso, 185. Detroit: Gale Research Company, 1977.
     A brief profile of DeMatteo's life and work.

Reviews

Dear Mr. G

861. Gussow, Mel. *New York Times* (Dec. 6, 1975): 20.
862. Loney, Glenn. *After Dark*, 8 (Mar. 1976): 83.

The Silver Fox

863. Lovenheim, Barbara. *New York Times* (Aug. 9, 1987), sect. 21: 21.

Lovenheim highlights the career of Uta Hagen, star of *The Silver Fox.*

864. Stone, Laurie. *Village Voice* (Sep. 1, 1987): 96-97.

DeVeaux, Alexis

Selected Plays

865. *Boudoir Pieces* (see *Onile*)
866. *Circles* (Frederick Douglass Creative Arts Center, 1973)
867. *No* (New Federal Theater, 1981)
868. *Onile* (with Kevin Winn, Merce Cunningham Studio, 1983)
869. *A Season to Unravel* (Negro Ensemble Company, 1979)
870. *The Tapestry: A Play Woven in 2* (Harlem Performance Center, 1976)
    Playscript: *9 Plays by Black Women.* Edited by Margaret B. Wilkerson, 138-195. New York: New American Library, 1986.

Profiles and Interviews

See items 77, 98.

871. *Black Writers: A Selection of Sketches from Contemporary Authors.* Edited by Linda Metzger, 151-152. Detroit: Gale Research Inc., 1989.
    This entry gives concise biographical information, general comments on DeVeaux's work, and lists her achievements as a writer, illustrator, and playwright.

872. *Contemporary Authors: A Bio-Bibliographical Guide.* Volume 26. New Revision Series. Edited by Hal May, 118-119. Detroit: Gale Research Inc., 1989. A brief profile of the life and work of DeVeaux.

873. Peterson, Bernard L. *Contemporary Black American Playwrights and Their Plays: A Biographical Directory and Dramatic Index,* 142-144. New York: Greenwood Press, 1989.

Peterson provides a biographical sketch and brief staging history of DeVeaux's plays.

874. Ramsey, Priscilla R. "Alexis DeVeaux." *Dictionary of Literary Biography.* Volume 38. *Afro-American Writers After 1955: Dramatists and Prose Writers.* Edited by Thadious M. Davis and Trudier Harris, 92-97. Detroit: Gale Research Company, 1985. The author surveys and analyzes the life and works of DeVeaux. Unfortunately, scant attention is paid to her work as a playwright. The essay includes a selected list of primary and secondary works.

Reviews

See item 104.

Boudoir Pieces

See item 877.

No

See item 93.

875. Gussow, Mel. *New York Times* (June 6, 1981): 14.
876. Hill, Stephanie. *Village Voice* (May 6-12, 1981): 92.

Onile

877. Anderson, Jack. *New York Times* (Oct. 11, 1983): C15. Anderson also reviews *Boudoir Pieces.*

A Season To Unravel

See item 13.

878. Barnes, Clive. *New York Post* (Jan. 26, 1979): 36.
879. Gussow, Mel. *New York Times* (Jan. 26, 1979): C3.
880. Oliver, Edith. *New Yorker,* 54 (Feb. 5, 1979): 100.

Diggs, Elizabeth

Selected Plays

881. *Close Ties* (Long Wharf Theater, New Haven, Connecticut,
     1981)
     Playscript: *Close Ties*. Garden City, New York:
     Nelson Doubleday, 1981.
882. *Comrades* (INTAR, 1987)
883. *Dumping Ground* (Ensemble Studio Theatre, 1981)
     Playscript: *Dumping Ground*. New York:
     Dramatists Play Service, 1982.
884. *Goodbye, Freddy* (Manhattan Punch Line, 1985)
     Playscript: *Goodbye, Freddy*. New York:
     Dramatists Play Service, 1986.
885. *Saint Florence* (Circle Repertory Theatre, 1988)

Profiles

886. *Contemporary Authors: A Bio-Bibliographical Guide.*
     Volume 109. Edited by Hal May, 111-112. Detroit:
     Gale Research Company, 1983.
     A brief profile of Diggs's life and work. Includes a
     brief discussion of her plays *Close Ties* and
     Dumping Ground, which incorporates critics'
     comments from reviews of the plays. A selected
     primary and secondary bibliography accompanies
     the entry.

887. *Contemporary Theatre, Film, and Television.* Volume 3.
     Edited by Monica M. O'Donnell, 130-131. Detroit:
     Gale Research Company, 1986.
     The entry offers a succinct biography and includes a
     selected list of Diggs's plays and awards.

888. Christon, Lawrence "*Close Ties* Bloodlines Revisited." *Los
     Angeles Times* (Mar. 22, 1986), Calendar sect.: 2.
     Christon converses with Diggs on the eve of the
     opening of *Close Ties,* which has been called by
     some the "new important American play." In
     addition to discussing the loose autobiographical
     connection to the play, Diggs comments on her
     early years in the theatre, which she "resisted" for

many years because she was "scared of being a
writer." Apparently, Jungian psychology has
helped her overcome her fear, "I learned that
darkness is creative if it's understood and
expressed."

Reviews

Close Ties

889. Christiansen, Richard. *Chicago Tribune* (Feb. 1, 1982),
       sect. 3: 7.
890. Christon, Lawrence. *Los Angeles Times* (Mar. 22, 1986),
       sect. 6: 1.
891. Gussow, Mel. *New York Times* (Mar. 22, 1981): 58.
892. Jonas, Larry. *Drama-Logue* (Aug. 24-30, 1989): 11.
893. Koehler, Robert. *Los Angeles Times* (Aug. 18, 1989), sect.
       6: 28.
894. Kerr, Walter. *New York Times* (Mar. 1, 1981), sect. 2: D3.
895. Massa, Robert. *Village Voice* (June 17-23, 1981): 77.
896. Novick, Julius. *Village Voice* (Mar. 25-31, 1981): 96.
897. Rosenfeld, Megan. *Washington Post* (June 9, 1983), sect.
       C: 1.
898. Sullivan, Dan. *Los Angeles Times* (Mar. 31, 1986), sect.
       2: 5,6.

Dumping Ground

899. Gussow, Mel. *New York Times* (June 11, 1981): C14.
900. Massa, Robert. *Village Voice* (June 17-23, 1981): 77.
901. Simon, John. *New York,* 14 (Nov. 9, 1981): 71.

Goodbye, Freddy

902. Christon, Lawrence. *Los Angeles Times* (Apr. 17, 1983),
       Calendar sect.: 40.
903. Sullivan, Dan. *Los Angeles Times* (Apr. 26, 1983), sect.
       6: 1, 6.

Saint Florence

904. Gussow, Mel. *New York Times* (Oct. 15, 1988): 19.

905. Mitgang, Herbert. *New York Times* (Feb. 23, 1988): C13.
Mitgang notes that Diggs's *Saint Florence* was
runner-up in the tenth annual Susan Smith
Blackburn Prize. Caryl Churchill won the award
for her play *Serious Money*. Other finalists
included: Maria Irene Fornes (*Abingdon Square*),
Beth Henley (*The Lucky Spot*), and Casey Kurtii
(*Three Ways Home*).

906. Wilson, Edwin. *Wall Street Journal* (Nov. 1, 1988): A26.

Donahue, Nancy

Selected Plays

907. *The Beach House* (Circle Repertory Company, 1985)
Playscript: *The Beach House*. New York: Samuel
French, 1985.
908. *Death and the Matron* (staged reading, Women's Project,
1984-1985)

Reviews

The Beach House

909. Oliver, Edith. *New Yorker*, 61 (Dec. 30, 1985): 58-59.
910. Rich, Frank. *New York Times* (Dec. 20, 1985): C3.

911. Ryzuk, Mary S. *The Circle Repertory Company: The First
Fifteen Years*, 259, 277. Ames: Iowa State
University Press, 1989.
Ryzuk briefly discusses the production of *The
Beach House*.

Drahos, Mary

Selected Plays

912. *Eternal Sabbath* (Blackfriars' Guild, 1963)
913. *Go, Go, Go, God Is Dead: A New Play about the New
Morals* (Blackfriars' Guild, 1963)

914. *Reunion of Sorts* (Blackfriars' Guild, 1969)

Profiles

915. *Contemporary Authors: A Bio-Bibliographical Guide.*
       Volume 116. Edited by Hal May, 124-125. Detroit:
       Gale Research Company, 1986.
       The entry provides biographical information as well
       as comments from Drahos herself and a list of
       primary and secondary sources.

Reviews

Eternal Sabbath

916. Calta, Louis. *New York Times* (Oct. 19, 1963): 17.
917. Lewis, Theophilus. *America,* 109 (Oct. 26, 1963): 497-498.

Go, Go, Go, God Is Dead

918. Fiske, Edward B. *New York Times* (Oct. 12, 1966): 37.

Reunion of Sorts

919. Gussow, Mel. *New York Times* (Oct. 15, 1969): 40.
920. Lewis, Theophilus. *America,* 121 (Oct. 18, 1969): 341-342.

Drayton, Mary

Selected Plays

921. *Ducks in a Row* (Santa Fe Theater Festival, New Mexico,
       1984)
922. *The Playroom* (Brooks Atkinson Theater, 1965)
       Playscript: *The Playroom.* New York: Random
       House, 1966.

Profiles

923. Nellhaus, Arlynn. *Denver Post* (July 26, 1984), sect. B: 1.
       Nellhaus profiles the professional career of Drayton
       and discusses her play *Ducks in a Row.*

Reviews

Ducks in a Row

See item 923.

The Playroom

924. Chapman, John. *New York Daily News* (Dec. 6, 1965).
     Reprinted in item 928.
925. *Drama-Logue* (July 27-Aug. 2, 1989): 9.
926. Kerr, Walter. *New York Herald Tribune* (Dec. 6, 1965).
     Reprinted in item 928.
927. McCulloh, T.H. *Los Angeles Times* (Sep 15, 1989), sect.
     6: 18.
928. *New York Theatre Critics' Reviews*, 26 (Dec. 13, 1965):
     235-238.
929. Taubman, Howard. *New York Times* (Dec. 6, 1965): 49.
930. Wadel, Norman. *New York World Telegram* (Dec. 6, 1965).
     Reprinted in item 928.
931. Watts, Richard. *New York Post* (Dec. 6, 1965): 40.
     Reprinted in item 928.

Dreher, Sarah

Selected Plays

932. *Alumnae News* (Celebration Theatre, Los Angeles, 1987)
     Playscript: *Lesbian Stages: Plays by Sarah Dreher*.
     Norwich, Vermont: New Victoria Publishers, Inc.,
     1988.
933. *Backward, Turn Backward*
     Playscript: see item 932.
934. *Base Camp*
     Playscript: see item 932.
935. *The Doris Day Years*
     Playscript: see item 932.
936. *8 x 10 Glossy* (Stonewall Repertory Theater, 1985)
937. *Hollandia '45*
     Playscript: see item 932.
938. *Ruby Christmas* (Peoples' Theatre, Massachusetts, 1981)

939. *This Brooding Sky*
   Playscript: see 932.

  Reviews

  Alumnae News

940. Koehler, Robert. *Los Angeles Times* (May 8, 1987), sect.
   6: 10.

  8 x 10 Glossy

  See item 19.

Drexler, Roslyn

  Selected Plays

941. *The Bed Was Full* (New Dramatists, 1965)
   Playscript: see item 950.
942. *Dear* (SoHo Repertory, 1983)
943. *Delicate Feelings* (Theatre for the New City, 1984)
944. *Graven Image* (Theatre for the New City, 1980)
945. *The Heart That Eats Itself* (Theatre for the New City, 1987)
946. *Home Movies* (Judson Poets Theatre, 1964)
   Playscript: *The Off -Off Broadway Book: The
   Plays, People, Theatre.* Edited by Albert Poland,
   30-43. New York: Bobbs-Merrill, 1972; see item
   950.
947. *Hot Buttered Roll* (New Dramatists 1970)
   Playscript: *Theatre Experiment.* Edited by Michael
   Benedikt, 197-233. Garden City, New York:
   Doubleday & Company, 1967.
948. *The Ice Queen* (The Proposition, Boston, 1973)
949. *The Investigation* (New Dramatists, 1966)
950. *The Line of Least Existence* (Judson Poets Theatre, 1968)
   Playscript: *The Line of Least Existence and Other
   Plays.* New York: Random House, 1967.
951. *The Mandrake* (Center Stage, Baltimore, 1983)
952. *A Matter of Life and Death* (Theatre for the New City,
   1986)
953. *Message From Garcia* (New Dramatists, 1971)

954. *Molly's Dream* (Writer's Conference, Boston University, Tanglewood, Massachusetts, 1968)
    Playscript: see item 946.
955. *Room 17C* (Omaha Magic Theatre, Omaha, 1983)
    Playscript: see item 961.
956. *She Who Was He* (New York Theatre Strategy, 1976)
957. *Skywriting* (included in *Collision Course*, an Off Broadway presentation of eleven plays, Cafe Au GoGo, 1968)
    Playscript: *Collision Course*. Edited by Edward Parone, 53-63. New York: Random House, 1986; *A Century of Plays by American Women*. Edited by Rachel France, 174-178. New York: Richards Rosen Press, 1977.
958. *Softly and Consider the Nearness* (Judson Poets Theatre, 1964)
    Playscript: see item 950.
959. *Sorry About That* (New Dramatists, 1964-1965)
960. *Starburn* (Theatre for the New City, 1983)
961. *Transients Welcome* (includes *Room 17-C* and *Utopia Parkway*, Theatre for the New City, 1985)
    Playscript: *Transients Welcome: Three One-Act Plays*. New York: Broadway Play Publishers, Inc., 1984.
962. *The Tree Artist* (Gateway, Long Island, 1981)
963. *Utopia Parkway* (see item 961)
964. *Vulgar Lives* (La Mama Experimental Theatre, 1979)
965. *Was I Good?* (New Dramatists, 1971)
966. *What Do You Call It?* (Theatre for the New City, 1986)
967. *The Writer's Opera* (Theatre for the New City, 1979)

Profiles and Interviews

See items 9, 33, 45,47, 67, 87, 103, 957 and pages 5, 7, 9.

968. *Contemporary Authors: A Bio-Bibliographical Guide.* Volumes 81-84. Edited by Frances Carol Locher, 134-135. Detroit: Gale Research Company, 1979. The entry includes a concise biography, a list of Drexler's works and awards, and brief comments from critics about some of Drexler's plays.

969. *Contemporary Theatre, Film, and Television*. Volume 1.
      Edited by Monica M. O'Donnell, 148-149. Detroit:
      Gale Research Company, 1984.
      This source offers a brief profile, including theatre-
      related activities, and a list of works, media
      appearances, and awards.

970. Drexler, Roslyn. "Notes on the Occasion of Having *Line of
      Least Existence & Other Plays* Remaindered at
      Marboro Book Shops." *New York Times* (Nov. 7,
      1971), sect. 2: 1, 13.
      In her unique style, Drexler reflects on her plays, "I
      wrote *Home Movies* in secret . . . as if I were
      gestating a bizarre mutant which only I could
      love." She also discusses *Hot Buttered Roll*, *The
      Investigation*, and *The Line of Least Existence*.

971. McNaughton, Howard. *Contemporary Dramatists*. 3rd
      edition. Edited by James Vinson, 124-125.
      Chicago: St. James Press, 1982.
      McNaughton briefly discusses the work of Drexler.
      Included is a list of her plays.

Reviews

See items 47, 49, 68, 78, 79.

The Bed Was Full

See item 12.

Delicate Feelings

972. Day, Susie. *Women & Performance*, 2, i (1984): 88-89.
973. Feingold, Michael. *Village Voice* (June 12, 1984): 89.
974. Gold, Sylviane. *Wall Street Journal* (Aug. 1, 1984): 22.

Graven Image

975. Gussow, Mel. *New York Times* (May 17, 1980): 14.
976. Sommer, Sally. *Village Voice* (May 19, 1980): 92.

Home Movies

See item 989.

977. Calta, Louis. *New York Times* (May 12, 1964): 32.
978. Gottfried, Martin. *A Theater Divided: The Postwar American Stage,* 208-209. Boston: Little, Brown, 1968.
979. Oliver, Edith. *The New Yorker,* 40 (May 23, 1964): 134.
980. Simon, John. *Uneasy Stages: A Chronicle of the New York Theater, 1963-1973,* 56. New York: Random House, 1975.
981. Sontag, Susan. *Partisan Review,* 31, iii (Summer 1964): 396.

Hot Buttered Roll

See item 970.

982. Leonard, Hugh. *Plays and Players,* 17 (Apr. 1970): 43.

The Investigation

See item 970.

983. Leonard, Hugh. *Plays and Players,* 17 (Apr. 1970): 43.

The Line of Least Existence

See item 970.

984. Barnes, Clive. *New York Times* (Mar. 25, 1968): 53.
985. *Contemporary Literary Criticism: Excerpts from the Criticism of the Works of Today's Novelists, Poets, Playwrights, and other Creative Writers.* Edited by Carolyn Riley. Detroit: Gale Research Company, 1974.
986. Duberman, Martin. *Partisan Review,* 35, iii (Summer 1968): 415.
987. Kroll, Jack. *Newsweek,* 75 (Feb. 9, 1970): 95.
988. _____. *Newsweek,* 71 (Apr. 1, 1968): 88.

989. Lamont, Rosette C. "Roslyn Drexler's Semiotics of Instability." *Theater,* 17 (Winter 1985): 70-77. Lamont observes, "In all of [Drexler's] lampoon plays she destabilizes the accepted forms of discourse, social stereotypes, and the very genre of drama. She exposes cultural myths (the doctor, the psychiatrist, the artist, the American family, the work of literature) and constructs alternative representations." Drexler creates a new discourse by dramatizing women's experience as their experience not as it has been staged through the consciousness of male playwrights. Lamont analyzes *Vulgar Lives, Utopia Parkway, The Writer's Opera, The Line of Least Existence, Home Movies,* and several other plays.

990. Smith, Michael. *Village Voice* (Mar. 28, 1968): 39, 50.
991. Sontag, Susan. *Partisan Review*, 31, iii (Summer 1964): 396.
992. Morgan, Edwin. *Times* (London) (Jan. 13, 1969): 5.

A Matter of Life and Death

993. Bruckner, D.J.R. *New York Times.* (Apr. 20, 1986): 68.

Room 17C

See items 1000, 1001.

Skywriting

994. Barnes, Clive. *New York Times* (May 9, 1968): 55.
995. Kerr, Walter. *New York Times* (May 19, 1968), sect. 2: 1.
996. Pasolli, Robert. *Nation*, 206 (June 10, 1968): 772-774.
997. Weales, Gerald. *Harper's Magazine*, 237 (Oct. 1968): 113-115.

Softly, And Consider the Nearness

998. Calta, Louis. *New York Times* (May 12, 1964): 32.

Starburn

999. Gussow, Mel. *New York Times* (Mar. 13, 1983): 62.

Transients Welcome

1000. Kroll, Jack. "Introduction." In item 961.
1001. Rogoff, G. *Village Voice* (Apr. 23, 1985): 105- 106.

Utopia Parkway

See items 961, 989.

Vulgar Lives

See item 989.

The Writer's Opera

See item 989.

1002. Clurman, Harold. *Nation*, 226 (May 5, 1979): 516.
1003. Feingold, Michael. *Village Voice* (Mar. 19, 1979): 85-86.
1004. Gussow, Mel. *New York Times* (Mar. 16, 1979): C1, C4.
1005. Loney, Glenn. *After Dark*, 12 (May 1979): 26.

Dworkin, Susan

Selected Plays

1006. *Deli's Fable* (Playhouse 46, 1979)
1007. *The Public Good* (Playwrights Horizons, 1976)

Reviews

Deli's Fable

1008. Corry, John. *New York Times* (Oct. 4, 1979), sect. C:16.

Eisenberg, Deborah

Selected Plays

1009. *Pastorale* (Second Stage, 1982)

Reviews

Pastorale

1010. Brustein, Robert. *New Republic*, 186 (May 19, 1982): 25.
1011. Hoffman, Jan. *Village Voice* (Apr. 20, 1982): 93.
1012. Kroll, Jack. *Newsweek*, 99 (Apr. 19, 1982): 102.
1013. Oliver, Edith. *The New Yorker*, 58 (Apr. 19, 1982): 151.
1014. Rich, Frank. *New York Times* (Apr. 12, 1982): C11.
1015. Simon, John. *New York*, 15 (Apr. 26, 1982): 83-84.
1016. *Variety* (Apr. 28, 1982): 102.

Ensler, Eve

Selected Plays

1017. *Cinderella/Cendrillon* (with Anne Bogart and Jeff Halpern,
          Music Theater Group, 1988)
1018. *The Depot* (Interart Theater, 1987)
1019. *Ladies* (music Joshua Schneider, Music Theater Group and
          the Women's Project, 1989)
1020. *Scooncat* (Samuel Beckett Theater, 1987)

Reviews

The Depot

1021. Klein, Alvin. *New York Times* (Mar. 15, 1987), sect. 23:
          14.

Ladies

1022. Stone, Laurie. *Village Voice* (Apr. 11, 1989): 97.

Scooncat

1023. Goodman, Walter. *New York Times* (Nov. 15, 1987): 78.

Faigao, Linda

Selected Plays

1024. *State Without Grace* (Pan Asian Repertory Theater, 1984)

Profiles

1025. Winn, Steven. "Filipino Artists Make a Play for More Visibility." *San Francisco Chronicle* (Oct. 6, 1985), Datebook sect.: 18, 20.
Winn's article, written shortly before the opening of Faigao's *State Without Grace* at Fort Mason's People's Theater, is not a typical preview article in that playwright Faigao focuses on the problems confronting Filipino theatre artists. She emphasizes the paucity of scripts by Filipino writers and ones that center around Filipino experiences. Faigao explains that "[t]here is a basic reticence among Filipinos to be singled out, to be heard. There is a strong desire to be invisible." The dramatist also articulates the difficulties Filipino-American writers face, such as locating professional Filipino actors, finding producers, and "overcom[ing] . . . self-consciousness about a 'baroque' prose style," as well as the anxiety of the possibility of their plays being misinterpreted as a consequence of the Marcos regime.

Reviews

State Without Grace

See item 1025.

1026. Gussow, Mel. *New York Times* (Nov. 28, 1984): C21.

Fales, Nancy

See **Garrett, Nancy Fales**

Fornes, Maria Irene

Selected Plays

1027. *Abingdon Square* (Women's Project, American Place
Theater, 1987)
Playscript: *WomensWork: Five New Plays from
the Women's Project.* Edited by Julia Miles, 1-42.
New York: Applause Theatre Book Publishers,
1989; *American Theatre,* 4 (Feb. 1988): 30-40.

1028. *And What of the Night?* (Milwaukee Repertory Theater,
Milwaukee, 1989)

1029. *The Annunciation* (Judson Poets Theater, 1967)

1030. *Aurora* (New York Theatre Strategy, 1974)

1031. *Baboon!!* (New Dramatists, 1970-1971)

1032. *Cap-a-Pie* (INTAR, 1975)

1033. *Cold Air* (Virgilio Pinero, translated and adapted by Fornes,
INTAR, 1985)
Playscript: *Maria Irene Fornes' Plays.* New York:
PAJ Communications Group, 1985.

1034. *Blood Wedding* (adaption of Lorca's *Blood Wedding,* Padua
Hills Playwrights Festival, 1988)

1035. *The Conduct of Life* (Theatre for the New City, 1985)
Playscript: *On New Ground: Contemporary
Hispanic-American Plays.* Edited by M. Elizabeth
Osborn, 45-72. New York: Theatre
Communications Group, 1987; see item 1049.

1036. *The Curse of the Langston House* (Playhouse in the Park,
Cincinnati, 1972)

1037. *The Danube* (American Place Theater, 1984)
Playscript: see item 1049.

1038. *Dr. Kheal* (New Dramatists, 1968)
Playscript: *A Century of New Plays by American
Women.* Edited by Rachel Smith, 79-184. New
York: Richards Rosen, 1979. *The Best of Off-Off
Broadway.* Edited by Michael Smith, 70-85. New
York: E.P. Dutton Company, 1969.

1039. *Drowning* (Part of *Orchards,* a bill of 7 one-acts, Lucille
Lortel Theater, 1986)
Playscript: *Orchards, Orchards, Orchards.* New
York: Broadway Play Publishing, 1987.

1040. *Evelyn Brown (A Diary)* (Theatre for the New City, 1980)

1041. *Eyes on the Harem* (INTAR Theater, 1979)

1042. *Fefu and Her Friends* (New York Theatre Strategy, 1977)

Playscript: *Performing Arts Journal* 2, iii (Winter
1978): 112-170; *Word Plays: An Anthology of
New American Drama*, 5-41. New York:
Performing Arts Journal Publications, 1980.

1043. *The Hunger* (part of *Three Pieces for a Warehouse*, En
Garde Arts, 1988)

1044. *Joan of Arc* (Theatre for the New City, 1986)

1045. *Life Is a Dream* (adaptation of Pedro Calderon de la Barca's
La Vida Es Sueno, New Dramatists, 1981)

1046. *Lovers and Keepers* (INTAR, 1986)
Playscript: *Lovers and Keepers: A Musical Play*.
New York: Theatre Communications Group, 1987.

1047. *Molly's Dream* (New York Theatre Strategy, 1973)

1048. *The Mothers* (Padua Hills Playwrights Festival, Los
Angeles, 1986)

1049. *Mud* (Padua Hills Playwrights Festival, Los Angeles,
1983)
Playscript: *Plays: Mud, The Danube, The Conduct
of Life, Sarita*. New York: PAJ Publications,
1986.

1050. *No Time* (Padua Hills Playwrights Festival, Los Angeles,
1984)

1051. *The Office* (Henry Miller's Theatre, 1966)

1052. *Oscar and Bertha* (Padua Hills Playwrights Festival, Los
Angeles, 1989)

1053. *Promenade* (music Al Carmines, Judson Poets Theatre,
1968)
Playscript: *Promenade and Other Plays*. New York:
PAJ Publications, 1987; *The New Underground
Theatre*. Edited by Robert J. Schroeder, 1-32. New
York: Bantam Books, 1968.

1054. *The Red Burning Light; or Mission XQ3* (La Mama, 1969)

1055. *Sarita* (INTAR, 1984)
Playscript: see item 1049.

1056. *The Successful Life of Three: A Skit for Vaudeville*
(Sheridan Square Playhouse Theatre, 1965)
Playscript: *Eight Plays from Off-Off Broadway*.
Edited by Nick Orze and Michael Smith. New
York:Bobbs-Merrill, 1966; see item 1057.

1057. *Tango Palace* (revised version, *There! You Died*, Actor's
Workshop, San Francisco, 1963)

Playscript: *Playwrights for Tomorrow: A Collection of Plays.* Edited by Arthur Ballet. Minneapolis: University of Minnesota Press, 1966.

1058. *A Vietnamese Wedding* (Washington Square Methodist Church, 1967)

1059. *A Visit* (Theatre for the New City, 1981)

1060. *The Widow* (New York Actors Studio, 1961)

Profiles and Interviews

See items 3, 9, 33, 46, 47, 75, 87, 91, 1076.

1061. Carranza, Ruth. "Profile: Maria Irene Fornes." *Intercambios Femeniles,* 3 (Winter 1989): 19-20.
        Cuban-American playwright Fornes talks about her formative years, her early years in the theatre, and her workshops as well as her current theatre project, *Abingdon Square.* According to Fornes, some spectators "adored it and applauded . . . [o]thers were rude and made cracks, but still with a lot of excitement." Fornes counsels aspiring Hispana playwrights to resist writing for the conventional theatre yet they should not assume that they must limit themselves to Hispanic drama "[w]hen people think of writing a Hispanic play, they lose the sense of who is Hispanic."

1062. *Contemporary Authors: A Bio-Bibliographical Guide.* Volume 28. New Revision Series. Edited by Hal May, 174-180. Gale Research Inc., 1990.
        The entry includes a biographical sketch, a list of Fornes's plays, and an interview with the playwright.

1063. *Contemporary Theatre, Film, and Television.* Volume 1. Edited by Monica M. O'Donnell, 181. Detroit: Gale Research Company, 1984.
        The entry includes a brief biographical profile and a list of her plays.

1064. Cummings, Scott. "Maria Irene Fornes." *American Playwrights Since 1945: A Guide to Scholarship, Criticism, and Performance.* Edited by Philip C. Kolin, 111-123. New York: Greenwood Press, 1989.
Cummings provides an assessment of Fornes's critical reputation, an historical survey of her productions, a brief analysis of her plays, and suggestions for future areas of study. Includes a primary and secondary bibliography of sources.

1065. _____. "Seeing With Clarity: The Vision of Maria Irene Fornes." *Theater,* 17 (Winter 1985): 51-56.
Cummings's interview with Fornes took place during a period of her life when she "has been receiving a lot of praise lately." Fornes, who started out as a painter, remarks that her first play, *Tango Palace,* was the product of an obsession, "I didn't want to do anything but write." Cummings's questions elicit from Fornes a discussion of the various theatres she has been affiliated with. Earlier in her career as a director she learned how to work with actors by taking acting courses and observing Strasberg's critiques and the acting and directing workshops that were held at the Actor's Studio Playwright's Unit. Fornes also talks about her plays. For example, she refers to *Fefu and Her Friends* as her "breakthrough" play. "My style of work in *Fefu,* "explains Fornes," was very different from my work before." To deepen her understanding of her characters, Fornes describes how she writes scenes for the characters that ultimately would not be part of the script, "you realize how much you learn about the characters when you put them in situations that are not going to be in the play." In addition, Fornes converses briefly about feminism and aesthetic concerns such as the relationship between character and language and the role.

1066. Dasgupta, Gautam. "Portrait in Words." *Performing Arts Journal,* 6, ii (1982): 27-28.

Maria Irene Fornes and Elizabeth Swados are
among several theatre artists who reminisce about
their initial introduction to Ellen Stewart, artistic
director La Mama Experimental Theatre Club.

1067. *Dictionary of Literary Biography.* Volume 7. *Twentieth
Century American Dramatists.* Edited by John
MacNicholas, 188-191. Gale Research Company,
1981.
This introductory article includes an extensive
biographical and critical survey of Fornes's
theatrical career. A primary and secondary
bibliography of her works is included.

1068. Drake, Sylvie. "Fornes Acts To Foster Hispanic
Playwrights." *Los Angeles Times* (July 9, 1987),
sect. 6: 5.
At the time of this article Fornes was dramaturg for
three of the readings at the South Coast Repertory's
Hispanic Playwrights Project, performed July 9,
1987. Fornes is cautious in her consideration of
the state of Hispanic theatre. "What I see is an
enormous potential rather than something that's
been realized." Drake blends biographical details of
Fornes's professional career with her comments on
her approach to teaching playwrights at INTAR.
She also talks briefly about two of her newest
plays, *Oscar and Bertha* and *Abingdon Square.*

1069. _____. "Introduction to *The Conduct of Life.*" In *On New
Ground: Contemporary Hispanic-American Plays.*
Edited by M. Elizabeth Osborn, 46-72. New York:
Theatre Communications Group, 1987.
As a preface to the text of her play *The Conduct of
Life,* Fornes profiles herself. She describes her
early years, her arrival to the United States from her
native Cuba, and her affiliation with INTAR and
the Padua Hills Playwrights' Festival where *The
Conduct of Life* originated.

1070. Kuhn, John. *Contemporary Dramatists*. 3rd Edition. Edited
by James Vinson, 158-160. Chicago: St. James
Press, 1982.
Kuhn briefly assesses the life and work of Fornes.
The entry includes a list of her plays.

1071. Marranca, Bonnie. "Interview: Maria Irene Fornes."
Performing Arts Journal, 2 (Winter1978): 106-111.
Marranca opens the interview by commenting that
Fornes's play *Fefu and Her Friends* differs from her
earlier works in that it is grounded in realism.
Fornes responds by saying, "Whether the play is
realistic or less realistic has to do with the distance
I have from it. I feel that the characters of *Fefu* are
standing around while other plays I see more at a
distance." Fornes explains how she manipulates
environmental concepts to create a more intimate
atmosphere for the spectators. "The fact that in
Fefu you are enclosed inside the rooms with the
actors is really the difference." In addition to the
discussion about the play's plot and structure,
Fornes also affirms the feminist perspective of
Fefu. The play is about women. "I show the
women as I see them and if it is different from the
way they've been seen before, it's because that's
how I see them. The play is not fighting anything,
not negating anything."

1072. Wetzsteon, Ross. "Maria Irene Fornes: The Elements of
Style." *Village Voice* (Apr. 29, 1986): 42-46.
In this insightful profile of Fornes, Wetzsteon
asserts that although Fornes is virtually ignored by
the commercial theatres and major regional theatres,
this multi-Obie winning playwright is "one of the
half-dozen most gifted playwrights in the American
theatre." Wetzsteon says the reason Fornes remains
invisible is her constant experimentation with
dramatic styles, thus, "There's no Fornes 'signature'
to capture the attention of either the casual
theatergoer or the middlebrow critic." By the time
the spectators recognize her particular style, "she's
already moved on" to other forms. During the

course of the article, Wetzsteon provides ample
quotes from Fornes herself, who discusses several
of her plays, including *The Danube, Lovers and
Keepers*, and *Fefu and Her Friends*.

General Criticism and Discussions

See items 22, 47, 49, 53, 67, 68, 102, 1064, 1065, 1066
and pages 4, 5, 7, 10, 21, 23.

1073. Fornes, Maria Irene. "I Write These Messages That Come."
       Drama Review, 21, iv (Dec. 1977): 25-40.
       This article is excellent for an understanding of
       Fornes's imaginative processes and aesthetic
       methodology. Fornes's energy and enthusiasm
       imbues her articulation of her "stages of creativity."
       She says she rarely starts with a central idea; most
       of her plays begin from her "scribblings," that is,
       "messages [coming from] a thought, like a
       statement . . . an insight, or . . . a line of dialog."
       The reader also receives insight into Fornes's mode
       of creating theatrical spaces, her perceptions of the
       audience and the development of her characters,
       "there is a point when the characters become
       crystallized. When that happens I have an image in
       full color, technicolor."

1074. Stuart, Jan. "Women's Work: Tina Howe and Maria Irene
       Fornes Explore the Woman's Voice in Drama."
       American Theatre, 2 (Sep. 1985): 11-15.
       Fornes and Howe's essays attempt to explore what
       it means to be a woman writing plays. Fornes, in
       her essay, comments that "I am in an odd position
       in relation to feminism: radical feminists don't
       consider me a feminist and see my characterizations
       of men as a harsh criticism." Fornes claims that
       she writes with a woman's sensibilities but she
       does so unselfconsciously. In effect Fornes is
       unwilling to inhibit her creative system by
       thinking and writing according to the expectations
       of society. And Howe remarks that she fuses her
       "antic vision" with her feminist perspective.

Women playwrights should proceed with caution, Howe warns, in applying the feminist aesthetic to their work, because the word "feminist" connotes too many impressions of dogma. Howe recommends "that the only way a woman can have a career in the theatre at this time is to cover her scent a bit." Needless to say, Howe is not suggesting that women dramatists ape their male counterparts, but that women have to maintain a "balancing act . . . it forces us to be inventive and precise."

Reviews

Abingdon Square

See items 905, 1061, 1068.

1075. Colvin, Clare. *Plays and Players*, 430 (Aug. 1989): 31-32.
1076. *Contemporary Literary Criticism: Excerpts of Criticism from the Works of Today's Novelists, Poets, Playwrights and Other Creative Writers.* Volume 61. Edited by Roger Matuz, 125-143. Detroit: Gale Research Inc., 1990.
1077. Green, Alexis. *Women & Performance*, 4, viii (1989): 151-152.
1078. Gussow, Mel. *New York Times* (Oct. 17, 1987): 16.
1079. Kingston, Jeremy. *Times* (London) (Mar. 31, 1990), Features sect.: n.p.
1080. Munk, Erica. *Village Voice* (Oct. 27, 1987): 112.
1081. Peter, John. *Sunday Telegraph* (London) (June 11, 1989): C8b.
1082. Wardle, Irving. *Times* (London) (June 10, 1989): 39b.
1083. Wilders, John. *Times Literary Supplement*, (Apr. 13-19, 1990): 396.
       Reprinted in item 1076.
1084. Woertendyke, Ruis. *Theatre Journal*, 40, ii (May 1988): 264-65.
       Reprinted in item 1076.

Aurora

1085. Barnes, Clive. *New York Times* (Sep. 30, 1974): 53.

Blood Wedding

1086. Kakutani, Michiko. *New York Times* (June 3, 1980): C19.

Cap-a-Pie

1087. Mackay, Barbara. *Saturday Review*, 2 (Aug. 9, 1975): 50.

Cold Air

1088. Holden, Stephen. *New York Times* (Apr. 10, 1985): C21.

The Conduct of Life

See items 1069, 1076, 1102, 1179.

1089. Berman, Paul. *Nation*, 240 (Apr. 6, 1985): 412-413
1090. Brown, Joe. *Washington Post* (Nov. 19, 1987): D6.
1091. Christiansen, Richard. *Chicago Tribune* (Feb. 16, 1988), sect. 2: 8.
1092. Feingold, Michael. *Village Voice* (Mar. 12, 1985): 79-81.
1093. Kingston, Jeremy. *Times* (London) (Nov. 15, 1988): 37.
1094. Mitgang, Herbert. *New York Times* (Mar. 20, 1985): C16.
1095. Munk, Erica. *Village Voice* (Apr. 2, 1985): 93.

1096. O'Malley, Lurana D. "Pressing Clothes/Snapping Beans/Reading Books: Maria Irene Fornes's Women's Work." *Studies in American Drama 1945-Present*, 4 (1989): 103-117.
O'Malley asserts that household work figures prominently in the later plays of Fornes. Drawing mainly upon *Mud*, *The Conduct of Life*, *Fefu and Her Friends*, and *Sarita*, O'Malley demonstrates how Fornes employs housekeeping tasks not to make a statement of female oppression but to dramatize how women are able to "transform this work into a holy rite, related to their senses of self." With commitment and devotion Fornes's protagonists perform household tasks as if they

were religious rituals. The author suggests that while others may regard housework as boring and tedious Fornes's characters, in performing such duties, transcend to meditative states that allow them to realize self. In other words, for Mae in *Mud* and Nena in *The Conduct of Life* housework "elevate[s] the woman who keeps house to the status of priestess/magician."

1097. Schuler, Catherine. *Theatre Journal*, 38, iv (Dec. 1986): 514-515.
1098. Stasio, Marilyn. *New York Post* (Mar. 9, 1985).
Reprinted in *Contemporary Literary Criticism: Yearbook: 1985*. Edited by Sharon K. Hall. Detroit: Gale Research Company, 1986.

The Danube

See items 1072, 1076, 1154, 1179.

1099. Feingold, Michael. *Village Voice* (Mar. 20, 1984): 83.
1100. Rich, Frank. *New York Times* (Mar. 13, 1984): C13.
1101. Schuler, Catherine. *Theatre Journal*, 38, iv (Dec. 1986): 514-515.
1102. Smith, Sid. Chicago Rediscovers a Theater Secret." *Chicago Tribune* (Feb. 8, 1988), sect. 5: 3.
In Smith's preview article for the opening of *The Danube*, which Fornes was commissioned to do for an anti-nuclear group, Fornes talks about the purpose of drama, in which she endeavors not to persuade, "I think it would be ridiculous to do so," but, she says, "[y]ou write because it concerns you, because you're obsessed with something." One of Fornes's obsessions created *The Danube*, whose structure is based on a set of Hungarian language lesson albums she found in an antique store. "I fell in love with [them], [j]ust the sound of the Hungarian and the arched sound of the voices speaking the English translation." Interwoven throughout the piece, Smith provides a profile of Fornes's professional background and Fornes's comments on her other play, *The Conduct of Life*.

Dr. Kheal

See item 1076.

1103. Barnes, Clive. *New York Times* (Mar. 21, 1974): 50.

1104. Marranca, Bonnie and Gautam Dasgupta. "Maria Irene
        Fornes." In *American Playwrights: A Critical
        Survey,* 53-63. Volume 1. New York: Drama
        Book Specialists, 1981.
        In this overview, the author provides a general
        critique of Fornes's major plays: *Dr. Kheal,
        Promenade, Tango Palace, The Successful Life of
        Three, Molly's Dream, A Vietnamese Wedding,
        The Red Burning Light,* and *Fefu and Her Friends.*

Drowning

1105. Gold, Sylviane. *Wall Street Journal* (Apr. 28, 1986): 22.
1106. Gussow, Mel. *New York Times* (Apr. 23, 1986): C15.
1107. Koehler, Robert. *Los Angeles Times* (July 23, 1988), sect.
        4: 1, 4.
1108. Rogoff, Gordon. *Village Voice* (May 6, 1986): 96.
1109. Shewey, Don. *New York Times* (Aug. 25, 1985), sect. 2:
        4, 26.

Evelyn Brown (A Diary)

See item 1076.

1110. Munk, Erica. *Village Voice* (Apr. 21, 1980): 83.

Eyes of the Harem

See item 1140.

1111. Eder, Richard. *New York Times* (Apr. 25, 1979): C17.
        Reprinted in item 1076.
1112. Oliver, Edith. *New Yorker,* 55 (May 7, 1979): 131.
        Reprinted in item 1076.
1113. Feingold, Michael. *Village Voice* (May 7, 1979): 104.

Fefu and Her Friends

See items 16, 1065, 1071, 1072, 1076, 1096, 1104, 1158, 1179.

1114. Aaron, Jules. *Theatre Journal*, 32, ii (May, 1980): 266-267.

1115. Austin, Gayle. "The Madwoman in the Spotlight: Plays of Maria Irene Fornes." In *Making a Spectacle: Feminist Essays on Contemporary Women's Theater.* Edited by Lynda Hart, 76-85. Ann Arbor: University of Michigan Press, 1989.
Austin observes that the dramatic canon is replete with madwomen. But rarely does the audience identify with these characters because of the great distance the playwright creates between character and spectator. Yet Fornes, Austin contends, is the unique dramatist in her approach to the madwoman from a feminist perspective by positioning her in the "spotlight," within which the madwoman "speaks for herself." Consequently, the audience experiences her within the narrow space of her "social and actual confinement." Fornes uses the double motif to dramatize two sides of a character's nature in a similar fashion as Charlotte Bronte did with Jane and Bertha in her novel, *Jane Eyre.* In Fornes's *Fefu and Her Friends,* for instance, the characters Fefu and Julia resemble Jane and Bertha in that Julia and Bertha and Fefu and Jane act out their anger and repressions. Still, maintains Austin, there are differences between the two sets of doubles; unlike Bertha, "Julia is not in the attic, but in the spotlight speaking the truth for herself."

1116. Baker, Rob. *After Dark*, 10 (Mar. 1978): 83-84.
1117. Barnes, Clive. *New York Post* (Jan. 14, 1978): 12.
1118. Byers-Pevitts, Beverley. In *Women in American Theatre.* Edited by Helen Krich Chinoy and Linda Walsh Jenkins, 316. New York: Crown, 1981.
1119. Christiansen, Richard. *Chicago Tribune* (Oct. 3, 1984), sect. 2:9.

1120. Clurman, Harold. *Nation*, 226 (Feb. 11, 1978): 154.
Reprinted in item 1076.
1121. Duberman, Martin. *Harper's Magazine*, 256 (May 1978): 83-84, 127-128.
Reprinted in item 1076.
1122. Eder, Richard. *New York Times* (Jan. 14, 1978): 10.
1123. Feingold, Michael. *Village Voice* (Jan. 23, 1978): 75.
1124. Grove, Lloyd. *Washington Post* (July 15, 1983), Weekend sect: 9.
1125. Kauffmann, Stanley. *New Republic,* 178 (Feb. 25, 1978): 38.
1126. Kerr, Walter. *New York Times* (June 13, 1978), sect. 3: 1.
1127. Koehler, Robert. *Los Angeles Times* (Aug. 2, 1989), sect. 6: 7.
1128. Kroll, Jack. *Newsweek*, 91 (Jan. 23, 1978): 87.
1129. Larkin, Joan. *Ms.,* 6 (June 1978): 28-29.
Reprinted in item 1076.
1130. Lewis, Barbara. *N.Y. Amsterdam News* (Jan. 21, 1978):D-7.
1131. Munk, Erica. *Village Voice* (May 23, 1977): 79-80.
1132. Oliver, Edith. *The New Yorker*, 53 (Jan. 23, 1978): 45-46.
Reprinted in item 1076.
1133. Richards, David. *Washington Post* (July 9, 1983), sect. C:1, 7.
1134. Sainer, Arthur. *Village Voice* (June 13, 1977): 73.
1135. Sullivan, Dan. *Los Angeles Times* (Sep. 17, 1979), sect. 4: 1, 11.
1136. Watt, Douglas. *New York Daily News* (Jan. 14, 1978): 12.
1137. Weiner, Bernard. *San Francisco Chronicle* (May 20, 1981): 62.
1138. Wetzsteon, Ross. *Plays and Players,* 24 (Aug. 1977): 36, 37.
Reprinted in item 1076.
1139. _____. *Village Voice* (June 6, 1977): 91, 93.

1140. "Women in the Theatre." *Centerpoint,* 3, iii & iv (Fall/Spring1979): 31-37.
A transcript of a session that was part of a symposium entitled "Women in the Arts." This particular session addressed the topic, "Women in the Theatre." The participants included writers, critics, and dramatists: Doris Abramson, Maria

Irene Fornes, Bonnie Marranca, and Rosette C.
Lamont. They talked in general terms about the
representation of women's vision on the stage and
the dialectic operating between "the private world of
the characters filtered through the author's own
private inner life" and its transference to the inner
consciousness of the audience. The transcript is
most useful, however, for the participants'
comments and reactions to Fornes's *Fefu and Her
Friends* and *Eyes on the Harem*, which was
playing at the INTAR theatre at the time of the
session.

Hidden Treasure

1141. Wetzsteon, Ross. *New York*, 18 (Mar. 18, 1985): 28.

Hunger

1142. Disch, Thomas M. *Nation*, 246 (Apr. 23, 1988): 580.
1143. Gussow, Mel. *New York Times* (Mar. 20, 1988): 59.
1144. Solomon, Alisa. *Village Voice* (Apr. 12, 1988): 98.

Life Is a Dream

1145. Feingold, Michael. *Village Voice* (June 3-6, 1981): 83-84.
1146. Gussow, Mel. *New York Times* (June 4, 1981): C15.

Lovers and Keepers

See item 1072.

1147. Feingold, Michael. *Village Voice* (Apr. 29, 1986): 92.
1148. Gussow, Mel. *New York Times* (Apr. 17, 1986), sect. 3:
      25.
1149. Smith, Sid. *Chicago Tribune* (May 27, 1988), sect. 5: 4.

Molly's Dream

See items 1076, 1104, 1167.

The Mothers

1150. Christon, Lawrence. *Los Angeles Times* (Aug. 6, 1986),
         sect. 6: 1,7.

Mud

See items 1076, 1096.

1151. Christon, Lawrence. *Los Angeles Times* (July 21, 1983),
         sect. 6: 2.
1152. Dolan, Jill. *Women & Performance*, 2, i (1984): 84-85.
1153. Feingold, Michael. *Village Voice* (Nov. 29, 1983): 130,
         132.

1154. Marranca, Bonnie. "The Real Life of Maria Irene Fornes."
         Performing Arts Journal, 8, i (1984): 29-34.
         Reprinted in *TheatreWritings*. Edited by Bonnie
         Marranca, 69-73. New York: PAJ Publications,
         1984.
         Marranca discusses Fornes's particular brand of
         realism, pointing out that in her plays (e.g., *Mud*
         and *The Danube*) Fornes "goes to the core of
         character . . . [they] exist in the world by their very
         act of trying to understand it." Fornes has "lift[ed]
         the burden of psychology, declamation, morality,
         and sentimentality from the concept of character."
         Diverging from the traditional stage setting,
         Fornes's sets are "more open cosmologically, its
         character iconic." And Marranca suggests that "this
         emotive, aggressive realism is rooted in
         expressionistic style."

1155. Schuler, Catherine. *Theatre Journal*, 38, iv, (Dec. 1986):
         514-515.

No Time

1156. Sullivan, Dan. *Los Angeles Times* (July 16, 1984), sect. 6:
         1, 7.
1157. DeRose, David J. *Theatre Journal*, 37, i (Mar, 1985): 110-
         111.

Oscar and Bertha

See item 1068.

1158. Arkatov, Janice. *Los Angeles Times* (July 6, 1989), sect.
6: 1.
Arkatov briefly discusses the twelfth annual season
of the Padua Hills Playwrights' Festival, which
includes Fornes's *Oscar and Bertha* and *Fefu and
Her Friends*.

1159. Sullivan, Dan. *Los Angeles Times* (July 25, 1989), sect. 6:
1, 6.

Promenade

See items 1076, 1104.

1160. Barnes, Clive. *New York Times* (June 5, 1969): 56.
Reprinted in item 1166.
1161. Cooke, Richard P. *Wall Street Journal* (June 6, 1969): 16.
1162. Davis, James. *New York Daily News* (June 5, 1969).
Reprinted in item 1166.
1163. Gottfried, Martin. *Women's Wear Daily* (June 5, 1969).
Reprinted in item 1166.
1164. Holden, Stephen. *New York Times* (Oct. 25, 1983): C8.
1165. Kerr, Walter. *New York Times* (June 15, 1969), sect. 2: 1.
1166. *New York Theatre Critics' Reviews*, 30 (Nov. 3, 1969):
213-216.

1167. Shepard, Richard F. "Lyrics Preceded a Hit Musical's
Music." *New York Times* (June 6, 1969): 32.
Shepard highlights Fornes, who "relaxed yesterday
in the morning afterglow" of her hit musical
Promenade. Fornes talks about her "unusual"
collaboration with Al Carmines, who wrote the
music for the play, in that it "does not measure up
to the Hollywood-style version of wordman and
musicman in artistic haggle over whose work
should fit what." According to Fornes she created
the book and lyrics and then Carmines wrote the
music based on her work. The playwright

discusses the application of her "words-before-music" method with previous musicals such as *Molly's Dream* and *The Red Burning Light.* Fornes also believes that "a revolution is taking place." And though Fornes identifies with the "revolutionary group," she feels they are neglecting "the positive things of revolution. I think they miss a sense of compassion and tenderness."

1168. Kerr, Walter. *New York Times* (June 15, 1969), sect. 2: 1, 10.

1169. Massa, Robert. *Village Voice* (Oct. 25, 1983): 98.

1170. *New York Times.* "*Promenade*—Is It Wrong to Boo?" *New York Times* (July 6, 1969), sect. 2: 4, 8.
This item contains letters to the editor commenting on *Promenade.*

1171. *New York Times* (Jan. 8, 1970): 45.
The *Times* announces the closing of *Promenade* on Jan. 18, 1970 at the Promenade Theatre after 259 performances.

1172. Pasolli, Robert. *Village Voice* (Apr. 17, 1969): 57.
1173. Smith, Michael. *Village Voice* (Apr. 15, 1965): 20.
1174. Watts, Richard. *New York Post* (June 5, 1969): 78.
Reprinted in item 1166.

The Red Burning Light

See items 1076, 1104, 1167.

Sarita

See items 1076, 1104.

1175. Dolan, Jill. *Women & Performance*, 2, i (1984): 84-85.
1176. Munk, Erica. *Village Voice* (Feb. 14, 1984): 95-96.
1177. Schuler, Catherine. *Theatre Journal*, 38, iv (Dec. 1986): 514-515.

The Successful Life of Three

See items 1076, 1104.

1178. Pasolli, Robert. *Village Voice* (June 1, 1967): 20.

Tango Palace

See items 1065, 1076, 1104.

1179. Worthen, W.B. "Still Playing Games: Ideology and
     Performance in the Theater of Maria Irene Fornes."
     In *Feminine Focus: The New Women
     Playwrights.* Edited by Enoch Brater, 167-181.
     Cambridge: Oxford University Press, 1989.
     Worthen focuses on Fornes's interest in the
     relationship of the mise-en-scene and performance.
     According to Worthen, "Fornes' plays suspend the
     identification between drama and its staging. The
     rhetoric of [her] major plays . . . is sparked by this
     ideological dislocation." To illustrate his points,
     the author examines Fornes's *Tango Palace, The
     Danube, The Conduct of Life,* and *Fefu and Her
     Friends.*

Vietnamese Wedding

See item 1076, 1104.

A Visit

1180. Feingold, Michael. *Village Voice* (Dec. 30-Jan. 5, 1981):
     69-70.
1181. Gussow, Mel. *New York Times* (Dec. 30, 1981): C8.
     Reprinted in item 1076.
1182. Wetzsteon, Ross. *Village Voice* (Apr. 29, 1986): 42-45.

Franklin, J.E. (Jennie Elizabeth)

   Selected Plays

1183. *Black Girl* (New Federal Theater, 1969)

Playscript: *Black Girl: A Play in Two Acts.* New York: Dramatists Play Service, 1971.

1184. *The Prodigal Sister* (with Micki Grant, New Federal Theater, 1974)

1185. *Cut Out the Lights and Call the Law* (Negro Ensemble Theater, 1972)

1186. *The In-Crowd* (New Federal Theater, 1977)

1187. *Mau Mau Room* (Negro Ensemble Company, 1972)

1188. *Two Flowers* (New Feminist Theatre, 1960s)

1189. *The Enemy* (Eureka Theatre Group, 1973)

1190. *The Creation* (Eureka Theatre Group, 1975)

Profiles and Interviews

See items 48, 361.

1191. Beauford, Fred. "Conversation with *Black Girls'* Franklin." *Black Creation*, 3 (Fall 1971): 38-40.
Beauford interviews Franklin during the production of *Black Girl* at the Theater de Lys in New York.

1192. *Black Writers: A Selection of Sketches from Contemporary Authors.* Edited by Linda Metzger, 203-206. Detroit: Gale, 1989.
A list of Franklin's plays accompanies this concise biography.

1193. *Contemporary Authors: A Bio-Bibliographical Guide.* Volumes 61-64. Edited by Cythia R. Fadool, 198-199. Detroit: Gale, 1976.
This entry includes a brief biography and a list of Franklin's works.

1194. Hunter, Charlayne. "Black Women Combine Lives and Talent in Play." *New York Times* (July 13, 1971): 19.
Hunter profiles Franklin and Shaunielle Perry, director of *Black Girl.* The article focuses on how each woman got her start in the theatre.

1195. "9 Playwrights Win Rockefeller Grants." *New York Times* (Apr. 27, 1980): 70.

The *Times* announces Franklin as one of the
winners of the tenth Rockefeller Foundation
Playwrights in Residence award.

1196. Parks, Carol. "J.E. Franklin, Playwright." *Black World*, 21
(Apr. 1972): 49-50.
Parks profiles Franklin's life and work, touching
upon her playwriting techniques. For example,
Parks asks Franklin if there is a particular theme
inherent in her plays and stories. Franklin responds
that her "feelings shape the theme." Franklin's
plays and her works-in-progress are listed.

1197. Peterson, Bernard L. *Contemporary Black American
Playwrights and Their Plays: A Biographical
Directory and Dramatic Index*, 175-177. New York:
Greenwood Press, 1988.
Peterson provides a biography as well as a staging
history of Franklin's plays.

1198. "Scenes in New York Drama; Talented Directors, Producers,
Playwrights Work 'On' and 'Off' Broadway."
Ebony, 28 (Apr. 1973): 107-108, 110-111.
This feature article briefly describes the
collaborative efforts of Shaunielle Perry and
Franklin.

Reviews

Black Girl

See items 1191, 1194, 2016.

1199. Barnes, Clive. *New York Times* (June 17, 1971): 49.
1200. Beauford, Fred. *Black Creation*, 3 (Fall 1971): 38-40.
1201. *Black Enterprise*, 2 (Sep. 1971): 30-34.
1202. Clurman, Harold. *Nation*, 213 (Nov. 1, 1971): 444-445.

1203. Curb, Rosemary K. "'Goin' Through the Changes': Mother-
Daughter Confrontations in Three Recent Plays by
Young Black Women." *Kentucky Folklore Record*,
25 (1979): 96-102.

Curb examines the vicissitudes of the mother-
daughter bond in three plays by African-American
women: *Black Girl* by J.E. Franklin, *Black Cycle*
by Martie Charles, and *Toe Jam* by Elaine
Jackson. Although each playwright dramatizes the
maternal bond differently, all three depict the
struggle of the adolescent daughter to break free
from the family to experience life on her own
terms. But, the mother resists her daughter's bid
for freedom and is "convinced that the daughter is
taking the wrong path toward maturity." Thus, the
daughter inevitably rejects the mother and becomes
"suspicious of the older generation."

1204. Feingold, Michael. *Village Voice* (Mar. 11, 1986): 87.
1205. Garnett, Richard. *Race Relations Reporter*, 3 (Feb. 7, 1972):
         4-6.
1206. Kalem, T.E. *Time* (June 28, 1971).
         Reprinted in item 1215.
1207. Kerr, Walter. *New York Times* (July 4, 1971), sect. 2: 3.
1208. Kroll, Jack. *Newsweek*, 77 (June 28, 1971): 85.
1209. Kupa, Kushauri. *Black Theatre*, 6 (1972): 48-51.
1210. Lamb, Margaret. *Drama Review*, 18 (Sep. 1974): 49.
1211. Lester, Elenore. *New York Times* (July 11, 1971), sect. 2:
         5.
1212. Mazo, Joseph. *Women's Wear Daily* (June 18, 1971).
         Reprinted in item 1215.

1213. Murray, James P. *Black Creation*, 4 (Winter 1973): 67.
         Murray's piece describes the screen adaptation of
         Black Girl.

1214. Simon, John. *New York*, 4 (Mar. 2, 1971): 55.
1215. *New York Theatre Critics' Reviews*, 32 (Nov. 1, 1971):
         219-220.
1216. Oliver, Edith. *The New Yorker*, 47 (June 26, 1971): 76.
1217. Rich, Frank. *New York Times* (Mar. 4, 1986): C13.
1218. Winn, Steven. *San Francisco Chronicle* (Jan. 3, 1984): 39.
1219. Sinclair, Abiola. *N.Y. Amsterdam News* (Mar. 1, 1986):
         27.
1220. Tallmer, Jerry. *New York Post* (June 17, 1971).
         Reprinted in item 1215.

The Prodigal Sister

1221. Bailey, Peter. *Black World,* 24 (Apr. 1975): 22-23.
1222. Barnes, Clive. *New York Times* (Nov. 26, 1974): 30.
1223. Beaufort, John. *Christian Science Monitor* (Nov. 29, 1974): 12-14.
       Reprinted in item 1229.
1224. Brukenfeld, Dick. *Village Voice* (July 18, 1974): 57.
1225. Ettore, Barbara. *Women's Wear Daily* (Oct. 26, 1974).
       Reprinted in item 1229.
1226. Gill, Brendan. *The New Yorker,* 50 (Dec. 9, 1974): 69-70.
1227. Gottfried, Martin. *New York Post* (Nov. 26, 1974).
       Reprinted in item 1229.
1228. Gussow, Mel. *New York Times* (July 16, 1974): 42.
1229. *New York Theatre Critics' Reviews,* 35 (Dec. 16, 1974): 124-125.
1230. Simon, John. *New York,* 7 (Dec. 16, 1974): 96.
1231. Watt, Douglas. *New York Daily News* (Nov. 26, 1974).
       Reprinted in item 1229.

Friedman, Leah K.

Selected Plays

1232. *The Rachel Plays* (includes: *I'm Hiding! I'm Hiding!* and *Running Home,* American Jewish Theater, 1985)

Reviews

The Rachel Plays

1233. *American Theatre,* 1 (Mar. 1985): 15.
1234. Mitgang, Herbert. *New York Times* (Mar. 3, 1985): 50.
1235. Stone, Laurie. *Village Voice* (Mar. 12, 1985): 81.

Gallagher, Mary

Selected Plays

1236. *Buddies* (Ensemble Studio Theatre, 1982)

Playscript: *Buddies: A Play in One Act.* New
York: Dramatists Play Service, 1983)

1237. *De Donde?* (Main Street Theater, Houston, 1988)
Playscript: *De Donde?* New York: Dramatists
Play Service, 1988; *American Theatre*, 6 (Nov.
1989): 1-20.

1238. *Dog Eat Dog* (Hartford Stage Company, 1982-1983)
Playscript: *Dog Eat Dog.* New York: Dramatists
Play Service, 1984.

1239. *Father Dreams* (Ensemble Studio Theatre, 1981)
Playscript: *Father Dreams.* New York: Dramatists
Play Service, 1982.

1240. *Fly Away Home* (American Conservatory Theatre, San
Francisco, 1977)

1241. *How To Say Goodbye* (Vineyard Theatre, 1986)
Playscript: *How To Say Goodbye.* New York:
Dramatists Play Service, 1987)

1242. *Little Bird* (New Dramatists, 1979)
Playscript: *Little Bird.* New York: Dramatists Play
Service, 1984.

1243. *Love Minus*
Playscript: *Love Minus.* New York: Dramatists
Play Service, 1989.

1244. *Perfect* (Manhattan Punch Line, 1988)

1245. *Special Family Things* (with Ara Watson, Women's
Project, American Place Theater, 1984)

1246. *Win/Lose/Draw* (A bill of three one-act plays: *Little Miss
Fresno, Chocolate Cake,* and *Final Placement* with
Ara Watson, Provincetown Players, 1983)
Playscript: *Win/Lose/Draw.* New York:
Dramatists Play Service, 1983; *Chocolate Cake.*
In *Best Short Plays 1982.* Radnor, Pennsylvania:
Chilton Book Company, 1982.

Profiles and Interviews

See items 9, 48, and profile in *Best Short Plays of 1982*
(item 1246).

1247. *Contemporary Theatre, Film, and Television.* Volume 1.
Edited by Monica M. O'Donnell, 190-191. Detroit:
Gale Research Company, 1984.

A biographical sketch, which includes a list of
plays and other writings and awards.

1248. *Contemporary Authors: A Bio-Bibliographical Guide.*
Volumes 97-100. Edited by Frances C. Locher,
184. Detroit: Gale Research Company, 1981.
A brief biography, which lists Gallagher's plays
and her views on playwriting.

1249. Kushner, Tony. "De Donde?" *American Theatre,* 6 (Nov.
1989): 55-56.
Accompanying the text of *De Donde?* Kushner
provides a brief biography of Gallagher and a stage
history of the play.

Reviews

See item 79.

Buddies

1250. Massa, Robert. *Village Voice* (July 6, 1982): 81.
1251. Rich, Frank. *New York Times* (June 5, 1982): 11.

Chocolate Cake

1252. Christiansen, Richard. *Chicago Tribune* (Jan. 21, 1988),
sect. 5: 4.
1253. Dace, Tish. *Plays International,* 2 (July 1987): 38-39.
1254. Novick, Julius. *Village Voice* (May 27-June 2, 1981): 90.
1255. Oliver, Edith. *New Yorker,* 59 (May 9, 1983): 109-110.

De Donde?

See item 1249.

1256. Ervolino, Bill. *Backstage* (Aug. 3, 1990): 26.
1257. Gussow, Mel. *New York Times* (Jan. 8, 1990): C13.
1258. Novick, M. *Guardian,* 42 (June 27, 1990): 18.

Dog Eat Dog

1259. Gussow, Mel. *New York Times* (Mar. 4, 1983): C5.

Father Dreams

1260. Blumenthal, Eileen. *Village Voice* (Apr. 1-7, 1981): 88.
1261. Gussow, Mel. *New York Times* (Mar. 28, 1981): 11.

How To Say Goodbye

1262. Blumenthal, Eileen. *Village Voice* (Dec. 16, 1986): 128.
1263. Christiansen, Richard. *Chicago Tribune* (Mar. 30, 1986), sect. 13: 8-9.
1264. *Drama-Logue* (Jan. 15-21, 1987): 25.

1265. "A Dramatic First." *Houston Post* (Feb. 24, 1987), sect. C: 6.
       This article reports Gallagher and Ellen McLaughlin co-winners of the Susan Smith Blackburn Prize.

1266. Gussow, Mel. *New York Times* (Dec. 2, 1986): C13.

1267. Kleiman, Dena. "2 Playwrights Share Award." *New York Times* (Feb. 24, 1987): C13.
       Kleiman notes Gallagher was awarded the Susan Blackburn Prize for *How To Say Goodbye*.

1268. Liston, William T. *Theatre Journal*, 38, iv (Dec. 1986): 489.
1269. Simon, John. *New York,* 19 (Dec. 15, 1986): 94.

Special Family Things

1270. Kakutani, Michiko. *New York Times* (Mar. 28, 1984): C23.
1271. Solomon, Alisa. *Village Voice* (Apr. 3, 1984): 90.

Win/Lose/Draw

1272. Barnes, Clive. *New York Post* (Apr. 27, 1983).
       Reprinted in item 1278.

1273. Beaufort, John. *Christian Science Monitor* (May 16, 1983): 18.
1274. Brown, Joe. *Washington Post* (May 3, 1985), Weekend sect: 9a.
1275. Cohen, R. *Women's Wear Daily* (Apr. 28, 1983). Reprinted in item 1278.
1276. Christiansen, Richard. *Chicago Tribune* (Jan. 30, 1985), sect. 2: 8.
1277. Koehler, Robert. *Los Angeles Times* (Jan. 29, 1988), sect. 6:4.
1278. *New York Theatre Critics' Reviews*, 44 (June 13, 1983): 222-225.
1279. O'Haire, Patricia. *New York Daily News* (Apr. 28, 1983) Reprinted in item 1278.
1280. Oliver, Edith. *The New Yorker*, 59 (May 9, 1983): 109-110.
1281. Rich, Frank. *New York Times* (May, 5, 1983): C13. Reprinted in item 1278.
1282. _____. *New York Times* (Apr. 26, 1983): C13. Reprinted in item 1278.
1283. Simon, John. *New York* 16 (May 9, 1983): 90.
1284. Stone, Laurie. *Village Voice* (May, 17, 1983): 98.
1285. *Variety* (May 11, 1983): 108.

Garrett, Nancy Fales

Selected Plays

1286. *Ark* (La Mama ETC, 1974)
1287. *How They Made It* (La Mama ETC, 1970)
1288. *Nicole Waiting* (Cubiculo, 1977-1978)
1289. *Playing in Local Bands* (O'Neill Theatre Center National Playwrights' Conference, Waterford, Connecticut, 1982)
1290. *Predicates* (La Mama ETC, 1971)
1291. *Some Sweet Day* (Long Wharf Theater, New Haven, 1989)
1292. *Surviving Death in Three Acts* (Playwrights Cooperative, 1973)

Profiles and Interviews

1293. Weiner, Bernard. *San Francisco Chronicle* (July 15, 1983): 60.

Garrett talks about her play *Playing in Local Bands*. Garrett also converses on the current status of women playwrights: "women playwrights are in fashion today," but she hopes they will not suffer the same fate as black dramatists "who were in fashion a few years ago. Now they've fallen out of fashion."

Reviews

Playing in Local Bands

1294. Rich, Frank. *New York Times* (Aug. 1, 1982), sect. 2: 1.
1295. Shirley, Don. *Los Angeles Times* (July 5, 1985), sect. 5: 4.
1296. *Variety* (Feb. 9, 1983): 84.
1297. Weiner, Bernard. *San Francisco Chronicle* (July 15, 1983): 60.

Some Sweet Day

1298. *Variety* (Apr. 5-11, 1989): 100.

Garson, Barbara

Selected Plays

1299. *MacBird!* (Village Gate, 1967)
          Playscript: *MacBird!* New York: Grove Press, 1967.
1300. *The Co-op* (Theatre for the New City, 1972)
1301. *A Winner's Tale* (Village Gate, 1974)
1302. *The Department* (Theatre for the New City, 1983)
1303. *The Dinosaur Door* (children's play, Theatre for the New City, 1976)

Profiles and Interviews

1304. *Contemporary Authors: A Bio-Bibliographical Guide.* Volumes 33-36. First Revision. Edited by Ann Evory, 324. Detroit: Gale Research Company, 1978.

The entry includes a brief biographical sketch and a list of Garson's works.

1305. *Contemporary Theatre, Film, and Television.* Volume 1. Edited by Monica M. O'Donnell, 195. Detroit: Gale, 1984.
The entry contains a biographical sketch and a list of Garson's plays.

1306. Garson, Barbara. "The Non-Event of the Half-Century." *Confrontation,* 15 (1978): 157-158.
Garson says that the "non-event" is the "absence" of the responsive audiences that understood her plays in the 1960s. She yearns for those spectators or a "cohesive movement" that "can change the world" and once again "enjoy [her] plays."

Reviews

See items 68, 102.

The Department

1307. Day, Susie. *Women & Performance,* 1, i (Spring/Summer 1983): 80-81.
1308. Gordon, M. *In These Times,* 7 (June 1, 1983): 12.
1309. Munk, Erica. *Village Voice* (May 24, 1983): 92.

MacBird!

1310. Abel, Lionel. *Partisan Review,* 34 (Winter 1967): 110-114.

1311. Atchity, Kenneth. *Motive,* 27 (Feb. 1967): 16-21.
Atchity praises the play for its "brave attempt to produce a genre of writing almost unknown in this country—a combination of parody, burlesque, lampoon, and polemic that might be called invective satire." Although he cites the plays as a "brilliant" example of parody, Atchity argues that it fails because its invectiveness is overwhelming and thus obliterates the satire.

1312. *Atlas,* 13 (May 1967): 40-42.
1313. Brook, Peter. *New York Times* (Mar. 19, 1967), sect. 2: 1, 3.

1314. Brustein, Robert. *New Republic* 156 (Mar. 11, 1967): 30-32.
        Reprinted in Brustein's *The Third Theatre,* 55-59. New York: Knopf, 1969.
        For letters to the editor regarding Brustein's review, see *New Republic* (Apr. 8, 1967): 41-42.

1315. Bryden, Ronald. *National Observer* (Apr. 16, 1967): 24e.
1316. Clurman, Harold. *Nation,* 204 (Mar. 13, 1967): 348-349.
1317. Conlin, K. *Theatre Southwest,* 6, iii (Oct. 1980): 13-17.
1318. Diether, Jack. *American Record Guide,* 33 (June 1967): 974-976.
1319. Downer, Alan S. *Quarterly Journal of Speech,* 53, iii (Oct. 1967): 222.
1320. Esslin, Martin. *New York Times* (Apr. 16, 1967): D3.
1321. _____. *Plays and Players,* 14 (June 1967): 39-58.
1322. Funke, Lewis. *New York Times* (Feb. 19, 1967), sect 2: D1, D8.
1323. Gilman, Richard. *New American Review,* 1 (1967): 123-134.
1324. Gottfried, Martin. *Women's Wear Daily* (Feb. 23, 1967).
        Reprinted in Gottfried's *Opening Nights: Theatre Criticism of the Sixties,* 304-307. New York: G.P. Putnam's Sons, 1969.
1325. Gussow, Mel. *Time,* 69 (Feb. 27, 1967): 99.
1326. Hewes, Henry. *Saturday Review,* 50 (Mar. 11, 1967): 30.
1327. Higgins. John. *Financial Times* (Apr. 12, 1967): 30a.
1328. Hobson, Harold. *Sunday Times* (London) (Apr. 16, 1967): 49g.

1329. "Hoover Assails *MacBird!* Author." *New York Times* (Apr. 1, 1967): 29.
        The item reports on former FBI director J. Edgar Hoover's disapproval of *MacBird!,* which he described as "a satirical piece of trash."

1330. Jones, D.A.N. *New Statesman* (Apr. 21, 1967): 553.

1331. Kauffmann, Stanley. *Persons in the Drama*, 178-181. New York: Harper & Row, 1976.

1332. Kerr, Walter. *New York Times* (Feb. 23, 1967): 38.

1333. _____. *New York Times* (Mar. 12, 1967), sect. 2:1.
For letters to the editor commenting on Walter Kerr's review of *MacBird!* see: *New York Times* (Apr. 9, 1967), sect. 2: 4; *New York Times* (Apr. 23, 1967), sect. 2: 9, and *New York Times* (Mar. 26, 1967), sect. 2: 7.

1334. _____. *New York Times* (Apr. 16, 1967), sect. 2: 1.

1335. Kingston, Jeremy. *Punch* (Apr. 19, 1967): 578.

1336. Kroll, Jack. *Newsweek*, 69 (Mar. 6, 1967): 79.

1337. Lewis, Anthony. *New York Times* (Apr. 2, 1967), sect. 4: 8.

1338. Lewis, Peter. *Daily Mail* (Apr. 12, 1967): 12b.
Lewis reports that the Lord Chamberlain has refused to allow *MacBird!* to be performed in England.

1339. "London Production of *MacBird!* Scored." *New York Times* (Apr. 11, 1967): 54.
This item briefly describes the poor reception of a watered-down version of *MacBird!* at the Theatre Royal.

1340. Madden, David. *Massachusetts Review,* 8 (1967): 722-25.

1341. "Major Publisher in Paris Bids for *MacBird!* Rights." *New York Times* (Jan. 18, 1967): 47.

1342. *New York Times* (Apr. 5, 1967): 72.
This item notes the *New Yorker's* refusal to run an advertisement promoting *MacBird!*

1343. "Out, Damned *MacBird*." *New York Times* (Feb. 1, 1967): 29.
This item notes that because of financial and artistic disagreements between director Roy Levine and the management, the opening of *MacBird!* has been postponed from February 8, 1967 to February 22, 1967.

1344. Potter, Stephen. *American Record Guide*, 33 (June 1967): 974-976.

1345. Oliver, Edith. *The New Yorker*, (Mar. 11, 1967): 127.

1346. *Playboy*, 14 (Aug. 1967): 24-26.

1347. Preston, Peter. *Manchester Guardian* (Apr. 11, 1967): 5d.

1348. Richardson, Jack. *Commentary*, 43 (Mar. 1967): 86-89.

1349. Schechter, Joel. *Durov's Pig: Clowns, Politics and Theatre*, 165-167. New York: Theatre Communications Group, 1985.
    In his brief examination of *Macbird!*, Schechter asserts that its immense popularity reveals that "satire can have an impact on America's consciousness."

1350. Schneck, Stephen. *Ramparts*, 5 (May 1967): 54, 56.

1351. Shorter, Eric. *Daily Telegraph* (London) (Apr. 11, 1967): 17a.

1352. Simon, John. *Hudson Review*, 20, ii (Summer 1967): 298-299.

1353. Spurling, Hilary. *Spectator* (Apr. 21, 1967): 465.

1354. Sullivan, Dan. *New York Times* (Feb. 22, 1967): 22.

1355. *Time*, 89 (Mar. 3, 1967): 52.

1356. *Times* (London) (Apr. 11, 1967): 8c.

1357. West, Anthony. *Vogue*, 19 (Apr. 19, 1967): 48.

1358. Zolotow, Sam. *"MacBird!* Will Open at Village Gate." *New York Times* (Jan. 4, 1967): 32.
    This item announces the premiere of *Macbird!* at the Village Gate on February 8, 1967.

1359. _____. "Program Printer Rejects *M'Bird!;* Denounces Play as Effort to Exploit Nation's Loss." *New York Times* (Jan. 11, 1967): 53. See also: "MacBird! Finds a Printer." *New York Times* (Jan. 1, 1967): 47.

Gibson, P.J.

Selected Plays

1360. *Brown Silk and Magenta Sunsets* (Frederick Douglass
           Creative Arts Theater, 1981)
           Playscript: *9 Plays by Black Women*. Edited by
           Margaret Wilkerson, 425-508. New York: New
           American Library, 1986.
1361. *Clean Sheets Can't Soil* (Bites and Reason, Providence,
           1983)
1362. *Konvergence* (Chicago 1978)
           Playscript: *New Plays for the Black Theatre*. Edited
           by Woodie King, 73-96. Chicago: Third World
           Press, 1989.
1363. *Long Time Since Yesterday* (New Federal Theatre, 1984-
           1985)
           Playscript: *Long Time Since Yesterday*. New York:
           Samuel French, 1986.
1364. *My Mark, My Name* (Bushfire Theatre Company,
           Philadelphia, 1988-1989)
1365. *Miss Ann Don't Cry No More* (Frederick Douglass Creative
           Arts Center, 1980)

Profiles

See items 77, 1362.

1366. Peterson, Bernard L. *Contemporary Black American
           Playwrights and Their Plays: A Biographical
           Directory and Dramatic Index*, 189-190. New York:
           Greenwood Press, 1989.
           Peterson provides a brief biography as well as a
           staging history of Gibson's plays.

Reviews

See item 104.

Long Time Since Yesterday

1367. Gussow, Mel. *New York Times* (Feb. 10, 1985): 63.
1368. Massa, Robert. *Village Voice* (Feb. 26, 1985): 88-89.
1369. Thorpe, John C. *Crisis*, 92 (Mar. 1985): 11.

Miss Ann Don't Cry No More

1370. Fox, Terry Curtis. *Village Voice* (Mar. 10, 1980): 84-85.

Gideon, Patty

Selected Plays

1371. *Man Enough* (Apple Corps Theater, 1985)

Reviews

Man Enough

1372. Shepard, Richard F. *New York Times* (May 29, 1985): C18.
1373. Solomon, Alisa. *Village Voice* (July 23, 1985): 94.

Glass, Joanna M.

Selected Plays

1374. *Canadian Gothic* (Manhattan Theater Club, 1972)
       Playscript: *Canadian Gothic* and *American Modern: Two Plays*. New York: Dramatists Play Service, 1977.
1375. *American Modern* (Manhattan Theater Club, 1972)
       Playscript: see item 1374.
1376. *Artichoke* (Manhattan Theater Club, 1979)
       Playscript: *Artichoke*. New York: Dramatists Play Service, 1979.
1377. *To Grandmother's House We Go* (Biltmore, 1981)
       Playscript: *To Grandmother's House We Go: A Play in Two Acts*. New York: Samuel French, 1981.
1378. *Play Memory* (Longacre Theatre, 1983)
1379. *Santackua* (HB Playwrights Foundation, 1969)

Profiles

1380. *Contemporary Theatre, Film, and Television*. Volume 1. Edited by Monica M. O'Donnell, 203. Detroit: Gale Research Company, 1984.

Glass's entry contains a brief biography, including a list of her plays.

1381. Drake, Sylvie. "Drama With a Canadian Accent." *Los Angeles Times* (Oct. 28, 1982), sect. 6: 1, 4. Drake profiles Glass on the eve of the opening of *Artichoke* at Theater 40. A native of Canada, Glass began her early theatrical career as an actress in Hollywood, "I had very little money and ended up living at the Hollywood Studio Club with a lot of beauty-contest winners." Of her earlier plays such as *Santackua,* Glass comments "[s]itting through those plays now is like being out with your kids when their table manners are really rotten."

Reviews

American Modern

1382. *American Theatre Annual 1976-1977,* 84. Detroit: Gale Research Company, 1978.
1383. Barnes, Clive. *New York Times* (Nov. 30, 1976): 51.
1384. Gottfried, Martin. *New York Post* (Nov. 30, 1976): 44.

Artichoke

1385. Barnes, Clive. *New York Post* (Feb 26, 1979): 33.
1386. _____. *New York Times* (Oct. 19, 1975): 53.
1387. Clurman, Harold. *Nation,* 228 (Mar. 17, 1979): 284-285.
1388. Drake, Sylvie. *Los Angeles Times* (June 29, 1981),sect. 6: 1.
1389. _____. *Los Angeles Times* (Oct. 28, 1982), sect. 6: 1.
1390. Eder, Richard. *New York Times* (Feb. 26, 1979): C13.
1391. Fox, Terry. *Village Voice* (Mar. 12, 1979): 86.
1392. Lochte, David. *Los Angeles Magazine* 27 (Dec. 1982): 347-348.
1393. Oliver, Edith. *The New Yorker,* 55 (Mar. 5, 1979): 92-94.
1394. Richards, David. *Washington Post* (Aug. 7, 1986), sect. B: 9.
1395. Simon, John. *New York,* 12 (Mar. 26, 1979): 95-96.
1396. Stone, Judy. *San Francisco Chronicle* (July 8, 1978): 38.

1397. Sullivan, Dan. *Los Angeles Times* (Nov. 2, 1982), sect. 4: 1.
1398. Taitte, W.L. *Texas Monthly*, 7 (Apr. 1979): 160.
1399. Wardle, Irving. *Times (London)* (Oct. 12, 1982): 8h.
1400. Weiner, Bernard. *San Francisco Chronicle* (Mar. 11, 1981): 54.

Canadian Gothic

See items 1383, 1384.

Play Memory

See item 80.

1401. Klein, Alvin. *New York Times* (Oct. 9, 1983), sect. 11: 31.
      Director Harold Prince talks briefly about the staging of *Play Memory* at the McCarter Theatre.

1402. _____. *New York Times* (Oct. 16, 1983), sect. 11: 15.
1403. Simon, John. *New York*, 17 (May 7, 1984): 79.

To Grandmother's House We Go

1404. Stasio, Marilyn. *After Dark*, 13 (May, 1981): 81.
1405. Barnes, Clive. *New York Post* (Jan. 16, 1981).
      Reprinted in item 1411.
1406. Beaufort, John. *Christian Science Monitor* (Jan. 19, 1981): 20.
      Reprinted in item 1411.
1407. Feingold, Michael. *Village Voice* (Jan. 21-27, 1981): 78.
1408. Gill, Brendan. *The New Yorker*, 56 (Jan. 26, 1981): 61.
1409. Kerr, Walter. *New York Times* (Jan. 25, 1981), sect. 2: 5, 17.
1410. Kissel, Howard. *Women's Wear Daily* (Jan. 16, 1981).
      Reprinted in item 1411.
1411. *New York Theatre Critics' Reviews*, 42 (Jan. 12, 1981): 384-388.
1412. Rich, Frank. *New York Times* (Jan. 16, 1981): C3.
      Reprinted in item 1411.

1413.   Richards, David. *Washington Post* (Dec. 10, 1981), sect. B:
        20.
1414.   Sauvage, Leo. *New Leader,* 64 (Feb. 9, 1981): 19-20.

1415.   Schonberg, Harold C. *New York Times* (Jan. 1, 1981),
        sect. 2: 1, 16.
        Schonberg profiles Eva Le Gallienne, star of *Play
        Memory.* For related story see: Klein, Alvin. *New
        York Times* (Aug. 30, 1981), sect. 23: 24.

1416.   Simon, John. *New York* 14 (Feb. 2, 1981): 43-44.
1417.   Taitte, T.L. *Texas Monthly,* 8 (Dec. 1980): 212, 214.
1418.   Watt, Douglas. *New York Daily News* (Jan 16, 1981).
        Reprinted in item 1411.
1419.   Wilson, Edwin. *Wall Street Journal* (Jan. 23, 1981): 21.
        Reprinted in item 1411.

Goldemberg, Rose Leiman

Selected Plays

1420.   *The Cross Roads* (Carillon Hotel, Miami, 1975)
1421.   *Gandhiji* (O'Neill Theatre Center National Playwrights'
        Conference, Waterford, Connecticut, 1970)
1422.   *Letters Home* (American Place Theatre, 1979)
        Playscript: *The Women's Project: Seven New
        Plays by Women.* Edited by Julia Miles, 105-176.
        New York: Performing Arts Journal Publications
        & American Place Theatre, 1980. *Plays by
        Women.* Volume 2. Edited by Michelene Wandor,
        30-75. London: Methuen, 1982.
1423.   *Love One Another* (New Dramatists, 1974)
1424.   *Marching As To War* (East Village Theatre, 1971)
        Playscript: *Marching As To War.* New York:
        Dramatists Play Service, 1972.
1425.   *Personals* (Women's Project, 1979-1980)
1426.   *The Rabinowitz Gambit* (New Dramatists, 1973-1974)
1427.   *Rites of Passage* (Astor Place Theater, 1975)
1428.   *Sophie* (Jewish Repertory Theater, 1987)

Profiles

1429. *Contemporary Authors: A Bibliographical Guide.* Volume 2. New Revision Series. Edited by Ann Evory, 257-258. Detroit: Gale Research Company, 1981.
   The entry offers a biographical portrait, including a list of plays, teleplays, and screenplays.

1430. *Contemporary Theatre, Film, and Television.* Volume 1. Edited by Monica M. O'Donnell, 205-206. Detroit: Gale Research Company, 1984.
   This entry includes a biographical sketch and a list of Goldemberg's works.

1431. Goldemberg, Rose Leiman. "Woman Writer, Man's World." *New York Times* (Sep. 20, 1970), sect. 2: 1, 3.
   Goldemberg chronicles her experiences at the twelfth annual Eugene O'Neill Conference in Waterford, Connecticut. She remarks that her experience was intensified because she was the only woman dramatist selected to participate, forcing her "to confront what it means to be a woman playwright."

Reviews

See item 79.

Gandhiji

See item 1431.

1432. Sullivan, Dan. *Los Angeles Times* (Oct. 17, 1982); Calendar sect: 46.

Letters Home

1433. *American Theatre Annual 1979-1980,* 123. Detroit: Gale Research Company, 1981.
1434. Barnes, Clive. *New York Post* (Oct. 24, 1979): 35.
1435. Christon, Laurence. *Los Angeles Times* (June 12, 1983), Calendar sect.: 44.
1436. Currie, Glenne. *Los Angeles Times* (Nov. 14, 1979), sect. 4: 31.

1437. Gill, Brendan. *The New Yorker*, 55 (Nov. 5, 1979): 81.

1438. Helle, Anita Plath. "Re-Presenting Women Writers Onstage: A Retrospective to the Present." In *Making a Spectacle: Feminist Essays on Contemporary Women's Theatre*. Edited by Lynda Hart, 195-208. Ann Arbor: University of Michigan Press, 1989. Helle briefly discusses Goldemberg's *Letters Home* in her examination of biographical dramas about women writers in which she addresses the question "Do women become the subject of their own discourse when they are re-presented on stage?"

1439. Kerr, Walter. *New York Times* (Oct. 22, 1979): C14.
1440. Munk, Erica. *Village Voice* (June 18, 1979): 100.
1441. Watt, Douglas. *New York Daily News* (Oct. 22, 1979): 25.

Rites of Passage

1442. Gussow, Mel. *New York Times* (Aug. 30, 1975): 14.

Gonzalez, Gloria

Selected Plays

1443. *Celebrate Me* (with Edna Schappert, Playbox Theatre, 1971)
1444. *Curtains* (Hudson Guild Theatre, 1975) Playscript: *The Best Short Plays 1976*. Edited by Stanley Richards, 161-192. Radnor, Pennsylvania: Chilton Book Company, 1976.
1445. *Cafe con Leche* (Gramercy Arts Theater, 1984)
1446. *Chicken Little's Ass Is Falling* (Playbox Theatre, 1970)
1447. *A Former Gotham Gal* (New Playwrights' Theatre, Washington D.C., 1980)
1448. *Love Is a Tuna Casserole* (New York Theatre Ensemble, 1971)
1449. *Let's Hear It For Miss America* (Omni Theater Club, 1971-1972.)
1450. *Moving On!* (Playbox Theatre, 1972, includes three one-act plays: *Moving On!*, *Cuba: Economy Class*, *The New America*.

Playscript: *Moving On! Three One-Act Plays.*
New York: Samuel French, 1971.

1451. *Night Travellers* (Playbox Theatre, 1972)

1452. *Port Authority* (Theater-At-Noon, 1974)

1453. *A Sanctuary in the City* (Theatre Americana, Altadena, 1975)

1454. *Tidings, Comfort and Joy* (with Edna Schappert and Joseph Gath, Playbox Theatre, 1971)

1455. *Waiting Room* (Theater-at-Noon, 1974)

Profiles and Interviews

See item 1444.

1456. *Contemporary Authors: A Bio-Bibliographical Guide.*
Volume 24. New Revision Series. Edited by
Deborah C. Straub, 208. Detroit: Gale Research
Inc., 1988.
The entry includes a brief biography, and a list of
Gonzalez's plays, novels, teleplays, and awards.

1457. Gonzalez, Gloria. "Happiness Is Being a Playwright."
Dramatists Guild Quarterly, 12, ii (Summer 1975):
20-21.
Gonzalez satirically explains the joys of working in
the theatre, a business she refers to as "insane,
impulsive, exciting, tragic and triumphant."

1458. _____. "Members Warn: Beware the Showcase Code!"
Dramatists Guild Quarterly 17, i (Spring 1980): 8,
13-14.
Dramatists Guild Quarterly invited several
members, including Gonzalez, to talk about their
experiences with the Actor's Equity Showcase
Code, which many Guild members see as
discriminatory to playwrights.

1459. _____. "A Playwright Explores the Strange World of
Acting." *Dramatists Guild Quarterly,* 15, iii
(Autumn 1978): 38-40.
Gonzalez humorously describes her first experience
as an actress. She wanted the experience because

"to hear some people tell it, you've got no right
being a playwright until you've served an
apprenticeship as an actor." In short, acting,
Gonzalez claims, "is supposed to familiarize you
with the unique problems of the actor, thereby
gaining insights into the craft of playwriting."

Reviews

Cafe con Leche

1460. Fernandez, Enrique. *Village Voice* (Dec. 25, 1984): 122.

1461. Robertson, Nan. *Cafe con Leche:* A Bit of Home Brew."
        New York Times (Nov. 2, 1984): C3.
        Robertson's profile of Gonzalez reflects her cultural
        and artistic diversity—she is Cuban and Spanish;
        she grew up in a multi-generational household; and
        in addition to writing plays, she writes novels and
        screenplays. Gonzalez talks about her play *Cafe
        con Leche*, currently playing at the Gramercy Arts
        Theater in New York. Until this play, Gonzalez
        claims, she wrote about subjects remote from her
        Hispanic heritage, "I've done plays about Miss
        America and a movie mogul." She says she
        disbelieved the timeless advice of writing what you
        know, "[t]hat's boring and confining." In her most
        recent play, *Cafe con Leche,* however she draws
        upon her rich cultural background to portray a
        lower-middle class Cuban family residing in New
        York. Ironically, Gonzalez points out that many in
        the Hispanic community have criticized the play
        —"some people think it portrays us in a bad light."

1462. Shepard, Richard F. *New York Times* (Sep. 23, 1984): 64.

Double Play

1463. Christon, Lawrence. *New York Times* (May 31, 1984),
        sect. 6: 1.
1464. Lochte, Dick. *Los Angeles*, 29 (July 1984): 44-45.

A Former Gotham Gal

1465. Lardner, James. *Washington Post* (Feb. 13, 1980), sect. B: 7.
1466. Mahoney, John C. *Los Angeles Times* (Dec. 15, 1978), sect. 4: 36.

Grant, Micki

Selected Plays

See also **Carroll, Vinnette**

1467. *Bury the Dead* (Urban Arts Corps, 1970)
1468. *An Evening of Black Folktales* (Urban Arts Corps, 1974)
1469. *The Prodigal Sister* (with J.E. Franklin, New Federal Theatre, 1974)
1470. *It's So Nice to Be Civilized* (Martin Beck Theater, 1980)

Profiles

1471. Flatley, Guy. "Don't Worry, Micki Can Cope." *New York Times* (May 7, 1972), sect. 2: 1, 7.
Grant talks about herself in the wake of the successful *Don't Bother Me, I Can't Cope.* She reminisces about her childhood, her early years writing music and acting in community theatre, her subsequent move to Off Broadway, and her years working with the Urban Arts Corps, founded by Vinnette Carroll. Grant reflects on collaborating with Carroll, "we've had our fights; Vinnette is a hard taskmaster," to the position of black theatre in America—"I believe there is room for all kinds of theater; it doesn't have to be one or the other. There's room for angry Black theater and there's room for a show like ours, a show that has pride and dignity and music that is indigenous to our background."

1472. Peterson, Bernard L. *Contemporary Black American Playwrights and Their Plays: A Biographical*

Directory and Dramatic Index. New York:
Greenwood Press, 1988.
Peterson provides a biographical sketch as well as a
staging history of Grant's plays.

Reviews

See item 370.

It's So Nice To Be Civilized

See item 397.

1473. Gussow, Mel. *New York Times* (June 4, 1980): C22.
1474. *New York Theatre Critics' Review* (June 1980): 220-22.

1475. *New York Times* (June 10, 1980): C7.
    The Times notes that *It's So Nice To Be Civilized*
    closed after eight performances, excluding previews.

1476. Stasio, Marilyn. *New York Post* (June 4, 1980).
    Reprinted in item 1474.
1477. Watt, Douglas. *New York Daily News* (June 4, 1980).
    Reprinted in item 1474.
1478. Wilson, Edwin. *Wall Street Journal* (June 6, 1980): 17.

The Prodigal Sister

See **Franklin, J.E.**

Greth, Roma

Selected Plays

1479. *But What Will We Do About Betty?* (Shelter West, 1987)
1480. *The Color of the World* (The Cubiculo, 1973-1974)
1481. *The Greatest Day of the Century* (staged reading, Women's
    Project, 1979-1980)
1482. *The Heaven Mother* (Old Reliable Free Theater, 1970-1971)
1483. *Interview*
    Playscript: *Scene,* 1 (1972): 66-69.
1484. *A Quality of Mercy* (Syracuse Stage, 1976)

1485. *Windfall Apples* (Impossible Ragtime Theatre, 1978)
1486. *Women! Women!* (includes: American War Mothers;
          Captain Hannah; Fifth of July; and *Gas and*
          Shock, WPA Theater, 1974)
1487. *Worms* (Omni Theater Club, 1970)
          Playscript: *Scene,* 1 (1972): 33-64.

Profiles

1488. *Contemporary Theatre, Film, and Television.* Volume 2.
          Edited by Monica M. O'Donnell, 218-219. Detroit:
          Gale Research Company, 1984.
          This entry provides a biographical sketch and a list
          of Greth's works.

Reviews

American War Mothers

1489. Calta, Louis. "*Women! Women!* Due in January." *New*
          York Times (Dec. 30, 1973): 30.
          Calta notes that four of Greth's one-act plays,
          American War Mothers, Captain Hannah, Fifth of
          July and *Gas and Shock,* will open as part of the
          collective show *Women Women!* at the WPA
          Theatre, January 18, 1973. The show also includes
          one-act plays by Diane Kagan and Avra Petrides.

Windfall Apples

See item 16.

1490. Fox, Terry Curtis. *Village Voice* (Jan. 1, 1979): 75.

Griffin, Susan

Selected Plays

1491. *Voices* (St. Clement's Church, 1978)
          Playscript: *Voices: A Play.* New York: Samuel
          French, 1979.

Profiles

1492. *Contemporary Authors: A Bio-Bibliographical Guide.*
Volume 3. New Revision Series. Edited by Ann
Evory, 248-249. Detroit: Gale Research Company,
1981.
This entry provides a biographical sketch of
Griffin.

Reviews

Voices

See item 16.

1493. Bardacke, Frances. *San Diego Magazine,* 30 (May 1978):
50.
1494. Brantley, Robin. *New York Times* (May 26, 1978), sect. 3:
4.
1495. Craig, Randall. *Drama,* 127 (Winter 1977-1978): 74.
1496. Drake, Sylvie. *Los Angeles Times* (Sep. 7, 1977), sect. 4:
12.

1497. Mael, Phyllis. "Rainbow of Voices." In *Women in
American Theatre.* Edited by Helen Krich Chinoy
and Linda Walsh Jenkins, 317-321. New York:
Theatre Communications Group, 1987.
Mael examines three plays, *Voices* (Susan
Griffin), *Out Of Our Father's House* (Eve
Merriam), and *for colored girls who have considered
suicide/when the rainbow is enuf* (Ntozake Shange)
and how each uses the consciousness-raising group
as a dramatic structure to express the individual and
collective female quest for self-definition.
According to Mael, consciousness-raising groups,
which aim to help women become aware of how
they are assigned certain roles in society, assembles
women on stage, allowing "the individual voices
[to] merge to speak to the collective journey of
women. The distinct voices thus interact with and
respond to each other."

Hagedorn, Jessica

> Selected Plays

1498. *The Art of War/Nine Situations* (with Blondell Cummings,
          Bessie Schonberg Theater, 1984)
1499. *Holy Food* (Magic Theatre, San Francisco, 1988-1989)
1500. *Mango Tango* (Other Stage, Public Theatre, 1978)
1501. *Where the Mississippi Meets the Amazon* (with Ntozake
          Shange and Thulini Nkabinde, Public Theatre
          Cabaret, 1977)

> Profiles

See item 8.

> Reviews

> *The Art of War/Nine Situations*

1502. Dunning, Jennifer. *New York Times* (Nov. 15, 1984): 20.
1503. Tobias, Tobi. *New York,* 17 (Nov. 19, 1984): 70.

> *Mango Tango*

1504. Eder, Richard. *New York Times* (May 30, 1978), sect. 3: 6.
1505. Fox, Terry Curtis. *Village Voice* (June 5, 1978): 71.

> *Where the Mississippi Meets the Amazon*

1506. Gussow, Mel. *New York Times* (Dec. 20, 1977): 44.
1507. Harris, Jessica. *Village Voice* (Jan. 30, 1978): 68-70.

Haufrecht, Marcia

> Selected Plays

1508. *Bliss Street* (Open Stage Theater, Sarasota, 1984)
1509. *In Exchange* (Quaigh Theater, 1986)
1510. *Flat Tire* (Quaigh Theater, 1986)
1511. *Full Moon and High Tide in the Ladies Room* (Company
          of Angels, Los Angeles, 1988)

1512. *It's Me Marie* (Actors Studio, 1981)
1513. *Leaving Home* (Ensemble Studio Theater, 1978)
1514. *Lucky Star* (Ensemble Studio Theater, 1979)
1515. *The Store* (Ensemble Studio Theater, 1980)
1516. *Welfare* (Ensemble Studio Theater, 1979)

Reviews

Bliss Street

1517. *Variety* (Apr. 11, 1984): 98.

Full Moon and High Tide in the Ladies Room

1518. Loynd, Ray. *Los Angeles Times* (Sep. 30, 1988), sect. 6: 18, 19.
1519. McCulloh, T.H. *Drama-Logue* (Oct. 20-26, 1988): 8.

The Store

1520. Faber, R.M. *Village Voice* (June 16, 1980): 80, 85.
1521. Gussow, Mel. *New York Times* (June 7, 1980): 11.

Welfare

1522. Gussow, Mel. *New York Times* (May 11, 1977), sect. C: 3.

Havard, Lezley

Selected Plays

1523. *Hide and Seek* (Belasco Theater, 1980)
      Playscript: *Hide and Seek*. New York: Dramatists Play Service, 1980.
1524. *In the Bag* (Actors Theatre of Louisville, Kentucky, 1982)
1525. *Termination Point* (Actors Theatre of Louisville, Kentucky, 1982-1983)
1526. *Victims*
      Playscript: *Victims*. Toronto: Playwrights Co-Op, 1976.

Reviews

Hide and Seek

1527. *American Theatre Annual 1979-1980*, 71. Detroit: Gale
      Research Company, 1981.
1528. Beaufort, John. *Christian Science Monitor* (May 7, 1980):
      19.
1529. Gill, Brendan. *The New Yorker*, 56 (May 19, 1980): 106.
1530. Rich, Frank. *New York Times* (May 5, 1980): C13.

1531. *New York Times* (May 10, 1980): 14
          The *Times* notes that *Hide and Seek* closed at the
          Belasco after nine performances.

1532. Simon, John. *New York,* 13 (May 19, 1980): 59-60.

Havoc, June

Selected Plays

1533. *I'm Still Here* (Warehouse Theatre, London, 1985)
1534. *I, Said the Fly* (Guthrie Theatre Company, Minneapolis,
      1973)
1535. *Marathon '33* (ANTA Theater, 1963)
          Playscript: *Marathon '33*. New York: Dramatists
          Play Service, 1969.
1536. *Oh Glorious Tintinnabulation* (Actors Studio, 1974)
1537. *Vaudeville* (Omaha Magic Theatre, Omaha, 1984-1985)

Profiles

See item 87.

1538. *Contemporary Authors: A Bio-Bibliographical Guide.*
          Volume 107. Edited by Hal May, 198-200.
          Detroit: Gale Research Company, 1983.
          A biographical sketch, which describes Havoc's
          work as an actress, director, and playwright and also
          provides general comments about her life and work
          in the theatre.

Reviews

I'm Still Here

1539. Morley, Sheridan. *Punch*, 289 (July 3, 1985): 48.

Marathon '33

1540. Garebian, K. *Journal of Canadian Studies*, 22 (Winter 1987/1988): 136-137.

1541. *New York Times* (Jan. 29, 1964): 22.
   The *Times* notes the closing of *Marathon '33*.

1542. Nichols, Lewis. *New York Times* (Dec. 23, 1963): sect. 10: 3.
1543. Taubman, Howard. *New York Times* (Dec. 23, 1963): 20.

Henley, Beth

Selected Plays

1544. *Abundance* (South Coast Repertory, Costa Mesa, 1989)
1545. *Am I Blue* (Circle Repertory Company, 1982)
   Playscript: *Am I Blue: A Play*. New York: Dramatists Play Service, 1982; *The Best Short Plays 1983*. Edited by Ramon Delgado, 131-150. Radnor, Pennsylvania: Chilton Book Company, 1983.
1546. *Crimes of the Heart* (Manhattan Theatre Club, 1980)
   Playscript: *Crimes of the Heart*. New York: Viking Press, 1982; *Plays From Actors Theatre of Louisville*, 71-140. New York: Broadway Play Publishing Inc., 1989. *Plays from the Contemporary American Theatre*. Edited by Brooks McNamara, 227-291. New York: New American Library, 1988.
1547. *The Debutante Ball* (South Coast Repertory, Costa Mesa, 1985)

1548. *Hymn in the Attic* (Back Alley Theatre, Van Nuys,
                California, 1982)
                Playscript: *West Coast Plays*, 17/18 (1985): 312-
                316.
1549. *The Lucky Spot* (Manhattan Theatre Club, 1987)
                Playscript: *The Lucky Spot: A Play*. New York:
                Dramatists Play Service, 1987.
1550. *The Miss Firecracker Contest* (Manhattan Theatre Club,
                1984)
                Playscript: *The Miss Firecracker Contest: A Play*.
                Garden City, New York: Doubleday, 1985.
1551. *The Wake of Jamey Foster* (O'Neill Theater Center National
                Playwrights' Conference, Waterford, Connecticut,
                1982)
                Playscript: *The Wake of Jamey Foster*. New York:
                Dramatists Play Service, 1983.

Profiles and Interviews

See item 9, 48, 75 and pages 4, 23.

1552. Bent, Ted. "Playwright Beth Henley's Only Crime Is
                Stealing Hearts of Broadway Critics." *People
                Weekly* 16 (Dec. 21, 1981): 124-125.
                Bent's article treats Henley's biography in the
                traditonal pop magazine fashion—light and casual.
                Written shortly after Henley won the Pulitzer Prize,
                Bent provides bits and pieces about Henley's
                personal life, her theatrical achievements and
                includes her comments about her artistic vision, her
                "eccentric eye." See also a briefer updated profile of
                Henley in *People Weekly* 26 (Dec. 22-29, 1986):
                91.

1553. Berkvist, Robert. "Act I: The Pulitzer, Act II: Broadway."
                New York Times (Oct. 25, 1981), sect. 2: D4,
                D22.
                This article anticipates the opening of *Crimes of
                the Heart* on Broadway at the John Golden Theater
                in November 1981. As to suddenly finding herself
                a Pulitzer Prize winner, Henley reveals her
                ambivalent feelings; on the one hand it's

"wonderful" yet "pretty terrifying." Berkvist also asks Henley about the staging history of *Crimes,* her strategies for writing plays, and the reasons for setting her plays in the South.

1554. Buckley, Peter. "Beating the Odds." *Horizon,* 2 (Dec. 1982): 48-55.
Buckley asks "What does it take to skyrocket to fame?" and explores this question by surveying the theatrical careers of several American playwrights, including two women dramatists, Beth Henley and Wendy Wasserstein.

1555. *Contemporary Authors: A Bio-Bibliographical Guide.* Volume 32, New Revision Series. Edited by James G. Lesniak, 199-200. Detroit: Gale Research Inc., 1991.
This entry includes a biographical sketch and general comments concerning Henley's work.

1556. *Contemporary Theatre, Film, and Television.* Volume 1. Edited by Monica M. O'Donnell, 239. Detroit: Gale Research Company, 1984.
Henley's entry contains a brief biography, including a list of her awards and plays.

1557. Corliss, Richard. "I Go With What I'm Feeling." *Time,* 119 (Feb. 8, 1982): 80. This article succinctly surveys Henley's achievements as a Pulitzer Prize winning dramatist; it includes insightful quotes from Henley on her aesthetic vision and approach to writing plays.

1558. *Current Biography Yearbook: 1983.* Edited by Charles Moritz, 185-188. New York: H.W. Wilson, 1983.
The entry provides an extensive biography on Henley's life and career.

1559. Drake, Sylvie. "Chat With a Pulitzer Dramatist." *Los Angeles Times* (Apr. 15, 1981), sect. 6: 1, 7.

Drake's short profile is based on a telephone interview with Henley shortly after she won the Pulitzer Prize for *Crimes of the Heart.*

1560.　＿＿＿. "Henley's Heart Is in the Theatre." *Los Angeles Times* (Apr. 16, 1983), sect. 5: 1, 8. Reprinted in *San Francisco Chronicle* (June 5, 1983), Datebook sect.: 31.
Drake profiles Henley's life and work as a playwright and actress. Henley reminisces about her childhood, her early theatrical career, her successful plays and not-so successful plays, and works-in-progress.

1561.　Durham, Ayne C. "Beth Henley." *Critical Survey of Drama: Supplement.* Edited by Frank McGill, 192-197. Pasadena: Salem Press, 1987.
Durham provides a biographical sketch of Henley's life and achievements as well as an analysis of her major plays.

1562.　Haller, Scot. "Her First Play, Her First Pulitzer." *Saturday Review,* 8 (Nov. 1981): 40-44.
Haller wrote this profile shortly after Henley received a Pulitzer Prize for *Crimes.* To capture Henley's unique personality and talent as a dramatist, Haller incorporates comments from Jon Jory, artistic director of Actors Theatre of Louisville, Melvin Bernhardt, director of the Broadway production of *Crimes,* playwrights James McClure and Fred Baile, John Simon's rave review, and quotes from Henley herself.

1563.　Jones, John. "Interview with Beth Henley." *Mississippi Writers Talking,* 169-190. Volume 1. Jackson: University Press of Mississippi, 1982.
Jones's interview of Henley took place at her mother's house in Jackson, Mississippi, on March 10, 1981, one month before the announcement that Henley had won the Pulitzer Prize for her play, *Crimes of the Heart.* Jones encourages Henley to talk about the genesis of each of her plays,

including the lesser-known *Am I Blue* and the
book she wrote for the musical *Parade*. Henley
also talks about the influence of the South on her
work, her playwriting methods, and her ambitions
about being an actress.

1564. Kinser, Jerry. "Mississippians in Rank of Pulitzers." *Biloxi-
Gulfport Daily Herald*. (Apr. 14, 1981): 4.
This brief article announces Henley as the winner
of the Pulizer Prize for drama and includes a brief
profile of her life.

1565. Kullman, Colby H. and Miriam Neuringer. In *American
Playwrights Since 1945*. Edited by Philip Kolin,
169-178. New York: Greenwood Press, 1989.
Kullman provides an assessment of Henley's
critical reputation, a historical survey of her stage
productions, a brief analysis of her plays, and
suggestions for future areas of study. Includes a
primary and secondary bibliography of sources.

1566. McDonnell, Lisa J. *Contemporary Authors Bibliographical
Series: American Dramatists*. Volume 3. Edited by
Matthew C. Roudane, 91-108. Detroit: Gale
Research Inc., 1989.
A bibliographical essay assessing the critical
reputation of Henley's work. Includes a primary
and secondary bibliography of sources.

1567. Meserve, Walter J. *Contemporary Dramatists*. 4th edition.
Edited by D.L. Kirkpatrick, 245-46. Chicago: St.
James Press, 1988.
Meserve briefly assesses the life and work of
Henley. The entry includes a list of her plays.

1568. Mullener, Elizabeth. "Beth Henley." *Times-Picayune* (New
Orleans) (Nov. 8, 1981), Dixie sect.: 7.
In this highly personal interview, Henley describes
her childhood struggle to find her niche, which
became especially painful when the results of a
school achievement test indicated that "I was tone
deaf, color blind and had no real creative powers,

but that I was kind of good in mathematics."
Rehearsals for the first staging of *Crimes* in
Louisville, Henley reveals, were extremely
stressful. "Sometimes people take your play and
do it better than you imagine it, and then it's really
like a high. But mainly, they don't do it like you
want it." And she confesses that winning the
Pulitzer Prize for *Crimes* was an overwhelming
experience. "It was a lot of attention for me. I'm
sure it would be nothing for Suzanne Somers."

1569. Rochlin, Margy. "The Eccentric Genius of *Crimes of the
Heart.*" *Ms.,* 15 (Feb. 1987): 12-14.
Rochlin presents a casual look at Henley as a writer
of plays, screenplays, and as an actress.

1570. Rosenfeld, Megan. "Beth Henley." *Washington Post*
(Dec.12, 1986): C1, C10.
Rosenfeld's insightful profile of Henley focuses on
her professional life and her approach to writing
plays.

1571. Sessums, Kevin. "Beth Henley." *Interview* 17 (Feb. 1987):
85.
Henley's responses to Sessums's penetrating
questions make for an intimate interview. She
talks about her early induction into politics, "I was
taken around to politic for my father . . . and I just
loathed it." Henley describes how she has coped
with her successes (e.g., *Crimes of the Heart*) and
failures (e.g., *The Wake of Jamey Foster).* The
dramatist also reflects on the vital role writing
plays in her life.

1572. Sharbutt, Jay. "Beth Henley." *Times-Picayune* (New
Orleans) (Oct. 3, 1982): 8.
Sharbutt's interview, written shortly before the
opening of *The Wake of Jamey Foster* on
Broadway, is short and reveals nothing that cannot
be found in other interviews except that here she
expresses her reasons why she did not pursue
television work. Unlike "many gifted young

playwrights of comic mind" who "flee to
Sitcomville . . . [and the] easy money" to be made
in television, "she has no desire to foal a comedy
series for any network."

1573. Tarbox, Lucia. "Beth Henley. *Dictionary of Literary
Biography: Yearbook 1986.* Edited by J.M. Brook,
302-305. Detroit: Gale Research Company, 1987.
Tarbox surveys Henley's personal life and theatrical
career. She also provides general critical remarks
about Henley's plays, especially *Crimes of the
Heart.* The entry includes a list of Henley's plays,
screenplays, television scripts, and selected
secondary sources commenting on her work.

1574. Wilson, Edwin. "Beth Henley: Aiming For the Heart."
Wall Street Journal (Nov. 5, 1981): 35.
Wilson refers to Henley as the "busiest playwright
around," describing her achievements in the theatre
as well as in film. Following a profile of Henley,
Wilson briefly discusses *Crimes of the Heart,* a
play replete with "resonance and complexity."

Reviews

See items 54, 79.

Abundance

1575. Cohen, Ron. *Contemporary Literary Criticism: Yearbook
1989.* Edited by Roger Matuz, 21. Detroit: Gale
Research Inc., 1990.
1576. Drake, Sylvie. *Los Angeles Times* (Apr. 24, 1989), sect.
5: 1.
1577. Henry, William A. *Time,* 133 (June 12, 1989): 72.
1578. McCulloh, T.H. *Drama-Logue* (Apr. 21, 1989): 8-9.

Am I Blue

See items 1563, 1610.

1579. Barnes, Clive. *New York Post* (Jan. 11, 1982).

Reprinted in item 1584.

1580. Beaufort, John. *Christian Science Monitor* (Jan. 19, 1982): 19.

1581. Feingold, Michael. *Village Voice* (Jan. 13-19, 1982): 101, 103.
Reprinted in item 1596.

1582. Kerr, Walter. *New York Times* (Jan. 24, 1982), sect. 2: 3, 10.
Reprinted in item 1596.

1583. Kissel, Howard. *Women's Wear Daily* (Jan. 11, 1982).
Reprinted in item 1584.

1584. *New York Theatre Critics' Reviews*, 43 (Feb. 1, 1982): 360-363.

1585. Rich, Frank. *New York Times* (Jan. 11, 1982): C14.
Reprinted in item 1584.

1586. Simon, John. *New York*, 15 (Jan. 25, 1982): 56.

1587. Watt, Douglas. *New York Daily News* (Jan. 11, 1982).
Reprinted in 1584.

1588. Weiner, Bernard. *San Francisco Chronicle* (Jan. 22, 1985): 58.

Crimes of the Heart

See items 1568, 1573, 1574.

1589. Barnes, Clive. *New York Post* (Nov. 5, 1981).
Reprinted in item 1628.

1590. Beaufort, John. *Christian Science Monitor* (Nov. 9, 1981): 20.

1591. Bent, Ted. *People Weekly,* 16 (Dec 21, 1981): 125.

1592. Bronski, M. *Gay Community News*, 11 (Nov. 19, 1983): 13.

1593. Brustein, Robert. *New Republic*, 185 (Dec. 23, 1981): 25-27.

1594. Cassidy, Claudia. *Chicago*, 33 (Feb 1984): 20.

1595. Christiansen, Richard. *Chicago Tribune* (Dec. 15, 1983), sect. 2: 24.

1596. *Contemporary Literary Criticism: Excerpts from Criticism of the Works of Today's Novelists, Poets, Playwrights and Other Creative Writers.* Volume

23. Edited by Sharon R. Gunton, 214-218. Detroit:
Gale Research Company, 1983.

1597. Currie, Glenne. *Los Angeles Times* (Jan. 5, 1981), sect. 6:
5.

1598. Demastes, William W. *Beyond Naturalism: A New
Realism in American Theatre.* New York:
Greenwood Press, 1988.
In his penultimate chapter, Demastes examines the
Pulitzer Prize-winning plays of Beth Henley
(Crimes of the Heart) and Marsha Norman *('night
Mother),* whom he considers as representing the
"second generation of new realists." The author
claims these dramatists deserve closer scrutiny
because their works have been "confused as
belonging to the old school of realism."
Furthermore, these writers infuse the new realist
mode with elements of black, Southern, and
feminist perspectives, which have been
underrepresented.

1599. Drake, Sylvie. *Los Angeles Times* (Nov. 5, 1981), sect. 6:
1, 5.

1600. Feingold, Michael. *Village Voice* (Nov. 18-24, 1981): 104,
106.
Reprinted in item 1596.

1601. Fox, Terry Curtis. *Village Voice* (Jan. 7-13, 1981): 71
Reprinted in item 1596.

1602. Frank, Leah D. *New York Times* (Nov. 14, 1989), sect.
21: 18.

1603. Gagen, Jean. "Most Resembling Unlikeness, and Most
Unlike Resemblance: Beth Henley's *Crimes of the
Heart* and Chekov's *Three Sisters." Studies in
American Drama 1945-Present,* 4 (1989): 119-128.
Gagen contends that the study of Henley's *Crimes
of the Heart* and Chekov's *Three Sisters* reveals
that the two playwrights share similarities in their
approach to drama. And the most "striking
similarity" is in the way both dramatists fuse the
comic with the serious. Gagen observes, however,

that the dramatists differ in the way they blend the comic with the characters' fears, frustrations, and disappointments. On the one hand, although Henley's sisters' lives are filled with tragedy, Gagen maintains that their reponses to calamitous situations "are believable . . . they are so utterly unexpected that they produce a moment of bewilderment and shock which finds release in outbursts of laughter." Chekov's infusion of "bizarre humor" is "less frequent than Henley's but more complex and often more subtle."

1604.   Gill Brendan. *The New Yorker*, 57 (Nov. 16, 1981): 182. Reprinted in item 1596.

1605.   Grove, Lloyd. *Washington Post* (June 8, 1984), Weekend sect.: 11.

1606.   Guerra, Jonnie. "Beth Henley: Female Quest and the Family-Play Tradition. In *Making a Spectacle: Feminist Essays on Contemporary Women's Theatre*. Edited by Lynda Hart, 118-130. Ann Arbor: University of Michigan Press, 1989. Guerra uses Carol Christ's paradigm (see item 4264) of the female quest to examine Henley's plays. Christ's model of the female quest, according to Guerra, requires that "women progress through experiences of nothingness, awakening, insight, and new naming . . . on their journey to selfhood." Guerra concedes that Henley's "decisions about form and dramaturgy undermine to some degree her thematic intention; for example, Henley's choice of the traditional family drama, which has been developed using male standards," perpetuates expectations about women's representation on stage that are inherently restrictive. In addition, the conventions of the family drama inhibit Henley from dramatizing the multiple dimensions of women on a quest of self-identity or envisioning alternative realities for her protagonists. Guerra suggests that Henley experiment with "transformation" and other alternative dramatic forms.

1607. Gussow, Mel. *New York Times* (Feb. 20, 1979): C7.

1608. _____. *New York Times* (June 11, 1981): C17.
Gussow announces *Crimes of the Heart* has won
the Drama Critics Circle award for best new
American play.

1609. Hargrove, Nancy D. "The Tragicomic Vision of Beth
Henley's Drama." *Southern Quarterly*, 22, iv
(1984): 54-70.
Hargrove disagrees with critics who view Henley's
plays as "amusing comedies." Through the
medium of comedy, Henley conveys a tragic-comic
vision of the human condition. The dominant
theme, according to Hargrove, running through
three of Henley's plays, *Crimes of the Heart, The
Wake of Jamey Foster,* and *The Miss Firecracker
Contest,* is that life is full of pain, cruelty,
unfulfilled dreams, and of the characters' problems,
many of which are brought on by their flaws and
bad choices. This rather cynical attitude is
counterbalanced by the assertion that pain
strengthens individuals and deepens their awareness
of themselves and others; and that much can be
endured with the love and support of the family.

1610. Harbin, Billy J. "Familial Bonds in the Plays of Beth
Henley." *Southern Quarterly*, 25, iii (Spring 1987):
81-94.
Underlying the comedy of Henley's plays (*Crimes
of the Heart, Am I Blue, The Miss Firecracker
Contest, The Debutante Ball* and *The Wake of
Jamey Foster*) lies the theme of stifling societal
pressures of the community and disintegrating
familial bonds. Because of familial alienation, the
characters end up with "psychological wounds" and
problems with intimacy. When the pain of
loneliness and isolation begins to overwhelm them,
these characters embark on a "quest of emotional
and spiritual fulfillment." However, in the later

plays such as *Jamey Foster*, Harbin asserts the
protagonists "possess little potential for change
... [they] remain bereft and unenlightened
prisoners of their own anxieties."

1611. Heilpern, John. *Times* (London) (Dec. 5, 1981): 11h.
1612. Kalem, T.E. *Time*, 113 (Mar. 5, 1979): 73.
1613. _____. *Time*, 118 (Nov. 16, 1981): 122.
         Reprinted in item 1628.
1614. Kauffmann, Stanley. *Saturday Review*, 9 (Jan.1982): 54.
         Reprinted in item 1596.
1615. Kelly, Kevin. *Boston Globe* (Jan. 18, 1990), Arts sect.: 74.
1616. Kerr, Walter. *New York Times* (Nov. 15, 1981): 3, 31.
         Reprinted in item 1596.
1617. Kingston, Jeremy. *Times* (London) (Aug. 18, 1989): 14.
1618. Kissel, Howard. *Women's Wear Daily* (Nov. 6, 1981).
         Reprinted in item 1628.
1619. Koyama, Christine. *Chicago Tribune* (May 24, 1984), sect.
         5: 13b.
1620. Kroll, Jack. *Newsweek*, 98 (Nov. 16, 1981): 123.
         Reprinted in item 1628.

1621. Laughlin, Karen L. "Criminality, Desire, and Community:
         A Feminist Approach to Beth Henley's *Crimes of
         the Heart*." *Women & Performance*, 3, i (1986):
         35-51.
         Laughlin agrees with many feminist critics that
         Crimes is not a "revolutionary play"; its form is
         conventional and "thematically compromised." On
         one level the play can be seen as reinforcing the
         stereotype of the passive female oppressed by the
         patriarch. However, Laughlin asserts that the
         significance of the play lies in its "double-voiced
         discourse." Paralleling the "'dominant' story of
         female criminality and violence, the 'muted' story
         of *Crimes* offers striking and significant images of
         the oppressive through the unseen presence of
         patriarchal forces, of their impact on women's
         desires, and of their ultimate rejection in favor of a
         vision of female bonding and community."

1622. McDonnell, Lisa J. "Diverse Similitude: Beth Henley and Marsha Norman. *Southern Quarterly*, 25, iii (Spr. 1987): 95-104.
McDonnell asserts Henley and Norman "have more in common than gender, geography and awards." For instance, both dramatists are unique storytellers, their protagonists seek to control their own destinies, the family is central to their dramatic themes, and both use Southern gothic humor "to demonstrate the poetic lyricism of the commonplace." Yet, McDonnell observes, the dramatists use different ways of approaching their similarities. In depicting her characters, Henley "is affectionate, if mildly ridiculing" but Norman is "realistic and frequently harsh." And McDonnell contends Henley "writes comedy with serious dimensions [while Norman writes] serious drama with comic overtones."

1623. Mason, Deborah. *Vogue*, 171 (Dec 1981): 58.
1624. Masters, Anthony. *Times* (London) (May 19, 1983): 15g.
1625. Megar, R. *Washington Post* (June 8, 1984), sect. B: 1, 6.
1626. Morrison, Hobe. *Variety* (Nov. 11, 1981): 84.

1627. Morrow, Laura. "Orality and Identity in *'night, Mother* and *Crimes of the Heart.*" *Studies in American Drama, 1945-Present*, 3 (1988): 23-39.
Morrow demonstrates how the self-concept of the protagonists in *'night, Mother* and *Crimes* is formulated by the food they eat, the cigarettes they smoke, and the words they speak. In short, the characters' oral behavior measures how they feel about themselves and the quality of their relationships. Morrow, for example, examines the mother-daughter relationship in these plays by studying the oral habits of the characters.

1628. *New York Theatre Critics' Reviews*, 42, (Nov. 2, 1981): 136-41.
1629. Nightingale, Benedict. *New Statesman*, (May 27, 1983): 25-26.
1630. Nelsen, Don. *New York Daily News* (Nov. 5, 1981).

Reprinted in items 1596, 1628.

1631. Novick, Julius. *Village Voice* (Mar. 12, 1979): 87.
1632. Oliver, Edith. *The New Yorker,* 56 (Jan. 12, 1981): 81-82.
       Reprinted in item 1596.
1633. Morley, Sheridan. *Punch,* 284 (June 8, 1983): 52.
1634. Rich, Frank. *New York Times* (Dec. 22, 1980): C16.
1635. _____. *New York Times* (Dec. 27, 1980): C16.
1636. _____. *New York Times* (Nov. 5, 1981): C21.
       Reprinted in item 1628.
1637. _____. *New York Times* (Dec. 27, 1981), sect. 2: D6.
1638. Rosenfeld, Megan. *Washington Post* (Dec. 12, 1986), Style
       sect.: 1.
1639. Sauvage, Leo. *New Leader,* 65 (Nov. 15, 1982): 20.
1640. _____. *New Leader,* (Nov. 30, 1981): 19-20.
       Reprinted in item 1596.
1641. Simon, John. *New York,* 14 (Jan. 12, 1981): 42-44.
1642. _____. *New York,* 14 (Nov. 16, 1981): 125.
       Reprinted in item 1596.
1643. Stasio, Marilyn. *After Dark,* 13 (Mar. 1981): 28-29.
1644. _____. *Penthouse,* 13 (June 1982): 44.
1645. Sullivan, Dan. *Los Angeles Times* (Apr. 19, 1983), sect.
       6: 1, 4.
1646. Thornber, Robin. *Guardian* (Oct. 3, 1986): 14.
1647. Travers, Peter. *People Weekly,* 26 (Dec 15, 1986): 12.
1648. *Variety* (Dec. 31, 1980): 60.

1649. Weiner, Bernard. "First Place Prize Stuns Playwrights." *San
       Francisco Chronicle* (Apr. 25, 1979): 52.
       Weiner announces *Crimes of the Heart* is the co-
       winner of the Great American Play Contest
       sponsored by Actors Theatre of Louisville.

1650. _____. *San Francisco Chronicle* (May 2, 1979): 55.
1651. _____. *San Francisco Chronicle* (May 15, 1984): 41
1652. _____. *San Francisco Chronicle* (Nov. 16, 1985): 37.
1653. Wilson, Edwin. *Wall Street Journal* (Nov. 6, 1981): 35.

The Debutante Ball

See item 1610.

1654. James, John. *Times Educational Supplement* (June 16, 1989): B31.
1655. Koenig, Rhonda. *Punch*, 296 (June 9, 1989): 44.
1656. Peter, John. *Sunday Times* (London) (June 4, 1989): C9f.
1657. Ross, Laura. *American Theatre*, 2 (Apr. 1985): 19.
1658. Sullivan, Dan. *Los Angeles Times* (Apr. 11, 1985), sect. 6: 1, 4.
1659. *Variety* (Apr.17,1985): 228.
1660. Wardle, Irving. *Times* (London) (May 31, 1989): 21b
1661. Wolf, Matt. *Plays and Players*, 429 (July 1989): 31.

The Lucky Spot

See item 905.

1662. Novick, Julius. *Village Voice* (May 12, 1987): 99, 102.
1663. Oliver, Edith. *The New Yorker*, 63 (May 11, 1987): 80-81.
1664. Popkin, Henry. *Plays and Players*, 406 (July 1987): 32-33.
1665. Rich, Frank. *New York Times* (Apr. 29, 1987): C22.
1666. Simon, John. *New York*, 20 (May 11, 1987): 83-84.
1667. *Variety* (May 6, 1987): 615.

The Miss Firecracker Contest

See items 1609, 1610.

1668. Barnes, Clive. *New York Post* (May 29, 1984).
       Reprinted in item 1686.
1669. Beaufort, John. *Christian Science Monitor* (June 6, 1984).
       Reprinted in item 1686.
1670. Brown, Joe. *Washington Post* (Aug. 16, 1985), Weekend sect.: 7.
1671. Chaillet, Ned. *Times* (London) (Apr. 28, 1982): 10f.
1672. Christiansen, Richard. *Chicago Tribune* (July 1, 1983), sect. 3: 10.
1673. Colodner, Joel. *Theatre Journal*, 34, ii (May 1982): 260-261.
1674. Cohen, Ron. *Women's Wear Daily* (May 30, 1984).
       Reprinted in item 1686.
1675. Drake, Sylvie. *Los Angeles Times* (Mar. 15, 1980), sect. 2: 8, 9.

1676. Fenton, James. *Sunday Times* (London) (May 2, 1982): 39g.
1677. Gold, Sylviane. *Wall Street Journal* (June 20, 1984): 28.
1678. *Guardian* (July 16, 1986): 11.

1679. Harris, Laurilyn J. "Delving Beneath the Stereotypes: Beth Henley's *The Miss Firecracker Contest.*" *Theatre Southwest* (May, 1987): 4-7.
Harris discusses Carnelle, Elaine, and Popeye's struggle for a definition of self in the face of the roles assigned to them by society: "the fallen woman," "the Southern belle," and "the homely spinster," respectively. Each woman attempts to create an image acceptable to society by emphasizing a few characteristics of her personality, but in the process denies the major part of her nature. As Harris points out, "[t]he issues in this play center around masochistic security versus hazardous freedom, style versus substance, part versus whole. The interest lies in watching each character challenge her own particular stereotype, stretching it until it either breaks or recoils upon her." Ultimately, these three women realize, through their journeys of painful self-discovery, that the attainment of an acceptable image does not result in a life devoid of pain or suffering; Henley's message is it's best to know and accept self and that life offers no guarantees but "there's always eternal grace."

1680. Heilpern, John. *Sunday Times* (London) (Dec. 5, 1981): 11h.
1681. Kauffmann, Stanley. *Saturday Review*, 9 (Jan. 1982): 54-55.
1682. Klein, Alvin. *New York Times* (Mar. 20, 1988), sect. 22: 18, 19.
1683. _____. *New York Times* (July 24, 1988), sect. 12: 19.
1684. Merrill, Lisa. *Women & Performance*, 2, ii (1985): 74-76.
1685. Myers, Leslie R. *Clarion-Ledger/Jackson Daily News* (May 22, 1988), sect. E: 3.
1686. *New York Theatre Critics' Reviews*, (May 21, 1984): 250-254.

1687. Nightingale, Benedict. *New York Times* (June 3, 1984): H3, H7.
1688. Oliver, Edith. *The New Yorker*, 60 (June 11, 1984): 112.
1689. Morley, Sheridan. *Punch*, 282 (May 5, 1982): 742.
1690. Rich, Frank. *New York Times* (May 28, 1984): 11. Reprinted in item 1686.
1691. Richards, David. *Washington Post* (July 8, 1984), sect. H:5.
1692. _____. *Washington Post* (Aug. 8, 1985), sect. B: 1, 10.
1693. Schickel, R. *Time*, 123 (June 11, 1984): 80. Reprinted in item 1686.
1694. Simon, John. *New York*, 17 (June 4, 1984): 79-80.
1695. Smith, Douglas. *Variety* (Nov. 4, 1981): 84.
1696. Watt, Douglas. *New York Daily News* (May 28, 1984). Reprinted in item 1686.
1697. Winn, Steven. *San Francisco Chronicle* (May 7, 1986): 66.

The Wake of Jamey Foster

See items 1609, 1610.

1698. Barnes, Clive. *New York Post* (Oct. 15, 1982). Reprinted in item 1708.
1699. Blau, Eleanor. *New York Times* (Aug. 13, 1982): C2.
1700. Brustein, Robert. *New Republic*, 187 (Nov. 29, 1982): 24-26.
1701. Davis, Curt. *After Dark*, 15 (Dec. 1982-Jan.1983): 10.
1702. Gill, Brendan. *The New Yorker*, 58 (Oct. 25, 1982): 161.
1703. Grove, Lloyd. *Washington Post* (June 1, 1984), Weekend sect.: 11.
1704. Kissel, Howard. *Women's Wear Daily* (Oct. 15, 1982). Reprinted in item 1708.

1705. Lawson, Carol. "Henley's *Wake of Jamey Foster* Taking Shape." *Clarion-Ledger* (Sep. 22, 1982): 6d. Lawson's brief profile of Henley and Susan Kingsley, who plays Jamey's widow, anticipates the opening of *The Wake of Jamey Foster* at the Eugene O'Neill Theater, October 14, 1982. Henley discusses the play, which is about how one family confronts the loss of a loved one. Henley comments that she likes to write about "stressful situations, where people are not acting normally. These situations make people act bigger than life . . . they intensify the family situation, which is always volatile anyway."

1706. _____. *New York Times* (Jan. 29, 1982): C2.
1707. _____. *New York Times* (Sep. 14, 1982): C9.
1708. *New York Theatre Critics' Reviews,* 43, (Nov. 1, 1982): 180-182.
1709. Novick, Julius. *Village Voice* (Oct. 26, 1982): 103.
1710. Rich, Frank. *New York Times* (Oct. 15, 1982): C3
       Reprinted in item 1708.
1711. Richards, David. *Washington Post* (June 2, 1984): C5.

1712. Shewey, Don. "A Director With an Eye For the Telling Detail." *New York Times* (Oct. 10, 1982), sect. 2: 28.
       Ulu Grosbard, director and co-producer of *The Wake of Jamey Foster,* discusses the play, which opens at the Eugene O'Neill Theater Center. Although Grosbard is not known for directing comedies, Henley chose him because "he understood where the sense of humor was coming from immediately. He makes it real *real*."

1713. Sauvage, Leo. *New Leader,* 65 (Nov. 15, 1982): 20.
1714. Simon, John. *New York,* 15 (Oct. 25, 1982): 78.
1715. Smith, Sid. *Chicago Tribune* (Apr. 10, 1985), sect. 5: 4.
1716. *Variety.* (Oct. 20, 1982): 331.
1717. *Variety.* (Jan. 27, 1987): 90.
1718. Watt, Douglas. *New York Daily News* (Oct. 15, 1982).
       Reprinted in item 1708.
1719. Wilson, Edwin. *Wall Street Journal* (Oct. 20, 1983): 32.
       Reprinted in item 1708.

Houston, Velina

Selected Plays

1720. *Asa Ga Kimashita* (Studio Theatre, Los Angeles, 1981)
1721. *American Dreams* (Negro Ensemble Company, 1984)
1722. *Shinsekai* (Asian American Theater, San Francisco, 1985)

1723. *Tea* (Manhattan Theatre Club, 1987)

Profiles

1724. Croon, Diana Y. "Writer Finds Creativity in Ice Cream."
Los Angeles Times (Apr. 24, 1984), sect. 6: 1.
Houston reflects upon her multi-ethnic background
and how it has affected her work in the theatre. For
instance, Houston claims she moved to Los
Angeles from Kansas "because of being Amerasian,
I never would have been produced . . . Asians just
don't fit in Kansas." Croon briefly discusses
Houston's plays: *Asa Ga Kimashita*, *American
Dreams*, and her forthcoming work *Shinsekai*.

1725. Njeri, Itabari. "The Melting Pot Myth." *Los Angeles Times*
(Nov. 2, 1988), sect. 5: 1.
Njeri discusses interminority relations in Los
Angeles and finds that the city fails somewhat as
the "perfect melting-pot metaphor." Houston,
among others, talks about her experiences as a
person of mixed race (Japanese, African-American,
and Blackfoot Indian) living and writing in Los
Angeles.

1726. Peterson, Bernard L. *Contemporary Black American
Playwrights and Their Plays: A Biographical
Directory and Dramatic Index*, 251-252. New York:
Greenwood Press, 1988.
Peterson provides a biographical sketch as well as a
staging history of Houston's works.

Reviews

See item 1.

American Dreams

See item 1724.

1727. Bardacke, Frances. *San Diego Magazine*, 40 (May 1988):
60.

1728. Beaufort, John. *Christian Science Monitor* (Feb. 17, 1984): 21.
1729. Gussow, Mel. *New York Times* (Feb. 2, 1984): C17.
1730. Oliver, Edith. *The New Yorker*, 60 (Feb. 20, 1984): 104.
1731. Stone, Laurie. *Village Voice* (Feb.14,1984): 98.
1732. Tapley, Mel. *N.Y. Amsterdam News* (Feb. 25, 1984): 21.

Asa Ga Kimashita

See also 1724.

1733. Hamilton, Camille. "An Amerasian Writes of Japanese War Brides." *San Francisco Chronicle* (Mar. 3, 1985), Datebook sect.: 20.
Hamilton interviews Houston on the eve of the debut of two of her plays *Asa Ga Kimashita* and *Tea*. Houston says her plays "are about love, fear, cultural conflict and the struggle to break out of tradition." Her depiction of the Japanese war bride often generates controversy. "I'm not trying to glorify the war bride experience or the Amerasian experience. I'm writing about what I know."

1734. Shirley, Don. *Los Angeles Times* (Jan. 27, 1984), sect. 6: 9.

Tea

1735. Bardacke, Frances. *San Diego Magazine*, 40 (May 1988): 60.
1736. Churnin, Nancy. *Los Angeles Times* (Apr. 1, 1988), sect. 6: 4.
1737. Drake, Sylvie. *Los Angeles Times* (Apr. 24, 1988), Calendar sect.: 47.
1738. *Drama-Logue* (Apr. 7-13 1988): 11.
1739. Goodman, Walter. *New York Times* (Oct. 21, 1987): C23.

Shinsekai

See item 1724.

Howe, Tina

Selected Plays

1740. *The Art of Dining* (New York Shakespeare Festival, 1979)
      Playscript: *The Art of Dining: A Comedy.* New
      York: Samuel French, 1980; see item 1744.
1741. *Appearances* (Ensemble Studio Theatre, 1981-1982)
1742. *Approaching Zanzibar* (Second Stage, 1989)
      Playscript: *Approaching Zanzibar.* New York:
      Theater Communications Group, 1990.
1743. *Birth and After Birth* (Gotham Art Theatre, 1974)
      Playscript: see item 73.
1744. *Coastal Disturbances* (Second Stage, 1986)
      Playscript: *Coastal Disturbances: Four Plays.*
      New York: Theatre Communications Group, 1989.
1745. *Museum* (New York Shakespeare Festival, 1977)
      Playscript: see item 1744.
1746. *The Nest* (Mercury Theatre, 1970)
1747. *Painting Churches* (Second Stage, 1983)
      Playscript: *Painting Churches.* New York: Samuel
      French, 1984; *Three Plays.* New York: Avon
      Books, 1984; *Plays from the Contemporary
      American Theatre.* Edited by Brooks McNamara.
      New York: New American Library, 1988; see item
      1744.
1748. *Urban Blight* (with Christopher Durang, Wendy
      Wasserstein, Ted Tally, Manhattan Theater Club,
      1988)

Profiles and Interviews

See items 9, 46, 48, 73, 75, 87, 90, 100, 1074.

1749. Barlow, Judith E. *Contemporary Dramatists.* 4th edition.
      Edited by D.L. Kirkpatrick, 271-272. Chicago: St.
      James Press, 1988.
      Barlow briefly assesses the life and work of Howe.
      The entry includes a list of her plays.

1750. _____. "An Interview With Tina Howe." *Studies in
      American Drama 1945-Present,* 4 (1989): 159-175.

Especially informative about this interview is the discussion of Howe's newest play, *Approaching Zanzibar*, by the playwright and the interviewer. Howe remarks that although "it was harrowing to write," *Zanzibar* is the play she is "proudest of . . . [it] says everthing I've been trying to say all along." Howe reveals that she identifies with Absurdist playwrights, in particular Beckett and Ionesco who have "inspired [her] the most." But she concedes she is not "nearly experimental enough." The playwright attributes her lack of "daring" as a reaction to having been criticized for her early "daring plays." Howe talks about her comic vision as well as the darker side of her self, "Tina the Destroyer," "the part that's frightening to me," which she tries to suppress from her writing but admits "there is a violent side that I haven't let out yet."

1751.   Bennetts, Leslie. "Five Top Playwrights in a Dialogue, with Arthur Miller Adding Drama." *New York Times* (June 18, 1988): 9.
Bennetts reports on a symposium sponsored by First New York International Festival of the Arts at the City University of New York. A panel of five dramatists, including Tina Howe, Arthur Miller, Athol Fugard, August Wilson, and Tom Stoppard addressed issues regarding the festival's theme: "The Challenges of Writing for the Theater Today."

1752.   Brenson, Michael. "Art Given a Role in Tina Howe's Play." *New York Times* (Feb. 18, 1983): C3.
Brenson primarily discusses *Painting Churches*; however, he includes information about Howe's personal background, especially as it pertains to *Painting Churches*. Of the parallels between the play and her life, Howe says, "all of it is true, but none of it happened."

1753.   *Contemporary Authors: A Bio-Bibliographical Guide.* Volume 109. Edited by Hal May, 212. Detroit: Gale Research Company, 1983

A biographical sketch is provided, along with brief critical comments about Howe's work.

1754. *Contemporary Theatre, Film, and Television*. Volume 7. Edited by Monica M. O'Donnell, 186. Detroit: Gale Research Inc., 1988.
This entry provides a brief biography of Howe's life and works.

1755. Simon, John. "The Powers That Be: Theater." *New York*, 19 (Dec. 22-29, 1986): 96-97.
Tina Howe is one of the individuals identified by *New York* who "will shape life in New York as we careen around the curve into the next century." Although Simon, who wrote the section on theatre, profiles the careers of four promising young theatre artists, he predicts the "next champion" will be Tina Howe. The critic briefly describes Howe's achievements and discusses *Museum, The Art of Dining* and *Coastal Disturbances*.

1756. "Taking the Stage." *Harper's Bazaar* (Aug. 1989): 153, 188.
Harper's profiles several women theatre artists, one of whom is Tina Howe.

1757. Walker, Lou Ann. "Comedies With a Dash of Menace." *New York Times* (Apr. 30, 1989), sect. 2: 7, 14.
Walker profiles Howe prior to the opening of *Approaching Zanzibar*, which the playwright considers her "breakthrough play" because "she has taken a play out of a single setting and attempted a more complex subject." Howe also recalls the critical reviews of her early plays such as *The Nest*, "[they were] so vitriolic it closed in one night" and *Birth and After Birth*, which "[n]obody would touch." Lacking the "right director" was the problem according to Howe; her plays did not become "accepted" until Carol Rothman began directing them, whom she feels "set the style."

1758. Wetzsteon, Ross. "The Mad, Mad World of Tina Howe."
New York, 16 (Nov. 28, 1983): 58-71.
Wetzsteon stresses how Howe pulls much of her
"antic vision" from her personal life. He, as well
as Howe, draws parallels between her life and the
lives of the characters in her plays, especially
Painting Churches. As Howe says, "[m]y parents
were like that—such comical people, but so
unutterably sad at the same time. I want that double
sense to come across in my plays." Howe also
states that the negative reception of Birth and After
Birth, which people "found too horrifying a
depiction of motherhood," caused her to take
measure of her theatrical career. "My antic side was
. . . just too wild . . . so I decided to explore other
aspects of my imagination. She discovered that she
could retain her "lunatic vision" if she
communicated it through unconventional settings.
Thus she created Museum and The Art of Dining.
"What I wanted to do . . . was to present a lovely
exterior, then seduce the audience into the dark and
mysterious places inside."

Reviews

See item 79.

Appearances

1759. Oliver, Edith. *The New Yorker*, 58 (May 24, 1982): 104.
1760. Rich, Frank. *New York Times* (May 14, 1982): C4.

Approaching Zanzibar

1761. Beaufort, John. *Christian Science Monitor* (May 24, 1989):
10.
1762. Henry, William A. *Time*, 133 (May 15, 1989): 87.
1763. Oliver, Edith. *The New Yorker*, 65 (May, 15, 1989): 94.
1764. Rich, Frank. *New York Times* (May 5, 1989): C3.
1765. Rogoff, Gordon. *Village Voice* (May, 16, 1989): 99-100.
1766. Simon, John. *New York*, 22 (May 15, 1989): 124-125.
1767. *Variety* (May 10, 1989): 119.

1768. Winer, Laurie. *Wall Street Journal* (May 12, 1989): A12.

The Art of Dining

See items 1755, 1758, 1781.

1769. *American Theatre Annual,* 1979-1980, 138. Detroit: Gale Research Company, 1980.

1770. Barnes, Clive. *New York Post* (Dec. 7, 1979): 31.

1771. *Contemporary Literary Criticism: Excerpts from Today's Novelists, Poets, Playwrights and Other Creative Writers.* Volume 48. Edited by Daniel G. Marowksi, 171-179. Detroit: Gale Research Company, 1988.

1772. Clurman, Harold. *Nation,* 230 (Jan. 5-Jan.12, 1980): 30. Reprinted in item 1771.

1773. Kearns, Nancy. *Theatre Journal,* 38, iii (Oct. 1986): 367-369.

1774. Kerr, Walter. *New York Times* (Dec. 7, 1979): C6. Reprinted in item 1771.

1775. Gill, Brendan. *The New Yorker,* 55 (Dec. 17, 1979): 100-101. Reprinted in item 1771.

1776. Simon, John. *New York,* 12 (Dec. 24, 1979): 73. Reprinted in item 1771.

1777. Smith, Sid. *Chicago Tribune* (Sep. 19, 1986), sect. 5: 3.

1778. Sullivan, Dan. *Los Angeles Times* (Nov. 21, 1983), sect. 6: 1.

1779. Weiner, Bernard. *San Francisco Chronicle* (Dec. 13, 1985): 102.

Birth and After Birth

See items 12, 16, 1757, 1758, 1781.

1780. Backes, Nancy. "Body Art: Hunger and Satiation in the Plays of Tina Howe." In *Making a Spectacle: Feminist Essays on Contemporary Women's Theatre.* Edited by Lynda Hart, 41-60. Ann Arbor: University of Michigan Press, 1989.
Backes views Howe's plays as excellent examples of the symbolic power of food in reflecting men's

control over the lives of women. In *Birth and After Birth,* for instance, Howe uses the bingeing and purging of food to dramatize how chaos and control "uneasily coexist" in a woman. Ultimately, each of Howe's protagonists learns that she can control her body without depriving it of nourishment. But, for these "hungry women controlling their bodies is rarely enough ... [they] manage to transform their hungers, cravings, and excess energies in art."

1781.   Barlow, Judith E. "The Art of Tina Howe." In *Feminine Focus: The New Women Playwrights.* Edited by Enoch Brater, 241-251. New York: Oxford University Press, 1989.
Barlow discusses Howe's "obsession with art," where she levels her "satiric eye" on the act of creation, the creator, the critic, and the consumer of the art to expose the absurdities of the human condition and the "savagery underneath the civilized veneer." Barlow includes in her examination Howe's major plays: *The Nest, Birth and After Birth, Museum, The Art of Dining, Coastal Disturbances,* and *Painting Churches.*

Coastal Disturbances

See items 1755, 1781.

1782.   Barnes, Clive. *New York Post* (Nov. 20, 1986).
Reprinted in items 1771, 1796.
1783.   Beaufort, John. *Christian Science Monitor* (Dec. 10, 1986).
Reprinted in item 1796.
1784.   Brustein, Robert. *New Republic* (Jan. 5&12, 1987): 25-27.
Reprinted in item 1771.
1785.   Cohen, Ron. *Women's Wear Daily* (Nov. 21, 1986).
Reprinted in item 1796.
1786.   Christiansen, Richard. *Chicago Tribune* (Sep. 30, 1988), sect. 2C: 9.
1787.   Dace, Tish. *Play International,* 2 (Jan. 1987): 41.

1788.   Gerard, Jeremy. "A Hit Play That Found No Takers." *New York Times* (Jan. 7, 1987): C19.

Gerard reports a producer has yet to move *Coastal Disturbances*, which had a successful run at a small Off Broadway theatre.

1789. Gold, Sylviane. *Wall Street Journal* (Dec. 10, 1986):32. Reprinted in item 1796.
1790. Greene, Alexis. *Theatre Journal*, 40, i (Mar. 1988): 101-102.
1791. Hill, Holly. *Times* (London) (Jan. 26, 1987): 9e.
1792. Hodgson, Moira. *Nation*, 244 (Jan. 10, 1987): 24-26. Reprinted in item 1771.
1793. Kerr, Walter. *New York Times* (May 17, 1987), sect. 2: H43.
1794. Kissel, Howard. *New York Daily News* (Nov. 26, 1986). Reprinted in item 1796.
1795. Levett, Karl. *Drama*, 164 (2nd Quarter, 1987): 44-45.
1796. *New York Theatre Critics' Reviews*, 47 (Nov. 24, 1986): 127-131.
1797. Novick, Julius. *Village Voice* (Dec. 2, 1986): 127-128.
1798. Oliver, Edith. *The New Yorker*, 62 (Dec. 1, 1986): 111.
1799. Rich, Frank. *New York Times* (Nov. 20, 1986): C25. Reprinted in item 1771.
1800. _____. *New York Times* (Dec. 28, 1986): H3, H17.
1801. Simon, John. *New York*, 19 (Dec. 1, 1986): 148-149.
1802. _____. *New York*, 20 (Mar. 30, 1987): 97.
1803. Smith, Sid. *Chicago Tribune* (Sep. 25, 1988), sect. 13: 18.
1804. *Variety* (Nov. 26, 1986): 146.
1805. Wallach, Allan. *New York Newsday* (Nov. 20, 1986). Reprinted in item 1796.
1806. Watt, Douglas. *New York Daily News* (Dec. 5, 1986). Reprinted in item 1796.

1807. Winn, Steven. "ACT Graduate Finds Broadway Stardom." *San Francisco Chronicle* (May 17, 1987), Datebook sect.: 38.
      Winn highlights the career of Annette Bening, "ingenue-turned-Broadway star," who plays Holly Dancer in Howe's *Coastal Disturbances* at the Circle in the Square in New York.

Museum

See items 16, 1755, 1758, 1781.

1808. *American Theatre Annual 1977-1978,* 122. Detroit: Gale
        Research Company, 1979.
1809. Barnes, Clive. *New York Post* (Feb. 28, 1978): 17.
        Reprinted in items 1771, 1814.
1810. Beaufort, John. *Christian Science Monitor* (Mar. 1, 1978):
        26.
        Reprinted in item 1771.
1811. Eder, Richard. *New York Times* (Feb. 28, 1978): 28.
1812. Fox, Terry Curtis. *Village Voice* (Mar. 6, 1978): 75.
1813. Loney, Glenn. *After Dark,* 11 (June 1978): 84.
1814. *New York Theatre Critics' Reviews* 39 (Mar. 20, 1978):
        343-346.
1815. Oliver, Edith. *The New Yorker,* 54 (Mar. 6, 1978): 67-68.
        Reprinted in item 1771.
1816. Sharp, Christopher. *Women's Wear Daily* (Feb. 28, 1978).
        Reprinted in item 1814.
1817. Sullivan, Dan. *Los Angeles Times* (May 12, 1976), sect.
        4: 1.
1818. _____. *Los Angeles Times* (June 4, 1976), sect. 4: 1,
        21.
1819. Watt, Douglas. *New York Daily News* (Feb. 28, 1978).
        Reprinted in item 1814.

The Nest

See items 1757, 1781.

1820. Barnes, Clive. *New York Times* (Apr. 10, 1970): 46.

Painting Churches

See items 1752, 1758, 1781.

1821. Beaufort, John. *Christian Science Monitor* (Feb. 24, 1983):
        19.
1822. Blumenthal, E. *Village Voice* (Feb. 15, 1983): 87, 89.
1823. Brown, Joe. *Washington Post* (July 19, 1985), Weekend
        sect.: 9.

1824. Brustein, Robert. *New Republic*, 188 (Apr. 4, 1983): 22-25.
Reprinted in item 1771.

1825. Christiansen, Richard. *Chicago Tribune* (May 10, 1985),
sect. 2: 10.

1826. Christon, Laurence. *Los Angeles Times* (Nov. 13, 1985),
sect. 6: 1, 2.

1827. Drake, Sylvie. *Los Angeles Times* (July 22, 1985), sect.
6: 1, 6.

1828. Friedman, Zelda Pilshaw. *New Directions for Women*, 12,
iii (May 1983): 7.

1829. Grove, Lloyd. *Washington Post* (July 13, 1985), sect. C:
5.

1830. Kalem, T.E. *Time*, 121 (Feb. 21, 1983): 74.
Reprinted in item 1835.

1831. Kissel, Howard. *Women's Wear Daily* (Nov. 23, 1983).
Reprinted in item 1835.

1832. Klein, Alvin. *New York Times* (Apr. 26, 1987), sect. 23:
33.

1833. Lieberman, Susan. *Theatre Crafts*, 19 (May 1985): 18, 44-
45.

1834. Morley, Sheridan. *Punch*, 295 (Oct. 7, 1988): 66.

1835. *New York Theatre Critics' Reviews*, 44 (Dec. 12, 1983): 74-
77.

1836. Nightingale, Benedict. *New York Times* (Dec. 4, 1983):
H5.

1837. O'Connor, John. *New York Times* (May 19, 1986): C20.
O'Connor reviews production for public TV's
"American Playhouse" series.

1838. Oliver, Edith. *The New Yorker*, 59 (Feb. 21, 1983): 104.

1839. Rich, Frank. *New York Times* (Nov. 11, 1982): C2.

1840. _____. *New York Times* (Feb 9, 1983): C16.
Reprinted in item 1771.

1841. _____. *New York Times* (Nov. 23, 1983): C13.
Reprinted in item 1835.

1842. Rossman, Kathleen. *Studies in American Drama 1945-
Present*, 4 (1989): 284-286.

1843. Simon, John. *New York*, 16 (Feb. 21, 1983): 52, 54.
Reprinted in item 1771.

1844. _____. *New York*, 16 (Dec. 12, 1983): 95-96.

1845. Sullivan, Dan. *Los Angeles Times* (Dec. 11, 1983), Calendar sect.: 53.
1846. Swisher, Kara. *Washington Post* (Mar. 24, 1988), Virginia sect.:14.
1847. *Variety* (Feb. 23, 1983): 102.
1848. Watt, Douglas. *New York Daily News* (Nov. 23, 1983). Reprinted in item 1835.
1849. Weales, Gerald. *Commonweal*, 111 (Jan. 13, 1984): 16-17. Reprinted in item 1771.
1850. Wetzsteon, R. *New York*, 16 (Nov. 28, 1983): 60.
1851. Winn, Steven. *San Francisco Chronicle* (May 5, 1985), Datebook: 29.
1852. Wilson, Edwin. *Wall Street Journal* (Nov. 30, 1983): 26.

Urban Blight

See *Wasserstein, Wendy*

Iko, Momoko

Selected Plays

1853. *Boutique Living and Disposable Icons* (Pan Asian Repertory Company, 1988)
1854. *Flowers and Household Gods* (Pan Asian Repertory Company, 1981)
1855. *The Gold Watch*
Playscript: *Aiiieeee!: An Anthology of Asian-American Writers*. Edited by Frank Chin, 88-114. Washington D.C.: Howard University Press, 1974.
1856. *Hollywood Mirrors* (Asian American Theater Workshop, 1978)

Profiles

1857. *Contemporary Authors: A Bio-Bibliographical Guide.* Volume 14. New Revision Series. Edited by Linda Metzger, 243. Detroit: Gale Research Company, 1985.

1858. Iko, Momoko. "Redress: Act of Atonement So They Can Face Their Gods." *Los Angeles*

Times (Aug. 11, 1988), sect. 2: 7.
Iko, a Japanese-American, reflects upon the
movement to redress the wrongs done to Japanese-
Americans during World War II. She does not,
however, discuss her plays or playwriting.

Reviews

See item 1.

Boutique Living and Disposable Icons

1859. Gussow, Mel. *New York Times* (June 30, 1988): C20

Flowers and Household Gods

1860. Francia, Luis H. *Village Voice* (Apr. 29, 1981): 88.
1861. Gussow, Mel. *New York Times* (Apr. 21, 1981): C7.

Hollywood Mirrors

1862. Weiner, Bernard. "Taking Flight from Soul-Pounding." *San
Francisco Chronicle* (Nov. 13, 1978): 47.
Weiner announces the opening of Iko's *Hollywood
Mirrors* on Friday at the Asian American Theater
Workshop in San Francisco and briefly profiles the
playwright's achievements.

1863. Gussow, Mel. *New York Times* (Dec. 7, 1982): C23.

Jacker, Corinne

Selected Plays

1864. *After the Season* (Academy Festival Theatre, Chicago,
1978)
1865. *Bits and Pieces* (Manhattan Theater Club, 1974)
Playscript: *Bits and Pieces*. New York: Dramatists
Play Service, 1975; see item 73.
1866. *Domestic Relations* (Circle Repertory Company, 1983)
Playscript: *Domestic Issues*. New York: Dramatists
Plays Service, 1983.

1867. *Harry Outside* (Circle Repertory Club, 1975)
> Playscript: *Harry Outside: A Play in Two Acts.*
> New York: Dramatists Play Service, 1975.

1868. *In Place*
> Playscript: *The Best Short Plays 1984.* Edited by
> Ramon Delgado, 181-182. Radnor, Pennsylvania:
> Chilton Book Company, 1984; see item 1873.

1869. *Later* (Marymount Manhattan Theatre, 1979)
> Playscript: *Later.* New York: Dramatists Play
> Service, 1979.

1870. *My Life* (Circle Repertory Company, 1977)
> Playscript: *My Life.* New York: Dramatists Play
> Service, 1977.

1871. *Night Thoughts* (Circle Repertory Theater, 1977)
> Playscript: *Night Thoughts* and *Terminal: Two
> Short Plays.* New York: Dramatists Play Service,
> 1977.

1872. *Other People's Tables* (bill of three one-acts, *Among
> Friends, Breakfast, Lunch and Dinner*, and *Chinese
> Restaurant Syndrome*, Billy Munk Theater, 1976)
> Playscript: *Breakfast, Lunch and Dinner.* New
> York: Dramatists Play Service, 1977.

1873. *Chinese Restaurant Syndrome*
> Playscript: *In Place* and *The Chinese Restaurant
> Syndrome.* New York: Dramatists Play Service,
> 1983; *The Best Short Plays 1979.* Edited by
> Stanley Richards, 179-194. Radnor, Penn.: Chilton
> Book Company, 1979.

1874. *Project Omega: Lillian* (Eugene O'Neill Theater Center
> National Playwrights' Conference, Waterford,
> Connecticut, 1971)

1875. *The Scientific Method* (New York Shakespeare Festival,
> 1970)

1876. *Songs from Distant Lands* (Long Wharf Theater, New
> Haven, 1989)

1877. *Terminal* (Circle Repertory Company, 1975-1976)
> Playscript: See item 1871.

1878. *Travellers* (Cincinnati Playhouse, Cincinnati, 1976-1977)

Profiles

See items 9, 48, 52, 73, 75, 86 and page 13.

1879. "The American Playwright in the Seventies: Some
Problems & Perspectives." *Theatre Quarterly,* 8
(Spring 1978): 45-58.
A lively discussion between seven American
dramatists, including Corinne Jacker. Barnet
Killman, a director, acts as moderator. The
discussion centers on questions concerning the
"how rather than the why of playwriting" and
perceived similarities and differences with
contemporary British playwrights. The panelists
tackle such issues as "is there a community of
playwrights?," "Do American playwrights follow
the British tradition of writing plays on
commission?," "Who are we writing for?," and
"How do playwrights feel about directors?"

1880. *Contemporary Authors: A Bio-Bibliographical Guide.*
Volumes 17-20. Gale Research Company, 1976.
The entry includes a biographical sketch and general
comments on Jacker's work.

Reviews

See item 68.

After The Season

1881. Lawson, Carol. "Michael Learned of *Waltons* to Star in
Corinne Jacker Play." *New York Times* (Feb. 22,
1980): C2.
Lawson's preproduction article discusses the play
and announces actress Michael Learned will appear
in the starring role.

1882. _____. *New York Times* (Mar. 14, 1980): C2.
Lawson notes the upcoming rehearsals for *After the
Season.*

Bits and Pieces

See item 16.

1883. Coe, Richard L. *Washington Post* (June 5, 1978), sect. B: 2.
1884. Fox, Terry Curtis. *Village Voice* (June 9, 1980): 85.
1885. Gussow, Mel. *New York Times* (Nov. 19, 1974): 52.
1886. Rich, Frank. *New York Times* (June 9, 1980): C12.

Domestic Issues

1887. Berman, Paul. *Village Voice* (Mar. 22, 1983): 109.
1888. Gussow, Mel. *New York Times* (Feb. 5, 1981): C21.
1889. Oliver, Edith. *The New Yorker*, 59 (Mar. 21, 1983): 98.
1890. Pace, Eric. *New York Times* (Jan. 11, 1981), sect. 2: D5.
1891. Rich, Frank. *New York Times* (Mar. 14, 1983): C12.
1892. Simon, John. *New York*, 16 (Mar. 28, 1983): 76.

Harry Outside

1893. Buckley, Tom. "About New York." *New York Times* (May 6, 1975): 20.
      Kevin McCarthy talks about his role in *Harry Outside*.

1894. Clurman, Harold. *Nation*, 220 (May 31, 1975): 668-669.
1895. Gussow, Mel. *New York Times* (May 13, 1975): 31.
1896. Oliver, Edith. *The New Yorker*, 51 (May 26, 1975): 77-78.

1897. Ryzuk, Mary S. *The Circle Repertory Company: The First Fifteen Years.* Ames: Iowa State University Press, 1989.
      Ryzuk briefly discusses the production of *Harry Outside* and *My Life*.

Later

See item 16.

1898. *American Theatre Annual 1978-1979*, 143. Detroit: Gale Research Company, 1980.
1899. Barnes, Clive. *New York Post* (Jan. 16, 1979): 48.
1900. Blumenthal, Eileen. *Village Voice* (Jan. 29, 1979): 77.
1901. *Variety* (Jan. 24, 1979): 96.

My Life

See item 1897.

1902. Clurman, Harold. *Nation*, 224 (Feb. 12, 1977): 190.
1903. Gold, Sylviane. *New York Post* (Jan. 24, 1977): 16.
1904. Gussow, Mel. *New York Times* (Jan. 24, 1977): 19.
1905. Oliver, Edith. *The New Yorker*, 52 (Feb. 7, 1977): 67-68.
1906. Sainer, Arthur. *Village Voice* (Feb. 7, 1977): 75.
1907. Simon, John. *New York*, 10 (Feb. 14, 1977): 88.
1908. Stasio, Marilyn. *Cue*, (Feb. 14, 1977): 37.

Other People's Tables

See item 52.

1909. Gussow, Mel. *New York Times* (Oct. 29, 1976): C5.

Jackson, Elaine

Selected Plays

1910. *Afterbirth* (staged reading, Women's Project, 1982-1983)
1911. *Birth Rights* (American Folk Theatre, 1987)
1912. *Cockfight* (American Place Theater, 1977)
1913. *Paper Dolls* (Richard Allen Center for Culture and Art, 1983)
       Playscript: *9 Plays by Black Women*. Edited by Margaret Wilkerson, 351-423. New York: New American Library, 1986.
1914. *Toe Jam* (New Federal Theater, 1975)
       Playscript: *Black Drama*. Edited by Woody King and Ron Milner, 641-671. New York: New American Library, 1971.

Profiles

See items 77, 1923.

1915. Peterson, Bernard L. *Contemporary Black American Playwrights and Their Plays: A Biographical*

Directory and Dramatic Index, 266. New York: Greenwood Press, 1988.
Peterson provides a biography as well as a staging history of Jackson's plays.

Reviews

Cockfight

1916. *American Theatre Annual 1977-1978,* 85. Detroit: Gale Research Company, 1979.
1917. Davis, Curt. *Encore,* 6 (Nov. 7, 1977): 31.
1918. Eder, Richard. *New York Times* (Oct. 17, 1977): 39.
1919. Evers, L.M. *Show Business* (Oct. 27, 1977): 23.
1920. Gottfried, Martin. *New York Post* (Oct. 17, 1977): 27.

1921. Harris, Jessica B. *N.Y. Amsterdam News* (Oct. 29, 1977): D10.
Following the review Jackson briefly discusses her play.

1922. Mahoney, John C. *Los Angeles Times* (Dec. 15, 1978), sect. 4: 36, 37.

1923. *Michigan Chronicle.* (Oct. 15, 1977), sect. B: 7.
This item announces the opening of *Cockfight* in New York and briefly profiles "Detroiter" Jackson.

1924. Munk, Erica. *Village Voice* (Nov. 7, 1977): 83-84.
1925. Oliver, Edith. *The New Yorker,* 53 (Oct. 31, 1977): 116-117.

Toe Jam

See item 1203.

1926. Gussow, Mel. *New York Times* (Nov. 18, 1975): 29.

Johnson, Cindy Lou

Selected Plays

1927. *Blesse* (Eugene O'Neill Theater Center National
      Playwrights' Conference, Waterford, Connecticut,
      1986)
1928. *Brilliant Traces* (Circle Repertory Company, 1989)
      Playscript: *Brilliant Traces.* New York: Dramatists
      Play Service, 1977.
1929. *The Person I Once Was* (INTAR,1986)
      Playscript: *The Person I Once Was: A One-Act
      Play.* New York: Dramatists Play Service, 1985.
1930. *Moonya* (Eugene O'Neill Theater Center National
      Playwrights' Conference, Waterford, Connecticut,
      1984)

Profiles and Interviews

See item 90.

1931. Rothstein, Mervyn. "A Play Grows Out of Family Art and
      Tradition." *New York Times* (Feb. 16, 1989):
      C27.
      Written shortly after the opening of Johnson's play,
      Brilliant Traces, Rothstein presents an illuminating
      vignette of Johnson's life and development as a
      playwright. He provides an abundance of quotes
      from Johnson about the themes of her current play,
      which the dramatist says is about the pain people
      experience because of loss and the necessity of
      reconnecting with others so that "through living,
      we can grow and heal and change. And as strong as
      our urge might be to fight it because of the pain it
      might cause, it's absolutely imperative that we
      connect."

Blesse

1932. Aucoin, Don. "Where Playwrights Take Center Stage."
      Boston Globe (July 25, 1986): 29.
      Aucoin talks briefly about Johnson's *Blesse* and
      includes quotes from her on playwriting in his
      article about the 22nd annual O'Neill National
      Playwrights' Conference in Waterford, Connecticut.

1933. *Variety* (Apr. 1, 1987): 84.

Brilliant Traces

See item 1931.

1934. Brown, Patricia Leigh. "A Working Girl Who Acts on Her
          Own." *New York Times* (Feb. 5, 1989): H5.
          Brown profiles Joan Cusack (*Working Girl*) who
          will play the lead in Johnson's comic drama
          Brilliant Traces at the Cherry Lane Theater.

1935. *Drama-Logue* (Mar. 9-15, 1989): 24.
1936. Kramer, Mimi. *The New Yorker*, 65 (Feb. 20, 1989): 89.
1937. Rich, Frank. *New York Times* (Feb. 6, 1989): C11.
1938. _____. *New York Times* (Dec. 24, 1989), sect. 2: 3, 26.
1939. Simon, John. *New York*, 22 (Feb. 20, 1989): 72.

The Person I Once Was

1940. Bruckner, D.J.R. *New York Times* (June 17, 1986): C14.
1941. *Drama-Logue* (Aug. 10-16, 1989): 9.

Jones-Meadows, Karen

Selected Plays

1942. *Henrietta* (Negro Ensemble Company, 1985)
1943. *Major Changes* (Hudson Guild Theater, 1988)
1944. *Tap Man* (Hudson Guild Theater, 1988)

Reviews

Henrietta

1945. Beaufort, John. *Christian Science Monitor* (Feb. 4, 1985),
          Arts sect.: 32.
1946. Rich, Frank. *New York Times* (Jan. 29, 1985): C13.

Tap Man

1947. Beaufort, John. *Christian Science Monitor*. (Mar. 3, 1988),
         Arts sect.: 22.
1948. Gussow, Mel. *New York Times* (Mar. 1, 1988): C17.

1949. Hurley, Joseph. "Moses Gunn on Tap As a Blues Singer."
         Newsday (Mar. 4, 1988), Weekend sect.: 14.
         Hurley interviews Moses Gunn, who plays the title
         role of *Tap Man*.

1950. Wallach, Allan. *Newsday* (Mar. 2, 1988), sect. 2: 9.

Kagan, Diane

Selected Plays

1951. *Corridor* (staged reading, Women's Project, 1978-1979)
1952. *High Times* (with Avra Petrides, WPA Theater, 1974)
1953. *Luminosity Without Radiance* (New Dramatists, 1970-
         1971)
1954. *Marvelous Gray* (New Dramatists, 1979-1980)
1955. *On the Rocks* (with Avra Petrides, WPA Theater, 1974)
1956. *Stolen Goods* (staged reading, Women's Project, 1985-
         1986)

Reviews

Corridor

1957. Shafer, George. *Theatre Journal*, 33, iv (Dec. 1981): 545-
         546.

High Times

1958. Calta, Louis. *New York Times* (Dec. 30, 1973): 30.
         Calta announces that Kagan's *High Times* and *On
         the Rocks* will be part of the bill *Women!
         Women!*, which includes several of Roma Greth's
         plays.

1959. Gussow, Mel. *New York Times* (Jan. 25, 1974): 18.

Marvelous Gray

1960. Gussow, Mel. *New York Times* (Dec. 7, 1982): C23.
1961. Stone, Laurie. *Village Voice* (Dec. 21, 1982): 122.

On the Rocks

1962. Gussow, Mel. *New York Times* (Jan. 25, 1974): 18.

Kava, Caroline

Selected Plays

1963. *Constance and the Musician* (Women's Project, American
        Place Theater, 1980-1981)
1964. *The Early Girl* (Circle Repertory Company, 1986)
        Playscript: *The Early Girl*. New York: Samuel
        French, 1986.
1965. *The Prevaricated Life of Constance McMalley* (staged
        reading, Women's Project, 1980-1981)

Profiles and Interviews

1966. Arkatov, Janice. "*Gate* Opened New Frontier for Kava." *Los
        Angeles Times* (Aug. 19, 1987), sect. 6: 5.
        Arkatov announces the opening of Kava's *The
        Early Girl* at the Back Alley in Los Angeles. In
        her interview with the reporter, Kava reveals she
        got the idea for her play while researching her role
        as a prostitute in the film *Heaven's Gate*. The
        actress turned playwright explains that in her play
        she does not focus on how one ends up as a
        prostitute but rather the consequences of choosing
        that lifestyle. Kava also reflects on her dual role as
        actress and writer, "I'd thought the writing was
        going to support my acting, but it's turned out the
        other way."

Reviews

The Early Girl

1967. Feingold, Michael. *Village Voice* (Nov. 11, 1986): 92.
1968. Gussow, Mel. *New York Times* (Oct. 31, 1986): 63.
1969. Hill, Holly. *Times* (London) (Jan. 26, 1987): 9d.
1970. Lochte, Dick. *Los Angeles,* 32 (Nov. 1987): 314-316.
1971. Sessions, Robert J. *Drama-Logue* (Apr. 27-May 3, 1989):
      8.
1972. Simon, John. *New York*, 19 (Nov. 10, 1986): 114.
1973. Sullivan, Dan. *Los Angeles Times* (Aug. 25, 1987), sect.
      6: 1, 8.
1974. Tokarczyk, M. *Women & Performance*, 3, ii (1987 &
      1988): 166-169.
1975. *Variety* (Nov. 19, 1986): 98.

Kelly, Casey

Selected Plays

1976. *Grand's Finale* (Quaigh Theatre, 1984-1985)
1977. *The Other Woman* (Three of Us Studios, 1984)
      Playscript: *The Best Short Plays 1984.* Edited by
      Ramon Delgado, 35-60. Radnor, Pennsylvania:
      Chilton Book Company, 1984.
1978. *Ready or Not* (Pennsylvania Stage Company, Allentown,
      1983)

Profiles

See items 100, 1977.

Reviews

Grand's Finale

1979. Lawson, Carol. *New York Times* (June 26, 1981): C2.
      Lawson's piece focuses on Orson Bean, who will
      direct *Grand's Finale.*

Ready or Not

1980. *Variety* (Jan. 26, 1983): 78.

Kennedy, Adrienne

Selected Plays

1981. *A Beast's Story*
　　　See item 1983.
1982. *Boats* (Mark Taper Forum, Los Angeles, 1969)
1983. *Cities in Bezique: Two One-Acts* (Public Theater, 1969)
　　　Playscript: *Cities in Bezique: Two One-Act Plays.*
　　　New York: Samuel French, 1969; *Kuntu Drama:*
　　　Plays of the African Continuum. Edited by Paul
　　　Carter Harrison, 169-202. New York: Grove Press
　　　Inc., 1974.
1984. *Electra* (adapted from Euripides, Juilliard School of Music,
　　　1980)
　　　Playscript: see 1985.
1985. *Funnyhouse of a Negro* (Circle in the Square, 1962)
　　　Playscript: *Adrienne Kennedy in One Act.*
　　　Minneapolis: University of Minnesota Press, 1988.
　　　Includes: *Funnyhouse of a Negro. The Owl*
　　　Answers, A Lesson in Dead Language, A Rat's
　　　Mass, Sun; A Movie Star Has to Star in Black and
　　　White, Electraf, and *Orestes; Contemporary Black*
　　　Drama. Edited by Oliver Clinton. New York:
　　　Charles Scribner's Sons, 1971; *Black Drama: An*
　　　Anthology. Edited by William Brasmer, 247-272.
　　　Columbus, Ohio: Charles S. Merrill, 1970; *The*
　　　Best Short Plays 1970. Edited by Stanley Richards,
　　　123-147. Philadelphia: Chilton Book Company,
　　　1970.
1986. *An Evening With Dead Essex* (American Place Theater,
　　　1973)
　　　Playscript: *Theater*, 9, ii (Spring 1978): 66-78.
1987. *A Lancashire Lad* (Empire State Youth Theatre, SUNY,
　　　Albany, 1980)
1988. *The Lennon Play: In His Own Write* (Arena Summer
　　　Theatre, 1969)
　　　Playscript: John Lennon, Adrienne Kennedy, Victor
　　　Spinetti. *The Lennon Play: In His Own Write.*
　　　New York: Simon and Schuster, 1969.
1989. *A Lesson in Dead Language* (Theatre Genesis, 1970)

Playscript: *Collision Course*. Edited by Edward
Parone, 33-40. New York: Random House, 1968;
see item 1985.

1990. *A Movie Star Has to Star in Black and White* (Public
Theatre, 1976)
Playscript: *Wordplays 3*, 51-68. New York: PAJ
Publications, 1984; see 1985.

1991. *Orestes* (adapted from Euripides, Juilliard School of Music,
1980)
Playscript: see item 1985.

1992. *The Owl Answers*
Playscript: *New American Plays II*. Edited by William
Hoffman, 249-268. New York: Hill/Wang, 1968;
see item 1985.

1993. *A Rat's Mass* (La Mama ETC, 1969)
Playscript: *New Black Playwrights*. Edited by William
Couch, Jr., 61-69. Baton Rouge: Louisiana State
University Press, 1968; *The Off-Off Broadway
Book: The Plays, People, Theatre*. Edited by
Albert Poland, 352-356. New York: Bobbs-Merrill,
1972. *More Plays From Off-Off Broadway*. Edited
by Michael Smith, 345-357. New York: Bobbs-
Merrill Company, 1972.

1994. *She Talks to Beethoven* (River Arts Repertory International
Writers Festival, Woodstock, New York, 1989)

1995. *Solo Voyages* (selected scenes from Kennedy's plays,
Interart Theater, 1985)

1996. *Sun: A Poem for Malcolm X Inspired by His Murder* (La
Mama ETC, 1970)
Playscript: *Scripts* 1 (Nov. 1971): 51-54.;
*Spontaneous Combustion: Eight New American
Plays*. Edited by Rochelle Owens, 3-13. New York:
Winter House LTD, 1972; see item 1985.

Profiles and Interviews

See items 9, 33, 87, 103 and pages 5-6, 9, 23.

1997. Binder, Wolfgang. "A *Melus* Interview: Adrienne
Kennedy." *Melus*, 12, iii (Fall 1985): 99-108.
Binder's questions touch upon several facets of
Kennedy's life and work. She talks about how her

home environment influenced her early themes.
For example, she recalls, "inside our house we had
these seemingly endless conflicts, these arguments.
How could we be a certain way on the outside and
another inside our house?" The dramatist also
describes the evolution of the production of
Funnyhouse of a Negro, which evolved from a
workshop presentation to Edward Albee's
production in 1964, and its controversial reception
by critics and audiences. Kennedy also speaks of
her activities after winning the Obie in 1964.
Binder includes a selective bibliography of primary
and secondary sources.

1998. *Black Writers: A Selection of Sketches from Contemporary*
Authors. Edited by Linda Metzger, 320-321.
Detroit: Gale Research Inc., 1989.
This entry provides a biographical sketch on
Kennedy as well as general comments on her plays.

1999. *Contemporary Authors: A Bio-Bibliographical Guide.*
Volume 26. New Revision Series. Edited by Hal
May, 199-201. Detroit: Gale Research Company,
1989.
Kennedy's entry includes a biographical sketch and
a list of her works.

2000. Diamond, Elin. *Contemporary Dramatists.* 3rd edition.
Edited by James Vinson, 293-294. New York: St.
Martin's Press, 1982.
A short biography is included with a list of
Kennedy's plays and general critical comments
about her work.

2001. _____. "An Interview with Adrienne Kennedy." *Studies in*
American Drama 1945-Present, 4 (1989): 129-141.
Diamond uses Kennedy's memoir *People Who Led*
to My Plays as a springboard from which to
awaken reflections from the playwright. According
to Kennedy, many individuals have proved to be
powerful forces in her life and work, and not all of
them real. She cites Humpty-Dumpty and the

figures on the Old Maid cards, for example, as
creating strong impressions, "[they] were as real to
me as my brother." Interspersed throughout the
interview, Kennedy talks about encounters with
racism that have affected her life, contending she
has "come to grips with that." Kennedy's plays are
discussed to a very limited extent throughout the
interview. A biographical profile prefaces the
interview.

2002. "Dramatus Instructus: How Six Playwriting Teachers Fire
up Their Students' Imaginations." *American
Theatre*, 6 (Jan. 1990): 22-26.
Six playwrights, including Kennedy and Maria
Irene Fornes, talk about the methods they use to
inspire experimentalism and individuality.

2003. Kennedy, Adrienne. "Becoming a Playwright." *American
Theatre*, 4 (Feb. 1988): 26-27.
Kennedy reminisces about the original production
of *Funnyhouse of a Negro* at the Circle in the
Square, which evolved from a class taught by
Edward Albee. She recollects telling Albee that she
was going to drop the class because she was unable
to stage her play, which she believed "was too
revealing" and that she was "embarrassed to have it
done." Albee told her a "playwright is someone
who lets his guts out on the stage and that's what
you've done in this play." Although terrified at the
prospect of staging *Funnyhouse*, Kennedy, after
talking to Albee, decided to witness the "anguish
that most often I had carefully blotted out as it
unfolded on the stage."

2004. _____. "A Growth of Images." *Modern Drama*, 21, iv
(Dec. 1977): 41-48.
Kennedy discusses the ways in which she writes
plays. Although autobiograpical topics concern her
the most, Kennedy wishes she could refrain from
writing about her family. However, writing helps
her work out her "psychological confusion" about
family problems, which "overwhelm" her.

Kennedy believes her dramas develop from images, emanating from her unconsious, which she records in her journals. For example, *A Rat's Mass* originated from a dream she had in which she was "being pursued by red, bloodied rats." According to the playwright, her admiration for Tennessee Williams and Federico Garcia Lorca influenced *Funnyhouse of a Negro*, which focuses on the protagonist's struggle with the ambivalent forces within her.

2005. _____. *People Who Led to My Plays*. New York: Knopf, 1987.
A memoir of a playwright "slowly find[ing] her direction." She provides a glimpse of the motley collection of family, friends, writers, movies stars, story-book characters, souls, and witches, who have given a profound "impetus and energy to [her] writing." For more information on this memoir, see item 2001.

2006. Overbeck, Lois More. *Contemporary Authors Bibliographical Series: American Dramatists*. Volume 3. Edited by Matthew C. Roudane, 109-124. Detroit: Gale Research Inc., 1989.
A bibliographical essay assessing the critical reputation of Kennedy's work. Includes a primary and secondary bibliography of sources.

2007. Peterson, Bernard L. *Contemporary Black American Playwrights and Their Plays: A Biographical Directory and Dramatic Index,* 287-290. New York: Greenwood Press, 1988.
Peterson provides a biography as well as a staging history of Kennedy's plays.

2008. Wilkerson, Margaret B. "Adrienne Kennedy." *Dictionary of Literary Biography*. Volume 38. *Afro-American Writers After 1955: Dramatists and Prose Writers*. Edited by Thadious M. Davis and Trudier Harris, 162-168. Detroit: Gale Research Company, 1985.

This introductory article includes an extensive biographical and critical survey of Kennedy's achievements. A primary and secondary bibliography of her works is included.

Reviews and Criticism

See items 22, 23, 38, 49, 50, 53, 68, 72, 78, 101, 370.

A Beast's Story

See also *Cities in Bezique*

2009.   Sullivan, Dan. *Los Angeles Times* (Dec. 22, 1972), sect. 4: 21.

Cities in Bezique (includes *The Beast's Story* and *The Owl Answers*)

See items 35, 55, 2016, 2050.

2010.   Barnes, Clive. *New York Times* (Jan. 13, 1969): 26.

2011.   Benston, Kimberly W. "*Cities in Bezique*: Adrienne Kennedy's Expressionistic Vision." *CLA Journal,* 20, ii (Dec. 1976): 235-244.
Benston asserts Kennedy's expressionistic plays anticipated Baraka in breaking away from naturalism. Kennedy's surreal vision of the black psyche and the "strange power" of her dramas, such as *Cities of Bezique,* and two one-acts, *The Owl Answers* and *A Beast's Story,* emanates from her unique dramatic method, which includes "the breakdown of autonomous characters; the elaboration of a pattern of verbal themes; and rejection of the representational stage." The plays complement each other thematically (sexuality, family structure, death) and symbolically (animals, light and dark, music). The surreal use of theme and symbol converts action into "another signature of emotion . . . invok[ing] . . . the intimacies,

ecstacies, and anguish of the Afro-American's soul-
life."

2012. Cooke, Richard P. *Wall Street Journal* (Jan. 14, 1969): 18.

2013. Curb, Rosemary K. "Fragmented Selves in Adrienne
Kennedy's *Funnyhouse of a Negro* and *The Owl
Answers.*" *Theatre Journal*, 32, ii (May 1980): 180-
195.
Curb asserts Kennedy's uniqueness lies in her
startling symbolic representations of "archetypal
female obsessions" as well as her innovative use of
space and time on stage. Kennedy breaks away
from the traditional linear plot, dramatizing her
theme of the double horror of being black and
female by depicting the fragmented selves of Sarah
and She symbolically as other personalities, such
as Queen Victoria and Anne Boleyn. Noting the
dramatic structure of *Funnyhouse* and *Owl* is
concentric rather than linear, Curb says the
"concentric accumulation of images and symbols
creates poetic unity."

2014. Duberman, Martin. *Partisan Review*, 36, iii (1969): 483-
500.

2015. Kerr, Walter. *New York Times* (Jan. 19, 1969), sect. 2: 3.

2016. Miller, Jeanne-Marie. "Images of Women in Plays by Black
Playwrights." *CLA Journal*, 20, iv (June 1977):
494-507. Reprinted in *Women in American
Theatre*. Edited by Helen Krich Chinoy and Linda
Walsh Jenkins, 256-262. New York: Theatre
Communications Group, 1987.
Miller briefly discusses the position of the black
woman in selected plays of several African-
American playwrights, including Kennedy's *The
Owl Answers* and *Funnyhouse of a Negro*, Alice
Childress's *Trouble in Mind, Wedding Band, Wine
in the Wilderness*, and *Florence*, and J.E.
Franklin's *Black Girl*.

2017. Oliver, Edith. *The New Yorker*, 44 (Jan. 25, 1969): 77.

2018. Pasolli, Robert. *Village Voice* (Jan. 23, 1969): 43.
2019. Rudin, Seymour. *Massachusetts Review,* 10 (Summer 1969): 583-593.
2020. Sainer, Arthur. *Village Voice* (Sep. 25, 1969): 42-43.

2021. Splawn, P. Jane. "Adrienne Kennedy." In *Critical Survey of Drama: Supplement.* Edited by Frank Magill, 212-217. Pasadena, California: Salem Press, 1987.
Splawn provides a biographical sketch of Kennedy's life and achievements as well as a cursory analysis of her major plays.

2022. Simon, John. *Uneasy Stages: A Chronicle of the New York Theater, 1963-1973,* 181. New York: Random House, 1975.

2023. Tener, Robert L. "Theatre of Identity: Adrienne Kennedy's Portrait of the Black Woman." *Studies in Black Literature,* 6 ii (1975): 1-5.
Kennedy's play *The Owl Answers* is a complex mosaic of image, myth and metaphor used to portray the character She's fragmented self and her quest for psychic integration. Tener explores Kennedy's use of the complex symbolic associations of the owl as a controlling metaphor, which "anchors the heroine's problem of identity with the worlds of her white and black parents and her many self-images."

An Evening With Dead Essex

See item 3844.

2024. Gussow, Mel. *New York Times* (Mar. 18, 1974): 42.
2025. Sullivan, Dan. *Los Angeles Times* (Dec. 22, 1972), sect. 4: 21.

Funnyhouse of a Negro

See items 23, 2016, 2050, 3128.

2026.   Berson, Misha. "*Funnyhouse of a Negro:* Unusual Play
That Keeps Kicking." *San Francisco Chronicle*
(June 19, 1983), Datebook sect.: 45.
Berson discusses *Funnyhouse* prior to its opening
at the Lorraine Hansberry Theater in San Francisco.
Kennedy remarks that *Funnyhouse* "represents to
me 10 years of writing and struggling with
concepts." Although the play has continued to be
produced over the last 20 years, Kennedy was so
"devastated" by the hostile reaction of the critics to
the first commercial Off-Broadway production that
she avoided the theatre and went to England to
recover.

2027.   Blau, Herbert. "The American in American Gothic: The
Plays of Sam Shepard and Adrienne Kennedy."
Modern Drama, 27, iv (Dec. 1984): 520-539.
Reprinted in Blau's *The Eye of Prey: Subversions
of the Postmodern,* 42-64. Bloomington: Indiana
University Press, 1987.
Blau examines the work of Shepard and Kennedy,
whom he considers to be the "most original"
writers of their generation, to discuss "the
persistence of desire in language to overcome the
failed promise" of the American Dream. Kennedy,
Blau asserts, was "out of place" with the black
activists of the sixties, using indirect modes of
expressing issues of racial prejudice,
miscegenation, and black nationalism on stage.
Kennedy's highly expressionistic style, Blau
contends, depends on a complex symbolic system
using arcane and enigmatic images. Blau further
argues Kennedy "is . . . [not] entirely sure . . . that
she wouldn't rather be white. Whiteness is very
much engrained, maybe against her wishes, in her
lyrical quest for roots."

2028.   Brown, Lorraine A. "For the Characters of Myself":
Adrienne Kennedy's *Funnyhouse of a Negro.*"
Negro American Literature Forum, 3 (Sep. 1975):
86-88.

Brown maintains that Kennedy's plays "have gone
unheralded and unappreciated" and considers her to
be one of the most significant contemporary
American playwrights. The author describes how
Kennedy employs surrealistic and expressionistic
modes, dramatizing the struggle of Sarah, the
educated daughter of a black father and white mother
in overcoming the obstacles to achieving psychic
integration caused by her color, gender, and
intellectual enlightenment. The play demonstrates
through Sara's fragility "the age-old necessity of
possessing one's own soul. Her view that the
modern world is oblivious, if not downright
hostile, to spiritual struggles links her work to that
of many others writing for the contemporary
theater."

2029. Clurman, Harold. *Nation,* 198 (Feb. 10, 1964): 154.

2030. Dodson, Owen. "Who Has Seen the Wind? Playwrights and
the Black Experience." *Black American Literature
Forum,* 11, iii (Fall 1977): 108-116.
Dodson surveys the major works of several
contemporary African-American playwrights,
including Kennedy's *Funnyhouse of a Negro* and
Ntozake Shange's *for colored girls who have
considered suicide/when the rainbow is enuf.*

2031. Fletcher, Winona. "Who Put the 'Tragic' in the Tragic
Mulatto?" In *Women in American Theatre.* Edited
by Helen Krich Chinoy and Linda Walsh Jenkins,
262-268. New York: Theatre Communications
Group, 1987.
Fletcher traces the history of the portrayal of the
"tragic mulatto" by black and white writers of the
American theatre. "The myriad associations of
'white' with right, might, and superiority and
'black' with backwardness and inferiority set the
stage for the entrance of the tragic mulatto." The
author highlights some of the mulatto characters in
American drama that represent the older stereotype
of the mulatto as "docile, saintly, noble, forgiving"

as seen in Dion Boucicault's plays to the "new
tragic mulatto," such as in Adrienne Kennedy's
works, in which she "displays[s] the tortures and
nightmares . . . of a tragic mulatto searching for an
identity that is. . . . torn by the paradoxes of living
in a no man's (nor woman's) land." Ultimately,
Fletcher does not accuse any one party of "put[ting]
the tragic in the mulatto," and its portrayal,
Fletcher predicts, will continue to appear on stage,
as long as "the mulatto is viewed as a social
problem rather than as human being."

2032. Harrison, Paul Carter. "The Revolution of Black Theatre."
          American Theatre, 6 (Oct. 1989): 31-32, 116-118.
2033. Hay, Samuel. *Negro History Bulletin*, 36 (Jan. 1973): 5-8.
2034. Oliver, Edith. *The New Yorker*, 39 (Jan. 25, 1964): 76-77.
2035. Sontag, Susan. *Partisan Review*, 31 (Spring 1964): 284-
          293.
2036. Sullivan, Dan. *Los Angeles Times* (Dec. 22, 1972), sect.
          4: 21.
2037. Talbot, William. *Drama Critique*, 7 (Spring 1964): 92-96.
2038. Tapley, Mel. *N.Y. Amsterdam News* (Dec. 1, 1984): 26.
2039. Taubman, Howard. *New York Times* (Dec. 12, 1963): 46.
2040. _____. *New York Times* (Jan. 15, 1964): 25.

2041. Turner, Beth. "Beyond *Funnyhouse*: Adrienne Kennedy."
          Black Masks, 1 (Dec. 1984): 1, 8-9.
          Turner profiles Kennedy's playwriting activities
          focusing on *Funnyhouse*. This play, according to
          Turner, established Kennedy as a gifted dramatist
          and "catapulted [her] into the upper echelon of
          avant-garde playwrights," despite the fact that
          Kennedy was heavily criticized for the surreal and
          expressionistic forms she used to depict the tortured
          protagonist, Sarah.

2042. Turner, Darwin T. "Negro Playwrights and the Urban
          Negro." *CLA Journal*, 12, i (Sep. 1968): 19-25.
          Turner examines ways in which African-American
          playwrights dramatize the conflicts blacks face in
          the city. Kennedy's *Funnyhouse of a Negro* and

Alice Childress's *Trouble in Mind* are among the
plays discussed.

2043. Wilkerson, Margaret B. "Diverse Angles of Vision: Two
Black Women Playwrights." *Theatre Annual* 40,
(1985): 91-114.
Wilkerson contends Kennedy and Lorraine
Hansberry are mutually concerned with dramatizing
the socio-political forces that affect an individual,
making a statement about the human condition.
However, the playwrights' approach to style,
language and the depiction of the perceptions of
their characters are entirely different. Hansberry's
method is grounded in realism: "she insisted on
meaning, on affirmation, willing it into being,
even though she was deeply aware of the absurdity
and irrationality of human beings." Whereas,
Kennedy set her dramas "in the thin line between
fantasy and consciousness, between dream and
reality."

2044. Winn, Steven. *San Francisco Chronicle* (June 30, 1983):
64.

2045. Zolotow, Sam. "Actors Equity Gives New Play Permission
for 12 Weekly Shows." *New York Times* (Dec.
12, 1963): 46.
Zolotow announces the opening of *Funnyhouse of
a Negro* at the East End theater, starring Billie
Allen.

In His Own Write

2046. Barnes, Clive. *New York Times* (July 9, 1968): 30.
2047. Esslin, Martin. *New York Times* (July 14, 1968), sect. 2:
4.
2048. Wardle, Irving. *New York Times* (June 20, 1968): 50.

A Lancashire Lad

2049. Rich, Frank. *New York Times* (May 21, 1980): C3.

A Lesson in Dead Language

2050. Curb, Rosemary. "'Lesson I Bleed': Adrienne Kennedy's
       Blood Rites." In *Women in American Theatre.*
       Edited by Helen Krich Chinoy and Linda Walsh
       Jenkins, 50-56. New York: Theatre
       Communications Group, 1987.
       Curb asserts Kennedy employs the image of blood,
       charged with symbolic meaning, to "dramatize the
       horrors attendant on female adolescent rites of
       passage under patriarchy," in five of her plays: *A
       Lesson in Dead Language, A Rat's Mass, The
       Beast's Story, The Owl Answers,* and *Funnyhouse
       of a Negro.* In these plays, blood represents the
       ambiguousness of the teenage girl's transition to
       womanhood. On the one hand, the bleeding
       resulting from the menstrual cycle is natural. But,
       on the other hand, because the menstrual process is
       regarded as a "curse," and therefore should be hidden
       from the male-dominated society, the young girl
       "learns to hate her imperfect and uncontrollable
       body . . . menstrual blood is the sin . . . of the
       inherited guilt of womanhood."

A Movie Star Has to Star in Black and White

See item 19.

2051. Sainer, Arthur. *Village Voice* (Nov. 29, 1976): 97, 99.

2052. Stein, Ruthe. "She's Got Her Own Place In the Sun." *San
       Francisco Chronicle* (Jan. 31, 1980): 22.
       Kennedy, whose play *A Movie Star Has to Star in
       Black and White* opens in February at the Durham
       Studio Theater in Berkeley, remarks that it took
       many years to work through the fact that she would
       never "be a really famous playwright." But,
       Kennedy claims, she has "made peace" with herself.

A Rat's Mass

See item 2050.

2053. Ansorge, Peter. *Plays and Players*, 17 (July 1970): 51.
2054. Barnes, Clive. *New York Times* (Nov. 1, 1969): 39.
2055. Huges, Catharine R. *Plays and Players*, 17 (Nov. 1969): 14-
       15.
2056. Scott, John S. *Players*, 47 (Feb.-Mar. 1972): 130-131.

She Talks to Beethoven

2057. *American Theatre*, 6 (June 1989): 11.
       Jacobson announces that *She Talks to Beethoven*
       will be performed at River Arts Repertory
       International Writers Festival in Woodstock, New
       York.

Solo Voyages

2058. Gussow, Mel. *New York Times* (Sep. 20, 1985): C3.

Kerr, E. Kathryn

Selected Plays

2059. *Juno's Swans* (Second Stage, 1985)
       Playscript: *Juno's Swans*. New York: Dramatists
       Play Service, 1986.
2060. *Lloyd Nolan Was My Co-Pilot* (unproduced)

Profiles

See item 100

2061. Lawson, Carol. "Broadway." New York Times (Aug. 7,
       1981): C2.
       Lawson briefly profiles Kerr's theatrical career.

Reviews

Juno's Swans

2062. Bardacke, Frances. *San Diego Magazine*, 40 (May 1988): 66.
2063. Barnes, Clive. *New York Post* (May 29, 1985). Reprinted in item 2065.
2064. Beaufort, John. *Christian Science Monitor* (June 7, 1985). Reprinted in item 2065.
2065. *New York Theatre Critics' Reviews*, 46 (Sep. 16, 1985): 226-229.
2066. Rich, Frank. *New York Times* (May 29, 1985): C18. Reprinted in item 2065.
2067. Simon, John. *New York*, 18 (June 10, 1985): 93.
2068. Winer, Linda. *USA Today* (May 29, 1985). Reprinted in item 2065.

Kesselman, Wendy

Selected Plays

2069. *Becca* (Interart, 1970)
2070. *The Cameo* (Actors Theatre of Louisville, Kentucky, 1982-1983)
2071. *The Griffin and the Minor Canon* (lyrics by Ellen Fitzhugh, Music-Theater Group, 1988-1989)
2072. *I Love You, I Love You Not* (Ensemble Studio Theatre, 1983)
       Playscript: *I Love You, I Love You Not*. New York: Samuel French, 1983.
2073. *The Juniper Tree: A Tragic Household Tale* (St. Clement's Church, 1983)
       Playscript: *The Juniper Tree: A Tragic Household Tale*. New York: Samuel French, 1985.
2074. *Maggie Magalita* (Lamb's Theatre Company, 1986)
2075. *Merry-Go-Round* (78th Street Theatre Lab, 1983)
2076. *My Sister in This House* (Second Stage, 1981)
       Playscript: *My Sister in This House*. New York: Samuel French, 1982.

Profiles

See items 87, 100.

2077. Swain, Elizabeth. *Contemporary Dramatists*. 4th edition.
Edited by D.L. Kirkpatrick, 294-296. Chicago: St.
James Press, 1988.
Swain briefly assesses the life and work of
Kesselman. The entry includes a list of her plays.

Reviews and Criticism

See item 54.

I Love You, I Love You Not

2078. Dace, Tish. *Plays International*, 2 (May 1987): 50-51.
2079. *Drama-Logue* (May 7-13, 1987): 25.
2080. Gussow, Mel. *New York Times* (June 1, 1983): C17.
2081. Holden, Stephen. *New York Times* (Mar. 29, 1987): 54.
2082. Massa, Robert. *Village Voice* (June 14, 1983): 100.
2083. Rogoff, Gordon. *Village Voice* (Apr. 7, 1987): 85-86.

The Juniper Tree

2084. Stone, Laurie. *Village Voice* (May 10, 1983): 85.

Maggie Magalita

2085. Feingold, Michael. *Village Voice* (May 20, 1986): 95-96.
2086. Gussow, Mel. *New York Times* (May 8, 1986): C18.
2087. Simon, John. *New York*, 19 (May 19, 1986): 100.

My Sister in This House

See item 23.

2088. Billington, Michael. *Guardian* (May 30, 1987): 12.
2089. Bronski, M. *Gay Community News*, 11 (Sep. 24, 1983): 6.
2090. Christiansen, Richard. *Chicago Tribune* (Nov. 24, 1983),
sect. 2: 26.
2091. Churnin, Nancy. *Los Angeles Times* (Sep. 22, 1987),
Calendar sect.: 5.
2092. Gussow, Mel. *New York Times* (Mar. 29, 1981): 61.

2093. Hart, Lynda. "They Don't Even Look Like Maids
        Anymore": Wendy Kesselman's *My Sister in This
        House.*" In *Making a Spectacle: Feminist Essays
        in Women's Theatre.* Edited by Lynda Hart, 131-
        146. Ann Arbor: University of Michigan Press,
        1989.
        Hart provides a feminist analysis of Kesselman's
        play, which is based on a true story of the brutal
        murder of two French women by their maids who
        happened to be sisters. Kesselman's interpretation
        of the murder and the motives of the sisters is
        contrary to how the sisters have been popularly
        viewed as "horrifying perversions[s] of woman."
        Kesselman also diverges from Genet's version of
        the murder. In his play *The Maids,* Genet
        dramatizes the two sisters as "monstrous
        psychological aberrations." As Hart demonstrates,
        Kesselman chose to explain the maids' motives
        from a feminist vantage point. The playwright's
        feminist strategy includes pushing the male
        characters off stage, leaving the four women
        characters: the two mistresses and the two maids.
        Thus, Kesselman re-tells the story from the point
        of view of the maids. Hart approaches her analysis
        by examining two social taboos the sisters
        transgress and the consequences these infractions
        have for the mistresses as well as the sisters. First,
        by savagely murdering their mistresses, they
        violate the "patriarchal prescription" which
        stipulates that women are docile and gentle
        creatures. The second taboo the maids transgress is
        their lesbianism by which they "break with
        heterosexuality." Hart concludes Kesselman "looks
        at Christine and Lea Papin [the maids] and finds in
        their lives sisters to all of us who would dare to
        claim them."

2094. Hoffman, Jan. *Village Voice* (Nov. 25, 1981): 89.
2095. Kalem, T.E. *Time,* 117 (Apr. 6, 1981): 74.
2096. Kilkelly, Ann Gavere. *Women & Performance,* 3, i (1986):
        28-34.
2097. Koyama, Christine. *Chicago,* 33 (Jan. 1984): 32.

2098. Radin, Victoria. *New Statesman*, 113 (June 12, 1987): 25.

2099. Ray, Robin. *Punch*, 292 (June 10, 1987): 58.

2100. Rich, Frank. *New York Times* (Nov. 23, 1981), sect. 3: 17.

2101. Richards, David. *Washington Post* (Sep. 8, 1984), sect. C: 1.

2102. Schroeder, Patricia R. "Locked Behind the Proscenium: Feminist Strategies in *Getting Out* and *My Sister In This House*." *Modern Drama*, 32, i (Mar. 1989): 104-114.
Helene Keyssar, among other scholars, contends feminist values can only be successfully dramatized by replacing conventional dramatic modes with experimental theatrical techniques. Schroeder challenges this assumption, asserting that formal realism and traditional dramatic structures can sustain feminist principles. Furthermore, the author questions the degree to which realistic plays are "necessarily as conventional as they appear." Schroeder explores "the potential power of formal realism when appropriated for feminist purposes" by analyzing Kesselman's *My Sister In This House* and Marsha Norman's *Getting Out*. Although grounded in formal realism in depicting the female protagonists entrapped in an "unyielding, traditional society" these plays also include experimental elements such as divided characters and pantomime.

2103. Simon, John. *New York*, 14 (Dec. 7, 1981): 159, 162.

2104. Wardle, Irving. *Times* (London) (May 28, 1987): 23a

2105. Warnick, Clay. *Washington Post* (Sep. 7, 1984), Weekend sect.: 9.

2106. Winn, Steven. *San Francisco Chronicle* (Jan 20, 1984): 61.

2107. Wolf, Matt. *Plays and Players*, 407 (Aug. 1987): 25-26.

Kurtti, Casey

Selected Plays

2108. *Catholic School Girls* (Douglas Fairbanks Theater, 1982)

Playscript: *Catholic School Girls*. New York: Samuel French, 1982.

2109. *The Concept* (conceived by Lawrence Sacharow, text by Kurtti, Circle in the Square, 1986)

2110. *Three Ways Home* (Astor Place Theater, 1988)
Playscript: *Three Ways Home*. New York: Samuel French, 1989.

Reviews

Catholic School Girls

2111. Corliss, Richard. *Time*, 119 (April 12, 1982): 77.
2112. Faber, Roderick M. *Village Voice* (Apr. 13, 1982): 83.
2113. Gussow, Mel. *New York Times* (Apr. 6, 1982): C14.
2114. Kerr, Walter. *New York Times* (Apr. 11, 1982): D3.
2115. Shirley, Don. *Los Angeles Times* (July 22, 1983), sect. 6: 14.

The Concept

2116. DeVries, Hilary. *Christian Science Monitor* (Jan. 9, 1987): 1.

2117. Freedman, Samuel G. "Drug Play To Reflect New Area." *New York Times* (Sep. 22, 1986), sect. B: 1. Freedman discusses the "reshaped" revival of *The Concept*, which was originally produced Off Broadway in 1968.

2118. Gussow, Mel. *New York Times* (Oct. 8, 1986): C19.

Three Ways Home

See item 905.

2119. Beaufort, John. *Christian Science Monitor* (May 20, 1988), Arts and Leisure sect.: 22.
2120. Bingham, Carolyn. *Los Angeles Sentinel* (Apr. 13, 1989): B6.
2121. *Chicago Defender* (Oct. 7, 1989): 30.
2122. Gussow, Mel. *New York Times* (May 12, 1988): C27.

2123. Lewis, Barbara Brewster. *N.Y. Amsterdam News* (June 11, 1988): 29.

Lamb, Myrna

Selected Plays

2124. *Apple Pie* (New York Shakespeare Festival, Public Theatre, 1976)
Playscript: *Women & Performance,* 1, ii (Winter 1984): 73.
2125. *Ballad of Brooklyn* (Brooklyn Academy, 1979)
2126. *Because I Want To* (Interart, 1974)
2127. *Crab Quadrille* (Women's Interart Center, 1976)
2128. *I Lost a Pair of Gloves Yesterday* (New Feminist Repertory Theatre, 1972)
Playscript: see item 73.
2129. *The Mod Donna; A Space-Age Musical Soap Opera with Breaks for Commercials* (Public Theatre, 1970)
Playscript: *The Mod Donna and Scyklon Z: Plays of Women's Liberation.* New York: Pathfinder Press, Inc., 1971.
2130. *Olympic Park* (Interart, 1978)
2131. *The Sacrifice* (AMDA Theater, 1977)
2132. *Scylon Z; A Group of Pieces With a Point* (1969)
Includes:
But What have You Done For Me Lately?
The Butcher Shop
Playscript: *Aphra,* 1, ii (Winter, 1970): 28-50.
In the Shadow of the Crematoria
Monologia
Pas de Deux
The Serving Girls and the Lady
Playscript: see item 2129.
Yesterday Is Over (Interart, 1980)
2133. *Two Party System* (Interart, 1974)
2134. *With a Little Help from My Friends* (Town Hall Theatre, 1974)

Profiles and Interviews

See items 73, 87 and page 7.

2135. Thurston, Linda. "An Interview with Myrna Lamb." *Second Wave*, 1 (1971): 12-15.

Lamb reveals how her experiences of being a woman, a feminist and a writer affect the creation of her plays. The vital role of politics in Lamb's plays is reflected in her comment, "I'm very hurt when people interpret my work as purely personal and psychological and don't see the political . . . substructure." She hopes her plays will effect social change. Lamb also talks about the feminist movement and how it has revolutionized the image women have of themselves, of "seeing themselves differently, seeing themselves as potential artists, not merely cooks and bottle-washers." Lamb foresees a "renaissance of rather magnificent nature" in women's art.

Reviews and Critical Studies

See items 38, 54, 68, 78, 99.

Apple Pie

2136. Barnes, Clive. *New York Times* (Feb. 13, 1976): 18.
Reprinted in item 2141.
2137. Beaufort, John. *Christian Science Monitor* (Feb. 23, 1976): 25.
Reprinted in item 2141.
2138. Glover, William. *San Francisco Chronicle* (Feb. 17, 1976): 39.
2139. Gottfried, Martin. *New York Post* (Feb. 13, 1976): 18.
Reprinted in item 2141.
2140. Kerr, Walter. *New York Times* (Feb. 22, 1976), sect. 2: 7.
2141. *New York Theatre Critics' Review*, 37 (Mar. 1, 1976): 340-43.

2142. Patraka, Vivian M. "Notes On Technique in Feminist Drama: *Apple Pie* and *Signs of Life*." *Women & Performance*, 1, ii (Winter 1984): 58-71.

Patraka observes Lamb's *Apple Pie* and Joan
Schenkar's *Signs of Life* have several things in
common. First, Patraka contends that the plays
have been largely ignored by the critics because
they deviate from conventional dramatic forms and
are imbued with a feminist sensibility. Secondly,
both playwrights employ themes and images from
the feminist experimental theatre: mourning, rage,
empowerment, and celebration. And thirdly, the
politicization of gender is central to their dramatic
purpose. Yet, Patraka asserts, the plays do differ in
the way each dramatist "produces recognition and
response." These divergent approaches, Patraka
maintains, reflect "a path of evolution in feminist
theatre. Lamb, for example, uses "hot" techniques,
drama that is "confrontational and explosive" and
that represents earlier modes on Patraka's
evolutionary scale, while Schenkar utilizes "cool"
techniques, "analytical and restrained" in approach
and which signify later modes in feminist theatre
development.

2143. Sharp, Christopher. *Women's Wear Daily* (Feb. 17, 1976).
Reprinted in item 2141.
2144. Simon, John. *New York,* 9 (Mar. 1, 1976): 60.
2145. Watt, Douglas. *New York Daily News* (Feb. 13, 1976).
Reprinted in item 2141.

But What Have You Done for Me Lately?

See items 16, 2156.

Crab Quadrille

2146. Crossette, Barbara. *New York Times* (Nov. 19, 1976): C8.
2147. Gussow, Mel. *New York Times* (Dec. 6, 1976): 46.
2148. Munk, Erica. *Village Voice* (Dec. 13, 1976): 113.
2149. *N. Y. Amsterdam News* (Dec. 25, 1976): D-16.

2150. *New York Times* (Nov. 11, 1976), sect. C: 8.

> A brief report, written on the first day of rehearsals, discussing *Crab Quadrille* and Lamb's theatrical background.

I Lost a Pair of Gloves Yesterday

2151.   Weiner, Bernard. *San Francisco Chronicle* (Mar. 8, 1972): 52.

Mod Donna

See page 23.

2152.   Barnes, Clive. *New York Times* (May 4, 1970): 48.

2153.   Bender, Marilyn. "Women's Liberation Taking to the Stage." *New York Times* (Mar. 26, 1970): 60. Bender previews *Mod Donna,* shortly to open at the New York Shakespeare Festival. In an interview, Lamb comments feminists criticize her for selecting a male director (Joe Papp), "I'm a feminist but I can't be a female chauvinist."

2154.   Bruckenfeld, Dick. *Village Voice* (May 7, 1970): 53.
2155.   Gluek, Grace. *New York Times* (May 10, 1970), sect. 2: 1, 24.

2156.   Gornick, Vivian. "Toward a Definition of the Female Sensibility." In *Essays in Feminism,* 108-127. New York: Harper & Row, 1978. Gornick examines several literary works, which she sees as signaling the development of female sensibility. Of the works she examines two are plays by Myrna Lamb: *Mod Donna* and *What Have You Done For Me Lately?* Gornick views these pieces as "fine examples of the femaleness of life operating to illuminate human experience." Lamb relies heavily on language to pursue the quest of the female self. Through dialogue, Lamb pierces through the layers of anger and defensiveness in order to "bring them to the light of consciousness" and in turn re-create self.

2157. _____. *Village Voice* (May 28, 1970): 47, 50.
2158. Kerr, Walter. *New York Times* (May 10, 1970), sect. 2: 1, 3.

2159. _____. *New York Times* (May 31, 1970), sect. 2: 6, 28. Readers respond to Grace Gluek and Walter Kerr's reviews of *Mod Donna*.

Olympic Park

2160. Dunning, Jennifer. *New York Times* (Dec. 21, 1978): C16.
2161. Sainer, Arthur. *Village Voice* (Jan. 1, 1978): 78.

Yesterday Is Over

2162. Feingold, Michael. *Village Voice* (July 2, 1980): 63-65.

Lauro, Shirley

Selected Plays

2163. *The Contest* (Ensemble Studio Theatre, 1976)
2164. *Nothing Immediate* (Actors Theatre of Louisville, Kentucky, 1980)
2165. *The Coal Diamond* (Circle Repertory Company, 1980) Playscript: *The Coal Diamond*. New York: Dramatists Play Service, 1979; *The Best Short Plays 1980*. Edited by Stanley Richards, 1-19. Radnor, Pennsylvania: Chilton Book Company, 1980.
2166. *Open Admissions* (Ensemble Studio Theatre, 1981) Playscript: *Open Admissions*. New York: Samuel French, 1982.
2167. *Pearls on the Moon* (staged reading, Women's Project, 1984-1985)
2168. *A Piece of My Heart* (Harold Prince Theatre, Philadelphia, 1989).
2169. *Sunday Go to Meetin'* (Actors Theatre of Louisville, Kentucky, 1985-1986)

Profiles and Interviews

2170. *Contemporary Authors: A Bio-Bibliographical Guide.*
　　　　　Volume 126. Edited by Susan M. Trosky, 251-
　　　　　255. Detroit: Gale Research Inc., 1989.
　　　　　The entry includes a biographical sketch, list of
　　　　　plays, and an interview with Lauro.

2171. *Contemporary Theatre, Film, and Television.* Volume 1.
　　　　　Edited by Monica M. O'Donnell, 308-309. Detroit:
　　　　　Gale Research Company, 1984.
　　　　　The entry provides a biographical sketch of Lauro's
　　　　　life, education, and career as well as a list of her
　　　　　plays and awards.

2172. Gussow, Mel. *New York Times* (Dec. 16, 1983): C2.
　　　　　Gussow briefly profiles Lauro on the eve of the
　　　　　Broadway opening of *Open Admissions.*

Reviews

The Coal Diamond

See also items 2179, 2180.

2173. Gussow, Mel. *New York Times* (June 15, 1979), sect. C:
　　　　　4.
2174. _____. *New York Times* (Mar. 23, 1980): 55.

The Contest

2175. Cook, Bruce. *National Observer* (June 21, 1975): 20.
2176. Gussow, Mel. *New York Tmes* (Oct. 27, 1976): 52.
2177. Tucker, Carll. *Village Voice* (Nov. 22, 1976): 97.

First and Thirty

See *The Coal Diamond*

Lost and Found

See *The Coal Diamond*

Nothing Immediate

2178. Christiansen, Richard. *Chicago Tribune* (Aug. 15, 1985), sect. 5: 10.
2179. Gussow, Mel. *New York Times* (Mar. 23, 1980), sect. 1: 55.
2180. Koehler, Robert. *Los Angeles Times* (Aug. 29, 1983), sect. 6: 6.
2181. Kroll, Jack. *Newsweek,* 95 (Mar. 31, 1980): 70.

Open Admissions

2182. Albright, William. *Houston Post* (May 5, 1985), sect. J: 4.
       Albright previews the Alley Theatre's production of *Open Admissions* at the Arena Stage. To the criticism that the play lacks a solution to the problem of educating children, Lauro responds, "I'm a creative writer, not an urban education planner. The goal of the playwright is to communicate experience."

2183. _____. *Houston Post* (May 11, 1985), sect. C: 11.
2184. Barnes, Clive. *New York Post* (Jan. 30, 1984).
       Reprinted in item 2195.
2185. Beaufort, John. *Christian Science Monitor* (Feb. 9, 1984), Arts and Leisure sect.: 29.
       Reprinted in item 2195.
2186. Crouch, Stanley. *Village Voice* (Feb. 14, 1984): 96-97.
2187. Freedman, Samuel. *New York Times* (Jan. 22, 1984), sect. 2: H4, H10.
2188. Gill, Brendan. *The New Yorker,* 59 (Feb. 13, 1984): 118-119.
2189. Gussow, Mel. *New York Times* (June 14, 1981): 66.
2190. _____. *New York Times* (Feb. 2, 1984): C14.
2191. Hughes, Catherine. *America,* 150 (Mar. 24, 1984): 216.
2192. Kissel, Howard. *Women's Wear Daily* (Jan. 30, 1984).
       Reprinted in item 2195.

2193. Lauro, Shirley. "A Playwright Finds a Subject Worth a Play." *Christian Science Monitor* (Nov. 1, 1988): 26.

Lauro explains that *Open Admissions* emerged
from her experiences as a college speech instructor
in New York City. The college's admissions
policy was "open," which meant that anyone could
attend provided they had a high school diploma.
Lauro remarks that such an policy created a
"schizoid situation"—her class was a jumble of
students whose reading levels ranged from
minimally literate to college level.

2194. Massa, Robert. *Village Voice* (June 17-23, 1981): 77.
2195. *New York Theatre Critics' Reviews*, 45 (Jan. 16, 1984):
       380-85
2196. Nightingale, Benedict. *New York Times* (Feb. 5, 1984):
       H5.
2197. Piette, Alain. *Theatre Journal*, 35, iv (Dec. 1983): 553-554.
2198. Rich, Frank. *New York Times* (Dec. 27, 1981): D6, D24.
2199. _____. *New York Times* (Jan. 30, 1984): C13.
       Reprinted in item 2195.

2200. Robertson, Nan. *New York Times* (May 17, 1985): C2.
       Robertson announces Lauro was awarded two
       fellowships for playwriting. See related articles:
       Shepard, Richard F. *New York Times* (Sep. 8,
       1988): C22 and *Variety* (Oct. 5, 1988): 118.

2202. Schickel, Richard. *Time*, 123 (Feb. 13, 1984): 75.
       Reprinted in item 2195.
2203. Simon, John. *New York*, 14 (Nov. 9, 1981): 72.
2204. _____. *New York*, 17 (Feb. 13, 1984): 69.
2205. _____. (Nov. 3, 1989): 80.
2206. Watt, Douglas. *New York Daily News* (Jan. 30, 1984).
       Reprinted in item 2195.
2207. Wilson, Edwin. *Wall Street Journal* (Feb. 10, 1984): 24.
       Reprinted in item 2195.

2208. Winer, Laura. "Lauro Wins Hull-Warriner Award." *New
       York Times* (Dec. 21, 1981): C15.
       The *Times* reports Lauro won the Dramatist Guild
       Council's Hull-Warriner Award for *Open
       Admissions*.

A Piece of My Heart

2209. Collins, William B. *Philadelphia Inquirer* (Mar. 6, 1989), Features sect.: E4.
2210. Santiago, Chiori. *American Theatre*, 6 (May 1989): 9. Santiago briefly describes *A Piece of My Heart*, which opened at the Philadelphia Festival Theatre for New Plays.

2211. *Variety* (Mar. 29, 1989): 61.

Lebow, Barbara

Selected Plays

2212. *Cyparis* (Academy Theater, Atlanta, 1987)
2213. *The Keepers* (Academy Theater, Atlanta, 1988)
2214. *A Shayna Maidel* (Westside Arts Theater, 1987) Playscript: *A Shayna Maidel*. New York: New American Library, 1988; *Southern Exposure*, 14, iii & iv (May/Aug. 1986): 97-98 (excerpt).

Profiles

See items 819, 820.

Reviews

A Shayna Maidel

2215. Dace, Trish. *Plays and Players*, 4 (Oct. 1988): 38-39.
2216. Gussow, Mel. *New York Times* (Oct. 30, 1987), sect. 3: 16.
2217. Kramer, Mimi. *The New Yorker*, 63 (Nov. 30, 1987): 121-122.
2218. Ransom, Rebecca. *Southern Exposure*, 14 (May/Aug 1986): 8.
2219. Sherbert, Linda. *Atlantic Journal-Constitution* (May 18, 1986), sect. J: 2.
2220. Shirley, Don. *Los Angeles Times* (July 4, 1990), sect. F: 7.

Long, Katherine

Selected Plays

2221. *Ariel Bright* (Ensemble Studio Theatre, 1984)
        Playscript: *The Best Short Plays 1986.* Edited by
        Ramon Delgado, 177-198. New York: Applause,
        1986.
2222. *Sedalia Run* (Ensemble Studio Theatre, 1988)
2223. *Two Part Harmony* (Ensemble Studio Theatre, 1980)

Profiles

See profile in item 2221.

Reviews

Ariel Bright

2224. Gussow, Mel. *New York Times* (June 1, 1984), sect. 3: 5.

Two Part Harmony

2225. Faber, R.M. *Village Voice* (June 16, 1980): 80, 85.
2226. Gussow, Mel. *New York Times* (June 7, 1980): 11.

Loomer, Lisa

Selected Plays

2227. *Accelerando* (reading, New Dramatists, 1989)
2228. *Birds* (South Coast Repertory, Costa Mesa, 1986)
2229. *A Crowd of Two* (with Rita Nachtmann, American Place
        Theatre, 1981)
2230. *Looking for Angels* (New York Shakespeare Festival,
        Public Theatre, 1986)
2231. *New Age Romance* (Omaha Magic Theatre, Omaha, 1987-
        1988)

Reviews

Birds

2232. *American Theatre*, 5, (June 1988): 5-6.

2233. Christon, Lawrence. *Los Angeles Times* (July 6, 1986),
       Calendar sect.: 44.
       Christon reports Loomer's *Birds* is part of a series
       of staged readings, *Second Series*, produced by
       South Coast Repertory. See also item 2234.

2234. Drake, Sylvie. *Los Angeles Times* (July 16, 1987), sect. 6:
       5, 7.
2235. *Variety* (Dec. 10, 1985): 102.

Looking for Angels

2236. Solomon, Alisa. *Village Voice* (July 29, 1986): 81.

Lott, Karmyn

Selected Plays

2237. *Hot Sauce* (Theater Off Park, 1984))
2238. *We Shall* (Theater Guinevere, 1987)

Profiles

2239. Peterson, Bernard L. *Contemporary Black American
       Playwrights and Their Plays: A Biographical
       Directory and Dramatic Index*, 310. New York:
       Greenwood Press, 1988.
       Peterson provides a biography as well as a staging
       history of Lott's major plays.

Reviews

Hot Sauce

2240. Shepard, Richard F. *New York Times* (June 11, 1984):
       C17.
       On the day of its opening, Shepard briefly discusses
       Hot Sauce, directed by Toni Dorfman.

We Shall

2241. Bruckner, D. *New York Times* (Jan. 29, 1987): C17.

McDonald, Heather

Selected Plays

2242. *Faulkner's Bicycle* (Yale Repertory Theater, New Haven, 1985)
2243. *Available Light* (Actors Theatre of Louisville, Kentucky, 1984-1985)

Reviews

Faulkner's Bicycle

See item 75.

2244. Austin, Gayle. "Woman/Text/Theatre." *Performing Arts Journal*, 9, ii & iii (1985): 185-191.
       Austin briefly mentions *Faulkner's Bicycle* as an example of the theme of errant daughter returning home to confront her past. According to Austin, the errant daughter "often displays the 'autobiographical fallacy': she is the most underwritten character on stage."

2245. Gussow, Mel. *New York Times* (June 16, 1985), sect. 2: 3, 10.
2246. Kupritz, S.H. *Plays International*, 4 (July 1989): 36.
2247. Rich, Frank. *New York Times* (June 10, 1985), sect. 3: 15.
2248. Feingold, Michael. *Village Voice* (June 10, 1985): 109-110.

Mack, Carol K.

Selected Plays

2249. *A.K.A. Marleen*
       Playscripts: see item 2258.

2250. *American Dreamer* (staged reading, Denver Center Theatre
         Company, Denver, 1985-1986)
2251. *Esther* (Promenade Theater, 1977)
2252. *From a Small Room* (staged reading, Women's Project,
         1984-1985)
2253. *Gazebo and Postcards* (staged reading, Women's Project,
         1980-1981)
2254. *Half Time At Halcyon Days* (staged reading, Women's
         Project, 1983-1984)
         Playscript: *The Best Short Plays of 1985*. Edited
         by Ramon Delgado, 147-175. Radnor,
         Pennsylvania: Chilton Book Company, 1985; see
         item 2258.
2255. *Hi-Tech* (Actors Theatre of Louisville, Kentucky, 1982-
         1983)
2256. *The Magenta Shift* (staged reading, Women's Project, 1984-
         1985)
2257. *Necessary Fictions* (New Dramatists, 1988)
2258. *Postcards* (Ensemble Studio Theatre, 1983)
         Playscripts: *Postcards and Other Short Plays*. New
         York: Samuel French, 1984.
2259. *Revisions on Eden Rock* (staged reading, Women's Project,
         1985-1986)
2260. *A Safe Place* (Berkshire Theatre Festival, Stockbridge,
         Maryland, 1981)
2261. *Survival Games* (Berkshire Theatre Festival, Stockbridge,
         Massachusetts, 1980)
2262. *Territorial Rites* (Women's Project, American Place
         Theater, 1983)
         Playscript: *Wordplays 2: An Anthology of New
         American Drama*. New York: Performing Arts
         Journal Publications, 1982.

Profiles

See profile in item 2254.

2263. *Contemporary Theatre, Film, and Television*. Volume 1.
         Edited by Monica M. O'Donnell, 333-334. Detroit:
         Gale Research Company, 1984.
         This entry provides a brief biography.

Reviews

Esther

2264. Gussow, Mel. *New York Times* (Nov. 30, 1977), sect. 3: 26.
2265. Mancini, Joseph. *New York Post* (Nov. 30, 1977): 61.
2266. Simon, John. *New York*, 10 (Dec. 12, 1977): 103.
2267. Speck, P. Gregory. *Show Business* (Dec. 1, 1977): 19.

Postcards

2268. Gussow, Mel. *New York Times* (May 13, 1983): C3.

Territorial Rites

2269. Gussow, Mel. *New York Times* (June 6, 1983): C12.
2270. Hoffman, Jan. *Village Voice* (June 14, 1983): 97-98.
2271. Simon, John. *New York*, 16 (June 20, 1983): 74-75.

MacKeaney, Grace

Selected Plays

2272. *Chicks* (Actors Space, 1986)
2273. *Deadfall* (Actors Theatre of Louisville, Kentucky, 1986-1987)
2274. *Fits and Starts* (Yale Repertory Theatre, New Haven, 1976)
2275. *How It Hangs* (Judith Anderson Theatre, 1989)
         Playscript: *The Best Short Plays of 1987*. Edited by Ramon Delgado, 93-123. New York: Applause, 1987.
2276. *Last Looks* (Center Stage, 1983)
         Playscript: *Last Looks*. New York: Dramatists Play Service, 1984.
2277. *Who They Are and How It Is With Them* (New American Plays Festival, Noyes Center, Evanston, 1979)

Profiles

See profile in item 2275.

Reviews

Deadfall

2278. Roberts, Peter. *Plays International*, 2 (May 1987): 49.
2279. DeVries, Hillary. *Christian Science Monitor* (Apr. 2, 1987): 31-32.

How It Hangs

2280. Loynd, Ray. *Los Angeles Times* (May 20, 1988), sect. 6: 11.

Last Looks

2281. Richards, David. *Washington Post* (Oct. 7, 1982): D11.

McLaughlin, Ellen

Selected Plays

2282. *Days and Nights Within* (Actors Theatre of Louisville, Kentucky,1985)
Playscript: *Days and Nights Within*. New York: Theatre Communications Group, 1985.
2283. *Infinity's House* (New Dramatists, 1989)
2284. *A Narrow Bed* (Perry Street Theatre, 1987)
Playscript: *A Narrow Bed*. New York: Samuel French, 1987.

Profiles and Interviews

2285. Eustis, Oskar. "Duet for One: Changing Roles—From Actress to Writer and Back—Keeps Ellen McLaughlin On Course. *American Theatre*, 6 (July/Aug. 1989): 19-21.
Eustis weaves facts about McLaughlin's life with her reflections concerning her dual career as actress and playwright about which McLaughlin says, "I'd go crazy if I was just an actress . . . being a writer gives me a feeling of control over my work and life that I could never have as just an actor. I can go

back to a world where I'm utterly in control. It's
mine, mine." Although her plays are not discussed
in detail, Eustis shows McLaughlin expressing
dissatisfaction with several theatrical conventions.
She is skeptical, for example, of the notion that
actions serve as the catalyst for change in a
character; that is, a character changes because of
something she does or in response to an event.
Rather, McLaughlin maintains "actions are
revelations of character." She also finds
"conventional theatrical progression" restrictive and
thus, is unable to follow the conventional rule of
playwriting: "every scene and everything anybody
says should contribute to the story." McLaughlin
prefers to "work with an image, a primary impulse
which is evocative in some way I don't understand."

Reviews

Days and Nights Within

2286.   Gussow, Mel. *New York Times* (Mar. 28, 1985): C16.
2287.   Sullivan, Dan. *Los Angeles Times* (Nov. 8, 1986), sect. 6:
        7.
2288.   Marshall, Kevin. *Theatre Journal*, 37, iv (Dec. 1985): 499-
        500.

Infinity's House

2289.   Gussow, Mel. *New York Times* (Apr. 5, 1990): C19.

2290.   Herman, Jan. "SCR [South Coast Repertory] Cancels
        Premiere of *Infinity's House.*" *Los Angeles Times*
        (Dec. 2, 1988), sect. 6: 26. See related article: Jan
        Herman. "Author Assails SCR for Dropping Play."
        Los Angeles Times (Dec. 15, 1988), sect. 6: 7.

2291.   Wilson, Edwin. *Wall Street Journal* (Apr. 5, 1990): A16.

Malpede, Karen

Selected Plays

2292. *Better People* (Theatre for the New City, 1990)
2293. *The End of War* (New Cycle Theatre, 1982)
2294. *Genetic Dreams* (Theatre for the New City, 1989)
       Playscript: *A Century of Plays by American
       Women*. Edited by Rachel France, 204-209. New
       York: Richards Rosen Press, 1979.
2295. *Making Peace: A Fantasy* (New Cycle Theater, 1979-1980)
2296. *A Monster Has Stolen the Sun* (New Cycle Theater, 1981)
       Playscript: *A Monster Has Stolen the Sun: And
       Other Plays*. Marlboro, Vermont: Marlboro Press,
       1987. Also includes: *The End of War* and *Sappho
       and Aphrodite*.
2297. *Rebeccah* (Playwrights Horizons, 1976)
2298. *Sappho and Aphrodite* (New Cycle Theatre, 1983)
2299. *Us* (Living Theater, Theatre for the New City, 1987)

Profiles

See items 3, 9, 83, 87.

2300. *Contemporary Authors: A Bio-Bibliographical Guide*.
       Volume 26. New Revision Series. Edited by Hal
       May, 258-259. Detroit: Gale Research Inc., 1989.
       This biographical sketch includes a list of
       Malpede's plays, works and awards. The
       playwright also comments on her achievements as
       a playwright and the role of women in the theatre.

General Criticism

See item 2296.

Reviews

The End of War

See items 65, 2296.

2301. Berman, Paul. *Village Voice* (June 15, 1982): 98.

Making Peace

2302. Armstrong, Gordon. *Theatre Journal*, 32, ii (May 1980):
          268-269.

A Monster Has Stolen the Sun

See items 2296.

2303. Massa, Robert. *Village Voice* (Mar. 11-17, 1981): 82.

Rebeccah

2304. Malpede, Karen. "*Rebeccah:* Rehearsal Notes." In *Women
          in American Theatre.* Edited by Helen Krich
          Chinoy and Linda Walsh Jenkins, 308-310. New
          York: Theatre Communications Group, 1987.
          Malpede's brief notes of the *Rebeccah* rehearsal
          reveal a few of the dramatic strategies used by the
          company.

Sappho and Aphrodite

See items 23, 2296.

2305. Klein, Alvin. *New York Times* (Jan. 22, 1984), sect. 21:
          16.
2306. Merrill, Lisa. *Women & Performance*, 1, i (Spring/Summer
          1983): 81-83.
2307. Munk, Erica. *Village Voice* (Oct. 25, 1983): 98.
2308. Talarico, Lori. *New Directions for Women*, 13 (Jan. 1985):
          12.

Us

2309. Goodman, Walter. *New York Times* (Dec. 28, 1987): C21.

2310. Lamont, Rosette C. "The Living Theater Lives On." *New
          York Times* (Dec. 13, 1987): H5.
          In discussing the staging of *Us,* director Judith
          Malina comments that what appeals to her is the
          play's "hotness . . . [it is] lush, lyrical as well as
          violent and angry."

Mann, Emily

Selected Plays

2310. *Annulla Allen: Autobiography of a Survivor* (New Theatre of Brooklyn, 1988)
Playscript: *Annulla: An Autobiography.* New York: Theatre Communications Group, 1985.

2311. *Betsey Brown : A Rhythm & Blues Musical* (with Ntozake Shange, American Musical Theatre Festival, Philadelphia, 1989)

2312. *Execution of Justice* (Actors Theatre of Louisville, Kentucky, 1983-1984)
Playscript: *Execution of Justice.* New York: Samuel French, 1986; *Out Front: Contemporary Gay and Lesbian Plays.* Edited by Don Shewey, 152-220. New York: Grove Press, 1988; *New Plays USA.* Volume 3. Edited by James Leverett, 39-112. New York: Theatre Communications Group, 1986; *American Theatre*, 2 (Nov. 1985): 1-20.

2313. *Fanny Kelly* (staged reading, Women's Project, 1982-1983)

2314. *Still Life* (American Place Theatre, 1981)
Playscript: *Still Life: A Documentary.* New York: Dramatists Play Service, 1982; *Coming to Terms: American Plays & the Vietnam War*, 213-274. New York: Theatre Communications Group, 1985. *New Plays USA.* Volume 1. Edited by James Leverett, 153-224. New York: Theatre Communications Group, 1982.

Profiles and Interviews

See items 9, 46, 75, 87, 91, 93, 2312, 2347.

2315. Breslauer, Jan and Susan Mason. "American Directors on Directing: Emily Mann." *Theatre*, 115, ii (Spring 1984): 27-33.
In this excerpt from an interview of Mann, which was conducted shortly after her completion of *Execution of Justice*, the focus is on Mann's

directorial efforts such as *A Doll's House* and
Kroetz's *Through the Leaves*, and the challenges of
being both a playwright and director. Mann
comments, "I think that my directing and
playwriting inform each other . . . I couldn't have
written *Execution of Justice* without having
directed *Oedipus* and written *Still Life*. Mann,
whose plays combine the "intimate with the
political," observes that America lacks a viable
political theatre as compared to the Europeans. She
believes the regional theatre groups will be
responsible for increasing the political
consciousness of American by creating "theater as a
place for ideas to be expressed." Mann also
discusses briefly her training, apprenticeships, and
experiences as a woman working in the theatre.

2316. *Contemporary Theatre, Film, and Television.* Volume 1.
       Edited by Monica M. O'Donnell, 340. Detroit:
       Gale Research Company, 1984.
       This entry provides a brief biography.

2317. Kolin, Philip C. and Lanelle Daniel. "Emily Mann: A
       Classified Bibliography." *Studies in American
       Drama*, 4 (1989): 223-266.
       The most extensive primary and secondary
       bibliography of Mann to date. The bibliography
       provides an overview of Mann's contributions as
       playwright and director, a list of primary works—
       published and unpublished—interviews, criticism,
       reviews of her work and biographical profiles.

2318. Nemy, Enid. "On Stage." *New York Times* (Dec. 8, 1989):
       B2.
       Nemy announces Mann will become the artistic
       director of the McCarter Theater at the Center for
       Performing Arts in Princeton, New Jersey.

2319. Schiff, Ellen. *Contemporary Dramatists.* 4th Edition. Edited
       by D.L. Kirkpatrick, 342-343. Chicago: St. James
       Press, 1988.

Schiff briefly assesses the work of Mann. The
entry includes a list of her works.

2320. Steckling, D. Larry. "Emily Mann's *Hedda Gabler*." *Drama-
Logue* (July 2-8, 1987): 6.
Steckling's profile of Mann is based on an
interview conducted shortly before her staging of
Hedda Gabler at the La Jolla Playhouse. The
article surveys Mann's salient contributions as a
writer and director as well as Mann's reflections on
her dual role as playwright and director; her views
on Ibsen; her opinions about sexual discrimination
in the theatre; and her observations about profit and
non-profit theatre.

Reviews

Annulla Allen: Autobiography of a Survivor

2321. Gussow, Mel. *New York Times* (Nov. 2, 1988): C23.
2322. Hersh, Amy. *American Theatre*, 5 (Nov. 1988): 8-9.
2323. Kramer, Richard E. *Studies in American Drama 1945-
Present*, 4 (1989): 286-289.
2324. Massa, Robert. *Village Voice* (Nov. 8, 1988): 10.
2325. Woods, Jeannie. *Women & Performance*, 4, viii (1989):
154-155.

Betsey Brown

See **Ntozake Shange**

Execution of Justice

2326. Aeschliman, M.D. *National Review*, 36 (May 18, 1984):
46.

2327. Bennetts, Leslie. "When Reality Takes To the Stage." *New
York Times* (Mar. 9, 1986), sect. 2: 1, 4.
Mann remarks that she chose the Dan White murder
case as a subject for *Execution of Justice*, a play
commissioned by the Eureka Theater in San
Francisco, because she realized that case continued

to be an "open wound . . . [San Franciscans] were
still walking around shell-shocked from this
sequence of events—the assassinations, the trial,
the verdict." For Mann, the trial and its aftermath
symbolizes the deep schism in America between
conservative and liberal values.

2328. Brown, Joe E. *Washington Post* (May 17, 1985), Weekend
　　　　sect.: 11.
2329. Christiansen, Richard. *Chicago Tribune* (Jan. 23, 1987),
　　　　sect. 2: 12.
2330. Collins, Robert. *MPLS St. Paul*, 13 (Oct. 1985): 60-62.
2331. Corliss, Richard. *Time*, 123 (Apr. 2, 1984): 88.
2332. *Drama-Logue*. (Oct. 29-Nov. 4, 1987): 8.
2333. Gill, Brendan. *The New Yorker*, 62 (Mar. 24, 1986): 108.
2334. Grove, Lloyd. *Washington Post* (June 10, 1983), Weekend
　　　　sect.: 9.
2335. Gussow, Mel. *New York Times* (Mar. 29, 1984): C21.
2336. _____. *New York Times* (May 29, 1985): C18.
2337. _____. *New York Times* (Mar. 14, 1986), sect. 3: 3.
2338. Hill, Holly. *Times* (London) (Apr. 8, 1986): 19.
2339. Langdon, Brown. *Theatre Journal*, 38, iv (Dec. 1986): 476-
　　　　477.
2340. McCulloh, T.H. *Drama-Logue* (Oct. 29-Nov. 4, 1987): 8.
2341. Massa, R. *Village Voice* (Mar. 25, 1986): 89.
2342. Moor, Paul. *Times* (London) (Aug. 23, 1985): 7a.
2343. Mootz, William. *Courier-Journal* (Louisville) (May 20,
　　　　1984), sect. 1: 1, 7.

2344. *New York Times* (Mar. 25, 1986), sect. 3: C21.
　　　　The *Times* notes the closing of *Execution of
　　　　Justice* after 20 performances.

2345. *New York Times* (Apr. 30, 1986): C26.
　　　　The *Times* reports Mann is one of five winners of
　　　　the 1986 Playwrights U.S.A. awards for her play
　　　　Execution of Justice.

2346. *New York Times* (Apr. 30, 1986): C26.
　　　　The *Times* reports Mann won the Helen Hayes
　　　　award for *Execution of Justice*.

2347. Richards, David. "The Passions of *Justice*: Playwright
       Emily Mann on the Trial of Dan White."
       Washington Post (May 5, 1985): K1.
       Richards' article, written a few days prior to a run
       of *Execution of Justice* at the Arena Stage,
       clarifies Mann's insights on the play as well as a
       profile of her professional career. Mann comments
       that while researching and writing the play, many
       of her preconceived notions concerning the crime
       and trial were smashed. "This is not a revenge
       play. In many ways, society itself was on trial—
       Dan White's conservative values . . . versus
       Moscone and Milk's liberal agenda." Mann also
       talks about her earlier plays and the influence of her
       family life on her art. "It was a constant challenge
       in our house that you had to know what you
       believed in."

2348. _____. *Washington Post* (June 8, 1983), sect. B: 1.

2349. *San Francisco Chronicle* (Mar. 15, 1986), Datebook sect.:
       38.
       The *Chronicle* reports on the New York critics'
       reactions to *Execution of Justice*.

2350. Sauvage, Leo. *New Leader*, 69 (Mar. 10, 1986): 22.
2351. Scott, Nancy. *San Francisco Chronicle* (Jan. 9, 1983), sect.
       A: 5.

2352. Shewey, Don. "Gay Theater." *American Theatre* 6 (May
       1988): 17.
       Shewey includes *Execution of Justice* in his
       discussion of contemporary Gay theatre.

2353. Shirley, Don. *Los Angeles Times* (Oct. 26, 1987), sect. 6:
       3.
2354. Simon, John. *New York*, 19 (Mar. 24, 1986): 96.

2355. Smith, Sid. *Chicago Tribune* (Jan. 18, 1987), sect. 3: 12.
       Smith previews *Execution of Justice* prior to its
       opening at the Bailiwick Repertory.

2356.   *Variety* (Mar. 19, 1986): 84.

2357.   Weiner, Bernard. "A Powerful Dan White Docu-Drama." *San Francisco Chronicle* (June 2, 1985), Datebook sect.: 35, 36.
           Weiner previews Mann's *Execution of Justice*, which opened at the Berkeley Repertory Theater. Mann comments that she is surprised the play has been staged several times around the country, "I thought it would be of interest to 500 people in San Francisco." She believes the play challenges audiences intellectually and emotionally, requiring them to scrutinize how justice is "being executed in our society." Mann agrees with Weiner's opinion that the play was rough when it first appeared at Actors Theatre of Louisville, "I knew the play wasn't finished. It's focused better, better balanced between the prosecution and defense, fact vs. emotion."

2358.   _____. *San Francisco Chronicle* (Mar. 28, 1984): 65.
2359.   _____. *San Francisco Chronicle* (June 11, 1985): 42.
2360.   Wilson, Edwin. *Wall Street Journal* (Mar. 31, 1986): 16.
2361.   Winn, Steven. *San Francisco Chronicle* (June 30, 1985), Datebook sect.: 38.

Still Life

2362.   Brown, Joe. *Washington Post* (Mar. 27, 1987), Weekend sect.: 7.
2363.   Brustein, Robert. *New Republic*, 184 (Mar. 28, 1981): 24.
2364.   Feingold, Michael. *Village Voice* (Feb. 25, 1981): 75.
2365.   Grove, Lloyd. *Washington Post* (June 10, 1983), Weekend sect.: 9.
2366.   Hurwitt, Robert. *California*, 7 (May 1982): 116-118.
2367.   Kart, Larry. *Chicago Tribune* (Oct. 28, 1980), sect.3: 6.
2368.   Oliver, Edith. *The New Yorker*, 57 (Mar. 2, 1981): 62.

2369.   Reston, James. "Coming To Terms: American Plays Offer New Truths About the Collective Trauma of Vietnam." *American Theatre*, 2 (1985): 16-19.

Reston includes Mann's play in a discussion on how playwrights wrestle with the Vietnam war in their plays.

2370. Rich, Frank. *New York Times* (Feb. 20, 1981), sect. C: 3.
2371. Simon, John. *New York*, 14 (Mar. 2, 1981): 52, 54.
2372. Smith, Sid. *Chicago Tribune* (Jan. 25, 1984), sect. 5: 8.
2373. Sullivan, Dan. *Los Angeles Times* (June 1, 1982), sect. 6: 1, 6.
2374. Weiner, Bernard. *San Francisco Chronicle* (Mar. 22, 1982): 41.

Martin, Jane

Selected Plays

2375. *The Boy Who Ate the Moon* (Actors Theatre of Louisville, Kentucky, 1981-1982)
Playscript: *What Mama Don't Know: Five Plays.* New York: Samuel French, 1988.
2376. *Cemetery Man* (Actors Theatre of Louisville, Kentucky, 1981-1982)
2377. *Coup/Clucks* (Actors Theatre of Louisville, Kentucky, 1982)
Playscript: *Plays from Actors Theatre of Louisville,* 1-70. New York: Broadway Play Publishing, 1989; *Coup/Clucks.* New York: Dramatists Play Service, 1989.
2378. *Cul-de-Sac* (Actors Theatre of Louisville, Kentucky, 1981-1982)
Playscript: see item 2375.
2379. Shasta Rue (Actors Theatre of Louisville, Kentucky, 1982-1983)
Playscript: see item 2375.
2380. *Stages* (collaborator, Actors Theatre of Louisville, Kentucky, 1981)
2381. *Summer* (Actors Theatre of Louisville, Kentucky, 1984)
Playscript: see item 2375.
2382. *Talking With* (Manhattan Theatre Club, 1982)
Includes eleven monologues:
Audition

Playscript: *Esquire,* 98 (Nov. 1982): 159-162.

Clear Glass Marbles
Playscript: *WordPlays 3: An Anthology of New American Plays,* 147-149. New York: PAJ Publications, 1984; see

Audition.

Dragons
Fifteen Minutes
French Fries
Handler
Playscript: *The Burns Mantle Yearbook: The Best Plays of 1981-1982,* 56-55. Edited by Otis L. Guernsey, New York: Dodd, Mead & Company, 1983 (excerpts).

Lamps
Playscript: see *The Handler.*

Marks
Rodeo
Playscripts: *WordPlays 3: An Anthology of New American Plays, 150-152.* New York: PAJ Publications, 1984; see *Handler.*

Scraps
Twirler
Playscript: The Best Short Plays of 1982. Edited by Ramon Delgado, 250-253. Radnor, Pennsylvania: Chilton Book Company, 1982; *see Audition.*

2383. *Stages* (collaborator, Actors Theatre of Louisville, Kentucky, 1981)

2384. *Travellin' Show*
Playscript: see item 2375.

2385. *Vital Signs* (Actors Theatre of Louisville, Kentucky, 1990)

Reviews

See page 4.

Coups/Clucks

2386. Richards, David. *Washington Post* (May 20, 1987): D1.

2387. Moe, Christian H. *Theatre Journal*, 36, i (Mar. 1984): 105-
       106.

Summer

2388. Moe, Christian H. *Theatre Journal*, 37, iv (Dec. 1984): 499-
       500.

Talking With

2389. Arkatov, Janice. *Los Angeles Times* (Oct. 2, 1987), sect.
       6: 13.
2390. Barnes, Clive. *New York Post* (Oct. 4, 1982).
       Reprinted in item 2402.
2391. Beaufort, John. *Christian Science Monitor* (Oct. 14, 1982),
       Arts sect.: 19.
       Reprinted in item 2402.
2392. Brustein, Robert. *New Republic*, 187 (Nov. 1, 1982): 26.
2393. Cohen, Ron. *Women's Wear Daily* (Oct. 4, 1982).
       Reprinted in item 2402.
2394. DeVries, Hilary. *Christian Science Monitor* (July 14,
       1983): B1.
2395. Frank, Leah D. *New York Times* (Mar. 24, 1985), sect. 21:
       14.
2396. Grove, Lloyd. *Washington Post* (Feb. 17, 1984), Weekend
       sect.: 9.
2397. Gussow, Mel. *New York Times* (Apr. 4, 1982): 58.
2398. Hill, Holly. *Theatre Journal*, 34, iv (Dec. 1982): 543-544.
2399. Kalem, T. E. *Time*, 119 (Apr. 12, 1982): 78.
2400. Koehler, Robert. *Los Angeles Times* (Sep. 22, 1987), sect.
       6: 5.
2401. Koyama, Christine. *Chicago*, 33 (Jan. 1984): 32.
2402. Kroll, Jack. *Newsweek*, 100 (Oct. 25, 1982): 101.
       Reprinted in item 2402.
2401. Munk, Erica. *Village Voice* (Oct. 12,1982): 91-92.
2402. *New York Theatre Critics' Reviews*, 43 (Nov. 15, 1982):
       167-170.
2403. Novick, Julius. *Village Voice* (Apr. 20, 1982): 96.
2404. Oliver, Edith. *The New Yorker*, 58 (Oct. 18, 1982): 160.
2405. Rich, Frank. *New York Times* (Oct. 4, 1982): C16.
       Reprinted in item 2402.

2406. Richards, David. *Washington Post* (Feb. 9, 1984), sect. D:
       13.
2407. Simon, John. *New York*, 15 (Oct. 18, 1982): 88.
2408. Watt, Douglas. *New York Daily News* (Oct. 4, 1982).
       Reprinted in item 2402.
2409. Wilson, Edwin. *Wall Street Journal* (Oct. 29, 1982): 31.

Twirler

2410. Kalem, T.E. *Time*, 117 (Apr. 6, 1981): 74.
2411. Novick, Julius. *Village Voice* (May 27-June 2, 1981): 90.

Vital Signs

2412. Gussow, Mel. *New York Times* (Apr. 5, 1990): C15.

Mason, Judi Ann

Selected Plays

2413. *Daughters of the Mock* (Negro Ensemble Company, 1978)
2414. *Indigo Blues* (Billie Holliday Theater, 1988)
2415. *Jonah and the Wonder Dog* (Negro Ensemble Company,
       1986)
2416. *Livin' Fat* (Negro Ensemble Company, 1976)
       Playscript: *Livin' Fat*. New York: Samuel French,
       1974.
2417. *A Star Ain't Nothin' But a Hole in Heaven* (Restoration
       Center, 1987)

Profiles and Interviews

2418. Lesem, Jeanne. "Writer's Plays Show Life As It Really Is."
       Chicago Defender (Aug. 20, 1977): 13. Reprinted
       in *Atlanta Daily World* (Sep. 11, 1977): 7.
       Mason shares her personal and professional history
       as well as her experiences as an African-American
       writer. The playwright says her plays depart from
       most black plays, which tend to focus on "keeping
       families together" whereas Mason contends her
       plays are "about young blacks who want to break
       away and become independent."

2419. Peterson, Bernard L. *Contemporary Black American Playwrights and Their Plays: A Biographical Directory and Dramatic Index,* 335-336. Westport, Connecticut: Greenwood Press, 1988.
Peterson provides a brief biography as well as a staging history of Mason's plays.

2420. Stinson, Patricia. "*Essence* Women: Judi Ann Mason." *Essence,* 8 (Nov. 1977): 6.
Stinson briefly profiles Mason, noting that not yet twenty-three, Mason has won two national awards for her plays *Livin' Fat* and *A Star Ain't Nothin But a Hole in Heaven.* For her dramatic material, Mason draws upon her early years growing up in the sixties in Bossier, Louisiana, especially the conflicting tensions of her family's reactions to racial unrest. "My father . . . was a moderate political leader in Bossier, while my older brother, president of the Shreveport NAACP, was calling for boycotts. I was caught in the middle of a family conflict."

Reviews

See item 370, 2436.

Daughters of the Mock

2421. *American Theatre Annual, 1978-1979,* 132. Detroit: Gale Research Company, 1979.
2422. Barnes, Clive. *New York Post* (Dec. 26, 1978): 43.
2423. Fox, Terry Curtis. *Village Voice* (Jan. 1, 1979): 75.
2424. Gussow, Mel. *New York Times* (Dec. 22, 1978): C3.
2425. Webster, Ivan. *Encore: American & Worldwide News,* 8 (Feb. 5, 1979): 36-37.

Jonah and the Wonder Dog

2426. Feingold, Michael. *Village Voice* (Mar. 11, 1986): 87.
2427. Rich, Frank. *New York Times* (Mar. 3, 1986): C13.
2428. *Variety* (Mar. 19, 1986): 84.

Livin' Fat

See item 2420.

2429. Byrd, William. *Atlanta Daily World* (Apr. 15, 1982): 6.
2430. *Chicago Defender* (Mar. 31, 1980): 17.
2431. *Cleveland Call and Post* (July 9, 1977), sect. A: 3.
2432. Dodds, Richard. *Times-Picayune* (New Orleans), sect. 2, 10.
2433. Drake, Sylvie. *Los Angeles Times* (June 23, 1979), sect. 2: 6.
2434. Durrah, James W. *N.Y. Amsterdam News* (May 6, 1978), sect. D: 4.
2435. Eder, Richard. *New York Times* (June 2, 1976): 43.

2436. Gagnard, Frank. "She Skips Shrinks and Sees Own Plays." *Times-Picayune* (New Orleans) (Oct. 27, 1979), sect. 4: 8.
    In addition to Gagnard's profile of Mason, the playwright talks about her play *Livin' Fat*, premiering at Dillard Coss Hall in New Orleans. She writes only about the South and says she is sensitive to the stereotypic way in which this region is treated in the media, "people are unique here . . . it's not like anywhere else." Mason also writes for television and describes the life of a "roving term writer," meaning she develops television scripts for several different shows.

2437. Keating, Douglas J. *Philadelphia Inquirer* (Oct. 15, 1988), Features sect.: D5.
2438. Mitchell, Lionel. *N.Y. Amsterdam News* (Dec. 24, 1983): 24.
2439. *National Observer* (Mar. 15, 1979), sect. 2: 10.
2440. Oliver, Edith. *The New Yorker*, 52 (June 14, 1976):77-78.
2441. Lardner, James. *Washington Post* (Mar. 15, 1979), sect. B: 10.
2442. Weiner, Bernard. *San Francisco Chronicle* (Jan. 22, 1985): 58.

A Star Ain't Nothing But a Hole in Heaven

See item 2420.

2443. Bruckner, D.J.R. *New York Times* (Apr. 12, 1987): 70.

2444. Coleman, Wanda. "Black Writers in the Theater: A Gray Future?" *New York Times* (July 17, 1977): 56. Coleman mentions Mason as winner of the Lorraine Hansberry Award for *A Star Ain't Nothing But a Hole in Heaven.*

May, Elaine

Selected Plays

2445. *An Evening with Mike Nichols and Elaine May* (John Golden Theater, 1960)
2446. *Adaptation* (Greenwich Mews Theatre, 1969)
       Playscript: *Adaptation.* New York: Dramatists Play Service, 1971.
2447. *Hot Line* (Goodman Theatre, Chicago, 1983)
2448. *Matter of Position* (Booth Theatre, 1969)
2449. *Name of a Soup* (HB Studio Workshop, 1963)
2450. *Not Enough Rope* (Maidman Playhouse, 1962)
       Playscript: *Not Enough Rope.* New York: Samuel French, 1964.

Profiles

See item 87.

2451. *Contemporary Authors: A Bio-Bibliographical Guide.* Volume 124, New Revision Series. Edited by Hal May, 302-303. Detroit: Gale Research Inc., 1988. The entry includes a biographical sketch and a list of May's work.

2452. *Contemporary Theatre, Film, and Television.* Volume 5. Edited by Monica M. O'Donnell, 227. Detroit: Gale Research Company, 1988.

The entry includes a biographical sketch and a list of May's work.

2453. *Current Biography Yearbook: 1961.* Edited by Charles Moritz, 300-302. New York: H.W. Wilson, 1962. The entry provides a lengthy biography of May's life and career.

2454. Gottfried, Martin. *Contemporary Dramatists.* 2nd Edition. Edited by James Vinson, 527-528. New York: St. Martin's Press, 1977. This entry includes a biographical sketch, a list of May's professional activities, including her theatrical productions and general critical comments on her work.

2455. Malm, Linda. *Dictionary of Literary Biography.* Volume 44. *American Screenwriters.* Edited by Randall Clark, 251-253. Detroit: Gale Research Company, 1986. This introductory article includes an extensive biographical and critical survey of May's achievements, emphasizing her work in film.

Reviews

Adaptation

2456. Barnes, Clive. *New York Times* (Feb. 11, 1969): 27.
2457. _____. *New York Times* (Mar. 12, 1970): 46.
2458. Clurman, Harold. *Nation*, 208 (Mar. 3, 1969): 281-282.
2459. Cook, Richard P. *Wall Street Journal* (Feb. 12, 1969): 14. Reprinted in item 2465.
2460. Dettmer, Roger. *Chicago Tribune* (Feb. 13, 1975), sect. 3: 6.
2461. Gottfried, Martin. *Women's Wear Daily* (Feb. 11, 1969). Reprinted in item 2465.
2462. Hewes, Henry. *Saturday Review,* 52 (Mar. 1, 1969): 45.
2463. Kerr, Walter. *New York Times* (Feb. 23, 1969), sect. 2: D1, D5.
2464. Lowell, Sondra. *Los Angeles Times* (Oct. 15, 1976), sect. 4: 22.

2465. *New York Theatre Critics' Reviews*, 30 (June 16, 1969):
269-271.
2466. Novick, Julius. *Vogue*, 153 (Apr. 1969): 150.
2467. Oliver, Edith. *The New Yorker*, 45 (Feb. 22, 1969): 90, 92.
2468. Shepard, Richard F. *New York Times* (Sep. 23,1962), sect.
2: 1, 3.
2469. Simon, John. *Uneasy Stages: A Chronicle of the New
York Theater, 1963-1973.* New York: Random
House, 1975.
2470. *Time*, 93 (Feb. 21, 1969): 42.
2471. Watts, Richard. *New York Post* (Feb. 11, 1969).
Reprinted in item 2465.

An Evening with Elaine May and Mike Nichols

2472. Taubman, Howard. *New York Times* (Oct. 10, 1960): 37.

A Matter of Position

2473. Shepard, Richard F. "Elaine May: Q & A: About Her
Play." *New York Times* (Sep. 23, 1969), sect. 2:
1, 3.
Because of May's elliptical responses, Shepard's
interview reveals little about May's career, art, or
her play *A Matter of Position*, which opened at the
Booth Theatre.

Not Enough Rope

2474. Lowell, Sondra. *Los Angeles Times* (Oct. 15, 1976), sect.
4: 22.
2475. Taubman, Howard. *New York Times* (Mar. 2, 1962): 24.

Medley, Cassandra

Selected Plays

2476. *Ma Rose* (staged reading, Women's Project, 1988)
Playscript: *WomensWork: Five New Plays From
the Women's Project*, 43-114. New York: Applause
Theatre Book Publishers, 1989.
2477. *Ms. Mae* (Women's Project, 1984)

2478. *Terrain* (staged reading, Women's Project, 1983-1984)
2479. *Waking Women* (Ensemble Studio Theater, 1987)

Profiles

See profile in item 2476.

Reviews

Ma Rose

2480. Gussow, Mel. *New York Times* (Oct. 22, 1988): 14.
2481. Stone, Laurie. *Village Voice* (Nov. 1, 1988): 106.

Waking Women

2482. Gussow, Mel. *New York Times* (June 3, 1987): C18.

Mercier, Mary

Selected Play

2483. *Johnny No-Trump* (Cort Theatre, 1967)
        Playscript: *Johnny No-Trump: A Play In Two
        Acts*. New York: Dramatists Play Service, 1968.

Reviews

Johnny No-Trump

2484. Barnes, Clive. *New York Times* (Oct. 9, 1967): 60.
        Reprinted in item 2490.
2485. Cooke, Richard. *Wall Street Journal* (Oct. 10, 1967): 18.
        Reprinted in item 2490.
2486. Davis, James. *New York Daily News* (Oct. 9, 1967).
        Reprinted in item 2490.
2487. Gottfried, Martin. *Women's Wear Daily* (Oct. 9, 1967).
        Reprinted in item 2490.

2488. Jacobs, Susan. *On Stage*. New York: Knopf, 1972.

Jacobs traces the staging history of *Johnny No-Trump*, which she dubs Broadway's famous "fatality."

2489. Leonard, William Torbert. *Once Was Enough*, 94-96. Metuchen, New Jersey: Scarecrow, 1986. Leonard includes *Johnny No-Trump* in his discussion of Broadway flops. He describes the play's staging history and plot and provides excerpts of reviews from various drama critics.

2490. *New York Theatre Critics' Reviews*, 27 (Oct. 16, 1967): 269-271.

2491. Stasio, Marilyn. *Broadway's Beautiful Losers*. New York: Delacorte Press, 1972. Stasio analyzes five plays, including Mercier's *Johnny No-Trump*, all of which she refers to as the "beautiful losers." According to Stasio these "losers" were commercial flops but were "victimized by a system whose structure and values automatically pronounced them failures." Following the text of *Johnny No-Trump*, Stasio examines the play's strengths as well as its flaws. However, she devotes most of her discussion to the reasons why the show was a dismal failure. She concludes "the play's fast flop was the combination of a truly impressive number of converging phenomena, from the playwright's hard-headedness and the producer's petulance to the reviewers' misreadings and the jitters of the *Time's* neophyte critic."

2492. Watts, Richard. *New York Post* (Oct. 9. 1967): 58. Reprinted in item 2490.

2493. Zolotow, Sam. "Broadway Score: 8 Opened, 5 Closed; *Johnny No-Trump* Is Latest Fatality of New Season." *New York Times* (Oct. 10, 1967): 55.

Merriam, Eve

Selected Plays

2494. *And I Ain't Finished Yet* (Upstage Theater, 1981)
2495. *At Her Age* (Joseph Jefferson Theatre Company, 1979)
2496. *The Club* (Circle in the Square, 1976)
2497. *Dialogue For Lovers* (sonnets of Shakespeare adapted by
Merriam, Symphony Space, 1980)
2498. *Joan of Arc and Women Heroes* (with Yvonne Brewster and
others, Women's Project, 1987-1988)
2499. *Street Dreams, The Inner City Musical* (with Helen Miller,
La Mama ETC, 1984)
2500. *Out of Our Father's House* (adaptation of Merriam's
Growing Up Female in America: Ten Lives,
Lenox Arts Center, Maryland,1975)
Playscript: see item 73.
2501. *Viva Reviva* (Open Space in Soho, 1977)

Profiles

See items 9, 10, 73 and page 22-23.

2502. *Contemporary Authors: A Bio-Bibliographical Guide.*
Volumes 5-8. Edited by Barbara Harte, 775-776.
Detroit: Gale Research Company, 1969.
The entry provides a biographical sketch of
Merriam and a list of her works.

2503. *Contemporary Theatre, Film, and Television*, Volume 1.
Edited by Monica M. O'Donnell. Detroit: Gale
Research Company, 1984.
A succinct biographical sketch is included with a
list of Merriam's plays and awards.

2504. "Short Plays and Small Musicals." *Dramatists Guild
Quarterly*, 17, iv (Winter 1981): 14-18, 27-39.
Reprinted in *Broadway Song and Story:
Playwrights/Lyricists/Composers Discuss Their
Hits*. Edited by Otis L. Guernsey, 405-420. New
York: Dodd, Mead & Company, 1985.
The Guild's Projects Committee held three
discussions on short theatre forms, one of which
Merriam moderated. The panelists included
playwrights Terrence McNally, David Mamet,

Albert Innaurato. Merriam contributes very little to the discussion.

Reviews

And I Ain't Finished Yet

2505. Rich, Frank. *New York Times* (Dec. 9, 1981): C28.

The Club

See item 16.

2506. *American Theatre Annual* 1976-1977, 75. Detroit: Gale Research Company, 1978.
2507. Beaufort, John. *Christian Science Monitor* (Oct. 26, 1976): 29.
2508. Chaillet, Ned. *Times* (London) (May 16, 1978): 13.

2509. "The Club: A Shift in Perspective." *New York Times* (Feb. 17, 1977): 48.
    Merriam remarks it took ten years to shape her feminist revue, *The Club*, which opened at the Circle in the Square. She set the drama during the Victorian era because "I think male chauvinism had its flowering in that society." Although the revue appeals to feminists and homosexuals, Merriam observes that "middle-aged heterosexuals seem to be among its most enthusiastic supporters."

2510. Drake, Sylvie. *Los Angeles Times* (Oct. 10, 1980), sect. 6: 1, 17.
2511. *Drama-Logue* (July 14-20, 1988): 8.
2512. Epstein, Renee. *Ms.*, 5 (Mar. 1977): 34-36.

2513. Ferris, Lesley. *Acting Women: Images of Women in Theatre*, 167-171. New York: New York University Press, 1989.
    In her concluding chapter, Ferris briefly discusses the following plays: Eve Merriam's *The Club*, Lavonne Mueller's *Little Victories*, Megan Terry's *Mollie Bailey's Traveling Circus*, Joan Schenkar's

> *Signs of Life*, Maria Irene Fornes's *Fefu and Her
> Friends*, Kathleen Collins's *The Brothers*, Ntozake
> Shange's *for colored girls who have considered
> suicide/when the rainbow is enuf*, Marsha Norman's
> *'night Mother*, and *The Daughters Cycle Trilogy*
> by Clare Coss, Sondra Segal and Roberta Sklar.

2514. Foley, F. Kathleen. *Drama-Logue* (July 14-20, 1988): 8.
2515. Gold, Sylviane. *New York Post* (Oct. 15, 1976): 22.
        Reprinted in item 2521.
2516. Gussow, Mel. *New York Times* (Oct. 15, 1976): C10.
        Reprinted in item 2521.
2517. Hughes, Catherine. *America*, 135 (Nov. 27, 1976): 373.
2518. Hughes-Hallet, Lucy. *Plays and Players*, 25 (July 1978): 32.
2519. Kerr, Walter. *New York Times* (Nov. 17, 1976): C21.
2520. Loynd, Ray. *Los Angeles Times* (July 22, 1988), sect. 6:
        20.
2521. *New York Theatre Critics' Reviews*, 38 (Nov. 8, 1976):
        122-123.
2522. Oliver, Edith. *The New Yorker*, 52 (Oct. 25, 1976): 64.
2523. Pacheco, Patrick. *After Dark*, 9 (Dec. 1976): 103-104.
2524. Rich, Alan. *New York*, 9 (Nov. 1, 1976): 75.
2525. Stasio, Marilyn. *Penthouse*, 8 (Apr. 1977): 42-43.
2526. Stein, Ellin. *San Francisco Chronicle* (June 25, 1980): 64.
2527. Stone, Elizabeth. *Village Voice* (Nov. 29, 1976): 19-20.

2528. *Times* (London) (Apr. 25, 1978): 19e.
        The *Times* announces the opening of *The Club* at
        the Regent Theatre London on May 15, 1978.

2529. Tucker, Carll. *Village Voice* (Nov. 29, 1976): 99-101.
2530. Watt, Douglas. *New York Daily News* (Oct. 15, 1976).
        Reprinted in item 2521.
2531. Wetzsteon, Ross. *Village Voice* (June 6, 1977): 91, 93.

Dialogue for Lovers

2532. Kakutani, Michiko. *New York Times* (Apr. 29, 1980),
        sect. C: 10.

Inner City, A Street Cantata

See item 4075.

2533. Gottfried, Martin. *Women's Wear Daily* (Dec. 21, 1971).
    Reprinted in item 2536.
2534. Barnes, Clive. *New York Times* (Dec. 20, 1971): 48.
2535. Kerr, Walter. *New York Times* (Dec. 26, 1971), sect. 2: 1,
    3
2536. *New York Theatre Critics' Reviews*, 32 (Dec. 20, 1971):
    147-149.
2537. Watt, Douglas. *New York Daily News* (Dec. 20, 1971).
    Reprinted in 2536.
2538. Watts, Richard. *New York Post* (Dec. 20, 1971): 57.
    Reprinted in item 2536.

Out of Our Father's House

See item 1497.

2539. Gussow, Mel. *New York Times* (Nov. 4, 1977): C2.
2540. Munk, Erica. *Village Voice* (Nov. 7, 1977): 83-84.
2541. Weiner, Bernard. *San Francisco Chronicle* (Oct. 15, 1983):
    37.

Street Dreams

2542. Christiansen, Richard. *Chicago Tribune* (Oct. 1, 1982),
    sect. 3: 3.
    Reprinted in: *Chicago Tribune* (Oct. 2, 1982),
    sect. 1: 13.
2543. Gussow, Mel. *New York Times* (Feb. 7, 1984): C15.
2544. Winer, Linda. *Chicago Tribune* (Mar. 19, 1979), sect. 2: 8.

Viva Reviva

2545. Eder, Richard. *New York Times* (Oct. 19, 1977): C22.
2546. Munk, Erica. *Village Voice* (Nov. 7, 1977): 83-84.

Meyer, Marlane

Selected Plays

2547. *Burning Bridges: What to Do When the Egg Won't Stick*
(with Reza Abdoh, 1989)
2548. *Etta Jenks* (Women's Project, American Place Theater,
1988)
Playscript: *WomensWork: Five New Plays from
the Women's Project*, 115-174. New York:
Applause Theatre Book Publishers, 1989.
2549. *The Geography of Luck* (Los Angeles Theater Center, Los
Angeles, 1989)
2550. *Kingfish* (New York Shakespeare Festival, 1989)

Profiles

See profile in item 2548 and page 4.

Reviews

Etta Jenks

2551. Arkatov, Janice. "A Think Piece on the Pornography
Industry." *Los Angeles Times* (Jan. 15, 1988),
sect. 6: 8.
According to Meyer her play *Etta Jenks,* which
opened recently at the Los Angeles Theater Center,
is about "an every woman, an everyperson who
comes out from the Midwest to be a star and ends
up in the porno business." Underlying her plays is
the theme of alienation, "I think there's a loneliness
in our society. People are unable to speak to each
other, address the important issues of their lives."
Because she sees the stage as "a surreal dimension,"
she avoids writing naturalistic theatre; she writes
dramas that are poetic "extended realism."

2552. _____. *Los Angeles Times* (Feb. 26, 1988), sect. 6: 19.
Arkatov interviews Roberta Levitow, director of
Etta Jenks, performing at the Los Angeles Theater
Center.

2553. Cohen, Ron. *Women's Wear Daily* (Apr. 19, 1988).
Reprinted in item 2559.
2554. *Drama-Logue* (Jan. 21-27, 1988): 8.

2555. Gussow, Mel. *New York Times* (Apr. 14, 1988): 26.
        Reprinted in item 2559.
2556. Kissel, Howard. *New York Daily News* (Apr. 19, 1988).
        Reprinted in item 2559.
2557. Lockte, Dick. *Los Angeles*, 33 (Mar. 1988): 188-193.
2558. Morris, Steven. *Drama*, 2 (2nd Quarter, 1988): 42-44.
2559. *New York Theatre Critics' Reviews*, 49 (Sep. 5, 1988): 200-202.
2560. Seligsohn, Leo. *New York Newsday* (Apr. 15, 1988).
        Reprinted in item 2559.
2561. Stasio, Marilyn. *New York Post* (Apr. 14, 1988).
        Reprinted in item 2559.
2562. Stone, Laurie. *Village Voice* (Apr. 19, 1988): 106.
2563. Sullivan, Dan. *Los Angeles Times* (Jan. 18, 1988), sect. 6: 1.
2564. *Variety* (Feb. 10, 1988): 128.

The Geography of Luck

2565. Field, Bruce. *Drama-Logue* (Sep. 14-20, 1989): 6.

2566. *Los Angeles Times* (Aug. 20, 1989): 53
        The *Times* announces the opening of *The Geography of Luck* at the Los Angeles Theater Center.

2567. Sullivan, Dan. *Los Angeles Times* (May 22, 1989), sect. 6: 1, 7.
2568. _____. *Los Angeles Times* (Aug. 28, 1989), sect. 6: 1, 7.

Kingfish

2569. Arkatov, Janice. "Buck Henry: A Cosmic Comic Searches for True Meaning." *Los Angeles Times* (Aug. 25, 1988), sect. 6: 1, 6.
        Arkatov's article highlights the life and times of Buck Henry, who plays the character of Wiley in *Kingfish*.

2570. _____. "Director Schweizer: The Strategies of Seduction." *Los Angeles Times* (Oct. 9, 1988), Calendar sect.: 49.

Schweizer, director of Meyer's *Kingfish*, talks about his approach to the play.

2571. _____. *Los Angeles Times* (Sep. 25, 1988), Calendar sect.: 58, 59.
This item consists of excerpts from several Los Angeles area critics' assessments of *Kingfish*. The critics include: Dan Sullivan (*Los Angeles Times*), Thomas O'Connor (*Orange County Register*), Richard Stayton (*Herald Examiner*), Tom Jacobs (*Daily News*), Timothy Gray (*Daily Variety*), and Lee Melville (*Drama-Logue*).

2572. Christon, Lawrence. *Los Angeles Times* (Aug. 6, 1986), sect. 6: 1, 7.
2573. Gray, Timothy. *Variety* (Sep. 21, 1988): 88.
2574. Gussow, Mel. *New York Times* (Dec. 22, 1989): C5.
2575. Sullivan, Dan. *Los Angeles Times* (Sep. 13, 1988), sect. 6: 1, 4.
2576. _____. *Los Angeles Times* (Oct. 9, 1988), Calendar sect.:48.

Miller, Susan

Selected Plays

2577. *Arts and Leisure* (American Theatre Association Conference, 1982)
2578. *Confessions of a Female Disorder* (Mark Taper Forum, Los Angeles, 1973-1974)
Playscript: *Gay Plays; The First Collection*. Edited by William M. Hoffman, 127-175. New York: Avon, 1979.
2579. *Cross Country* (Interart Theatre, 1977)
Playscript: *West Coast Plays*, 1 (Fall 1977): 41-80.
2580. *Daddy and a Commotion of Zebras* (Alice Theatre Company, 1970)
2581. *Denim Lecture* (Pennsylvania State University, 1970)
2582. *Flux* (New York Shakespeare Festival, 1977)
2583. *For Dear Life* (Public Theatre, 1989)

2584. *Nasty Rumors and Final Remarks* (New York Shakespeare
          Festival, Old Prop Shop/Public Theatre, 1979)
2585. *No One is Exactly 23* (Pennsylvania State University,
          1967)
          Playscript: *Pyramid*, 1 (1968): 51-60.
2586. *Prime Time: A Celebration of Aging* (with Christopher
          Quilter, Joseph Jefferson Theater Company, 1976)

Profiles

See profile in Hoffman's anthology (item 2578) and page 4.

2587. *Contemporary Authors: A Bio-Bibliographical Guide.*
          Volume 107. Edited by Hal May, 341-342. Detroit:
          Gale Research Company, 1983.
          The entry provides a biographical profile, including
          brief comments about Miller's plays.

2588. *Contemporary Theatre, Film, and Television.* Volume 1.
          Edited by Monica M. O'Donnell, 372-73. Detroit:
          Gale Research Company, 1984.
          The entry includes a thumbnail sketch of the
          playwright's achievements and a list of plays and
          awards.

2589. Keyssar, Helen. *Contemporary Dramatists.* 3rd Edition.
          Edited by James Vinson, 371-73. New York: St.
          Martin's Press, 1982.
          Keyssar provides a biographical sketch, a list of
          Miller's plays, and general comments concerning
          her work.

Reviews

See item 10.

Confessions of a Female Disorder

2590. Adler, Dick. *Los Angeles*, 8 (Nov. 1973): 75.
2591. Drake, Sylvie. *Los Angeles Times* (Oct. 18, 1973), sect. 4:
          17.

2592. Sullivan, Dan. *Los Angeles Times* (Oct. 21, 1973),
       Calendar sect.: 36.

Cross Country

2593. Drake, Sylvie. "The Inward Journey of a Playwright." *Los
       Angeles Times* (Mar. 18, 1976), sect. 4: 1, 21.
       Drake converses with Miller about her life and art
       on the day of the opening of her new play *Cross
       Country* at the Mark Taper Forum. Miller
       remarks that although her play is deeply "personal,"
       it confronts "a problem we all have: how to be
       with ourselves, how to be with other people, how
       to be with this craziness that's happening now."

2594. Fox, Terry Curtis. *Village Voice* (June 27, 1977): 92.
2595. Aaron, Jules. *Educational Theatre Journal*, 28, iv (Dec.
       1976): 556-557.
2596. Sullivan, Dan. *Los Angeles Times* (Mar. 30, 1976), sect.
       4: 1, 3.

Flux

2597. Wardle, Irving. *Times* (London) (Nov. 2, 1976): 9e.
2598. Wetzsteon, Ross. *Village Voice* (Sep. 5, 1977): 71.

For Dear Life

2599. Feingold, Michael. *Village Voice* (Jan. 17, 1989): 91.
2600. Simon, John. *New York,* 22 (Jan. 23, 1989): 56-57.
2601. *Variety* (Jan. 18, 1989): 160.

Nasty Rumors and Final Remarks

2602. Barnes, Clive. *New York Post* (Apr. 13, 1979): 31.
2603. Fox, Terry Curtis. *Village Voice* (Apr. 23, 1979): 91-92.
2604. Gussow, Mel. *New York Times* (Apr. 13, 1979): C3.

Molinaro, Ursule

Selected Plays

2605. *The Abstract Wife* (York Theatre, 1961)
   Playscript: *New American Plays.* Volume 2. Edited
   by Robert W. Corrigan and William Hoffman,147-
   153. New York: Hill & Wang, 1965.
2606. *Breakfast Past Noon* (East Village Theater, 1971)
   Playscript: *Women in Literature: Life Stages through*
    Stories, Poems, and Plays. Edited by Sandra
    Eagleton, 244-256. Englewood Cliffs, New Jersey:
    Prentice Hall, 1988; see item 73.
2607. *The Contest* (Judson Poets Theatre, 1962)
2608. *The Engagement* (Playwrights Unit, 1964)
2609. *Second Shepherd's Play* (Judson Poets Theatre, 1962)

Criticism

See items 10, 2605.

Moore, Honor

Selected Plays

2610. *Mourning Pictures* (Lyceum, 1974).
   Playscript: see item 73.
2611. *Years* (staged reading, Women's Project, 1978-1979)

Profiles

See item 73.

2612. *Contemporary Authors: A Bio-Bibliographical Guide.*
   Volumes 85-88. Edited by Frances Carol Locher,
   413. Detroit: Gale Research Company, 1980.
   The entry includes a biographical sketch and a list
   of Moore's work.

Reviews

Mourning Pictures

See items 10, 16.

2613. Barnes, Clive. *New York Times* (Nov. 11, 1974): 41.
          Reprinted in item 2619.
2614. Braudy, Susan. *Ms.*, 3 (Nov. 1974): 100-104.
2615. Ettorre, Barbara. *Women's Wear Daily* (Nov. 12, 1974).
          Reprinted in item 2619.
2616. Gill, Brendan. *The New Yorker*, 50 (Nov. 18, 1974): 113.
2617. Gottfried, Martin. *New York Post* (Nov. 11, 1974): 13.
          Reprinted in item 2619.

2618. Leonard, William Torbert. *Once Was Enough*, 131-132.
          Metuchen, New Jersey: Scarecrow, 1986.
          Leonard includes *Mourning Pictures* in his
          discussion of so-called Broadway flops. He
          describes the play's staging history and plot as well
          as includes comments from various drama critics.

2619. *New York Theatre Critics' Reviews*, 35 (Nov. 11, 1974):
          195-196.
2620. Simon, John. *New York*, 7 (Nov. 25, 1974): 101.
2621. Watt, Douglas. *New York Daily News* (Nov. 11, 1974).
          Reprinted in item 2619.

Moraga, Cherrie

Selected Plays

2622. *Giving Up the Ghost* (staged reading, Foot of the Mountain
          Theatre, Minneapolis, 1984)
          Playscript: *Giving Up the Ghost*. Los Angeles:
          West End Press, 1986.
2623. *A Shadow of a Man* (reading, South Coast Repertory, Los
          Angeles, 1989)

Profiles and Interviews

2624. Lomeli, Francisco A. *Dictionary of Literary Biography*.
          Volume 82. *Chicano Writers*. Edited by Francisco
          A. Lomeli and Carl R. Shirley, 165-178. Detroit:
          Gale Research Inc., 1989.

Lomeli provides an in-depth survey of Moraga's personal, literary, and theatrical life. The essay includes a primary and secondary bibliography.

2625. Umpierre, Luz Marie. "With Cherrie Moraga." *Americas Review,* 14, ii (Summer 1986): 54-67.
Although Umpierre focuses on Moraga's literary work, some of her questions elicit from Moraga a discussion on her theatre work, which she says "has allowed me to give voice to a lot . . . there have been numerous plays about Chicanos, but none particularly about Chicanas." Moraga talks about the themes she is primarily concerned with such as the Chicana living within the extended family. In addition, Moraga candidly talks about her lesbianism and her views on the feminist movement. Moraga also mentions her plays-in-progress, *Giving Up the Ghost, The Shadow of a Man,* and a musical *La Extranjera.*

Reviews and Criticism

Giving Up The Ghost

2626. Alarcon, Norma. "Making *Familia* from Scratch: Split Subjectivities in the Work of Helena Maria Viramontes and Cherrie Moraga." In *Chicana Creativity and Criticism: Charting New Frontiers in American Literature.* Edited by Maria Herrera-Sobek and Helena Maria Viramontes, 147-159. Houston: Arte Publico Press, 1988. Reprinted in *Americas Review,* 15 (Fall/Winter 1987): 147-159. Alarcon uses the work of Viramontes and Moraga's *Giving Up the Ghost* to show that "Chicana writers are increasingly employing female-speaking subjects who hark back to explore the subjectivity of women. The female-speaking subject that would want to speak from a different position than that of a mother, or a future wife/mother, is thrown into a crisis of meaning that begins with her own gendered personal identity and its relational position with others."

2627. Herrera-Sobek, Maria. The Politics of Rape: Sexual Transgression in Chicana Fiction." In *Chicana Creativity and Criticism: Charting New Frontiers in American Literature.* Edited by Maria Herrera-Sobek and Helena Maria Viramontes, 171-181. Houston: Arte Publico Press, 1988.
Herrera-Sobek examines the rape scenes in several short stories and plays, including Moraga's *Giving Up the Ghost* and Portillo-Trambley's *The Day of the Swallows* to demonstrate how the authors use rape as a motif to express the oppression and suppression of women in a "phallocratic" society.

2628. Huerta, Jorge. *Americas Review,* 15 (Summer 1987): 104-109.

2629. Paredes, Raymond. *Rocky Mountain Review of Language and Literature,* 41 (1987): 124-129.

2630. Yarbro-Bejarano, Yvonne. "Cherrie Moraga's *Giving Up the Ghost:* The Representation of Female Desire." *Third Woman,* 3 (1986): 113-120.
Recognizing that Moraga's *Giving Up the Ghost* can be interpreted on several levels, the author chooses to focus on the relationship between women's sexuality and the Chicano and Anglo cultures. Moraga, Yarbro-Bejarano contends, is not concerned with an "idealized vision of lesbian sexuality" but the way in which Chicanas internalize the sexist and homophobic values for their culture and how they have been adversely affected by oppression. Ultimately, says Moraga, the answer for the Chicana lesbian lies in "women's love for women."

2631. _____. "Chicana Literature From a Chicana Feminist Perspective." In *Chicana Creativity and Criticism: Charting New Frontiers in American Literature.* Edited by Maria Hererra-Sobek and Helena Maria Viramontes, 139-145. Houston: Arte Publico Press, 1988.

In this essay, Yarbro-Bejarano includes a brief
discussion of Moraga's *Giving Up the Ghost*,
exploring how the sexual identity of Chicanas is
dictated by their culture's perceptions of men and
women.

Morrison, Toni

Selected Plays

2632. *Dreaming Emmett* (Capitol Repertory Company, 1985)

Profiles

See items 2635, 2637.

2633. *Black Writers: A Selection of Sketches From the
Contemporary Author Series*. Edited by Linda
Metzger, 411-417. Detroit: Gale Research
Inc.,1989.
The entry provides a concise biography of
Morrison.

2634. *Contemporary Authors: A Bio-Bibliographical Guide*.
Volume 2. New Revised Series. Edited by Hal
May, 330-336. Detroit: Gale Research Inc., 1989.
Morrison's entry includes a biographical sketch and
a list of her works.

Reviews

Dreaming Emmett

2635. Croyden, Margaret. "Toni Morrison Tries Her Hand At
Playwriting." *New York Times* (Dec. 29, 1985),
sect. 2: 6, 16.
Croyden discusses Morrison's *Dreaming Emmett*
on the eve of its opening at the Market Theater.
She views Morrison's leap into theater as a "brave
act for a novelist" since traditionally most
established novelists fail to produce successful
plays. Morrison, however, feels that, unlike her

predecessors, she has something that perhaps other novelists have lacked "I write good dialogue. It's theatrical. It moves. It just doesn't hang there."

2636. Medwick, Cathleen. *Vogue,* 176 (Jan. 1986): 56.

2637. Robinson, Harlow. Dreams of a Prophetic Past: Novelist Toni Morrison Tries Her Hand At Playwriting." *American Theatre,* 2 (Jan. 1986): 17-19. Robinson's article was written shortly before the premier of *Dreaming Emmett* at the Capitol Repertory Company in Albany on January 4, 1986. Morrison chronicles the events and forces that influenced the development of her play, which she describes as "so much of a discovery." As a first-time dramatist, Morrison shares some of her insights as to how playwriting differs from novel writing. For instance, Morrison feels she is adept at dialogue but not as secure with "dramatizing, about linking the word to a visual image or a physical gesture. I need help in linking the word to visuality."

2638. *Variety* (Mar. 5, 1986): 108.

Mueller, Lavonne

Selected Plays

2639. *The Adjutant* (staged reading, Women's Project, 1986-1987)
2640. *The Assassination of Federico Garcia Lorca* (staged reading, Women's Project, 1986, 1987)
2641. *Breaking the Prairie Wolf Code* (Women's Project, American Place Theater, 1985)
   Playscript: *Breaking the Prairie Wolf Code.* New York: Dramatist Play Service, 1986.
2642. *Colette in Love* (with Alice Eve Cohen, staged reading, Women's Project, American Place Theater, 1986)
   Playscript: *Women Heroes: Six Short Plays from the Women's Project,* 1-23. New York: Applause Theatre Book Publishers, 1987.
2643. *Crimes and Dreams* (Theatre Four, 1980)

2644. *Five in the Killing Zone* (Women's Project, 1985)
        Playscript: *WomensWork: Five New Plays from the Women's Project*, 175-252. New York: Applause Theatre Book Publishers, 1989.

2645. *Killing on the Last Line* (American Place Theater, 1980)
        Playscript: *The Women's Project: Seven New Plays by Women*, 179-254. Edited by Julia Miles, 179-254. New York: Performing Arts Journal Publications & American Place Theater, 1980.

2646. *Letters to a Daughter from Prison: Nehru and Indira* (Women's Project, 1988)

2647. *Little Victories* (American Place Theater, 1982-1983)
        Playscript: *Little Victories*. New York: Dramatists Play Service, 1984.

2648. *Luring the Enemy Deep* (staged reading, Women's Project, 1986-1987)

2649. *Mutiny in the Silence After a Last Sniper* (staged reading, Women's Project, 1982-1983)

2650. *The Only Woman General* (staged reading, Women's Project, 1983-1984)

2651. *Private Fudge in the Killing Zone* (staged reading, Women's Project, 1984-1985)

2652. *Susan B* (staged reading, Women's Project, 1980-1981)

2653. *Violent Peace* (staged reading, Women's Project, 1988-1989)

2654. *War and Things* (Nat Horne Theater, 1989)

2655. *Warriors From a Long Childhood* (staged reading, Women's Project, American Place Theater, 1979)

2656. *A Working Breakfast* (staged reading, Women's Project, 1984-1985)

Profiles

See profile in item 2644 and page 4.

Reviews

See item 79.

Breaking the Prairie Wolf Code

2657. Gross, Brenda. *Women & Performance*, 3, i (1986): 99-101.

2658. Gussow, Mel. *New York Times* (Nov. 25, 1985), sect. 3: 16.

2659. Jacobs, Diane. *Village Voice* (Nov. 19, 1985): 56.

Crimes and Dreams

2660. *American Theatre Annual* 1979-1980, 172. Detroit: Gale Research Company, 1981.

2661. Fox, Terry Curtis. *Village Voice* (May 26, 1980): 84.

2662. Oliver, Edith. *The New Yorker*, 56 (May 26, 1980): 77.

2663. Rich, Frank. *New York Times* (May 16, 1980): C10.

2664. Stasio, Marilyn. *New York Post* (May 16, 1980): 39.

Killings on the Last Line

2665. Bigsby, C.W.E. *A Critical Introduction to Twentieth-Century American Drama*, 427. Volume 3. New York: Cambridge University Press, 1982.
In his survey of contemporary drama, Bigsby briefly discusses *Killings on the Last Line*.

2666. Blumenthal, Eileen. *Village Voice* (June 16, 1980): 80

2667. Gussow, Mel. *New York Times* (June 6, 1980): C4.

Little Victories

2668. Gussow, Mel. *New York Times* (Feb. 4, 1983): C3.

2669. Bennetts, Leslie. "Breakthrough Season Arrives for Linda Hunt." *New York Times* (Feb. 12, 1983): 11.
Little Victories is briefly mentioned in Bennetts' article highlighting the career of Linda Hunt, who was playing the character of Joan of Arc in *Little Victories* at the American Place Theater.

2670. Hoffman, Jan. *Village Voice* (Feb. 8, 1983): 74-75.

The Only Woman General

2671. Kakutani, Michiko. *New York Tmes* (Mar. 28, 1984): C23.

Violent Peace

2672. Gussow, Mel. *New York Times* (Mar. 3, 1990): 12.
2673. Simon, John. *New York*, 23 (Mar. 19, 1990): 75-76.

Warriors From a Long Childhood

2674. Gussow, Mel. *New York Times* (May 23, 1979), sect. 3: 23.
2675. _____. *New York Times* (June 8, 1979): C3.

Nanus, Susan

Selected Plays

2676. *Autumn Ladies* (Eugene O'Neill Theater Center National Playwrights' Conference, 1981-1982)
2677. *The Phantom Tollbooth* (based on the book by Norton Juster, Henry Street Settlement House, 1977) Playscript: *The Phantom Tollbooth: A Children's Play in Two Acts.* New York: Samuel French, 1977.
2678. *Playing Dolls* (Ensemble Studio Theatre, 1978)
2679. *The Survivor* (adapted from the book by Jack Elsner, Morosco Theatre, 1981)
2680. *Where Memories Are Magic and Dreams Invented* (Interart, 1978)

Reviews

Playing Dolls

2681. Gussow, Mel. *New York Times* (Dec. 9, 1978): 16.

The Survivor

2682. Barnes, Clive. *New York Post* (Mar. 4, 1981). Reprinted in item 2684.
2683. Kissel, Howard. *Women's Wear Daily* (Mar. 5, 1981). Reprinted in item 2684.
2684. *New York Theatre Critics' Reviews*, 42 (Mar. 9, 1981): 327-330.

2685. Rich, Frank. *New York Times* (Mar. 4, 1981): C20.
         Reprinted in item 2684.
2686. Simon, John. *New York*, 14 (Mar. 16, 1981): 44.
2687. *Variety* (Mar. 11, 1981): 228.
2688. Watt, Douglas. *New York Daily News* (Mar. 4, 1981).
         Reprinted in item 2684.

Where Memories Are Magic and Dreams Invented

2689. Gussow, Mel. *New York Times* (Feb. 4, 1978): 13.

Nemeth, Sally

Selected Plays

2690. *Millfire* (Women's Project, 1987-1988)
         Playscript: *WomensWork: Five New Plays from
         the Women's Project*, 253-310. New York:
         Applause Theatre Book Publishers, 1989.
2691. *Holy Days* (staged reading, Women's Project, 1984-1985)

Profiles

See profile in item 2690.

Reviews

Millfire

2692. Christiansen, Richard. *Chicago Tribune* (May 2, 1989): 16.
2693. Winer, Laurie. *New York Times* (Oct. 19, 1989): C22.

Holy Days

2694. Drake, Sylvie. *Los Angeles Times* (Jan. 29, 1990), sect. F:
         1, 8.
2695. *Variety* (Feb. 21, 1990): 348.

Newman, Molly

Selected Plays

2696. *Hoopla* (staged reading, Denver Center Theater Company, 1985-1986)

2697. *Quilters* (with Barbara Damashek, adapted from *The Quilters: Women and Domestic Art* by Patricia Copper and Norma Bradley Allen, Jack Lawrence Theater, 1984)
Playscript: *Quilters*. New York: Dramatists Play Service, 1986; *Early American Life*, 17 (Oct. 1986): 30-33 (excerpt).

2698. *Shooting Stars* (Actors Space, 1988)
Playscript: *Shooting Stars*. New York: Dramatists Play Service, 1988.

2699. *Urges* (The Changing Scene, Denver, 1987-1988)

Profiles

2700. Barr, Donald J. *Sports Illustrated*, 65 (Aug. 4, 1986): 1.
Barr briefly profiles Molly Newman and her brother who is a senior editor for *Sports Illustrated*.

Reviews

Quilters

2701. *American Theatre*, 1 (Sep. 1984): 21-22.
2702. Bardacke, Frances. *San Diego*, 36 (Feb. 1984): 18.
2703. Beaufort, John. *Christian Science Monitor* (Sep. 28, 1984): 23.
Reprinted in item 2713.

2704. Butruille, Susan G. "Acting Out! Curtain Going Up On Women's History." *Ms.*, 12 (Mar. 1984): 95-98.
Butruille includes a brief discussion of *Quilters* in this piece about writers and performers who are "bringing [women's] history alive by linking drama with music and other art forms."

2705. Christiansen, Richard. *Chicago Tribune* (Oct. 3, 1985), sect. 5: 10d.
2706. _____. *Chicago Tribune* (Nov. 20, 1985), sect. 2: 5.
2707. Cohen, Ron. *Women's Wear Daily* (Sep. 26, 1984).
Reprinted in item 2713.

2708. Gill, Brendan. *The New Yorker*, 60 (Oct. 8, 1984): 116.
2709. Kauffmann, Stanley. *Saturday Review*, 10 (Dec.1984): 58.
2710. Kroll, Jack. *Newsweek*, 102 (July 4, 1983): 70.
2711. Lochte, Dick. *Los Angeles*, 29, (Feb. 1984): 44-45.
2712. Koehler, Robert. *Los Angeles Times* (Oct. 10, 1986), sect. 6: 8.
2713. *New York Theatre Critics' Reviews*, 45 (Sep. 17, 1984): 206-208.
2714. Novick, Julius. *Village Voice* (Jan. 17, 1984): 104.
2715. Rich, Frank. *New York Times* (Sep. 26, 1984): C17.
       Reprinted in item 2713.
2716. Richards, David. *Washington Post* (Aug. 6, 1984): C1, 6.
2717. _____. *Washington Post* (Aug. 10, 1984, Weekend sect.: 11.
2718. Simon, John. *New York*, 17 (Oct. 8, 1984): 77.
2719. Stasio, Marilyn. *New York Post* (Sep. 26, 1984).
       Reprinted in item 2713.
2720. Weiner, Bernard. *San Francisco Chronicle* (Nov. 20, 1985): 71.
2721. *Variety* (June 15, 1983): 76.
2722. *Variety* (Sep. 26, 1984): 116.
2723. Watt, Douglas. *New York Daily News* (Sept. 26, 1984).
       Reprinted in item 2713.
2724. Wilson, Edwin. *Wall Street Journal* (Sep. 28, 1984): 24.
       Reprinted in item 2713.

Shooting Stars

2725. Gussow, Mel. *New York Times* (Nov. 7, 1988): C17.
2726. Solomon, Alisa. *Village Voice* (Nov. 22, 1988): 102.

2727. Stern, Alan. *Denver Post* (Mar. 18, 1987), sect. C: 1.
       Stern previews *Shooting Stars,* opening at the
       Denver Center Theater. Playwright Newman
       comments that while the play forced her to confront
       difficult challenges, the experience inspired her to
       move on to the next play and gave her the
       confidence to realize that her "career doesn't hang in
       the balance."

2728. *Variety* (Apr. 15, 1987): 221.

Norman, Marsha

Selected Plays

2729. *Circus Valentine* (Actors Theatre of Louisville, Kentucky, 1979)

2730. *Getting Out* (Phoenix Theater, 1978)
Playscript: *Four Plays*. New York: Theatre Communications Group, 1988; *Getting Out*. New York: Avon Books, 1979; *Plays from Actors Theatre of Louisville*, 213-252. New York: Broadway Play Publishing, 1989.

2731. *The Holdup* (Circle Repertory Company, 1983)
Playscript: see item 2730.

2732. *Merry Christmas* (Actors Theatre of Louisville, Kentucky, 1978-1979)

2733. *'night, Mother* (John Golden Theater, 1983)
Playscript: *night, Mother*. New York: Hill and Wang, 1983.

2734. *Traveler in the Dark* (American Repertory, Cambridge, 1984)
Playscript: see item 2730.

2735. *Sarah and Abraham* (Actors Theatre of Louisville, Kentucky, 1988)

2736. *The Secret Garden* (music by Lucy Simon, Virginia State Theater, Norfolk, 1990)

2737. *Third and Oak* (Actors Theatre of Louisville, Kentucky, 1978)
Includes two one-acts: *The Laundromat* (Ensemble Studio Theatre, 1979)
The Pool Hall (Actors Theatre of Louisville, Kentucky, 1978)
Playscript: see item 2730.

2738. *Winter Shakers* (Kentucky Center for the Arts, Louisville, 1983)

Profiles and Interviews

See items 9, 36, 75, 87, 91, 100, 2907 and pages 3, 23.

2739. *The Best Plays of 1978-1979*. Edited by Otis L. Guernsey. New York: Dodd, Mead & Company, 1979.

Guernsey provides a biographical profile of Norman and photographs of the production of *Getting Out*.

2740. Brustein, Robert. "Conversation with Marsha Norman." *Dramatists Guild Quarterly*, 21, iii (Autumn 1984): 8-21. Reprinted in *Broadway Song and Story: Playwrights, Lyricists, Composers Discuss Their Hits*. Edited by Otis L. Guernsey, 184-196. New York: Dodd, Mead & Company, 1985.
A transcript of a seminar, co-sponsored by the Dramatists Guild and Playwrights Platform, held at Emerson College, Boston. Brustein conducted the session with Norman whose candid responses to his queries reveal a great deal about her approach to playwriting. For example, according to Norman "I live in a very secret world" but she sees her role as a dramatist is to "make confusion clear." Norman reflects on the collaborative aspects of theatre in which she remarks that she learns from the director, actors, and designers. However, she warns that collaborating on a script can be "dangerous." To Brustein's question about the playwrights she most admires, she responds that Sam Shepard, Christopher Hampton, Lanford Wilson, and Samuel Beckett are her favorites. She also regards highly the rules of Aristotle, "rules really *are* the rule, and now I am not interested in breaking them or seeing how they could be stretched or changed." Norman discusses a variety of other topics: the critics, realism in the theatre, and working out glitches in her scripts. Throughout the course of the interview, Norman refers to several of her plays, including the lesser-known *Circus Valentine* and *The Holdup*.

2741. Cohen, Ron. "Marsha Norman's Journey into 'Night'." *Women's Wear Daily* (Apr. 22-29, 1983): 18.
Written during a run of *'night Mother* on Broadway, Cohen's conversation with Norman touches briefly upon her plays, her favorite writers, and her experiences writing for the movies.

2742. *Contemporary Authors: A Bio-Bibliographical Guide.*
Edited by Frances C. Locher, 361-362. Detroit:
Gale Research Company, 1982.
The entry includes a biographical sketch as well as
general comments about Norman's plays.

2743. *Contemporary Theatre, Film, and Television.* Volume 1.
Edited by Monica O'Donnell, 400-401. Detroit:
Gale Research Company, 1984.
This entry provides a brief biography of Norman.

2744. *Current Biography Yearbook: 1984.* Edited by Charles
Moritz, 302-305. New York: H.W. Wilson, 1984.
The entry provides a lengthy biography of
Norman's life and theatrical career.

2745. DeVries, Hillary. "Once Loved, Once Spurned, A
Playwright Now Returns." *Christian Science
Monitor* (June 8, 1988): 1. Reprinted in *Chicago
Tribune* (July 1, 1988), sect. 5: 3.
DeVries's profile of Norman was inspired by the
premiere run of *Sarah and Abraham,* at the Actors
Theatre of Louisville's Festival of New Plays. In
addition to talking about working in the theatre and
her new play *Sarah and Abraham,* she also reflects
upon her temporary withdrawal from the theatre
world after "being crushed" by critics who "just
slammed" *Traveler in the Dark.* She also expresses
her feelings toward critics, who, according to
DeVries, "remain one of Norman's sorest sore
points."

2746. Drake, Sylvie. "In the Wake of Norman's Pulitzer." *Los
Angeles Times* (Apr. 22, 1983), sect. 6: 1, 16.
Drake's article is based on an interview with
Norman shortly after the playwright learned she
won the Pulitzer Prize for *'night Mother.* In
addition to discussing her prize-winner, Norman
talks about her previous plays and her work-in-
progress, a musical entitled *The [Winter] Shakers.*

2747. Forman, Robert J. "Marsha Norman." In *Critical Survey of Drama*. Edited by Frank McGill, 288-293. Pasadena, California: Salem Press, 1986.
Forman provides a biographical survey and critical analysis of Norman's major plays.

2748. Franklin, Rebecca. "Playwright Marsha Norman is NOT a Sweet Little Thing." *Birmingham News* (Sep. 9, 1979), sect. E: 3.
Norman talks about the events of her life that led up to creating her play *Getting Out*.

2749. Gussow, Mel. "Marsha Norman Savors Pulitzer Prize for Drama." *New York Times* (Apr. 19, 1983): C13.
Gussow's piece is a biographical and professional profile of Norman, written shortly after she won the Pulitzer Prize for her one-act *'night Mother*.

2750. Hoffman, Tess. *Contemporary Dramatists*, 4th edition. Edited by D.L. Kirkpatrick, 403-04. Chicago: St. James Press, 1988.
Hoffman briefly assesses the life and work of Norman. The entry includes a list of her plays.

2751. Hubert, Linda. *Contemporary Authors Bibliographical Series: American Dramatists*. Volume 3. Edited by Matthew Roudane, 271-287. Detroit: Gale Research Inc., 1989.
A bibliographical essay assessing the critical reputation of Norman's canon. It includes a primary and secondary bibliography.

2752. Klemesrud, Judy. "She's Had Her Own Getting Out to Do." *New York Times* (May 27, 1979), sect. 2: 4, 19. Reprinted in *New York Times Biographical Service* (May 1979): 673-675.
Klemesrud, interviewing Norman one day at Sardi's, encourages the playwright to talk about her plays, especially *Getting Out,* her experiences as a dramatist in residence at the Actors Theatre of Louisville, and her methods of writing dramas. Of *Getting Out,* Norman implies that she identifies

with Arlie, "[t]hat person locked up was me. My
whole life I felt locked up, I felt in isolation, like
Arlie. My mother was a strict Methodist who . . .
wouldn't let me play with anybody, because she
didn't think any of the kids were good enough to
play with me."

2753.   Miller, Mary Ellen. "Marsha Norman." *Dictionary of
        Literary Biography: Yearbook* 1984. Edited by
        Jean W. Ross, 308-312. Detroit: Gale Research
        Company, 1985.
        This extensive introductory article includes a
        biographical profile as well as a critical survey of
        Norman's work.

2754.   Norman, Marsha. "Articles of Faith: A Conversation with
        Lillian Hellman." *American Theatre*, 1 (May
        1984): 10-15.
        Norman's brief but poignant interview with Lillian
        Hellman was conducted on Martha's Vineyard in the
        summer of 1983. Although Hellman is the focus,
        her reflections prompt Norman to voice her own
        thoughts about life and the theatre. See also
        Norman's article: "Lillian Hellman's Gift to a
        Young Playwright." *New York Times* (Aug. 26,
        1984): H1, H7.

2755.   _____. "Ten Golden Rules for Playwrights." *Writer*, 98
        (Sep. 1985): 13, 45.
        Norman provides writers with tips on writing
        plays. For example, she suggests "[d]on't write
        about your present life. You don't have a clue what
        it's about yet. Write about your past. Write about
        something that terrified you, something you still
        think is unfair."

2756.   Stone, Elizabeth. "Playwright Marsha Norman: An
        Optimist Writes About Suicide, Confinement and
        Despair." *Ms.*, 12 (July 1983): 56-59.
        Unlike most feature articles on Marsha Norman,
        which usually are biographical profiles, Stone's
        essay centers on Norman's modus operandi in

creating her plays, her choices of subject matter and how she sets the groundwork for her plays. Of central interest to Norman is "writ[ing] stories of what it is that keeps you alive. How do we survive? That's the only question we all keep asking." To enable her to answer that question she listens, which she claims is her one true capability—"I listen better than any other thing." Furthermore, Norman states, she is intrigued with the unspoken dialog that occurs within the individual. Stone's penetrating queries also elicit from Norman her attitudes toward feminism and the mother-daughter relationship, which figures prominently in her plays.

2757. Stout, Kate. "Marsha Norman: Writing for the 'Least of Our Brethren'." *Saturday Review*, 9 (Oct. 1983): 28-33. Stout's brief profile traces Norman's development as a playwright.

2758. "30 and Loving It." *Harper's Bazaar*, 116 (July 1983): 100-101, 138, 140. Marsha Norman joins Norris Church, painter, Donna Karan, fashion designer, and Fran Leibowitz, writer, in a breezy interview in which they talk about how they deal with their success, grapple with fears of failure, face the prospect of growing old, and discuss how their fame affects their friends, family, and the men in their lives.

2759. Wallach, Allan. "Women Writers Take Center Stage." *Newsday* (May 8, 1983), sect. 2: 1-5. The piece begins with a discussion of what Wallach perceives as the "explosion of women playwrights," but the article quickly turns the spotlight upon the achievements of Marsha Norman.

2760. Wolfe, Irmgard H. "Marsha Norman: A Classified Bibliography." *Studies in American Drama, 1945-Present*, 3 (1988): 149-173.

Wolfe provides one of the most extensive primary and secondary bibliograpies on Norman's dramatic works, fiction, and nonfiction. See also Wolfe's bibliographic essay in *American Playwrights Since 1945: A Guide to Scholarship, Criticism, and Performance*. Edited by Philip C. Kolin. New York: Greenwood Press, 1989.

Reviews and Criticism

See items 18, 50, 53, 79.

Circus Valentine

2761. Mootz, William. *Courier-Journal* (Louisville) (Feb. 2, 1979): C3.
2762. Saunders, Dudley. *Louisville Times* (Feb. 2, 1979): C7.

Getting Out

See items 16, 2102, 2853, 2858, 2888, 2907.

2763. *American Theatre Annual, 1978-1979*, 112. Detroit: Gale Research Company, 1979.
2764. *American Theatre Annual, 1979-1980*, 178. Detroit: Gale Research Company, 1980.
2765. Barnes, Clive. *New York Post* (Oct. 25, 1978): 90.
2766. _____. *New York Post* (May 16, 1979).
     Reprinted in item 2802.
2767. Beaufort, John. *Christian Science Monitor* (Oct. 25, 1978).
     Reprinted in 2802.
2768. Brown, Joe. *Washington Post* (Mar. 5, 1988), sect. B: 5.
2769. Clurman, Harold. *Nation*, 227 (Nov. 18, 1978): 557-558.
2770. *Contemporary Literary Criticism: Excerpts from Criticism of the Works of Today's Novelists, Poets, Playwrights and Other Creative Writers*. Volume 28. Edited by Jean C. Stine, 317-332. Detroit: Gale Research Company, 1984.
2771. DeVries, Hilary. *Christian Science Monitor* (Apr. 2, 1987): 31.
2772. Drake, Sylvie. *Los Angeles Times* (Jan. 5, 1978), sect. 6: 11.

2773. _____. *Los Angeles Times* (Feb. 12, 1978), Calendar sect.: 58.

2774. _____. *Los Angeles Times* (Aug. 9, 1988), sect. 6: 1, 8.

2775. _____. *Los Angeles Times* (Sep. 1, 1988), sect. 6: 7.
Drake reports that *Getting Out* will not perform at the California Institution for Women at Frontera. According to the public information officer for the institution, the play "has very negative connotations about correctional officers in relation to inmates." See related story in item 2788.

2776. Eder, Richard. *New York Times* (May. 16, 1979): C19. Reprinted in item 2802.

2777. Eichelbaum, Stanley. *San Francisco*, 23 (Feb. 1981): 24.

2778. Erstein, Hap. *Washington Times* (Mar. 2, 1988), sect. E: 3.

2779. Faber, Charles. *Los Angeles Free Press* (Mar. 2, 1978): 20.

2780. Feingold, Michael. *Village Voice* (May 28, 1979): 90.

2781. Fox, Terry Curtis. *Village Voice* (Nov. 6, 1978): 127, 129. Reprinted in item 2770.

2782. Gill, Brendan. *The New Yorker*, 55 (Dec. 24, 1979): 73.

2783. Glover, William. *Courier-Journal* (Louisville) (Oct. 24, 1978): B10.

2784. Gussow, Mel. *New York Times* (Oct. 14, 1979), sect. 2: 3.

2785. Kauffmann, Stanley. *New Republic*, 181 (July 7-14, 1979): 24-25.

2786. Kalem, T.E. *Time*, 113 (May 28, 1979): 80. Reprinted in item 2802.

2787. Kerr, Walter. *New York Times* (June 3, 1979), sect. 2: D5. Reprinted in items 2770, 2802.

2788. Koehler, Robert. "Rehearsals for *Getting Out* Go Inside for Firsthand Look; Actors Learn from Frontera Inmates about Life's Intricacies on Both Sides of Barbed Wire." *Los Angeles Times* (Aug. 1, 1988), sect. 6: 1, 2.
Koehler notes that several members of the cast of *Getting Out*, including Carole King who plays ex-con Ruby, enact scenes of the play for Frontera inmates. The purpose of the performance was to entertain as well as to elicit comments from the

inmates. See related article: Sylvie Drake. *Los Angeles Times* (Sep. 1, 1988), sect. 6: 7.

2789. Kroll, Jack. *Newsweek,* 93 (Mar. 19, 1979): 92-94.
Reprinted in item 2802.
2790. _____. *Newsweek,* 93 (May 28, 1979): 103.
2791. Lardner, James. *Washington Post* (Feb. 28, 1981), sect. B: 2.
2792. Latour, Martine. *Mademoiselle,* 85 (Apr. 1979): 60.
2793. Lochte, Dick. *Los Angeles,* 23 (Apr. 1978): 246.
2794. Loney, Glenn. *After Dark,* 11 (Jan. 1979): 85.
2795. McCulloh, T.H. *Drama-Logue* (Aug.11-17, 1988): 28.
2796. Mahoney, John. *Los Angeles Times* (Jan. 8, 1982), sect. 6: 13.
2797. Metzger, Deena. *Ms.,* 6 (June 1978): 26-27.

2798. Miner, Madonne. "'What's These Bars Doin' Here?'—The Impossibility of *Getting Out.*" *Theatre Annual,* 40 (1985): 115-137.
Miner describes *Getting Out* as a "radically feminist play in its critique of the most sacred tenets of capitalistic, patriarchal ideology." Characters continually find themselves in situations which apparently "free" them to make decisions; but Norman consistently undercuts this supposed freedom, pointing to the"barbed network of unspoken and unexamined beliefs which confine characters to a single day of being free, of identifying themselves and their desires." *Getting Out* suggests that "ghosts can be neither expelled nor conquered, that acts of decision merely doom the presumed self to incompletion and alienation, that finally, the self cannot be won."

2799. Mootz, William. *Courier Journal* (Louisville) (Nov. 5, 1978): H14.
2800. Morrow, Linda. *Studies in American Drama, 1945-Present,* 3 (1988): 22.

2801. Murray, T. "Patriarchal Panoticism, or The Seduction of a Bad Joke: *Getting Out* in Theory." *Theatre Journal,* 35, iii (Oct. 1983): 376-388.

Instead of focusing on analyzing the play according to dramatic critical standards, Murray "chooses to highlight how the play self-consciously emphasizes the institutional norms of interpreting and controlling [Arlie's] deviancy." Therefore, Murray addresses key questions relating to "the institutional codes of spectatorship." For example: what is the "legitimate self" that spectators wish for Arlene? How does the play depict "a viciously uncompromising macho theatre?" And, "how might *Getting Out* reflect a theatre whose search for new profit-making images delays our admission of the public crimes committed by our playwright fathers."

2802. *New York Theatre Critics' Reviews,* 40 (June 11, 1979): 243-246.
2803. *New West,* 3 (Mar. 13, 1978): Sc-29.
2804. Oliver, Edith. *The New Yorker,* 54 (Nov. 6, 1978): 152.
2805. Pacheco, Patrick. *After Dark* 12 (Nov. 1979): 73.
2806. Raidy, William A. *Play and Players,* 26 (July, 1979): 36-37.
2807. Saunders, Dudley. *Louisville Times* (Oct. 24, 1978): C1.

2808. Scharine, Richard G. "Caste Iron Bars: Marsha Norman's *Getting Out* as Political Theatre." *Themes in Drama,* 11 (1989): 185-197.
   According to Scharine, *Getting Out* is rarely discussed as an example of political theatre, which he defines as dramatizing the nature in which society's laws, norms, and codes "imping[e] unfairly and destructively upon private lives." More specifically, Norman's play represents the experience of a woman trapped, whether inside or outside prison walls, by a male-dominated society. Scharine further asserts that if to "'get out' is to assume sovereignty over one's own life, and if *Getting Out* is a political play then the factors that mitigate against Arlene taking charge of her life must be seen as a flaw in the social system and not purely personal problems." Scharine concludes from this assumption that the consequences of

Arlene's sexual abuse must be examined and then
proceeds to look at how the "sexually
discriminating legal system," which represents the
codes and norms of society, responded to those
consequences.

2809. Sharp, Chrisopher. *Women's Wear Daily* (Oct. 24, 1978).
         Reprinted in item 2802.
2810. Sherbert, Linda. *New York Times* (Jan. 23, 1987), sect. P:
         5.
2811. Simon, John. *New York*, 11 (Nov. 13, 1978): 152.
         Reprinted in item 2770.
2812. _____. *Hudson Review*, 32, i (Spring 1979): 81-84.
2813. Sullivan, Dan. *Los Angeles Times* (Nov. 20, 1977),
         Calendar sect.: 66.
2814. _____. *Los Angeles Times* (Feb. 17, 1978), sect. 5: 1,
         25.
2815. *Times-Picayune* (New Orleans) (May 25, 1979), Fanfare
         sect.: 8.
2816. *Variety* (Nov. 8, 1978): 68.
2817. Weales, Gerald. *Georgia Review*, 34 (Fall 1980): 506-508.
2818. _____. *Commonweal*, 110 (June 17, 1983): 370-371.
         Reprinted in item 2770.
2819. Watt, Douglas. *New York Daily News* (May 16, 1979).
         Reprinted in item 2802.
2820. Winn, Steven. *San Francisco Chronicle* (Dec. 2, 1980): 52.
2821. Wohlfert-Wihlborg, Lee. *People Weekly*, 19 (May 16,
         1983): 55-57.

The Holdup

See item 2907.

2822. Erben, Rudolf. "The Western Holdup Play: The Pilgrimage
         Continues." *Western American Literature* , 23, iv
         (Winter 1989): 311-322.
         Erben analyzes five dramas, one of which is
         Norman's *The Holdup*, that represent modern
         interpretations of "the holdup play." A unique
         genre, Erben claims it was introduced by
         Sherwood's *The Petrified Forest* and evolved from
         the earlier "snowbound" or "lifeboat" plays.

According to Erben, what distinguishes the holdup
play from its antecedents is its Western frontier
setting that operates as the central geographic and
symbolic focal point. As can be seen in Norman's
play, the transformations the characters undergo are
symbolic of the changes the West and the country
have experienced.

2823.　Sullivan, Dan. *Los Angeles Times*　(Apr. 22, 1983), sect.
　　　　6: 1, 14.
2824.　Weiner, Bernard. *San Francisco Chronicle*　(Apr. 14, 1983):
　　　　62.

2825.　Winn, Steven. "*Hold-Up:* No Escaping the Evils of Our
　　　　World." *San Francisco Chronicle*　(Apr. 10, 1983),
　　　　Datebook sect.: 40.
　　　　According to Norman, *The Holdup*, which at the
　　　　time of this article was premiering at the Geary
　　　　Theatre, was originally written for the Mark Taper
　　　　Forum in Los Angeles. The Forum, however, did
　　　　not produce the play because Norman claims it
　　　　"turned out to be a different kind of work from what
　　　　Gordon [Davidson, artistic director] and I discussed.
　　　　I was interested in real nature, real guns and death."

The Laundromat

See items 2858, 2888, 2907.

2826.　Gill, Brendan. *The New Yorker,* 55 (Dec. 24, 1979): 72
2827.　Gussow, Mel. *New York Times*　(Dec. 21, 1979): C5.
2828.　Lowell, Sondra. *Los Angeles Times*　(Feb. 3, 1978), sect.
　　　　4: 15.
2829.　O'Connor, John J. *New York Times*　(Apr. 4, 1985): C18.
2830.　*Variety*　(Apr. 10, 1985): 63.

'night Mother

See items 26, 35, 88, 1598, 1622, 1627, 2907.

2831. Adler, Thomas. *Mirror on the Stage: The Pulitzer Prize Play As a Approach to American Drama*. West Lafayette: Purdue Research Foundation, 1987. Adler's study is unique; it is one of the few works that analyze the Pulitzer Prize winning plays as a way of examining "the nature and development of serious American drama." The book treats the plays thematically rather than chronologically. For example, in chapter three, "The Ethic of Happiness," he analyzes six plays, including Beth Henley's *Crimes of the Heart*, which address the question of what is happiness. In *Crimes,* Adler contends the McGrath sisters' unhappiness is rooted in loneliness yet their loneliness is "mitigated by their solidarity, however fragile, with one another." In chapter one, Adler examines Marsha Norman's *'night Mother,* which he sees as an American version of Ibsen's *A Doll's House.* Adler approaches these plays employing Janet Brown's definition of feminism (see item 12), that is a woman's grappling for independence in a patriarchal society. The women in these plays strive for self-definition and the independence to make their own choices. In *'night Mother,* for instance, Adler views Jessie's suicide as "an ultimate act of existential definition of self . . . it is something she does not 'have to' do, but which she chooses to do just the same."

2832. Arkatov, Janice. *Los Angeles Times* (Apr. 29, 1986), sect. 6: 5. Arkatov reports on a discussion of suicide, moderated by the suicidologist, Edwin Schneidman, following a production of *'night Mother* at the Mark Taper Forum.

2833. Asahina, Robert. *Hudson Review,* 37 i (Spring 1984): 101.
2834. Barnes, Clive. *New York Post* (Apr. 1, 1983). Reprinted in item 2873.
2835. Beaufort, John. *Christian Science Monitor* (Apr. 22, 1983): 11.
2836. Bosworth, Patricia. *Working Woman,* 8 (Oct. 1983): 204.

2837. Brown, Joe. *Washington Post* (Oct. 25, 1985), Weekend
         sect.: 11.
2838. Brustein, Robert. *New Republic*, 188 (May 2, 1983): 25-27.
         Reprinted in Brustein's *Who Needs Theatre?*, 64-
         67. New York: Atlantic Monthly Press, 1987.
2839. Christiansen, Richard. *Chicago Tribune* (Feb. 28, 1986),
         sect. 2: 8.
2840. Crouch, Paula. *Atlanta Constitution* (Oct. 31, 1985), sect.
         C: 2.

2841. _____. *Atlanta Constitution* (Nov. 19, 1987), sect. C: 2.
         Crouch announces the opening of *'night Mother*
         by the A.R.T. Station Inc., in Stone Mountain.
         Following the play, local therapists discuss rational
         suicide and epilepsy.

2842. Denby, David. *Atlantic* (Jan. 1985): 44-45.
2843. Dolan, Jill. *Women and Performance*, 1, i (Spring/Summer
         1983): 78-79.
2844. Feingold, Michael. *Village Voice* (Apr. 12, 1983): 81.
2845. Frank, Leah. *New York Times* (Nov. 1, 1987), sect. 21:
         16.
         See also: Copeland, Roger. *New York Times*
         (Aug. 21, 1983), sect. 2: H3, H12.
2846. *Gambit*, 11 (1984): 135.
2847. Gilhooley, Jack. *Stages* (June 1984): 29.
2848. Gill, Brendan. *The New Yorker*, 59 (Apr. 11, 1983): 109-
         110, 112.
2849. Gilman, Richard. *Nation*, 236 (May 7, 1983): 585-586.
         Reprinted in item 2770.
2850. Gross, Amy. "Marsha Norman." *Vogue*, 173 (July 1983):
         200-201, 256-258.
         Norman explains that *'night Mother* is not a
         rationale for suicide but "to understand what a
         person feels who is planning to kill herself." Gross
         observes that while many plays deal with the
         "newly achieving woman," the "incompetence" of
         Norman's protagonists is "noticeable." "I'm
         interested in how life functions at its most basic
         level . . . how you continue living it without the
         skills that most people have to protect them."

Norman sees herself "representing" women like
Jessie and Arlene "who have no one on their side."

2851. Gulley, Paul. *Studies in American Drama 1945-Present*, 2
(1987): 133-135.

2852. Harmetz, Aljean. "Faith and Charity Make a Movie of a Hit
Play." *New York Times* (Aug. 10, 1986), sect. 2:
H1, H21.
This article discusses the filming of *'night Mother*,
starring Anne Bancroft and Sissy Spacek. See
related articles: Judith Michaelson. *Los Angeles
Times* (Mar. 23, 1986), Calendar sect.: 43, 52;
Linda Sherbert. "Marsha Norman Adapting
Winning Script for Screen." *Atlanta Constitution*
(May 1, 1984); 1B, 7B.

2853. Hart, Lynda. "Doing Time: Hunger for Power in Marsha
Norman's Plays." *Southern Quarterly*, 25, iii
(Spring 1987): 67-79.
Hart sees Arlene and Jessie, protagonists of *Getting
Out* and *'night Mother* respectively, as prisoners
of their inner and outer realities; yet, each woman
"hungers" for freedom and the power to control
their own destiny. Hart analyzes each play in terms
of how Norman uses "the hunger imagery [to]
capture the elemental struggle for autonomy that
her characters undergo; no metaphor could be more
basic to convey the deprivation or determination of
these women." The author, in addition, draws
analogies between the protagonists' relationship
with food, their mothers, and their sense of self.
As Hart asserts, "Jessie and Arlene share a struggle
to separate themselves from their mother's images
of them and a desire to transcend what their mothers
have themselves become. This tension between
identification and separation is a primary source of
their hunger." See related article, item 2870.

2854. Henry, William. *Time* 121 (Feb. 7, 1983): 85.
Reprinted in item 2873.
2855. Hughes, Catherine. *America,* 148 (May 7, 1983): 361.

2856. Isenberg, Barbara. *Los Angeles Times* (July 14, 1985), Calendar sect.: 40.
Isenberg briefly recounts the production history of '*night Mother* prior to its opening at the Mark Taper Forum.

2857. Johnson, Holly. *Sacramento Union* (Mar. 7, 1987): C2.

2858. Kane, Leslie. "The Way Out, The Way In: Paths To Self In the Plays of Marsha Norman." In *Feminine Focus: The New Women Playwrights*. Edited by Enoch Brater, 255-274. New York: Oxford University Press, 1989.
Kane explores the mother-daughter relationship, which forms an integral part of '*night Mother, Getting Out, Third and Oak: The Laundromat,* and *Traveler in the Dark.* The psychological and emotional gulf between mother and daughter is vast and rife with tensions, conflicts, and estrangements in these early plays. Therefore, Kane contends that underlying the relationship is "betrayal." Norman depicts daughters who live painful lives because of mothers who renege on their maternal responsibilities, they give "neither protection or guidance; they do not nourish with food or love." Norman's concern is to show the mother-daughter bond to be "crucial"; the bond prescribes how the daughter will feel about herself and how she will relate to others.

2859. Kauffmann, Stanley. *Saturday Review,* 9 (Oct. 1983): 47-48.
Reprinted in *Theater Criticisms* New York: Performing Arts Journal Publications, 1983; see item 2770.

2860. Kay, Alfred. *Sacramento Bee* (Mar. 7, 1987): A19.

2861. Kerr, Walter. *New York Times* (April 10, 1983), sect. 2: 5, 19.

2862. Kissel, Howard. *Women's Wear Daily* (Apr. 1, 1983).
Reprinted in item 2873.

2863. Kroll, Jack. *Newsweek,* 101 (Jan 3, 1983): 41-42.

2864. Lamont, Rosette C. *New York Times* (Mar. 24, 1985): H3, H27.
2865. Leydon, Joe. *Houston Post* (May 27, 1984), sect. F: 1.
2866. Lieberman, Susan. *Theatre Crafts*, 19 (Sep. 1985): 22, 46-47.
2867. Lochte, Dick. *Los Angeles*, 31 (May 1986): 52-53.
2868. Morley, Sheridan. *Punch*, 288 (Mar. 13, 1985): 82.
2869. Morris, Steven. *Drama*, 3 (3rd Quarter, 1986): 45.

2870. Morrow, Laura. "Orality and Identity in '*night, Mother* and *Crimes of the Heart*. *Studies in American Drama, 1945-Present* (1988): 23-39.
> Morrow asserts that the characters' oral behavior reflects how they feel about themselves and the quality of their relationships. In short, the self-concept of the protagonists in '*night Mother* and *Crimes* is formulated by the food they eat, by the cigarettes they smoke, and by the words they speak. For example, in '*night Mother*, Mama's love of sweets serves as a "happy substitut[tion] for genuine human interaction; they provide Mama with the sensual gratification and the sense of fullness she failed to obtain from her marriage." See related article, item 2853.

2871. Nachman, Gerald. *San Francisco Chronicle* (Sep. 8, 1983): 58.
2873. *New York Theatre Critics' Reviews*, 44 (Mar. 21, 1983): 333-337.
2874. Nightingale, Benedict. *New Statesman*, 109 (Mar. 15, 1985): 36.
2875. O'Hara, Jane. *Maclean's*, 97 (Nov. 5, 1984): 52.
2876. Radin, Victoria. *Plays & Players*, 379 (Apr. 1985): 28.
2878. Rich, Frank. *New York Times* (Apr. 1, 1983): C3.
> Reprinted in items 2770, 2873.
2879. _____. *New York Times* (July 28, 1983): C15.
2880. Richards, David. *Washington Post* (Oct. 25, 1985): D1, D3.
2881. _____. *Washington Post* (Nov. 19, 1985): E11.
2882. Sauvage, Leo. *New Leader*, 66 (Apr. 18, 1983): 21-22.
2883. Scott, Trudy. *Women & Performance*, 1, i (Spring/Summer 1983): 78.

2884.   Sherbert, Linda. *Atlanta Constitution* (Jan. 17, 1986), sect.
        P: 11.
2885.   Simon, John. *New York,* 16 (Apr. 11, 1983): 55-58.
        Reprinted in item 2770.
2886.   Smith, Patricia K. *Canadian Forum,* 65 (Apr. 1985): 38.

2887.   Spencer, Jenny S. "Norman's *'night Mother:* Psycho-
        Drama of Female Identity." *Modern Drama,* 30, iii
        (Sep. 1987): 364-375.
        Using *'night Mother* as a focal point, Spencer
        asserts there are gender differences in the way
        spectators interpret and respond to a theatrical
        production. Spencer approaches her analysis
        employing the "psychoanalytic premise that given
        the specific pressures, complications, and
        resolutions offered the female child within the
        Oedipal situation, the process whereby men and
        women gain their sexual identity is not identical,
        then it stands to reason that a literary work in
        which such issues are represented should provide for
        the audience of each sex a different *kind* of
        experience." Therefore, Spencer concludes, most
        male spectators feel Norman's play is too
        predictable and has too narrow a focus for their
        interest to remain engaged. Female theatergoers
        identify greatly with the play and undergo a
        cathartic experience—for women know that the
        play centers not around a predictable suicide but is
        grounded in the female quest for self, female
        autonomy, and self-determination.

2888.   _____. "Marsha Norman's *She-tragedies.*" In *Making a
        Spectacle: Feminist Essays on Contemporary
        Women's Theatre.* Edited by Lynda Hart, 147-165.
        Ann Arbor: University of Michigan Press, 1989.
        Spencer begins her essay by observing a
        resemblance of Norman's major plays to the *she-
        tragedies* identified with Nicholas Rowe and other
        eighteenth-century playwrights whose plots focused
        on heroines enmeshed in "pathetic situations,"
        which they have little power to control. Norman's
        dramas, maintains Spencer, are similar in that they

too "focus on female characters, address a female audience, and foreground issues of female identity." Like the eighteenth-century she-tragedies, Norman emphasizes the "potentially pathetic situation [rather] than advancing the action." Furthermore, Norman's plots revolve around female characters struggling to gain control of their lives, seeking self-validation and recognition from other women, and dealing with the reverberations that occur when they attain self-fulfillment in a society that persists in undervaluing the rights of women. Spencer discusses *Getting Out, 'night Mother,* and *The Laundromat.*

2889. Sullivan, Dan. *Los Angeles Times* (Jan. 8, 1983), sect. 5: 8.
2890. _____. *Los Angeles Times* (Mar. 28, 1986), sect. 6: 1, 18.
2891. _____. *Los Angeles Times* (Apr. 4, 1983), sect. 6: 1.
2892. Swisher, Kara. *Washington Post* (Jan. 28, 1988), Virginia sect.: 8.
2893. Tweeton, Leslie. *Boston Magazine,* 76 (Feb. 1984): 23-24.
2894. *Variety* (Apr. 6, 1983): 82.
   See also *Variety* (Jan. 26, 1983): 78-80.
2895. Wardle, Irving. *Times* (London) (Mar. 5, 1985): 10.
2896. Watt, Douglas. *New York Daily News* (Apr. 1, 1983): 3.
   Reprinted in item 2873.
2897. Weales, Gerald. *Commonweal,* 110 (June 17, 1983): 370-371.
2898. Wilson, Edwin. *Wall Street Journal* (Apr. 6, 1983): 30.
   Reprinted in item 2873.
2899. Wohlfert-Wihlborg, L. *People Weekly,* 19 (May 16, 1983): 55-56.

Sarah and Abraham

2900. Gussow, Mel. *New York Times* (Mar. 23, 1988): C26.
2901. Roberts, Peter. *Plays International,* 3 (July 1988): 35.

Third and Oak

See items 2858, 2888, 2907.

2902.   Mootz, William. *Courier-Journal* (Louisville) (Mar. 23, 1978): 4.

Traveler in the Dark

See items 2858, 2907.

2903.   DeVries, Hilary. *Christian Science Monitor* (Feb. 22, 1984): 19.
2904.   Fuchs, Elinor. *Village Voice* (Apr. 3, 1984): 92.

2905.   Gorfinkle, Constance. "Playwright Marsha Norman—A Talent For Listening." *Patriot Ledger* (Quincy, Massachusetts) (Feb. 7, 1984): 13, 17.
This preview article, written on the eve of the opening of Norman's *Traveler in the Dark* at the American Repertory Theater in Cambridge, provides a profile of her personal and professional life and her thoughts on the genesis of *Traveler*.

2906.   Gussow, Mel. *New York Times* (Jan. 16, 1990): C13.

2907.   Harriot, Esther. *American Voices: Five Contemporary Playwrights in Essays and Interviews,* 129-163. Jefferson, North Carolina: McFarland & Company, 1988.
Harriot assesses the work of five playwrights: Sam Shepard, Lanford Wilson, David Mamet, Charles Fuller, and Marsha Norman. Although lacking a label to connect these playwrights to a specific movement, Harriot contends they are related insofar as they represent a generation of writers. For each of the playwrights, Harriott includes an examination of their major plays as well as a transcript of an interview she conducted with the playwright. For Marsha Norman, Harriot provides a brief biography; the staging history of her plays; an interview, and interpretations of *Getting Out, The Laundromat, The Pool Hall, The Holdup, Traveler in the Dark,* and '*night Mother.*

2908. Henry, William A. *Time,* 123 (Feb. 27, 1984): 101.
2909. Kroll, Jack. *Newsweek,* 103 (Feb. 27, 1984): 76.
2910. Lawson, Carol. *New York Times* (Nov. 11, 1983): C2.
2911. Lochte, Dick. *Los Angeles,* 30 (Mar. 1985): 48-50.
2912. Sullivan, Dan. *Los Angeles Times* (Jan. 25, 1985), sect. 6: 1.
2913. *Variety* (Mar. 7, 1984): 402.
2914. Weales, Gerald. *Commonweal,* 117 (Feb. 23, 1990): 117.
2915. Weiner, Bernard. *San Francisco Chronicle* (Feb. 4, 1985): 41.

Winter Shakers

See item 2746.

2916. Lawson, Carol. "Marsha Norman Has Two New Works Ready for Staging." *New York Times* (Nov. 11, 1983): C2.
Lawson talks briefly about *Winter Shakers* and *Traveler in the Dark.*

Oates, Joyce Carol

Selected Plays

2917. *Daisy* (Music Theater Performing Group/Lenox Arts Center, 1980)
2918. *The Eclipse* (Ensemble Studio Theatre, 1990)
2919. *Faustus in Hell* (revue, with John Guare, Amlin Gray, Christopher Durang, and others, McCarter Theatre, 1985)
2920. *In Darkest America* (Actors Theatre of Louisville, Kentucky, 1990)
2921. *Miracle Play* (Phoenix Repertory Company, 1974)
2922. *Ontological Proof of My Existence* (Cubiculo, 1972)
Playscript: *Partisan Review,* 37, iv (1970): 471-497.
2923. *Presque Isle* (Theater of the Open Eye, 1984)
2924. *Psychiatric Service* (Hartley House, 1976)
2925. *Sunday Dinner* (American Place Theater, 1970)
2926. *Sweet Enemy* (Actors Playhouse, 1965)

2927. *The Triumph of the Spider Monkey* (Classical Theater
           Ensmble, 1983)
           Playscript: *Three Plays*. Ontario: Ontario Review
           Press, 1981.

Profiles

2928. *Contemporary Authors: A Bio-Bibliographical Guide.*
           Volume 25. New Revised Series. Edited by Hal
           May. Detroit: Gale Research Inc., 1989.
           The entry includes an interview with Oates in
           addition to a biographical sketch.

2929. Westcott, Holly Mims. *Dictionary of Literary Biography:
           Yearbook 1981.* Edited by Karen L. Rood, 119-
           125. Detroit: Gale Research Company, 1982.
           Westcott provides a biographical profile and a
           critical survey of Oates's works, emphasizing her
           novels.

Reviews

Daisy

2930. Lask, Thomas. *New York Times* (Feb. 22, 1980): C8.

Faustus in Hell

2931. Gussow, Mel. *New York Times* (Feb. 3, 1985): 55.
2932. Klein, Alvin. *New York Times* (Feb. 3, 1985), sect. 11:
           17.

In Darkest Africa

2933. Primm, Sandy. *In These Times* (Apr. 25, 1990): 20-22.
2934. Wilson, Edwin. *Wall Street Journal* (Apr. 5, 1990): A16.

Miracle Play

2935. Bruckenfeld, Dick. *Village Voice* (Jan. 10, 1974): 52.
2936. Gussow, Mel. *New York Times* (Jan. 1, 1974): 12.

Ontological Proof of My Existence

2937. Kroll, Jack. *Newsweek,* 79 (Feb. 21, 1972): 99.

Presque Isle

2938. Gussow, Mel. *New York Times* (Apr. 8, 1984): 63.

Sunday Dinner

2939. Barnes, Clive. *New York Times* (Nov. 3, 1970): 28.
2940. Kerr, Walter. *New York Times* (Nov. 8, 1970), sect. 2: 1,
      5.

Sweet Enemy

2941. Sheed, Wilfrid. *Commonweal,* 81 (Mar. 12, 1965): 764.
2942. *New York Times* (Feb. 15, 1965): 39.
      The *Times* announces the opening of *Sweet
      Enemy* at the Actors Playhouse.

Triumph of the Spider Monkey

2943. Arkatov, Janice. "Oates Spins 'Hairy' Tale about *Spider
      Monkey.*" *Los Angeles Times* (Oct. 30, 1985),
      sect. 6: 1, 4.
      Oates reflects upon her play, *Triumph of the Spider
      Monkey*, opening at the Los Angeles Theater
      Center.

2944. Blau, Eleanor. *New York Times* (Mar. 18, 1983): C2.
      Blau's preproduction article briefly describes the
      staging history of *Spider,* which would be
      performed in mid-May of 1983 at the Cubiculo
      Theater.

2945. Christiansen, Richard. *Chicago Tribune* (Oct. 21,1987),
      sect. 2: 13.
2946. Drake, Sylvie. *Los Angeles Times* (Nov. 2, 1985), sect. 5:
      1, 8.
2947. Massa, Robert. *Village Voice* (June 7, 1983): 81.

Ordway, Sally

Selected Plays

2948. *All Them Women* (with Megan Terry, Westbeth
           Playwrights Feminist Cooperative, 1973-1974)
2949. *Crabs* (Assembly Theater, 1971)
           Playscript: *Scripts*, 1 (Dec. 1977): 27-35.
2950. *Cross Country*
           Playscript: see item 2949.
2951. *Family, Family* (Westbeth Playwrights Feminist
           Collective, Joseph Jefferson Theatre, 1973)
           Playscript: *The Scene: Plays from Off-Off
           Broadway*. Edited by Stanley Nelson, 48-58. New
           York: The Smith/New Egypt, 1974.
2952. *Fanny Trollop* (staged reading Women's Project, 1982-
           1983)
2953. *No More Chattanooga Choo Choo* (staged reading,
           Women's Project, 1980-1981)
2954. *A Pretty Passion* (Interart, 1981-1982)
2955. *S.W.A.K* (staged reading, Women's Project, 1978-1979)
2956. *There's a Wall Between Us, Darling* (Theatre Genesis,
           1966)
2957. *Translators* (staged reading, Women's Project, 1984-1985)

Profiles

See item 87.

Family, Family

2958. Thompson, Howard. *New York Times* (May 26, 1973): 44.

Owens, Rochelle

Selected Plays

2959. *Beclch* (Theater of the Living Arts, Philadelphia, 1968)
           Playscript: *Beclch: A Play In Two Acts*. New
           York: Studio Duplicating Service, 1966; see item
           2964.
2960. *Chunky's Hunch* (Theatre for the New City, 1981)

Playscript: *Wordplays 2: An Anthology of New American Drama,* 1-26. New York: Performing Arts Journal Publications, 1982.

2961. *Coconut Folksinger*
Playscript: see item 2964.

2962. *Emma Instigated Me* (American Place Theater, 1976)
Playscript: *Performing Arts Journal,* 1 (Spring 1976): 71-94.

2963. *Farmer's Almanac*
Playscript: see item 2968.

2964. *Futz!* (La Mama ETC, 1967)
Playscript: *Futz! and What Came After,* 1-30. New York: Random House, 1968; *New Short Plays.* London: Methuen, 1969; *The Off-Off Broadway Book: The Plays, People, Theatre.* Edited by Albert Poland, 90-198. New York: Bobbs-Merrill, 1972; *New American Plays.* Volume 2. Edited by Robert W. Corrigan and William Hoffman, 1-24. New York: Hill & Wang, 1965.

2965. *Homo* (La Mama ETC, 1969)
Playscript: see item 2964.

2966. *He Wants Shih!* (New York Theater Strategy, 1975)
Playscript: *Spontaneous Combustion: Eight New American Plays.* New York: Winter House, 1972.

2967. *Istanboul* (Judson Poets Theatre, 1965)
Playscript: *The New Underground Theatre.* Edited by Robert J. Schroeder, 139-169. New York: Bantam Books, 1968.

2968. *The Karl Marx Play* (lyrics by Owens, music by Galt McDermott, American Place Theater, 1973)
Playscript: *The Karl Marx Play and Others.* New York: Dutton, 1974; *The Best Short Plays 1971.* Edited by Stanley Richards, 221-245. Philadelphia: Chilton Book Company, 1971.

2969. *Kontraption* (New York Theater Strategy, 1978)
Playscript: *Scripts,* 2 (Dec. 1971): 4-25; see item 2968.

2970. *Mountain Rites*
Playscript: *The Best Short Plays of 1978.* Edited by Stanley Richards, 299-328. Radnor, Pennsylvania: Chilton Book Company, 1978.

2971. *O.K. Curtaldo*

Playscript: see item 2968.
2972. *The Queen of Greece* (La Mama ETC, 1969)
2973. *The String Game* (Judson Poets Theatre, 1965)
Playscript: see item 2964.
2974. *Three Front* (Omaha Magic Theatre, Omaha, 1988)
2975. *The Widow and the Colonel*
Playscript: *The Widow and The Colonel: A Play In One-Act.* New York: Dramatists Play Service, 1977; *The Best Short Plays 1977.* Edited by Stanley Richards, 239-254. Radnor, Pennsylvania: Chilton Book Company, 1977.

Profiles and Interviews

See items 2, 9, 22, 33, 45, 67, 103, a profile in item 2970 and pages 5-6, 21.

2976. *Contemporary Theatre, Film, and Televison.* Volume 5. Edited by Monica M. O'Donnell, 265-266. Detroit: Gale Research Inc., 1988.
Owens's entry contains a brief biography and a list of her works.

2977. Lester, Eleanore. "Only Rochelle Escaped To Tell Us." *New York Times* (July 21, 1968), sect. 2: D1, D3.
Lester profiles the professional career of Owens and her first play *Futz!,* written at the age twenty-three. According to Owens, the play is a "tragic grotesquerie" about the "self-righteousness of our age."

2978. Owens, Rochelle. "Creative Consciousness: The Poet and the Theater Esthetic." *Dramatists Quarterly,* 11, iv (Winter 1975): 14-15.
According to Owens, the artist's responsibility to the theatre aesthetic is to break through the layers of conventionality—"contemporary theatre must make possible new perceptions of our disorderly, narcissistic and dangerous world."

2979. Shragge, Elaine. *Contemporary Dramatists.* 3rd edition.
Edited by James Vinson, 412-14. New York: St.
Martin's Press, 1982.
The author gives concise biographical information,
provides a list of plays and other works, and offers
general critical comments on several of Owens's
plays such as *Futz!, The String Game, Istanboul,
Beclch, The Karl Marx Play,* and *He Wants Shih!*

Reviews

See items 47, 78.

Beclch

2980. Barnes, Clive. *New York Times* (Dec. 17, 1968): 59.
2981. Cohn, Ruby. *Dialogue in American Drama,* 303-307.
Bloomington: Indiana University Press, 1971.
2982. Hewes, Henry. *Saturday Review,* 50 (Jan. 7, 1967): 111.
2983. Kerr, Walter. *God on the Gymnasium Floor and Other
Theatrical Adventures,* 105-112. New York: Simon
and Schuster, 1971.
2984. Frankel, Haskell. *National Observer* (Dec. 23, 1968): 16.
2985. Stone, Judy. *San Francisco Chronicle* (Mar. 29, 1976): 37.
2986. *Time,* 89 (Feb. 10, 1967): 58.

Chucky's Hunch

2987. Christon, Lawrence. *Los Angeles Times* (Jan. 21, 1983),
sect. 6: 2.
2988. Feingold, Michael. *Village Voice* (Mar. 2, 1982): 81.
2989. Gussow, Mel. *New York Times* (Feb. 19, 1982): C5.
2990. Hoffman, Jan. *Village Voice* (Mar. 25-31, 1981): 95.

2991. Murray, Timothy. "The Play of Letters: Possession and
Writing in *Chucky's Hunch.*" In *Feminine Focus:
The New Women Playwrights.* Edited by Enoch
Brater, 186-209. New York: Oxford University
Press, 1989.
Murray observes that Owens's "curious and
contradictory writing strategy motivates the 'play'
Chucky's Hunch." The dramatist's use of the

epistle to convey meaning suppresses two major
components of Western theatre, dialogue and
action, both of which develop characters as well as
"primal scenes." According to Murray, letter
writing and reading "constitutes the source of this
play's primal attraction." Chucky's phallic and
misogynistic letters reflect a fragile man dislocated
by two events, the demise of his dog and "Oedipal
displacement" due to an "erotic love affair" between
his mother and Chester Nickerson, both of whom
are over eighty.

2992. Rich, Frank. *New York Times* (Mar. 23, 1981): C13.

Emma Investigated Me

2993. Berkman, Len. *Parnassus: Poetry in Review,* 12/13, i,
        (1985): 552-576.
2994. Stone, Judy. *San Francisco Chronicle* (Apr. 22, 1976): 41.

Futz!

See items 22, 3845.

2995. Ansorge, Peter. *Plays and Players,* 15 (Nov. 1967): 45.
2996. Atcheson, Richard. *Holiday,* 44 (Oct. 1968): 60-65.
2997. Barnes, Clive. *New York Times* (June 14, 1968): 39.
        Reprinted in item 3010.
2998. _____. *New York Times* (Oct. 22, 1968): 37.
2999. Berkman, Len. *Parnassus: Poetry in Review,* 12.13, i
        (1985): 552-576.
3000. Brustein, Robert. *New Republic,* 159 (July 13, 1968): 31-
        32.
        Reprinted in Brustein's *The Third Theater,* 68-72.
        New York: Knopf, 1969.
3001. *Contemporary Literary Criticism: Excerpts from Criticism
        of the Works of Today's Novelists, Poets,
        Playwrights and Other Creative Writers.* Volume 8.
        Edited by Dedria Bryfonski, 434-435. Detroit: Gale
        Research Company, 1978.
3002. Davis, James. *New York Daily News* (June 14, 1968).
        Reprinted in item 3010.

3003. Feingold, Michael. *Yale/Theater*, 1, iii (Winter 1968): 28-30.
3004. Gottfried, Martin. *Women's Wear Daily* (June 26, 1968). Reprinted in Gottfried's *A Theater Divided: The Postwar American Stage*, 300. Boston: Little, Brown, 1968; and *Opening Nights: Theater Criticism of the Sixties*, 324-326. New York: Putnam, 1969.
3005. Hewes, Henry. *Saturday Review*, 51 (June 22, 1968): 57.
3006. Hughes, Catharine. *Nation*, 208 (Jan. 20, 1969): 91.
3007. Kerr, Walter. *New York Times* (June 30, 1968), sect. 2: 1, 5. Reprinted in Kerr's *Thirty Plays Hath November: Pain & Pleasure in the Contemporary Theatre*, 70-74. New York: Simon & Schuster, 1969.
3008. Kroll, Jack. *Newsweek*, 72 (July 1, 1968): 95.
3009. Lester, Elenore. *New York Times* (June 30, 1968), sect. 2: D1, D5.
3010. *New York Theatre Critics' Reviews*, 29 (Dec. 30, 1968): 142-144.

3011. *New York Times* (Dec. 25, 1968): 45. The *Times* announces the closing of *Futz!* at the Actors Playhouse after 233 performances.

3012. O'Connor, James J. *Wall Street Journal* (June 17, 1968). Reprinted in item 3010.
3013. Oliver, Edith. *The New Yorker*, 43 (Feb. 10, 1968): 88-90.
3014. Prideaux, Tom. *Life*, 65 (July 12, 1968): 10.
3015. Simon, John. *Commonweal*, 88 (June 28, 1968): 442-443. Reprinted in Simon's *Uneasy Stages: A Chronicle of the New York Stage, 1963-1973*, 143. New York: Random House, 1975; see item 3001.
3016. Tallmer, Jerry. *New York Post* (June 17, 1968). Reprinted in item 3010.
3017. *Time*, 91 (June 21, 1968): 67.
3018. Weiner, Bernard. *San Francisco Chronicle* (Feb. 21, 1978): 40.

He Wants Shih!

3019. Gussow, Mel. *New York Times* (Apr. 2, 1975): 25.

Homo

See item 22.

3020. Van Gelder, Lawrence. *New York Times* (Apr. 12, 1969): 40.

Istanboul

3021. Barnes, Clive. *New York Times* (Feb. 9, 1971): 34.

The Karl Marx Play

See item 22.

3022. Barnes, Clive. *New York Times* (Apr. 3, 1973): 51.
3023. Berkman, Len. *Parnassus: Poetry in Review,* 12/13, i (1985): 552-576.
3024. Gottfried, Martin. *Women's Wear Daily* (Apr. 3, 1973). Reprinted in item 3028.
3025. Kerr, Walter. *New York Times* (Apr. 8, 1973), sect. 2: 3.
3026. Kroll, Jack. *Newsweek,* 81 (Apr. 16, 1973): 117-118. Reprinted in items 3001, 3028.
3027. Oliver, Edith. *The New Yorker,* 49 (Apr. 7, 1973): 58-59. Reprinted in item 3001.
3028. *New York Theatre Critics' Reviews,* 34 (Aug. 20, 1973): 256-258.

3029. *New York Times* (Feb. 27, 1973): 30.
    The *Times* briefly describes *The Karl Marx Play* and announces the opening of the play at the American Place Theater on March 16 and at the Le Jeune Theatre Nationale de Paris in Paris on May 2.

3030. Simon, John. *New York,* 6 (Apr. 16, 1973): 88.
3031. Watt, Douglas. *New York Daily News* (Apr. 3, 1973). Reprinted in item 3028.
3032. Watts, Richard. *New York Post* (Apr. 3, 1973). Reprinted in item 3028.

The Queen Of Greece

3033. Van Gelder, Lawrence. *New York Times* (Apr. 12, 1969): 40.

The String Game

See item 22.

Pearson, Sybille

Selected Plays

3034. *Baby* (developed by Susan Yankowitz, book by Pearson, Ethel Barrymore, 1983)
3035. *A Little Going Away Party* (staged reading, Women's Project, 1978-1979)
3036. *Phantasie* (Vineyard Theatre, 1989)
3037. *Reunion* (Center Stage, Baltimore, 1986)
3038. *Sally and Marsha* (Manhattan Theater Club, 1982)
       Playscript: *Sally and Marsha*. New York: Dramatists Play Service, 1983.

Profiles

3039. Bosworth, Patricia. "The Arts: Some Uncommon Dramatists." *Working Woman*, 9 (Aug. 1984): 39-141.
       A cursory survey of the life and works of Pearson and three other successful playwrights, Beth Henley, Tina Howe, Wendy Wasserstein.

Reviews

Baby

3040. Beaufort, John. *Christian Science Monitor* (Dec. 14, 1983): 33.

3041. Blau, Eleanor. "A New Musical *Baby* Due To Be Delivered Nov. 6." *New York Times* (Aug. 12, 1983): C2.

Blau's pre-production article briefly discusses the play's unconventional aspects and quotes James B. Freydbert, producer of the show, as claiming the musical "is singing about things that people haven't sung about before."

3042. Czarnecki, Mark. *Maclean's,* 96 (Dec. 26, 1983): 41-42.

3043. Freedman, Samuel G. "Survival Tactics of 3 Broadway Musicals." *New York Times* (Feb. 2, 1984): C13. Freedman includes *Baby* in his discussion of how these musicals survive in the "risky territory" of Broadway.

3044. Gill, Brendan. *The New Yorker,* 59 (Dec. 12, 1983): 158.
3045. Hughes, Catherine. *America,* 150 (Feb. 25, 1984): 136.
3046. Klein, Alvin. *New York Times* (Oct. 28, 1984), sect. 11: 26.

3047. Lawson, Carol. "Musical *Baby* Is On the Way." *New York Times* (July 30, 1982): C2. Lawson's preview article briefly discusses *Baby*.

3048. Novick, Julius. *Village Voice* (Dec. 13, 1983): 116.
3049. Schickel, Richard. *Time,* 122 (Dec. 19, 1983): 71.
3050. Simon, John. *New York,* 16 (Dec. 19, 1983): 87.
3051. Wilson, Edwin. *Wall Street Journal* (Dec. 7, 1983): 26.

Phantasie

3052. Breslauer, Jan. *American Theatre,* 6 (Apr. 1989): 7-8.
3053. Gussow, Mel. *New York Times* (Jan. 4, 1989): C15.
3054. Simon, John. *New York,* 22 (Jan. 23, 1989): 56.

Sally and Marsha

3055. Beaufort, John. *Christian Science Monitor* (Mar. 2, 1982): 19.

3056. Corry, John. "New Road To Broadway." *New York Times* (June 3, 1981): C21.

Corry reports on the opening of *Sally and Marsha*
at the State University of New York on July 30,
1981.

3057. Drake, Sylvie. *Los Angeles Times* (Mar. 12, 1984), sect.
6: 1.
3058. Gussow, Mel. *New York Times* (Feb. 5, 1981): C2.
3059. Hughes, Catherine. *America,* 146 (Apr. 24, 1982): 320.
3060. _____. *Plays and Players,* 344 (May 1982): 30-31.
3061. Kerr, Walter. *New York Times* (Mar. 14, 1982): D3.
3062. Munk, Erica. *Village Voice* (Mar. 2, 1982): 83.
3063. Oliver, Edith. *The New Yorker,* 58 (Mar. 8, 1982): 98.
3064. Pace, Eric. *New York Times* (Jan. 11, 1981), sect. 2: D5,
D20.
3065. Rich, Frank. *New York Times* (Feb. 22, 1982): C18.
3066. Shirley, Don. *Los Angeles Times* (Dec. 14, 1985), sect. 5:
9.
3067. Simon, John. *New York,* 15 (Mar. 8, 1982): 82.
3068. Stasio, Marilyn. *Penthouse,* 13 (June 1982): 44-46.
3069. *Variety* (Feb. 24, 1982):114.

Perry, Shaunielle

Selected Plays

3070. *Aunt Willie Pays a Call* (Henry Street Settlement, 1980)
3071. *A Celebration* (American Place Theater, 1986)
3072. *Daddy Goodness* (National Theatre, Washington D.C.,
1979)
3073. *Mio* (Henry Street Settlement, 1978-1979)

Profiles

See items 361, 1194, 1198.

3074. *Contemporary Authors: A Bio-Bibliographical Guide.*
Volume 113. Edited by Hal May, 374-375. Detroit:
Gale Research Company, 1985.
A biographical sketch accompanies general critical
remarks on Perry focusing on her directorial efforts.

3075. "Creative Directions." *Essence,* 3 (May 1972): 76.

This article highlights the careers of several women artists including Perry.

3076. Peterson, Bernard L. *Contemporary Black American Playwrights and Their Plays: A Biographical Directory and Dramatic Index*, 379-380. New York: Greenwood Press, 1989.
Peterson provides a biographical sketch as well as a survey of Perry's work.

Reviews

Mio

3077. Supree, Burt. *Village Voice* (Feb. 5, 1979): 85.

Portillo-Trambley, Estela

Selected Plays

3078. *Blacklight* (reading, South Coast Repertory, Los Angeles, 1987)
3079. *Day of the Swallows* (Nosotros, Los Angeles, 1979)
Playscript: *El Grito*, 4, iii (Spring, 1971): 4-47; *Contemporary Chicano Theatre*. Edited by Roberto J. Garza, 205-246. Notre Dame: University of Notre Dame, 1976; *El Espejo/The Mirror*. Edited by Octavio I. Romano. Berkeley: Quinto Sol Publications, 1972; *We Are Chicanos: An Anthology of Mexican-American Literature*. Edited by Philip D. Ortego, 221-223. New York: Washington Square Press, 1973.
3080. *Morality Play*
Playscript: *El Grito*, 7 (Sep. 1973): 7-21 (excerpt).
3081. *Sun Images*
Playscript: *Revista Chicano-Riquena*, 7, i (Winter, 1979): 19-42; *Nuevos Pasos*: Edited by Nicholas Kanellos and Jorge A. Huerta, 19-64. Houston: Arte Publico Press, 1989.

Profiles and Interviews

3082. *Contemporary Authors: A Bio-Bibliographical Guide.*
Volumes 77-80. Edited by Frances Carol Locher,
552-53. Detroit: Gale Research Company, 1979.
The entry includes a brief biography and a list of
Portillo-Trambley's works.

3083. Garza, Roberto J. "Introduction to *The Day of the
Swallows.*" In *Contemporary Chicano Theatre.*
Edited by Roberto J. Garza, 205. Notre Dame:
University of Notre Dame, 1976.
Garza provides a concise profile of Portillo-
Trambley that accompanies the text of her play *The
Day of the Swallows.*

3084. Jalon, Allan. "3 Latino Writers in SCR Spotlight." *Los
Angeles Times* (July 10, 1987), sect. 6: 21.
Jalon profiles Portillo-Trambley and Ana Maria
Simo, whose plays *Blacklight* and *Passion*,
respectively, are to be given staged readings during
the South Coast Repertory's Hispanic Playwrights
Project. The third dramatist included in the profile
is Jose Rivera.

3085. Novoa, Bruce. "Estela Portillo [Trambley]." In *Chicano
Authors: Inquiry by Interview.* Austin: University
of Texas Press, 1980.
Novoa's interview, which is formal and less
conversational in structure than Vowell's (see item
3086), commences with Portillo's description of
her early life, family, and educational background.
The writer offers insights on Chicano literature and
its relation to the Anglo literary canon. To the
question of the position of Chicano literature
within American literature, Portillo maintains the
former is in its "revolutionary" phase in which it
emphasizes "complaint and condemnation" toward
Anglo society. But the author predicts that
Chicano writers will outgrow this phase and
Chicano literature will "find its own balance."
Very little of the interview is devoted to Portillo's

theatre activities; however, she does discuss briefly
the genesis of her play *The Day of the Swallows*.

3086.   Vowell, Faye Nell. "A *Melus* Interview: Estela Portillo-
Trambley." *Melus*, 9, iv (Winter 1982): 59-66.
Unlike Novoa's interview of Portillo-Trambley (see
item 3085), Vowell's interview yields more
information on her activities in the theatre. She
disagrees with what she views as the major tenet of
Chicano theatre: the purpose of the play is to
protest the social inequities of living in the Anglo
society. Portillo-Trambley argues that theatre
should be more than satisfying political ends, and
she claims her plays "go beyond social protest" to
dramatize the multifaceted sides of poverty—"I
show the wear and tear." The dramatist declares her
feminist perspective serves to counter the
traditional images of women extant in Chicano
literature. She affirms the perception that Chicano
male writers unfailingly image women according to
the stereotypic categories of "the adored, revered
mother . . . the suffering wife . . . then . . . the
lady who is there for fun and pleasure." Portillo-
Trambley claims she has "fought these images" and
that Chicanas "should be seen as a totality of
things." Thus, the playwright creates independent
women who "are not passive, they're alive, they
have a mind of their own, and they're not afraid."
And to those who criticize her for failing to depict
realistic Chicanas, Portillo-Trambley retorts, "I've
said that they are definitely images of women and
they're images of angry women."

Reviews and Criticism

The Day of the Swallows

See items 2627, 3097 and *We Are Chicanos* (item 3979)
and page 18.

3087. Castellano, Olivia. "Of Clarity of the Moon: A Study of
Two Women in Rebellion." *De Colores,* 3, iii
(1977): 25-30.
The "two women" in Castellano's title refer to
Josefa and Nian, protagonists from Portillo-
Trambley's play *The Day of the Swallows* and her
short shory *The Apple Trees* respectively.
Castellano observes both stories end with the
suicide of each woman; but, "even in their death,
they are triumphant." According to Castellano,
Portillo has diverged from the traditional depiction
of women in Chicano literature; her protagonists
rebel against the "senselessness of ritualized
behavior and. . . look deeply into their own
imagination and subconscious, the source from
which all myth springs." However, their rebellion
can only lead to death of self because of their
refusal to conform to the social values grounded in
patriarchy. Josefa's lesbianism, according to
Castellano, "represents change, a respite from the
self-perpetuating role of women as perfect." Josefa
attempts to find self-definition through her
lesbianism; she breaks away from the collective
myths of the community to create her own
mythology. To achieve success, Josefa must
disengage herself from emotional and psychological
boundaries. She makes an attempt but
unfortunately fails because she is unable to free
herself from the social or communal boundary. In
short, Josefa is unable to live openly as a lesbian
and still feel she is accepted by her community.

3088. Dewey, Janice. "Dona Josefa: Bloodpulse of Transition and
Change." In *Breaking Boundaries: Latina Writing
and Critical Readings.* Edited by Asuncio Delgado,
39-47. Amherst: University of Massachusetts,
1989.
Dewey observes that critics tend to categorize *Day
of the Swallows* as outside the main current of
Chicano literature because it focuses on themes of
"poetry, magic, and lesbianism" instead of the
traditional themes of socio-political protest.

However, Dewey argues that the protagonist Dona Josefa's suicide is a "symbolic protest" against both the violence that leads to her death and the "farce of the lie that she lived." Lesbians and Chicanos as distinct culture groups have much in common: they both live "marginal" lives and have an acute political awareness. Dewey reinforces her argument by comparing this play with Garcia Lorca's *The House of Bernardo Alba*. Both plays dramatize individuals rebelling against the social norms and mores of their communities, include issues of virginity and suicide, and incorporate ritual, poetic imagery, and symbolism to convey meaning.

3089. Gonzalez, Laverne. "Estela Portillo-Trambley." In *Chicano Literature: A Reference Guide*. Edited by Julio A. Marinez and Francisco A. Lomeli, 316-322. Westport, Connecticut: Greenwood Press, 1984. Gonzalez provides a cursory critical survey of the works of Portillo-Trambley.

3090. Mael, Phyllis. *Frontiers*, 5, ii (Summer 1980): 54-58.
3991. Mahoney, John C. *Los Angeles Times* (May 11, 1979), sect. 4: 24.

3092. Parr, Carmen Salazar."Surrealism in the Work of Estela Portillo." *Melus*, 7, iv (Winter 1980): 85-92. Parr suggests that Portillo-Trambley is among the female surrealist dramatists who are re-defining the image of women in surrealist drama, which venerates femininity yet continues to portray them in conventional images. Like other female surrealists, Portillo draws upon archetypal images to interpret feminine qualities. According to Parr, Portillo has imaged the protagonist, Josefa in *The Day of the Swallows* "in traditional surrealist terms . . . graceful, virtuous, intuitive, charitable" but intensified the character by not having Josefa "seek an androgynous union as the ultimate realization of totality."

3093. Ramirez, Arthur. "Estela Portillo: The Dialectic of
       Oppression and Liberation." *Revista Chicano-*
       Riquena, 8, iii (Summer 1980): 106-114.
       Ramirez focuses on Portillo's theme of the
       consequences of a woman engaged in a struggle
       against the oppressive social conditions imposed by
       a patriarchal value system. Her rebellion results in
       being torn between oppression and independence,
       submissiveness and assertiveness. Ramirez
       considers the public self and the private self of
       Josefa, the protagonist of *The Day of the*
       Swallows, as embodying the dialectic between
       oppression and liberation. The real but private self
       of Josefa is lesbian, which she accepts; but she
       realizes that the community, if it knows of her
       lesbianism, would "destroy her image of an almost
       venerated angel." To protect her private, secret self,
       Josefa maintains her public image of the ideal
       woman: saintly, good, pure. But, ultimately, her
       public image is "undone by her overextended grasp
       for power and appearances." Consequently, Josefa
       is unable to "reconcile the inward and outward
       images . . . the real and the ideal and commits
       suicide."

3094. Rodriguez, Alfonso. "Tragic Vision in Estela Portillo's *The*
       Day of the Swallows." *De Colores*, 5, 1&2 (1980):
       152-158.
       Rodriguez analyzes Portillo's play in terms of its
       tragic dimensions. He applies David D. Raphael's
       definition of the tragic conflict, which is one
       "between inevitable power, which we may call
       necessity, and the reaction to necessity of self-
       conscious effort . . . the victory always goes to
       necessity. . . the hero is crushed." Thus,
       "necessity" in *The Day of the Swallows* is
       personified by the values of Josefa's community,
       which run counter to Josefa's values. Privately
       Josefa rebels against these communal values, but
       because she is unable to transcend the judgments of
       her community she is "crushed" in the end.
       Roderiguez identifies several characteristics aligning

Josefa with protagonists of tragedy: she holds a
privileged place in the community; embodies
several paradoxes; exercises a "radical solitude" and
she is "defined by . . . her suffering, much of which
is brought on by guilt." The author concludes
"Josefa's death becomes the sacrificial offering as an
atonement for [her] guilt and for the evils of
society."

3095. Salinas, Judy. "The Image of Woman in Chicano Literature.
       Revista Chicano-Riquena, 4, iv (Autumn 1976):
       139-148.
       Salinas contends it is inevitable that Chicano
       literature contains the kinds of images of woman as
       its parent literatures (Spanish, Spanish-American,
       and Anglo-American) but "the portrayal of woman
       in Chicano literature [is] unique and totally distinct
       from the traditional . . . stereotypic influences of
       its parent literatures. Salinas cites two reasons for
       the distinctiveness of the images of women
       portrayed in Chicano literature. First, Chicano
       publishers encourage women writers. And second,
       women are represented realistically "and far more
       consistently presented as a duality of good and bad
       in several Chicano works." Salinas analyzes three
       works by Chicano writers, one of which is
       Portillo-Trambley's *The Day of the Swallows.*
       Salinas discusses the duality of Dona Josefa, who
       "was not totally bad as her acts condemned her nor
       was she totally good as her false image portrayed
       her to be."

Sun Images

3096. Kanellos, Nicolas and Jorge A. Huerta. "Introduction to *Sun
       Images.*" *Revista Chicano-Riquena,* 7 (1979): 19-
       42.
       In their introduction to Portillo-Trambley's play
       Sun Images Kanellos and Huerta claim that it is
       the "first musical to be published by a Chicano and
       represents a first step towards employing the style
       usually associated with Broadway and community

theatre." The editors maintain, however, that a
"possible shortcoming" of the play is the "absence
of a strong social or political statement."

3097. Tatum, Charles M. "Estela Portillo-Trambley." In *Chicano
Literature*, 75-76. Boston: Twayne Publishers,
1982.
Tatum briefly discusses the musical comedy *Sun
Images* as well as *The Day of the Swallows*.

Prida, Delores

Selected Plays

3098. *The Beggars Soap Opera* (with Paul Radelat, DUO Theater,
Spanish English Ensemble Theater, 1979)
3099. *Coser y Cantar* (Duo Theater, INTAR, 1981)
3100. *La Era Latina* (with Victor Gragoso, Puerto Rican
Traveling Theater, 1980)
3101. *Savings* (INTAR, 1985)

Profiles and Interviews

3102. Escarpenter, Jose and Linda S. Glaze. "Delores Prida." In
*Biographical Dictionary of Hispanic Literature in
the United States*. Edited by Nicolas Kanellos, 250-
255. New York: Greenwood, 1989.
Following a biographical sketch, the authors
briefly discuss the themes and motifs of Prida's
work, including her major dramas. Included is a
selected primary and secondary bibliography.

3103. Waldman, Gloria F. "Hispanic Theatre in New York."
Journal of Popular Culture, 19, iii (Winter 1985):
139-147.
Waldman briefly highlights the achievements of
Prida and Maria Irene Fornes in her assessment of
the theatrical work done by Hispanics in New
York.

3104. Prida, Delores. "The Show Does Go On (Testimonio)." In
Breaking Boundaries: Latina Writing and Critical

Readings. Edited by Asuncio Delgado, 181-186.
Amherst: University of Massachusetts, 1989.
Prida, a Cuban-American playwright, articulates
what the theatre means to her. She began her
creative career secretly writing poetry—"[it] wasn't
the 'in' thing among my peers," but upon seeing
her first play after moving to New York she
"became fascinated forever with the idea of people
bursting into song and dance at the least
provocation." In addition to her career in the
theatre, Prida reflects upon the situation of the
contemporary Hispanic theatre in the United States,
which she believes suffers from lack of visibility
among the audiences of the Hispanic as well as the
Anglo communities. To promote awareness and
increase audience attendance, Prida contends that
colleges and universities have "a large role to play
in bringing Hispanic-American theatre and literature
into the mainstream." But, Prida observes, because
many academic institutions lack understanding of
Hispanic literature and its position in the
curriculum, "they don't know, or don't want to
know, what to do with the whole darned big
enchilada."

Reviews and Criticism

Beggars Soap Opera

3105. Agueros, Jack. *Nuestro* 3 (Oct. 1979): 52-53.
3106. Corry, John. *New York Times* (July 24, 1979): C7.

Coser y Cantar

3107. Nordheimer, Jon. "Tempest In Miami Over a Playwright."
            New York Times (May 10, 1986): 6.
            Nordheimer reports the cancellation of Prida's play
            Coser y Cantar by the Miami theatre company,
            Teatro Nuevo, due to threats made against members
            of the production. Apparently, some Cuban-
            Americans regard Prida as an "enemy of Cuban
            exiles," because of her prior attempts "to improve

relations with . . . Castro's Cuba." But, Prida
maintains her plays are apolitical, "I've never even
read Karl Marx. If I'm to be called anything, I am a
liberal democrat and an activist."

3108. Pena, Amalia. *Village Voice* (July 29, 1981): 69.

3109. Sandoval, Alberto. "Delores Prida's *Coser y Cantar:*
Mapping the Dialectics of Ethnic Identity and
Assimilation." In *Breaking Boundaries: Latina
Writing and Critical Readings*. Edited by Asuncio
Delgado, 201-220. Amherst: University of
Massachusetts, 1989.
Examining Prida's *Coser y Cantar* from a socio-
cultural perspective, Sandoval's "aim is to
demonstrate how subjectivity is constructed,
configured, and articulated when an individual
moves dialectically between two cultures." He
declares that the play "is but the *re*-presentation of
Latina subjectivity in process: always in
movement, in flux, and oscillating in the dialectics
of a bicultural identity in the United States."
Prida's protagonists confront the "dilemma of a dual
selfhood that is demeaned, marginalized, and
silenced" by the repressive Anglo society and
political structure.

Savings

3110. Bruckner, D.J.R. *New York Times* (May 24, 1985): C3.

Pryor, Deborah

Selected Plays

3111. *Briar Patch* (Ensemble Studio Theater, 1989)
3112. *Burrhead* (New Playwrights Theatre, Washington D.C.,
1983)
3113. *The Love Talker* (Hudson Guild Theater, 1988)
Playscript: *The Best Short Plays 1988*. Edited by
Ramon Delgado, 255-80. New York: Applause,
1988.

3114.   *Rattlesnake Trap* (Actors Theatre of Louisville, Kentucky, 1986-1987)

Profiles and Interviews

See profile in item 3113.

3115.   Erstein, Hap. "Playwright Pryor Basks In Overnight Fame." *Washington Post* (Apr. 3, 1987), sect. M: 4.
Erstein profiles Pryor following a successful run of her one-act *The Love Talker* at the Humana Festival of New American Plays in Louisville. Erstein describes Pryor's professional career as well as her unique writing process. Pryor's ideas for her plays originate from her dreams. The characters of her subconscious "sort of come in . . . they talk to her for awhile and then they turn their backs on her and sulk." In addition, Pryor's colleagues comment on the challenging nature of her work. For example Jon Jory, director of the *The Love Talker,* remarks that the uniqueness of her plays makes it "difficult to bring [them] alive on stage."

3116.   Rosenfeld, Megan. "Backstage" *Washington Post* (July 4, 1983): B7.
Rosenfeld's article, written during a current production of Pryor's *Burrhead,* briefly describes Pryor's personal background, her start in the theatre, and current works in progress. The article also includes Pryor's comments on the creation of *Burrhead.*

Reviews

Burrhead

3117.   Richards, David. *Washington Post* (June 28, 1983): C1.

The Love Talker

3118.   DeVries, Hilary. *Christian Science Monitor* (Apr. 2, 1987): 30-31.

3119. Gussow, Mel. *New York Times* (Apr. 30, 1988): 17.
3120. Roberts, Peter. *Plays International,* 2 (May 1987): 49-50.

Rahman, Aishah

Selected Plays

3121. *Lady and the Tramp (1983)*
    Playscript: *Confirmation: An Anthology of African American Women.* Edited by Amiri Baraka, 284-299. New York: William Morrow, 1983.
3122. *Lady Day: A Musical Tragedy* (Brooklyn Academy of Music, Chelsea Theatre, 1972)
3123. *The Mojo and the Sayso* (Crossroads Theater Company, New Jersey, 1988)
    Playscript: *Massachusetts Review,* 39, i (Spring 1988): 169-216.
3124. *The Tale of Madame Zora* (Ensemble Studio Theatre, 1986)
3125. *Transcendental Blues* (Manhattan Theater Club, 1977)
    Playscript: see item 3121.
3126. *Unfinished Women Cry in No Man's Land While a Bird Dies in a Gilded Cage* (New York Shakespeare Festival, Public Theatre, 1977)
    Playscript: *9 Plays by Black Women.* Edited by Margaret Wilkerson, 197-237. New York: New American Library, 1986.

Profiles and Interviews

See item 77.

3127. Gossett, Hattie. "Aishah Rahman: Transcending the Black Woman's Blues." *N.Y. Amsterdam News* (Sep. 24, 1977), sect. D: 8.
    Gossett profiles Rahman during a run of her play *Unfinished Women Cry In No Man's Land While A Bird Dies In a Gilded Cage.* Rahman recounts her years "getting ready to write," her future projects as well as her desire to write for film and television. The versatile playwright comments that underlying all her plays is a message to her "sisters," to

"transcend these Black woman's blues and move on up to higher ground."

3128.   Rahman, Aishah. "To Be Black, Female, and a Playwright." *Freedomways*, 19 (1979): 256-60.
Rahman confronts the dilemmas facing black playwrights, especially African-American female dramatists, writing and producing for the predominately white American theatre audience. Rahman suggests that black women playwrights face a dual dilemma: hostility from the commercial theatre as well as from their male counterparts. As Rahman comments, "Black women playwrights are judged differently and with more hostility by both women and men than are black male playwrights." She cites Lorraine Hansberry, the first black playwright to be produced on Broadway, to support her contention. The playwright claims that many in the black community criticized Hansberry's plays as being too bourgeois and too commercial. And that being female made it easier for her to make it to Broadway because "women could get through the barrier more easily than black men." Rahman asserts black and white male playwrights distort the images of black women. Rahman is "determined to pick up the standard of the Hansberry legacy by portraying black women in real terms, not as the perverted characters of someone's nightmare." She briefly discusses the work of Adrienne Kennedy and Sonia Sanchez.

Reviews

See item 104.

Lady Day: A Musical Tragedy

3129.   Barnes, Clive. *New York Times* (Oct. 26, 1972): 39.
3130.   Gottfried, Martin. *Women's Wear Daily* (Oct. 27, 1972). Reprinted in item 3134.
3131.   Kart, Larry. *Chicago Tribune* (July 27, 1983): 46.
3132.   Kerr, Walter. *New York Times* (Nov. 11, 1972), sect. 2: 5.

3133. Kroll, Jack. *Newsweek*, 80 (Nov. 6, 1972): 133-134.
3134. *New York Theatre Critics' Reviews*, 33 (Dec. 4, 1972): 165-166.
3135. Tallmer, Jerry. *New York Post* (Oct. 26, 1972): 28. Reprinted in item 3134.

The Tale of Madame Zora

3136. Gussow, Mel. *New York Times* (Mar. 2, 1986): 64.

Transcendental Blues

3137. *N.Y. Amsterdam News* (Aug. 14, 1976): D-16.

Unfinished Women Cry in No Man's Land While a Bird Dies in a Gilded Cage

3138. Moore, Honor. *Ms.*, 6 (Dec. 1977): 37-38.
3139. Wadud, Ali. *N.Y. Amsterdam News* (Aug. 20, 1977): D-7.

Ross, Judith

Selected Plays

3140. *Almost a Perfect Person* (Belasco Theatre, 1977)
3141. *Via Galactica* (with Christopher Gore, Uris Theater, 1972)

Reviews

Almost a Perfect Person

3142. *American Theatre Annual* 1977-1978, 18. Detroit: Gale Research Company, 1978.
3143. Beaufort, John. *Christian Science Monitor* (Nov. 2, 1977). Reprinted in item 3154.
3144. Clurman, Harold. *Nation* (Nov. 19, 1977): 540.
3145. Eder, Richard. *New York Times* (Oct. 28, 1977), sect. 3: 3. Reprinted in item 3154.
3146. Gill, Brendan. *The New Yorker*, 53 (Nov. 7, 1977): 104.
3147. Gottfried, Martin. *New York Post* (Oct. 28, 1977): 44. Reprinted in item 3154.

3148. Gussow, Mel. *New York Times* (Aug. 3, 1977): 20.
      Gussow highlights the career of Zoe Caldwell,
      actress and director of the Broadway production of
      Almost A Perfect Person.

3149. Hughes, Catharine. *America,* 137 (Dec. 10, 1977): 423.
3150. Kerr, Walter. *New York Times* (Nov. 6, 1977), sect. 2: 3.
3151. Kissel, Howard. *Women's Wear Daily* (Oct. 28, 1977): 10.
3152. Moore, Honor. *Ms.,* 6 (Dec. 1977): 37-38.
3153. Munk, Erika. *Village Voice* (Nov. 7, 1977): 83-84.
3154. *New York Theatre Critics' Reviews,* 38 (Oct. 31, 1977):
      158-160.
3155. Simon, John. *New York,* 10 (Nov. 14, 1977): 92.
3156. Watt, Douglas. *New York Daily News* (Oct. 28, 1977).
      Reprinted in item 3154.

Via Galactica

3157. Barnes, Clive. *New York Times* (Nov. 29, 1972): 33.
3158. Gottfried, Martin. *Women's Wear Daily* (Nov. 30, 1972).
      Reprinted in item 3160.
3159. Kerr, Walter. *New York Times* (Dec. 10, 1972), sect. 2: 5.
3160. *New York Theatre Critics' Reviews,* 33 (Nov. 27, 1972):
      174-176.
3161. Watts, Richard. *New York Post* (Nov. 29, 1972): 52.
      Reprinted in item 3160.

Sanchez, Sonia

Selected Plays

3162. *The Bronx is Next* (Theatre Black, 1970)
      Playscript: *Drama Review,* 12, iv (Summer 1968):
      78-84; *New Plays from Black Theatre.* Edited by
      Ed Bullins. New York: Bantam Books, 1969.
3163. *Dirty Hearts* (New York Shakespeare Festival, 1971)
      Playscript: *Scripts,* 1 (Nov. 1971): 46-50.
3164. *Malcolm Man Don't Live Here No Mo!* (ASCOM
      Community Center, Philadelphia, 1979)
      Playscript: *Black Theatre,* 6 (1972): 24-27.
3165. *Sister Son/ji* (part of a bill of one-acts, *Black Visions,* New
      York Shakespeare Festival, Public Theatre, 1972)

Playscript: *New Plays from the Black Theatre.*
Edited by Ed Bullins. New York: Bantam Books,
1969.

3166. *Uh, Uh; But How Do It Free Us?*
Playscript: *New Lafayette Theatre Presents.* Edited
by Ed Bullins, 161-215. Garden City, New York:
Anchor Press, 1974.

Profiles and Interviews

See items 98, 3128.

3167. *Black Writers: A Selection of Sketches from
Contemporary Authors.* Edited by Linda Metzger.
Detroit: Gale Research Inc., 1989.
Sanchez's entry includes a biographical sketch and a
list of her plays.

3168. *Contemporary Authors: A Bio-Bibliographical Guide.*
Volume 24. New Revision Series. Edited by
Deborah Straub, 410-414. Detroit: Gale Research
Inc., 1988.
This biographical profile includes general
comments about Sanchez's work.

3169. Cornwell, Anita. "Attuned to the Energy: Sonia Sanchez."
Essence, 10 (July 1979): 10.
Sanchez briefly touches upon facets of her
professional life as a writer. She remarks that she
began writing at an early age because her stutter
made it difficult to communicate with people.

3170. Kalamu ya Salaam. "Sonia Sanchez." *Dictionary of Literary
Biography.* Volume 41. *Afro-American Poets Since
1955.* Edited by Trudier Harris, 295-306. Detroit:
Gale Research Company, 1985.
This is an extensive introductory article providing a
biographical and critical survey of Sanchez's poetry
and drama.

3171. Peterson, Bernard L. *Contemporary Black American
Playwrights and Their Plays: A Biographical*

Directory and Dramatic Index, 411-412. New York: Greenwood Press, 1988.
Peterson provides a biographical sketch as well a staging history of Sanchez's works.

3172. Sanchez, Sonia. "Ruminations/Reflections." In *Black Women Writers: A Critical Evalution*. Edited by Mari Evans, 415-418. Garden City, New York: Anchor Press, 1984.
"The truth of the Black condition" is that "America is killing us," says Sanchez. She exposes this condition in the hopes that it will serve as a catalyst for change.

Reviews and Criticism

See items 72, 101, 370, 3128.

The Bronx Is Next

See item 3190.

3173. Curb, Rosemary K. "Pre-Feminism in the Black Revolutionary Drama of Sonia Sanchez." In *Many Forms of Drama*. Edited by Karelisa Hartigan, 19-29. New York: University Press of America, 1985.
Curb asserts that although Sanchez is primarily concerned with the black separatist theme in her plays, sexual inequality dominates the subtexts of these dramas. Although Sanchez's women do not reflect feminist positions, "their portrayals of the victimization of strong women constitute a preliminary raising of consciousness." Sanchez's three revolutionary plays, *The Bronx Is Next, Sister Son/ji, and Uh, Uh; But How Do It Free Us?*, observes Curb, move progressively toward depicting the African-American woman's struggle for sexual as well political equality.

3174. Kupa, Kushauri. *Black Theatre*, 6 (1972): 38-43.

3175. Taylor, Willene Pulliam. "The Reversal of the Tainted
　　　　Blood Theme in the Works of Writers of the Black
　　　　Revolutionary Theater." *Negro American Literature
　　　　Forum*, 10 (Fall 1976): 89-94.
　　　　Taylor examines the use of the "tainted blood"
　　　　motif in the works of African-American as well as
　　　　white writers. Sanchez's *The Bronx Is Next* is
　　　　included in an examination of those writers who
　　　　attempt to debunk the age-old assumption that
　　　　white culture and its values can be fouled when
　　　　brought into close proximity to blacks. Sanchez
　　　　dramatizes ways in which African-Americans
　　　　become contaminated with the values of whites.
　　　　For example in the scene where Charles knocks
　　　　Black Bitch to the ground, he is in effect
　　　　repudiating the white value system.

Sister Son/ji

See items 55, 3172, 3173.

3176. Barnes, Clive. *New York Times* (Apr. 5, 1972): 37.

3177. Clayborne, Jon L. "Modern Black Drama and the Gay
　　　　Image." *College English*, 36, iii (1974): 381-384.
　　　　Clayborne uses a passage from *Sister Son/ji* to
　　　　illustrate the "black woman's obligation to her
　　　　man."

3178. Clurman, Harold. *Nation*, 214 (Apr. 17, 1972): 508-509.
3179. Gottfried, Martin. *Women's Wear Daily* (Apr. 5, 1972).
　　　　Reprinted in item 3183.
3180. Kalem, T.E. *Time*, 99 (May 1, 1972): 53.
　　　　Reprinted in item 3183.
3181. Kerr, Walter. *New York Times* (Mar. 26, 1972), sect. 2: 3.
3182. Kroll, Jack. *Newsweek*, 79 (Apr. 17, 1972): 91, 93.
　　　　Reprinted in item 3183.
3183. *New York Theatre Critics' Reviews*, 33 (June 12, 1972):
　　　　268-270.

3184. *New York Times* (Feb. 16, 1972): 27.

The *Times* announces *Black Visions,* a bill of one-act plays by African-Americans, will be produced by the Public Theatre on March 12, 1972.

3185. Newman, Jill. "The Player's the Thing At Clay Stevenson's Players Workshop." *Encore American & Worldwide News,* 6 (Feb. 21, 1977): 34-39.
Newman briefly mentions Sanchez's play *Sister Son/ji* in her article on the Player's Workshop in New York.

3186. Oliver, Edith. *The New Yorker,* 48 (Apr. 8, 1972): 97-98.

3187. Walker, Barbara. "Sonia Sanchez Creates Poetry for the Stage." *Black Creation,* 5 (Fall 1973): 12-14.
Walker's article is devoted to Sanchez's reflections on her play, *Sister Son/ji.*

3188. Watt, Douglas. *New York Daily News* (Apr. 5, 1972).
Reprinted in item 3183.
3189. Watts, Richard. *New York Post* (Apr. 5, 1972): 67.
Reprinted in item 3183.

Uh, Uh; But How Do It Free Us?

See item 3173.

3190. Sanchez, Sonia. "Preface to *Uh, Uh; But How Do It Free Us?* In *The New Lafayette Theatre Presents.* Edited by Ed Bullins, 161-163. New York: Doubleday, 1974.
To express particular concerns she is unable to communicate in her poems, Sanchez turns to the more expansive form of drama. As she puts it, "I have to stretch it out into a play." Of major concern for Sanchez is the effects of urban living on blacks. The cities are killing its African-American inhabitants, "the majority of Black children, Black young people [are] dying, being killed in . . . New York." For Sanchez, "to eliminate this dying was for us to leave the city. I know [African-Americans] would not."

Sanchez-Scott, Milcha

Selected Plays

3191. *The Cuban Swimmer* (INTAR, 1984)
        Playscript: *Dog Lady* and *The Cuban Swimmer*.
        New York: Theatre Communications Group, 1984;
        Dog Lady and *The Cuban Swimmer*. New York:
        Dramatists Play Service, 1988; *The Best Short
        Plays 1986*, Edited by Ramon Delgado. Radnor,
        Pennsylvania: Chilton Book Company, 1986.
3192. *Dog Lady* (INTAR, 1984)
        Playscript: see item 3191.
3193. *El Dorado* (South Coast Repertory, Costa Mesa, 1990)
3194. *Evening Star* (Cubiculo, 1988)
        Playscript: *Evening Star*. New York: Dramatists
        Play Service, 1988.
3195. *Latina* (with Jeremy Blahnik, AIPOP, Pilot Theatre, Los
        Angeles, 1980)
        Playscript: *Frontiers* (Summer 1980): 25-30;
        *Necessary Theater: Six Plays About the Chicano
        Experience*. Edited by Jorge Huerta, 76-141.
        Houston: Arte Publico Press, 1989.
3196. *Roosters* (INTAR, 1987)
        Playscript: *Roosters*. New York: Dramatists
        Play Service, 1988; *American Theatre*, 4 (Sep.
        1986): n.p.; *On New Ground: Contemporary
        Hispanic-American Plays*. Edited by Elizabeth M.
        Osborn, 243-280. New York: Theatre
        Communications Group, 1987.
3197. *Stone Wedding* (Latino Theatre Lab, L.A. Theatre Center,
        Los Angeles, 1988)

Profiles

See profiles in item 3195 and page 18.

3198. Henry, William A. "Visions of the Past." *Time*, 132 (July
        11, 1988): 82-83.

Henry includes Sanchez-Scott among the "emerging cadre" of Hispanic Americans writing for the American theatre.

3199. Fernandez, Enrique. "Nuestro Teatro." *Village Voice* (May 12, 1987): 100.
Fernandez examines Hispanic theatre and addresses the question "How Hispanic is Hispanic Theatre?" He includes in his assessment Sanchez-Scott and Fornes.

3200. Sanchez-Scott, Milcha. "Introduction to *Roosters*." *On New Ground: Contemporary Hispanic-American Plays*. Edited by Elizabeth M. Osborn. New York: Theatre Communications Group, 1987.
Sanchez-Scott's autobiographical profile precedes the text of her play, *Roosters*.

Reviews

The Cuban Swimmer

3201. Fernandez, Enrique. *Village Voice* (May 22, 1984): 83-94.
3202. Mitgang, Herbert. *New York Times* (May 10, 1984): C32.
3203. Radin, Victoria. *New Statesman*, 113 (May 15, 1987): 24.

Dog Lady

See items 3201-3203.

Evening Star

3204. Gussow, Mel. *New York Times* (May 16, 1988), sect. 3: 13.
3205. Feingold, Michael. *Village Voice* (May 24, 1988): 115.

Latina

3206. Henkel, Gretchen. *Drama-Logue* (June 12-18, 1980): 6.
3207. Sullivan, Dan. *Los Angeles Times* (June 11, 1980), sect. 6: 1, 7.

Roosters

3208. Billington, Michael. *Guardian* (Sep. 5, 1988): 17.
3209. Castillo, Ana. *Third Woman*, 4 (1989): 147-150.
3210. Gussow, Mel. *New York Times* (Mar. 24, 1987): C15.
3211. Smith, Sid. *Chicago Tribune* (Mar. 9, 1989), sect. 5: 7.
3212. Solomon, Alisa. *Village Voice* (Mar. 31, 1987): 98.
3213. Weiner, Bernard. *San Francisco Chronicle* (Sep. 18, 1987), sect. E: 7.

Stone Wedding

3214. Hewison, Robert. *Sunday Times* (London) (Jan. 29, 1989): C9e.
3215. McCulloh, T.H. *Drama-Logue.* (June 15-21, 1988): 10.

3216. "Return of the Wizard." *American Theatre*, 5 (Dec. 1988): 8. A brief note announcing the premiere of *Stone Wedding* at the L.A. Theatre Center's Latino Theatre Lab. The article also discusses the play and includes comments from Sanchez-Scott.

3217. *Variety* (Dec. 28, 1988): 38.

Sandler, Susan

Selected Plays

3218. *Crossing Delancey* (Jewish Repertory Theater, 1985)
3219. *The Moaner* (Manhattan Punchline, 1986-1987)
3220. *The Renovation* (Jewish Repertory Theater, 1987)

Reviews

Crossing Delancey

3221. Shepard, Richard F. *New York Times* (May 2, 1985), sect. 3: 24.

The Renovation

3222. Shepard, Richard F. *New York Times* (Mar. 20, 1987): C17.
3223. Stone, Laurie. *Village Voice* (Mar. 24, 1987): 86.

Scarborough, Janeice

Selected Plays

3224. *Majestic Kid* (with Mark Medoff, Golden Glow Unlimited, 1988)
3225. *Trinity Site* (WPA Theater, 1986)

Reviews

Majestic Kid

3226. Gussow, Mel. *New York Times* (Dec. 2, 1988): C3.

Trinity Site

3227. Massa, R. *Village Voice* (June 24, 1986): 184.
3228. Rich, Frank. *New York Times* (June 17, 1986): C13.

Schenkar, Joan

Selected Plays

3229. *Between The Acts* (Theater for the New City, 1989)
3230. *Cabin Fever* (New Dramatists, 1982-1983)
           Playscript: *Cabin Fever*. New York: Samuel French, 1980.
3231. *Death* (New Dramatists, 1985)
3232. *Family Pride in the Fifties* (Theater for the New City, 1987)
3233. *Fire in the Future* (New Dramatists, 1987-1988)
3234. *Fulfilling Koch's Postulate* (music by Christopher Drobny, New Dramatists, 1985-1986)
3235. *Hunting Down the Sexes #1: Bucks and Does* (New Dramatists, 1987)
3236. *In the Night Kitchen* (Theater for a New City, 1986)
3237. *The Last of Hitler* (Theater for a New City, 1984)

3238. *The Lodger: Hunting Down the Sexes #2* (Theater for a
      New City, 1988)
3239. *Nothing Is Funnier Than Death* (New Dramatists, 1983-
      1984)
3240. *Signs of Life* (Women's Project, 1978-1979)
      Playscript: *The Women's Project: Seven New
      Plays By Women.* Edited by Julia Miles, 307-362.
      New York: Performing Arts Journal Publications
      and American Place Theatre, 1980.

Profiles

See item 3 and page 4.

3241. *Contemporary Authors: A Bio-Bibliographical Guide.*
      Volume 133. Edited by Susan M. Trosky, 353-
      354. New York: Gale Research Inc., 1991.
      The entry provides a brief biography of Schenkar
      and comments on her theatrical career.

Reviews and Criticism

Between the Acts

3242. Stone, Laurie. *Village Voice* (Mar. 14, 1989): 96.

Cabin Fever

3243. Patraka, Vivian M. "Foodtalk In the Plays of Caryl
      Churchill and Joan Schenkar." *Theatre Annual,* 40
      (1985): 137-157.
      Although many dramatists use food images to
      convey statements about their characters, the plays
      of Churchill (*Top Girls* and *Fen)* and Schenkar
      (*Cabin Fever* and *The Last of Hitler)* are unique in
      that "all aspects of the processes connected to
      food—its production, preparation, consumption and
      excretion—are used to make meaning." Schenkar
      and Churchill use food and its rituals to portray
      economic and ideological constructs. For example,
      in Schenkar's two plays, people become "fodder for
      the physical and mental appetites of each other,

they convey structures of exploitation." Patraka
briefly mentions Sondra Segal and Roberta Sklar's
Foodtalk.

Family Pride in the Fifties

See item 3248.

3244. Rogoff, Gordon. *Village Voice* (May 26, 1987): 107-109.

Fulfilling Koch's Postulate

See item 3248.

The Last Hitler

See item 3248.

The Lodger: Hunting Down the Sexes #2

3245. Bruckner, D.J.R. *New York Times* (May 22, 1988): 49.
3246. Fuchs, Eleanor. *Village Voice* (May 24, 1988): 116.

Signs of Life

See items 23, 80.

3247. Munk, Erica. *Village Voice* (June 18, 1979): 100.

3248. Patraka, Vivian M. "Mass Culture and Metaphors of Menace
   in Joan Schenkar's Plays." In *Making A Spectacle:*
   Feminist Essays on Contemporary Women's
   Theatre. Edited by Lynda Hart, 25-40. Ann Arbor:
   University of Michigan Press, 1989.
   Patraka asserts Schenkar uses tropes, especially the
   metaphor, to dismantle the psyche's protective
   armor, thus threatening the individual's perception
   of the familiar, those deeply entrenched conventions
   and assumptions of the collective experience. In
   short, these metaphors make the familiar
   unfamiliar, therefore, "refamiliarizing us . . . to
   what we've repressed." Patraka examines

Schenkar's unique use of tropes in her major plays *Signs of Life, The Last of Hitler, Fulfilling Koch's Postulate,* and *Family Pride in the Fifties.*

3249. Rosenfeld, Megan. "Dream Weaver." *Washington Post* (Oct. 25, 1984): D7.
Rosenfeld talks to Schenkar during a run of her play *Signs of Life* by Horizons Theatre in Washington. The playwright prefers writing experimental over naturalistic plays, "life does not present resolutions, everything all neatly tied up by the end of the third act." Spectators, however, find her plays unsettling because they lack tidy endings, and thus, the audience "laugh[s] at things they think they shouldn't be laughing at." The dramatist claims her next project will be a trio of one-acts entitled *Nothing Is Funnier Than Death.*

3250. Wilson, Ann. "History and Hysteria: Writing the Body In *Portrait of Dora* and *Signs of Life.*" *Modern Drama*, 32, i (March 1989): 73-88.
Wilson demonstrates the relationship between hysteria and feminist theory by examining two plays whose protagonists are hysterics: Helene Cixous's *Portrait of Dora*, based on a patient of Freud's and Joan Schenkar's *Signs of Life*, which revolves around Henry James's sister, Alice. According to Wilson, both playwrights "inscribe themselves in their respective texts by identifying with these hysterics," and in so doing, dislocate the masculine-constructed portrayal of these figures as monsters. Instead, these playwrights pull the hysterics from their image of shame to center stage and allow them to voice their story.

Schneider, Barbara

Selected Plays

3251. *Crossings*
Playscript: see item 3253.

3252. *Details Without a Map* (Eugene O'Neill Theater Center
      Playwrights' Conference, 1980-1981)
3253. *Flight Lines* (Actors Theatre of Louisville, Kentucky,
      1982)
      Playscript: *Flightlines* and *Crossings: Two Short
      Plays*. New York: Dramatists Play Service, 1983.
3254. *I Want To Be an Indian* (Actors Theatre of Louisville,
      Kentucky, 1982-1983)

Reviews

Details Without a Map

3255. Gussow, Mel. *New York Times* (Oct. 29, 1982): C3.

3256. *New York Times* (Feb. 14, 1980): C19.
      This news item announces that Barbara Schneider
      won the 1979 Susan Smith Blackburn Prize for her
      play, *Details Without A Map;* runner-up for the
      award was Beth Henley. Included in the item is a
      brief biographical sketch of Schneider.

Schottenfeld, Barbara

Selected Plays

3257. *Greencard* (unproduced, 1987)
3258. *I Can't Keep Running in Place* (formerly *A Woman
      Suspended*, Westside Arts Theatre, 1981)
3259. *Sit Down and Eat Before Our Love Gets Cold* (American
      Kaleidoscope and West Side Y Arts Center, 1985)

Profiles

See item 100.

3260. *Contemporary Theatre, Film and Television.* Volume 1.
      Edited by Monica M. O'Donnell, 453-54. Detroit:
      Gale Research Company, 1984.
      The entry contains a biographical sketch of
      Schottenfeld.

Reviews

Greencard

3261. "Drama League Awards." *New York Times* (Dec. 14, 1987): C22.
    The *Times* reports Schottenfeld won a Drama League Playwrights Assistance award for her play *Greencard.*

I Can't Keep Running In Place

See item 100.

3262. Corry, John. *New York Times* (Mar. 1, 1980): 13.

3263. _____. *New York Times* (June 5, 1981), sect. C: 2.
    Corry briefly profiles Helen Gallagher, who appeared in *I Can't Keep Running in Place.*

3264. Faber, Roderick. *Village Voice* (Mar. 10, 1980): 86.
3265. Feingold, Michael. *Village Voice* (May 20, 1981): 93-94.

3266. Gardner, Sandra. "Writer-Actress Running Hard." *New York Times* (Aug. 23, 1981), sect. 2: 14.
    Gardner traces the creation of Schottenfeld's Off Broadway hit *I Can't Keep Running in Place* at the Westside Arts Theater. Although the play focuses on the experiences of a group of women, Schottenfeld rejects the label of it being a feminist play. That label, according to the playwright, politicizes the play: "I wanted to be entertaining first, and very few people have written political plays that are entertaining." The play originated from a creative thesis, entitled *A Woman Suspended,* which Schottenfeld wrote and produced at the University of Princeton.

3267. Gussow, Mel. *New York Times* (May 15, 1981): C4.

3268. Krebs, Alvin. "Moving From Princeton to Off-Broadway." *New York Times* (May 15, 1981): C27.

According to the *Times*, Schottenfeld's play *I Can't
Keep Running in Place*, originated as partial
fulfillment for her master's degree at Princeton.
Schottenfeld wrote and directed the first production,
which was entitled *A Woman Suspended*. Since
then the play had a tryout at La Mama and at the
time of this article the play was being performed at
the West Side Arts Theater on Off Broadway.

3269.   O'Neill, Rosary H. *Theater Journal*, 34, ii (May 1982): 262.
3270.   Simon, John. *New York*, 14 (May 25, 1981): 97-99.
3271.   *Variety* (May 20, 1981): 112.
3272.   Wilson, Edwin. *Wall Street Journal* (July 24, 1981): 21.

Sit Down and Eat Before Our Love Gets Cold

3273.   Gussow, Mel. *New York Times* (May 9, 1985): C22.

Segal, Sondra

Selected Plays

3274.   *Feast or Famine* (with Roberta Sklar, Women's Interart
          Center, 1985)
3275.   *Food* (with Roberta Sklar, Interart 1981-1982)
3276.   *The Daughters Cycle*
          see **Coss, Clare**

Reviews

Feast or Famine

3277.   Gussow, Mel. *New York Times* (May 10, 1985): C29.
3278.   Merrill, Lisa. *Women & Performance*, 3, i, (1986): 104-
          106.
3279.   Stone, Laurie. *Village Voice* (May 21, 1985): 116.

Daughters

see **Coss, Clare**

Electra Speaks

see **Coss, Clare**

Sister/Sister

see **Coss, Clare**

Sexton, Anne

Selected Plays

3280. *Mercy Street* (American Place Theater, 1969)
3281. *Transformations* (Westwood Playhouse, Los Angeles, 1980)

Profiles

3282. *Contemporary Authors: A Bio-Bibliographical Guide.* Volume 3. New Revision Series. Edited by Ann Evory, 490-492. Detroit: Gale Research Company, 1981.
This entry provides a brief biographical sketch as well as general comments on her poetry and plays.

3283. *Contemporary Authors Bibliographical Series: American Poets.* Volume 2. Edited by Ronald Baughman, 307-334. Detroit: Gale Research Company, 1986. A bibliographical essay assessing the critical reputation of Sexton's work. Includes a primary and secondary bibliography.

3284. *Dictionary of Literary Biography.* Volume 5. *American Poets Since World War II.* Edited by Donald J. Greiner, 225-234. Detroit: Gale Research Company, 1980.
This introductory article includes an extensive biographical and critical survey of Sexton's work.

Reviews

Mercy Street

3285. Barnes, Clive. *New York Times* (Oct. 28, 1969): 43.

3286. Berg, Beatrice. "'Oh, I Was Very Sick'." *New York Times* (Nov. 9, 1969), sect. 2: 1, 7.
Sexton, poet-turned-playwright, discusses the challenges of writing drama: "You have to keep a log of things in your mind at once . . . with a poem, you write it and that's that." Writing, Sexton claims, helps her work through bouts of mental illness. For example, Sexton drew upon her personal life experiences to create Daisy Cullen, the suicidal character in *Mercy Street,* "there is a lot of me in her."

3287. *Critical Essays on Anne Sexton.* Edited by Linda Wagner-Martin. Boston: G.K. Hall, 1989.
Brief comments about *Mercy Street* appear throughout this volume of essays.

3288. Hughes, Catherine. *America.* 121 (Dec. 20, 1969): 622.
3289. Kauffmann, Stanley. *New Republic,* 161 (Nov. 22, 1969): 33.

3290. Kevles, Barbara. "Anne Sexton." In *Writers At Work: The Paris Review Interviews, 4th Series.* Edited by George Plimpton, 399-424. New York: Viking Press, 1976.
In this interview, Anne Sexton remarks that her drama, which she refers to as a "morality play," continues the themes she explores in her poetry. Sexton "felt great" writing the play, she would "pac[e] up and down the living room shouting out the lines."

3291. Kerr, Walter. *New York Times* (Nov. 2, 1969), sect. 2: 3.

3292. Maryan, Charles. "The Poet on Stage." *Anne Sexton: The Artist and Her Critics.* Edited by J.D. McClatchy, 89-95. Bloomingdale: Indiana University Press 1978.
Maryan, who directed the first production of *Mercy Street* at The American Place, reflects on his

collaboration with Anne Sexton. Their work
together was done "joyfully." He recalls Sexton as
being a good listener and receptive to alternative
ideas. Although the play was a critical, if not a
financial, success, after the opening, Anne "never
seemed as excited about her [play]," the acceptance
of which "was not like that of her books." Maryan
remarks the only "real disagreement" he and Sexton
had was that he "thought Anne was a playwright."

3293. Middlebrook, Diane Wood. "Seduction In Anne Sexton's
Unpublished Play *Mercy Street*." In *Sexton:
Selected Criticism*. Edited by Diana Hume George,
19-26. Urbana: University of Illinois Press, 1988.
From a generally psychoanalytic perspective,
Middlebrook addresses the question of the daughter's
position within the male-ordered society in
Sexton's play *Mercy Street*. Middlebrook concludes
that the play is "an act of resistance to the
patriarchy in us all."

3294. O'Connor, John J. *Wall Street Journal* (Oct. 20, 1969): 20.

Transformations

3295. *Los Angeles Times* (Feb. 28, 1980), sect. 4: 6.
A brief note announcing that *Transformations* will
be performed at the Westwood Playhouse in Los
Angeles beginning March 10, 1980.

3296. Sullivan, Dan. *Los Angeles Times* (Nov. 12, 1979), sect.
4: 15.

Shange, Ntozake

Selected Plays

3297. *Betsey Brown: A Rhythm & Blues Musical* (with Emily
Mann, American Music Theater Festival,
Philadelphia, 1989)

Playscript: *Studies in American Drama, 1945-Present,* 4, 1989, 3-20 (excerpt).

3298. *Boogie Woogie Landscapes* (Symphony Space Theatre, 1979)
Playscript: *three pieces**. New York: St. Martin's Press, 1981.

3299. *Daddy Says*
Playscript: *New Plays for the Black Theatre.* Edited by Woodie King, Jr., 233-251. Chicago: Third World Press, 1989.

3300. *for colored girls who have considered suicide/when the rainbow is enuf* (New York Shakespeare Festival, New Federal Theater, 1976)
Playscript: *for colored girls who have considered suicide /when the rainbow is enuf.* New York: Bantam Books, 1981; *Totem Voice: Plays from the Black World Repertory.* Edited by Harrison Paul Carter. New York: Grove Press, 1989.

3301. *Mother Courage and Her Children* (adapted from Brecht's *Mother Courage,* Newman/Public Theatre, 1980)

3302. *A Photograph: A Study of Cruelty* (New York Shakespeare Theater Festival, Public Theatre, 1977; revised, *A Photograph: Lovers in Motion,* Equinox Theatre, Houston, 1979)
Playscript: *A Photograph: Lovers in Motion: A Drama.* New York: Samuel French, 1981; see item 3298.

3303. *Shapes, Sadness, and the Witch* (Wortham Theatre, University of Houston, Houston, 1984)

3304. *Spell #7: geechee jibara quik magic trance manual for technologically stressed third world people* (New York Shakespeare Festival, Public Theatre, 1979)
Playscript: *Spell #7: A Theater Piece in Two Acts.* New York: Samuel French, 1981; *9 Plays by Black Women.* Edited by Margaret Wilkerson, 239-292. New York: New American Library, 1986; see item 3298.

3305. *Three Views of Mt. Fuji* (New Dramatists, 1987)

3306. *Where the Mississippi Meets the Amazon* (with Jessica Hagedorn and Thulani Nkabinda, Public Theatre Cabaret, 1977)

Profiles and Interviews

See items 9, 48, 86, 87, 98 and pages 15-17.

3307. *Black Writers: A Selection of Sketches from Contemporary Authors.* Edited by Linda Metzger, 518-522. Detroit: Gale Research Company, 1989. This entry includes a biographical sketch as well as general comments about Shange's work.

3308. Blackwell, Henry. "An Interview With Ntozake Shange." *Black American Literature Forum,* 13, iv (Winter 1979): 134-138.
Blackwell's interview is the rare one that focuses on Shange's aesthetics. She candidly responds to Blackwell's queries: What makes a good poet? Does living in the South influence black writers in "distinctive ways?" Who are your role models? Has diminishment and neglect in and out of literature forced Black women to look at life in a special way, forced them to devise a special aesthetic? And for whom did you write *for colored girls?*

3309. Brown, Elizabeth. "Ntozake Shange." *Dictionary of Literary Biography.* Volume 38. *Afro-American Writers After 1955: Drama and Prose Writers.* Edited by Thadious M. Davis and Trudier Harris. Detroit: Gale Research Company, 1985.
This article introduces the reader to Shange's life and work and provides a general assessment of her poetry and choreopoems.

3310. Buckley, Tom. "The Three Stages of Ntozake Shange." *New York Times* (Dec. 16, 1977): C6.
Buckley writes about Shange's recent activities: writing a new play *In the Middle of a Flower;* lecturing at Rutgers; changing her "slave name" Paulette Williams to Ntozake Shange; and, "formalizing her relationship" with David Murray, a musician who performs in *Where the Mississippi Meets the Amazon,* a play she co-wrote with two

other writers. Shange also talks about her
"determined" feminism and the influence of the
Vietnam War on her political ideology.

3311. Considine, Shaun. "On Stage: Ntozake Shange." *People Weekly,* 6 (July 5, 1976): 68-69.
A light and breezy profile of Shange's life and how
she "began turning the psychic wounds of her
youth, many inflicted by black men . . . into her
autobiographical poetry."

3312. *Contemporary Authors: A Bio-Bibliographical Guide.*
Volume 27. New Revision Series. Edited by Hal
May, 426-430. Detroit: Gale Research Inc., 1989.
The entry includes a biographical sketch, general
critical remarks on Shange's work, and a list of her
works.

3313. *Contemporary Theatre, Film, and Television.* Volume 5.
Edited by Monica M. O'Donnell, 337-338.
Detroit: Gale Research Company, 1988.
Shange's entry contains a brief biography,
including a list of her awards and plays.

3314. Dong, Stella. "Ntozake Shange." *Publisher's Weekly,* 227
(May 3, 1985): 74-75.
Dong's portrait of Shange was written after the
recent publication of Shange's novel *Betsey Brown,*
which, Dong claims, will reappear as a musical at
Joseph Papp's Public Theatre. In addition to
discussing biographical details, Dong also describes
Shange's work. Dong observes, for example, that
"from *for colored girls,* Shange began to dissect her
earlier theme of sisterhood and feminism to analyze
smaller themes." She quotes Shange as saying "in
my successive pieces [e.g., *A Photograph, Spell #7*
and *Boogie Woogie Landscapes]* I've tried to look
at the choices available to their characters."

3315. Funke, Phyllis. "Beneath the Surface of Shange." *Los
Angeles Times* (Aug. 7, 1977), Calendar sect.: 54.

Funke wrote her article on the eve of the opening
of *for colored girls* at the Mark Taper Forum in
Los Angeles. Throughout Shange's description of
the genesis of her play and people's reactions to it,
Funke provides a character sketch of Shange and her
upcoming marriage to David Murray, a tenor
saxophonist.

3316. Futterman, Ellen. "Ntozake Shange Casts Her Eye On
Texas." *St. Louis Post Dispatch* (Apr. 15, 1987),
sect. F: 1, 4.
Futterman converses with Shange during her stay
in St. Louis to speak at the Heart of the Arts
festival. The poet/playwright talks about her latest
writings and her move to Houston, "I had to go
somewhere with the baby [her daughter Savannah]
that looked something like what I understood, and
New York wasn't that." Very little of the article
discusses Shange's work in the theatre, but she does
note that she was criticized for being "too angry
and anti-men" in *for colored girls*. Shange views
herself as "pro-women."

3317. Gillespie, Marcia Ann. "Ntozake Shange Talks With Marcia
Ann Gillespie." *Essence*, 16 (May 1985): 122-124,
203-208.
Shange talks about what has happened to her since
her Broadway hit *for colored girls* catapulted her
into the bright lights ten years earlier. The success
of her play and the intense attention from the
media, Shange remarks, was a painful experience
and "so overwhelming . . . [it] really tore a lot of
my friendships apart, and they are not repaired to
date." She left New York for Houston and she
reflects "I've tried to figure out if I was running
away. I think I would have been running away if I
had stopped writing." At any rate, since her move,
Shange says she has "some new visions" such as
"fight[ing] pornography and violence against
women and children." Gillespie encourages Shange
to talk about her daughter Savannah, and her
relationships with men, including Savannah's

father, "we're still friends, and we still support each
other as artists and as friends."

3318. "Interview: Ntozake Shange." *The New Yorker*, 52 (Aug. 2,
       1976): 17-19.
       The conversation with Shange took place at an
       unspecified restaurant near Joseph Papp's Public
       Theatre during a break from Shange's role in her
       choreopoem *for colored girls*. In between sips of
       coffee Shange reveals slices of her life: her
       childhood years in St. Louis, her close communion
       with the poets in San Francisco, and her loss of a
       "tactile or sensuous connection " to the city of New
       York, where she was living at the time. She
       concludes the conversation by talking about her
       writing, "I write about pain. Apathy stops me up."

3319. Jordan, June. "Shange Talks the Real Stuff." *The Dial*
       (Feb. 1982): 11-13.
       Written in anticipation of the airing of a production
       of *for colored girls* on PBS, poet June Jordan
       reminisces about her association with Shange and
       her reactions to a staged reading of *for colored girls*
       at the Public Theatre, which she was invited by
       Shange to attend in early 1975.

3320. King, Anne Mills. "Ntozake Shange." *Critical Survey of
       Drama: Supplement*. Edited by Frank Magill, 326-
       331. Pasadena, California: Salem Press, 1986.
       King provides a biographical sketch of Shange's
       life and achievements as well as a cursory analysis
       of her plays.

3321. Latour, Martine. "Ntozake Shange: Driven
       Poet/Playwright." *Mademoiselle*, 82 (Sep. 1976):
       182, 226.
       An intimate, if brief, profile of Shange, during a
       run of *for colored girls* at Joseph Papp's Public
       Theatre. Latour quotes Shange as saying that she
       is wary of all the hoopla surrounding her hit play
       because prior to *for colored girls* her poetry went
       virtually unrecognized. Shange maintains that "had

there been more respect for my poetry . . . my
suicide attempts wouldn't have happened." She
also talks about how she channels her "rage and
alienation" into her creative work.

3322. Lauerman, Connie. "Stage to Novel: Broadway Wasn't
'Enuf' for Author." *Chicago Tribune* (Oct. 21,
1982), sect. 4: 1, 6.
Lauerman's article, written soon after the
publication of *Sassafras, Cypress & Indigo*, focuses
on Shange's new novel. However, Shange does
talk in general terms about her life and writings.

3323. Lee, Catharine Carr. *Contemporary Authors Bibliographies
Series: American Dramatists*. Volume 3. Edited by
Matthew C. Roudane, 305-324. Detroit: Gale
Research Inc., 1989.
A bibliographical essay assessing the critical
reputation of Shange's work. Includes a primary
and secondary list of sources.

3324. Levine, Jo Ann. "'Bein' a Woman, Bein' Colored.'"
Christian Science Monitor (Sep. 9, 1976): 23.
This article anticipates the move of *for colored girls*
from the Public Theatre to Broadway. Levine has
Shange reflect on the consequences that the play
has had on her personal life. For example, Shange
remarks that since the play opened, she and her
parents "have been going through some fairly
traumatic, terribly painful discussions." Other
traumatic events in her life include being bused to a
white school, "I think it is unfortunate that we
buffaloed ourselves into thinking that the black
children who were integrated had a good time—
because it was the worst time of my life." Shange
talks candidly about her relations with white
people, "I do have white friends. But they are very
selected." The poet/playwright was "dumbfounded"
when one reporter labelled *for colored girls*
"racist." To which she responded, "if he wanted to
see me racist, he should have read the things I
wrote in 1968. I have some real racist things

there." But Shange claims she has "expiated all of that."

3325. Lewis, Barbara. *"For Colored Girls Who Have Considered Suicide." Essence,* 7 (Nov. 1976): 119-120.
Lewis's article, based on a conversation with Shange between shows of a production of *for colored girls,* begins with Shange's reflections on her childhood. She recalls the pain she experienced because of repeated moves to various cities where the "whole ostracism [by whites] process began again." Lewis traces Shange's college days, where she developed a passionate interest in the study of the black visual arts and literature. The article concludes with Shange's description of her works in progress such as a piece entitled *Slow Bolero Down Avenue 'C'* and *Closets,* a poem/dance piece, which Shange comments is "the underneath of *for colored girls."*

3326. Lyons, Brenda. "Interview With Ntozake Shange." *Massachusetts Review,* 28, iv (Winter 1987): 687-697.
Although the interviewer does not focus on Shange's dramatic aesthetics or her individual theatre pieces, Lyon's does reveal insights on Shange's writing process, the African-American woman writer's aesthetic, and her works in progress.

3327. Peterson, Bernard L. *Contemporary Black American Playwrights and Their Plays: A Biographical Directory and Dramatic Index,* 417-421. New York: Greenwood Press, 1989.
Peterson provides a biographical sketch as well as a staging history of Shange's plays.

3328. Richards, Sandra. *Contemporary Dramatists.* 3rd edition. Edited by James Vinson, 477-78. New York: St. Martin's Press, 1982.
Richards briefly assesses the life and work of Shange. The entry includes a list of her plays.

3329. Shange, Ntozake. "Ntozake Shange Interviews Herself."
Ms., 6 (Dec. 1977): 35, 70-72.
Shange indicates that she has been somewhat
disappointed in herself during the myriad of
interviews she has given so she decided to give
herself "a chance to talk to myself," to have a
"conversation with all her selves." In a highly
entertaining yet perceptive self-interview, Shange
responds to questions she asks herself: "how has yr
relationship with the world changed since becoming
an overnight sensation with *for colored girls?";*
"why did you always want to be an ikette?"; "how
do you account for yr reputation as a feminist, if
you listen to & get nourishment from all these
men?"; "how do you explain loving some men who
write . . . when yr work for almost three years has
been entirely woman-centered?"; and, "who did
help you understand yr craft?"

3330. "Showstoppers." *Essence,* 13 (Oct. 1982): 75-77.
This article provides casual vignettes of highly
successful black writers and entertainers, including
Shange.

3331. Umrani, Munir. "Ntozake Shange: Woman Behind *Colored
Girls." Bilalian News* (Jan. 6, 1978): 28.
Umrani's profile focuses on Shange's creation of
her choreopoem *for colored girls* and her perception
of those individuals who call the play "anti-male."
According to Shange, these individuals "are denying
interaction among human beings more so than
dealing with what kinds of things men need in
terms of ego support." Furthermore, women who
Shange refers to as "male dominated" or "the
executive type," dislike the play because they have
assumed the "same ego structure and the same
responses to the world as the people who oppress
them." Umrani also touches upon how Shange's
mysticism and experimentation with dance have
influenced her plays.

3332. Watson, Kenneth. In *American Playwrights Since 1945*.
          Edited by Philip C. Kolin, 379-386. New York:
          Greenwood Press, 1989.
          Watson provides an assessment of Shange's critical
          reputation, an historical survey of her productions,
          a brief analysis of her plays, and suggestions for
          future areas of study. Includes a primary and
          secondary bibliography.

3333. "Welcome to the Great Black Way!" *Time*, 108 (Nov. 1,
          1976): 72-76.
          Written at the time of an "explosion of all-black
          shows" this article briefly highlights Shange,
          among five other young black women, "who are
          now sovereign on Broadway."

3334. Wykoff, Peter C. *Houston Post*. (May 26, 1985), sect. F:
          11.
          Based on a "chat" with Shange at the Warwick
          Hotel restaurant in Houston, Wycoff's brief profile
          describes Shange's life in the Texas city, where she
          has been teaching drama at the University of
          Houston, her recently published works, and her
          works in progress.

Reviews and Criticism

See items 13, 38, 54, 68, 72, 79, 104, 370.

Betsey Brown

3335. Koenenn, Joseph C. "Unoriginal Play Titles: The
          Musical." *Newsday* (June 7, 1990), sect. 2: 5.
          Koenenn briefly discusses *Betsey Brown* in his
          article.

3336. Gussow, Mel. *New York Times* (Sep. 9, 1990), sect. 2:
          48.
          Gussow announces the opening of *Betsey Brown*
          on April 5, 1991 at the McCarter Theater.

3337. Swed, Mark. *New York Times* (Apr. 2, 1989), sect. 2: 25.

3338. *Variety* (Apr. 12-18, 1989): 108.

   Boogie Woogie Landscapes

   See item 55.

3339. Berson, Misha. *San Francisco Chronicle* (Jan. 8, 1984), Datebook sect.: 32-33.

3340. Fraser, C. Gerald. "New Shange Play Will Aid Writer's Workshop." *New York Times* (June 25, 1979): C16.
   Fraser announces *Boogie Woogie Landscapes* will be staged at the Symphony Space for the benefit of the Frank Silvera Writers' Workshop, a project that nurtures African-American playwrights.

3341. Winn, Steven. *San Francisco Chronicle* (Jan. 18, 1984): 51.

   for colored girls who have considered suicide/when the rainbow is enuf

   See items 12, 14, 15, 23, 80, 590, 1497, 2030 and pages 15-17.

3342. *American Theatre Annual* 1978-1979, 78. Detroit: Gale Research Company, 1979.
3343. Bambara, Toni Cade. *Ms.*, 5 (Sep. 1976): 36, 38.
3344. Barber, John. *Daily Telegraph* (London) (Oct. 11, 1979): 15f.
3345. Bardacke, Frances L. *San Diego Magazine*, 29 (Dec. 1976): 66.
3346. _____. *San Diego Magazine*, 29 (Oct. 1977): 45-50.
3347. Barnes, Clive. *New York Times* (June 2, 1976): 44.
3348. Barnes, Jessica. *N.Y. Amsterdam News* (Oct. 9, 1976): D10.
3349. Beaufort, John. *Christian Science Monitor* (Sep. 24, 1976). Reprinted in item 3305.
3350. Bell, Roseanne Pope. *Black Collegian*, 7 (May-June 1977): 48-49.

3351. Bond, Jean Carey. *Freedomways*, 16 (3rd Quarter, 1976):
       187-191.
3352. Brunazzi, Elizabeth. *Off Our Backs*, 9 (Feb. 1979): 18.
3353. Catinella, Joseph. *New York Times* (Apr. 27, 1980), sect.
       11: 19.

3354. *Chicago Defender* (Dec. 24, 1977), Accent sect.: 5.
               This item announces a run of *for colored girls* at
               the Blackstone Theatre in Chicago from December
               27 through February 19. The article also
               chronicles the staging history of the play and
               briefly profiles Shange, director Oz Scott, and
               actress Trazana Beverley.

3355. Calloway, Earl. *Chicago Defender* (Dec. 17, 1977),
               Entertainment sect.: 2.
               Calloway announces a touring production of *for
               colored girls* to be performed on December 27,
               1977 at the Blackstone Theatre. He also discusses
               the staging history, "[l]ike any new or different
               artistic or cultural form, the genesis of its concept
               and development is interesting and important,
               historically and socially."

3356. Christiansen, Richard. *Chicago Tribune* (Apr. 3, 1986),
               sect. 2: 9.
3357. *Cleveland Call and Post* (Dec. 3, 1977): 6A.
               For letters to the editor regarding the play, see *Call
               and Post* (Jan. 14, 1978), sect. B: 3.
3358. Clark, Rozelle. *Atlanta Daily World* (Jan. 10, 1980): 3, 6.
3359. Clurman, Harold. *Nation*, 222 (May 1, 1976): 542.
3360. Coe, Richard L. *Washington Post* (Oct. 10, 1976), sect. F:
               8.
3361. _____.*Washington Post* (Oct. 14, 1977), sect. F: 1.
3362. _____.*Washington Post* (Nov. 30, 1978), sect. G: 18.
3363. *Contemporary Literary Criticism: Excerpts from Criticism
               of the Works of Today's Novelists, Poets,
               Playwrights, and Other Creative Writers.* Volume
               8. Edited by Dedria Bryfonski, 484-485. Detroit:
               Gale Research Company, 1978.

3364. Christ, Carol P. "'i found god in myself . . . i loved her fiercely': Ntozake Shange." In *Diving Deep and Surfacing: Women Writers on Spiritual Quest*, 97-117. Boston: Beacon Press, 1980.
Christ states in her chapter on Shange's choreopoem *for colored girls* that the work is "a search for the meaning of nothing experienced and a quest for a new sacrifice of self for the love of a man." But Shange does more than just affirm the pain of these women and their invisible selves. She depicts how the women come to terms with the emptiness, which "enable[s] them to acknowledge their history while moving beyond it to the ends of their own rainbows." The poems in *for colored girls*, says Christ, "dramatize a spiritual rite of passage for these women who move through hope, defeat, and rebirth."

3365. DeShazer, Mary K. "Rejecting Necrophilia: Ntozake Shange and the Warrior Re-Visioned." In *Making a Spectacle: Feminist Essays on Contemporary Women's Theatre*. Edited by Lynda Hart, 86-100. Ann Arbor: University of Michigan Press, 1989.
DeShazer points out that "warrior" as metaphor "is a problematic term for many feminists." On the one hand, many women writers reject its use because of its "embody[ing] the destructive powers of patriarchy." On the other hand, the author has observed that warrior is used frequently by women writers of various races and cultures and thus has acquired new meaning. To these women, many of whom "lack class or color or heterosexual privilege, the warrior image reflects a profound commitment to combating not just sexism . . . but racism, elitist, and heterosexual oppressions as well." Therefore the warrior image has been "re-visioned" to symbolize not destructiveness but a "source of life-preservation and enhancement." The author observes that Shange uses the warrior image in her plays. Shange dramatizes the two sides of the "re-visioned" warrior—her characters' rage at their situation, as they struggle against racial,

sexual, and economic oppression yet resist destruction by "nurtur[ing] . . . strong selves and communities." For example, in *for colored girls* the women rage against male domination but transcend their anger by "staking out a new country beyond this war, defined by a nurturant female community." DeShazer also discusses *Spell #7*.

3366. Dodds, Richard. *Times-Picayune* (New Orleans) (Nov. 14, 1979), sect. 1: 26.

3367. Drake, Sylvie. *Los Angeles Times* (Aug. 12, 1977), sect. 4: 1, 26.

3368. _____. *Los Angeles Times* (Feb. 23, 1982), sect. 4: 2.
Drake's preview article announces the airing of American Playhouse's version of *for colored girls*.

3369. *Drama-Logue* (Feb. 12-18, 1987): 11.

3370. *Drama-Logue* (July 20-26, 1989): 9.

3371. Dunning, Jennifer. *Dance Magazine*, 51 (May 1977): 92.

3372. Eder, Richard. *New York Times* (July 22, 1979), sect. 2: D3.

3373. Elliot, Jeffrey. "Ntozake Shange: Genesis of a Choreopoem." *Negro History Bulletin*, 41 (Jan-Feb. 1978): 797-800.
Following a brief profile of Shange by Elliot, Shange describes how *for colored girls* evolved.

3374. *Encore American & Worldwide News*, 5 (Oct. 18, 1976): 33.

3375. Flowers, Sandra Hollin. "Colored Girls: Textbook for the Eighties." *Black American Forum*, 15, ii (Summer, 1981): 51-54.
Flowers disagrees with those spectators and critics who view *for colored girls* as a feminist harangue against the evil that black men do. Rather, Flowers contends the play conveys Shange's compassion towards men and the "crisis between black men and women." This crisis and the nature of relationships is the focal point of the play.

Shange's compassion for black men is most
noticeable in the Beau Willie poem. Here Flowers
demonstrates how Beau Willie is a "tragic figure,"
that Shange's anger is not directed toward Beau
Willie as a man but towards the circumstances
which compelled him to drop his children out the
window. For additional articles on reactions to the
portrayal of men in *for colored girls*, see item
3422.

3376. Geis, Deborah. "Distraught Laughter: Monologue in
Ntozake Shange's Theatre Pieces." In *Feminine
Focus: The New Women Playwrights*. Edited by
Enoch Brater. New York: Oxford University Press,
1989.
Geis points out that in her plays, Shange "develops
her narration primarily through monologues
because monologic speech inevitably places the
narrative weight of a play upon its spoken language
and upon the performances of the individual actors."
According to Geis, Shange does not use the
monolgue to "define and embody [the] characters"
as does Maria Irene Fornes, but Shange employs
the monologue to assume "multiple roles and
therefore to emphasize the centrality of *storytelling*
to her work." The author also discusses the
criticism voiced by critics Erskine Peters (see item
3409) and Andrea Benton Rushing (see item 3417)
and others who complain that the play's focus is
too narrow in that it deals with the personal
experiences of a few middle-class black women
rather than the socio-political ramifications that
affect all African-Americans.

3377. Glover, William. *Los Angeles Times* (Sep. 21, 1976), sect.
4: 14.
3378. Gordon, D. *Texas Monthly* (Jan. 1978): 94-96.
3379. Gottfried, Martin. *New York Post* (Sep. 16, 1976): 22.
3380. Griffin, Rita. *Michigan Chronicle* (May 27, 1978), sect. C:
12.
3381. Gussow, Mel. *New York Times* (Sep. 16, 1976): 53.
3382. Harris, Jessica. *Essence*, 7 (Nov. 1976): 87-89.

3383. Hayes, Donald. "An Analysis of Dramatic Themes Used by Selected Black-American Playwrights from 1950-1976 with a Backgrounder: The State of the Art of the Contemporary Black Theater and Black Playwriting." Ph.D., diss., Wayne State University, 1984.
Hayes hopes to fill the gap in the scholarship on black theatre and black playwrights by examining "the dogma, misconceptions, and conflicting schools of thought behind the themes" in eleven contemporary African-American dramatists, including Shange and her choreopoem *for colored girls*.

3384. Higgins, John. *Times* (London) (Apr. 12, 1978): 11c.
3385. Hughes, Catharine. *America*, 135 (Oct. 9, 1976): 214.
3386. Jarrett, Vernon. *Chicago Tribune* (Jan. 1, 1978): 19.

3387. Johnston, Laurie. "*Colored Girls* Goes to Rikers Island and Hits Home." *New York Times* (Jan. 14, 1977), sect. B: 2.
Johnston's article focuses on the reactions of the prisoners of the Women's House of Detention on Rikers Island to a performance of *for colored girls* staged at the prison.

3388. Kalem, T.M. *Time*, 107 (June 14, 1976): 74.
3389. Kart, Larry. *Chicago Tribune* (Oct. 5, 1978), sect. 2: 8.
3390. Kauffmann, Stanley. *New Republic*, 174 (July 3-10, 1976): 20-21.
3391. Kingston, Jeremy. *Times* (London) (July 6, 1990), Features sect.: n.p.
3392. Kroll, Jack. *Newsweek*, 87 (June 14, 1976): 99.
3393. Lardner, James. *Washington Post* (Mar. 3, 1981), sect. D: 3.

3394. Levin, Toby and Gwendolyn Flowers. "Black Feminism in *for colored girls*." In *History and Tradition in Afro-American Culture*. Edited by Gunter Lenz, 181-193. Frankfurt: Campus Verlag, 1984.

What might be considered a response to those
critics who believe that Shange's play is a diatribe
against the black male, Flowers and Levin assert
that because African-American men "have little
present need to be reminded of the devastating
effects of racism, Shange's primary purpose is to
bring to their attention the equally scathing effects
of sexism on the potential for black solidarity."
Their article is arranged in two parts: first the
principles of black feminism are discussed and in
the second part each author critiques the play "as a
black and a white woman, offering our independent
but mutally supportive experiences with the text."

3395. Lewis, Barbara. "Rikers Inmates Touched By *for colored
girls" N.Y. Amsterdam News* (Jan. 22, 1977),
sect. D: 7.
Lewis reports on the reactions of inmates of the
Women's House of Detention on Rikers Island to a
production of *for colored girls* staged on January
13, 1977. See also Lewis's article: *Essence, 7*
(Nov. 1976): 86, 119-120.

3396. Loynd, Ray. *Los Angeles Times* (July 31, 1987), sect. 6:
23.

3397. Miller, E. Ethelbert. *New Directions* (Washington, D.C.)
(Apr. 1980): 29-31.

3398. Miller, Jeanne-Marie A. "Three Theatre Pieces by Ntozake
Shange." *Theatre News,* 14 (Apr. 1982): 8.
Miller provides succinct comments on Shange's
dramatic pieces *Spell #7, A Photograph: Lovers in
Motion* and *Boogie Woogie Landscapes.*

3399. Miller, Lynn F. *Educational Theatre Journal*, 29, ii (May
1977): 262-263.

3400. Mitchell, Carolyn. "'A Laying On of Hands': Transcending
the City in Ntozake Shange's *For Colored Girls."
Women Writers and the City: Essays in Feminist
Literary Criticism.* Edited by Susan Merrill Squier,

230-248. Knoxville: University of Tennessee
Press, 1984.
Mitchell examines *for colored girls* within the
context of Paul Tillich's vision of the city, which
"supports equality of aspiration, mobility of action,
and freedom of community." Tillich's idealistic
vision of urban life, according to Mitchell, excludes
women because he bases it on the tenets of a
patriarchal system. Clearly, Mitchell asserts,
Shange repudiates Tillich's vision; her perception
of contemporary city life as depicted in her theatre
piece lacks the characteristics identified with
Tillich's model city. To the several women in
Shange's play, the city represents isolation,
repression and oppression. In their city, creativity
does not flourish but rather it is "perverted into
desperate schemes for survivial." Whereas Tillich
envisions the city as fostering equality at the
marketplace, in Shange's world "competition
becomes the dog-eat-dog syndrome." These women
neither succumb to nor are destroyed by the city.
Instead, they transcend to another community that
has arisen from the bleakness and horror of the city.

3401. Morley, Sheridan. *Punch,* 277 (Oct. 24, 1979): 731.
3402. Murray, William. *New West* (Sep. 12, 1977): SC-20.

3403. Narvaez, Alfonso A. "Broadway Show Is a Hit As It Goes
        Behind Walls of Jail." *New York Times* (Apr. 8,
        1977), sect. 2: B13.
        Narvaez reports on the reactions of the inmates of
        Essex County Jail to a production of *for colored
        girls* at their own "Jail Theater." One inmate,
        Leroy Harnette, said of the play, "[i]t shows that
        we should show more kindness, consideration and
        love for our women."

3404. *N.Y. Amsterdam News* (Sep. 3, 1977): D7.
3305. *New York Theatre Critics' Reviews,* 37 (Sep. 13, 1976):
        199-202.
3406. Nightingale, Benedict. *New Statesman,* 98 (Oct. 19, 1979):
        604-605.

3407. Novick, Julius. *Humanist*, 37 (Jan.-Feb. 1977): 56.

3408. Pacheco, Patrick. *After Dark*, 9 (Oct. 1976): 36-37, 88.

3409. Peters, Erskine. "Some Tragic Propensities of Ourselves: The Occasion of Ntozake Shange's *For Colored Girls.*" *Journal of Ethnic Studies*, 6, i (Spring 1978): 79-85.

Peters finds the "heaps upon heaps of praises" for *for colored girls* unfortunate. Peters complains that the "discriminating" spectator is "overcome with a sense of disappointment and betrayal." Shange portrays, Peters contends, black men as shallow, one-dimensional, and "pasteboards or beasts." Furthermore, Shange reneges on her responsibility as an artist because she fails to explore the underlying "tragic circumstances" that consume the male characters.

3410. Peterson, Maurice. *Essence*, 7 (Oct. 1976): 48.

3411. *Players*, 3 (Dec. 1976): 24-25.

3412. Ribowsky, Mark. "A Poetess Scores a Hit With Play On 'What's Wrong With Black Men'." *Sepia*, 25 (Dec. 1976): 42-46.

Shange comments that often male spectators "can't handle" the images of themselves in her play *for colored girls*. The play depicts black men "the way they can be—cruel, headstrong and patronizing to black women." However, Shange feels that many men are "being 'purified' because for the first time they can see in clear terms how ugly they can be."

3413. Rich, Alan. *New York*, 9 (June 14, 1976): 62.

3414. Richards, Sandra L. "Conflicting Impulses in the Plays of Ntozake Shange." *Black American Literature Forum*, 17, ii (Summer 1983): 73-78.

According to Richards, one of Shange's most effective dramatic strategies is the dialectic of "awareness of social oppression and commitment to struggle . . . [and] a desire to transcend or bypass, through music and dance, the limitations of social

and human existence." Richards sees as one aspect
of the dialectic an element that Shange terms
"combat breath," which Richards views as the
explanation "that Shange's plays not only startle
and energize but also infuriate and disturb many of
her audiences." *for colored girls* and *Spell #7* are
primarily discussed throughout the article.

3415.   Ridley, Clifford A. *National Observer* (July 31, 1976): 16.
3416.   Rogers, Curtis E. *N.Y. Amsterdam News* (Oct. 9, 1976):
         D-11.

3417.   Rushing, Andrea Benton. "*For Colored Girls,* Suicide or
         Struggle." *Massachusetts Review,* 22, iii (Autumn
         1981): 539-550.
         Although seeing a production of *for colored girls*
         moved her deeply, Rushing realized, upon
         reflection, that "the play was missing something."
         Not unlike a few other critics of the play (see items
         3409, 3422), Rushing criticizes the "ladies of the
         rainbow" as being unrepresentative of black
         women's culture and for having a too narrow focus,
         that is, zeroing in on "black women's shared pain"
         resulting from the treatment of the men in their
         lives. Shange, as maintained by Rushing,
         disregards other reasons for black women's
         suffering, namely, tensions between women and
         their parents, the effect of the political and sexual
         liberation on women, racism, and the capitalist
         system. In conclusion, Rushing expresses her
         disappointment that Shange "reject[s] political
         solutions . . . in favor of young African-American
         women seeking their solutions in themselves and
         with other young women who have the same
         troubles and scant resources."

3418.   Shange, Ntozake. "Introduction." In *for colored girls who
         have considered suicide/when the rainbow is enuf:
         a choreopoem,* ix-xvi. New York: Macmillan
         Publishing Company, 1977.
         In the introduction to the text of her play, Shange
         talks about its genesis. The choreopoem, she says,

began as a series of seven poems, based on Judy
Grahn's *The Common Woman*, that "were to
explore the realities of seven different kinds of
women." Shange also emphasizes the importance
of dance to her spirit as well as her work. "With
dance I discovered my body more intimately than I
had imagined possible. With the acceptance of the
ethnicity of my thighs & backside, came a clearer
understanding of my voice as a woman & as a
poet."

3419. _____. "uncovered losses/black theater traditions." In *three
pieces** 1981. Reprinted in Shange's *See No Evil:
Prefaces, Essays & Accounts 1976-1983*. San
Francisco: Momo's Press, 1984, 18-25; *Black
Scholar*, 10 (July/Aug. 1979): 7-9.
In her preface to *three pieces**, which includes the
texts of *Spell #7, A Photograph: Lovers In
Motion* and *Boogie Woogie Landscapes,* she
observes that the American theatre has become
"shallow/stilted & imitative." She fears that
African-Americans have succumbed to the "same
artificial aesthetics" as white playwrights. Black
playwrights should create their own aesthetic,
which would include developing more works
dealing with "the lives of our regular & precious"
rather than concentrating on "our geniuses" who are
portrayed in hits such as *Bubbling Brown Sugar,
Ain't Misbehavin', Mahalia* and others. Her
discussion of the plays in this collection reflect
Shange's attempts at experimenting with a new
aesthetic. These plays deal with contemporary
issues involving ordinary people, which are
dramatized in a variety of mediums including
visuals, music, and dance.

3420. Simon, John. *New Leader*, 59 (July 5, 1976): 21, 22.
Reprinted in item 3363.
3421. Smith, Cecil. *Los Angeles Times* (May 19, 1983), sect. 6:
3.

3422. Staples, Robert. "The Myth of Black Macho: A Response
       To Angry Black Feminists." *Black Scholar,* 10
       (Mar./Apr. 1979): 24-32.
       In the opinion of Staples, a sociologist of black
       sex roles, Shange shows no "compassion for
       misguided black men or a love of child, family and
       community" in her play *for colored girls.* He
       asserts Shange's anger towards black men is
       displaced and suggests that rather than focusing on
       blacks as monsters she should communicate
       through her art ways that black men and women
       might reconcile their differences and confront racial
       and sexual discrimination. He accuses Shange of
       failing to explore the reason "many black men feel
       their manhood . . . is threatened by black women."
       For a brief rebuttal to Staples' article, see Audre
       Lorde's "Feminism & Black Liberation: The Great
       American Disease." *Black Scholar* (May/June
       1979): 17-19 and Yvonne Smith's "Ntozake
       Shange." *Essence,* 12 (Feb. 1982): 12.

3423. Sullivan, Dan. *Los Angeles Times* (Feb. 7, 1977), sect. 4:
       1, 11.
3324. _____. *Los Angeles Times* (July 14, 1978), sect. 4: 1,
       25.
3425. Sumrall, Harry. *Washington Post* (Mar. 24, 1979), sect. B:
       2.
3426. *Sunday Times* (London) (May 15, 1977): 37c.

3427. Talbert, Linda Lee. "Ntozake Shange: Scarlet Woman and
       Witch/Poet." *Umoja,* 4 (Spring1980): 5-10.
       Ntozake Shange "is preoccupied with poetcraft-as-
       witchcraft," says Talbert. In examining two poems
       from the theatre piece *for colored girls, Sechita* and
       A Laying On of Hands, Talbert explores how
       Shange combines poetry and magic "as a mode of
       transforming patriarchal myths into a distinctive
       female mythology." In *Sechita,* for example, the
       dance hall girls represent—according to the world-
       view of a male-dominated society—"deity and slut,
       innocent and knowing" but their dances reflect

feminine creative powers, that is, as a means of "conjurin' the spirit."

3428. Tapley, Mel. *N.Y. Amsterdam News* (June 11, 1977), sect. D: 2.
Tapley profiles Trazana Beverley, who won the AUDELCO Award for her performance in *for colored girls*. See related article: "*Colored Girls: No Lynching of Black Men: Trazana Beverley*." *Afro-American* (Feb. 21-25, 1978): 7.

3429. Taylor, John Russell. *Plays and Players*, 27 (Dec. 1979): 16-17.
3430. *Variety* (Sep. 22, 1976): 72.
3431. Wallace, Michelle. *Village Voice* (Aug. 16, 1976): 108-09. Reprinted in item 3363.
3432. Ward, Francis. *Los Angeles Times* (Dec. 20, 1977), sect. 4: 1, 8.
3433. Watt, Douglas. *New York Daily News* (Sep. 16, 1976). Reprinted in item 3305.
3434. Wetzsteon, Ross. *Plays and Players*, 23 (Sep. 1976): 39.
3435. _____. *Village Voice* (June 6, 1977): 91, 93.
3436. Weiner, Bernard. *San Francisco Chronicle* (Aug. 3, 1978): 52.
3437. _____. *San Francisco Chronicle* (Jan. 26, 1979): 57.
3438. _____. *San Francisco Chronicle* (Sep. 4, 1979): 46.
3439. Willis, Ellen. *Rolling Stone* (Sep. 23, 1976): 19.
3440. Wilson, Edwin. *Wall Street Journal* (Sep. 21, 1976): 24.
3441. Winer, Linda. *Chicago Tribune* (Jan. 23, 1977), sect. 6: 2-3.
3442. _____. *Chicago Tribune* (Dec. 25, 1977), sect. 6: 2.

Mother Courage

3443. Allen, Bonnie. *Essence*. 11 (Aug. 1980): 21.
3444. *American Theatre Annual 1979-1980*, 171. Detroit: Gale Research Company, 1980.
3445. *Essence*, 12 (Feb. 1982): 12-14.
3446. Barnes, Clive. *New York Post* (May 14, 1980): 36. Reprinted in item 3453.
3447. Beaufort, John. *Christian Science Monitor* (May 19, 1980): 19.

Reprinted in item 3453.
3448. *Encore*, 9 (June 1980): 34.
3449. Gussow, Mel. *New York Times* (May 14, 1980), sect. C: 20.
3450. Kissel, Howard. *Women's Wear Daily* (May 14, 1980). Reprinted in item 3453.

3451. Munk, Erica. *Village Voice* (May 19, 1980): 89.
In addition to this review, Shange briefly discusses the production of *Mother Courage* on page 40 of this issue.

3452. *N.Y. Amsterdam News* (June 14, 1980): 33.
3453. *New York Theatre Critics' Reviews*, 41 (Aug. 4, 1980): 183-186.
3454. Oliver, Edith. *The New Yorker*, 56 (May 26, 1980): 77.
3455. Rich, Frank. *New York Times* (June 15, 1980), sect. 2: D5.
3456. Watt, Douglas. *New York Daily News* (May 14, 1980). Reprinted in item 3453.

A Photograph: A Study of Cruelty

3457. *After Dark*, 10 (Apr. 1978): 80.
3458. *American Theatre Annual, 1977-1978*, 107. Detroit: Gale Research Company, 1979.
3459. Barnes, Clive. *New York Post* (Dec. 22, 1977): 39.
3460. Eder, Richard. *New York Times* (Dec. 22, 1977): C11.
3461. Gottfried, Martin. *Saturday Review*, 5 (Feb. 18, 1978): 42.
3462. Nightingale, Benedict. *New Statesman*, 98 (Oct. 19, 1979): 604-605.
3463. Oliver, Edith. *The New Yorker*, 53 (Jan. 2, 1978): 48-49.
3464. Sharp, Christopher. *Women's Wear Daily* (Dec. 22, 1977): 7.
3465. Simon, John. *New York*, 11 (Jan. 16, 1978): 58.
3466. _____. *New York*, 13 (May, 26, 1980): 80-81.
3467. Stasio, Marilyn. *Cue* (Jan. 7-20, 1978): 31-32.
3468. Valentine, Dean. *New Leader*, 61 (Jan. 2, 1978): 29.

Shapes, Sadness, and the Witch

3469. Albright, Will. *Houston Post* (July 28, 1984), sect. C: 16.

Spell #7

3470. Albright, William. *Houston Post* (Jan. 27, 1988), sect. B: 5.
3471. *American Theatre Annual, 1979-1980,* 109. Detroit: Gale Research Company, 1980.
3472. Bailey, Peter. *Black Collegian,* 10 (Jan 1979): 70.
3473. Barnes, Clive. *New York Post* (July 16, 1979): 20.
3474. Beaufort, John. *Christian Science Monitor* (June 7, 1979): 19.
3475. Byrd, William. *Atlanta Daily World* (Feb. 12, 1982): 3.
3476. Campbell, Mary. *Chicago Tribune* (July 1, 1979), sect. 6: 14.
3477. Cooper, Martin. *Times* (Apr. 4, 1985): 11d.
3478. Eder, Richard. *New York Times* (June 4, 1979), sect. C: 13.
3479. _____. *New York Times* (July 16, 1979): C12.
       Reprinted in item 3487.
3480. _____. *New York Times* (July 22, 1979), sect. 2: D3.
3481. Fox, Terry Curtis. *Village Voice* (July 23, 1979): 77-79.
3482. Gelman, David. *Newsweek,* 94 (July 30, 1979): 65.
3483. Hill, Latham. *Norfolk Journal and Guide* (Feb. 19, 1986): 13.
3484. Nelson, Don. *New York Daily News* (July 16, 1979).
       Reprinted in item 3487.
3485. *N.Y. Amsterdam News* (Jan. 5, 1980): 21.
3486. *N.Y. Amsterdam News* (July 3, 1982): 34.
3487. *New York Theatre Critics' Reviews,* 40 (Nov. 19, 1979): 107-108.
3488. Oliver, Edith. *The New Yorker,* 55 (July 16, 1979): 73.
3489. Simon, John. *New York,* 12 (July 30, 1979): 57.
3490. Stasio, Marilyn. *New York Post* (June 5, 1979).
       Reprinted in item 3487.
3491. Winn, Steven. *San Francisco Chronicle* (Mar. 26, 1985): 44.
3492. Wood, William R. *Cleveland Call and Post* (June 6, 1981): 11B.
3493. Woodis, Carole. *Plays and Players,* 381 (June 1985): 28-29.
3494. *Variety* (July 25, 1979): 106.

Three Views of Mt. Fuji

3495. Arkatov, Janice. "A Less-Public Obie Winner Writes On."
       Los Angeles Times (July 28, 1987), sect. 6: 5.
       Arkatov profiles Shange shortly before her play
       Three Views of Mt. Fuji opens at New
       Dramatists. Shange remarks "I feel good about this
       play," which is about a birthday party that "ends up
       being about sex and lust and Third World debt." In
       all her plays Shange says of primary importance is
       the meaning of being a woman of "color and female
       in the 20th century."

3496. Guthmann, Edward. "Shange's Fond Memories." *San
       Francisco Chronicle* (June 19, 1987): 87.
       Shange talks about her new play, *Three Views of
       Mt. Fuji,* a dramatic piece that reflects Shange's
       imaginary vision "return[ing] to a fondly
       remembered time" to the days she spent in San
       Francisco "writing, dancing and teaching . . . [and]
       hanging out in bars like Minnie's Can Do," the
       days before her play *for colored girls* threw her into
       the spotlight. Shange says unlike *for colored girls,*
       her new play reflects her ability to be "a little more
       tolerant of frailty, of character flaws." The new
       piece also dramatizes Shange's concern for "the role
       of art and sex in a creative person's life, and how
       passions, whether sexual or literary/artistic, can
       become mixed together."

3497. Weiner, Bernard. *San Francisco Chronicle* (June 12, 1987):
       84.

Where the Mississippi Meets the Amazon

3498. Gussow, Mel. *New York Times* (Dec. 20, 1977): 44.
3499. Oliver, Edith. *The New Yorker*, 53 (Jan. 2, 1978): 48-49.
3500. Sharp, Christopher. *Women's Wear Daily* (Dec. 22, 1977):
       7.
3501. Stasio, Marilyn. *Cue*, 46 (Jan. 8-20, 1977): 31-32.

Shank, Adele Edling

Selected Plays

3502. *Fox & Co.* (adaptation of Volpone, University of
      California, Davis, 1978)
3503. *The Grass House* (Magic Theatre, San Francisco, 1983)
3504. *Sand Castles* (Actors Theatre of Louisville, Kentucky,
      1982)
      Playscript: *West Coast Plays*, 15/16
      (Winter/Spring, 1983): 256-324.
3505. *Stuck: A Freeway Comedy* (Magic Theatre, San Francisco,
      1981)
3506. *Sunset/Sunrise* (Actors Theatre of Louisville, Kentucky,
      1980)
      Playscript: *West Coast Plays* (Spring 1979): 1-57.
3507. *Tumbleweed* (Los Angeles Theater Center, Los Angeles,
      1986)
3508. *The War Horses* (Magic Theatre, San Francisco, 1985)
3509. *Winterplay* (Magic Theatre, San Francisco, 1980)
      Playscript: *New Plays USA 1*, 289-368. New
      York: Theatre Communications Group, 1982.

Profiles

See item 87.

Reviews

Sand Castles

3510. Gussow, Mel. *New York Times* (Mar. 31, 1983): C15.

3511. Jenner, C. Lee. "Theatrical Hyperrealism in the Plays of
      Adele Shank." *Contemporary Review*, 247 (Oct.
      1985): 202-207.
      Jenner contends that Shank uses superrealism, or
      what Shank refers to as "theatrical hyperrealism,"
      much like artists of photo-realism—"to describe a
      morally corrupt society . . . [to] stress surface
      qualities to capture a community obsessed with
      surfaces." Shank uses this approach in her cycle of
      plays called the California Series, which includes:

> Winterplay, Sunset/Sunrise, Stuck, and Sand
> Castles.

3512. Koehler, Robert. Los Angeles Times (Aug. 15, 1986), sect.
       6: 18.
3513. Wilson, Edwin. Wall Street Journal (Apr. 8, 1983): 27.

Stuck

3514. Shank, Theodore. "Stuck on a California Freeway." Theatre
       Design and Technology, 18, (Summer 1982): 14-
       16.
       Shank, who directed Stuck at the Magic Theatre in
       San Francisco, discusses the unique set of the play,
       which required "5 real cars, set on a California
       freeway."

3515. Winn, Steven. San Francisco Chronicle, (Oct. 25, 1981),
       Datebook sect.: 45-46.

Sunset/Sunrise

3516. Aratov, Janice. Playwright in Theory, Practice." Los
       Angeles Times (Mar. 28, 1986), sect. 6: 2.
       Arkatov briefly interviews Shank on the eve of the
       premiere of Tumbleweed at the Los Angeles
       Theater Center. Shank discusses playwriting and
       her unique use of hyperrealism, "I wanted a style . .
       . that could act as a mirror for the audiences to see
       themselves."

3517. Drake, Sylvie. Los Angeles Times (July 28, 1980), sect. 6:
       1, 2.
3518. Gussow, Mel. New York Times (Mar. 23, 1980): 55.
3519. Kalem, T.E. Time, 115 (Mar. 31, 1980): 58.
3520. Kroll, Jack. Newsweek, 95 (Mar. 31, 1980): 70-71.

3521. Shank, Theodore. "Hyperrealism in the Theatre: Shank
       Interviews Shank." West Coast Plays, 4 (Spring
       1979): 59-63.
       In Ted Shank's interview with Adele Shank, which
       follows the text of her play Sunset/Sunrise: A

Hyperreal Comedy, the playwright explains the hyperrealistic style whose elements she adapted for the theatre from painting. Hyperrealism heightens the spectators' perception because they are not distracted by the character's emotional life. Suspense, therefore, is replaced by a kind of "voyeuristic interest." Spectators are curious about the characters, "there is recognition of them by the audience, not an emotional identification." Moreover, suspense in the traditional sense does not occur, that is, "the audience [does not] hang on an evolving future."

3522. Wardle, Irving. *Times* (London) (Mar. 22, 1980): 8h.
3523. _____. *Sunday Times* (London) (Apr. 6, 1980): 10.
3524. Weales, Gerald. *Georgia Review,* 34 (1980): 497-508.

3525. Weiner, Bernard."The Success of *Sunrise.*" *San Francisco Chronicle* (Dec. 15, 1979): 34.
This item reports that Shank's *Sunset/Sunrise* was a co-winner of The Great American Play Contest sponsored by the Actors Theatre of Louisville. Also included is a brief discussion of her play *Winterplay.*

Tumbleweed

3526. Mason, Jeffrey. *Theatre Journal,* 39, i (Mar. 1987): 106-107.
3527. Sullivan, Dan. *Los Angeles Times* (Apr. 5, 1986), sect. 5: 1.

War Horses

3528. Weiner, Bernard. "The Feuding Actors Who Caused Fatal Riots." *San Francisco Chronicle* (January 13, 1985), Datebook sect.: 42
Weiner previews the premiere of Shank's *War Horses,* a play about two nineteenth-century actors whose volatile relationship resulted in the Astor Place Riots of 1849. Shank remarks that this play

differs substantially from her previous plays in the
California series, but she vows to return to the
series when she completes her work on *War
Horses.*

3529. Winn, Steven. *San Francisco Chronicle* (Feb. 17, 1985),
Datebook sect.: 31-32.

Winterplay

3530. Faber, Roderick. *Village Voice* (May 31, 1983): 96.
3531. Rich, Frank. *New York Times* (May 23, 1983): C14.
3532. Simon, John. *New York,* 16 (June 6, 1983): 89.
3533. Winn, Steven. *San Francisco Chronicle* (Oct. 30, 1980):
60.

Siefert, Lynn

Selected Plays

3534. *Coyote Ugly* (New York Theater Workshop, 1987)
Playscript: *Coyote Ugly.* New York: Dramatists
Play Service, 1987.
3535. *Little Egypt* (Steppenwolf Theater, Chicago, 1987)

Reviews

Coyote Ugly

3536. Christiansen, Richard. *Chicago Tribune* (Apr. 1, 1985),
sect. 2: 8.
3537. Gussow, Mel. *New York Times* (Dec. 5, 1987): 13.
3538. Smith, Sid. *Chicago Tribune* (June 17, 1985), sect. 4: 2.
3539. *Variety* (Feb. 9, 1983): 84.
3540. Weiner, Bernard. *San Francisco Chronicle* (Oct. 27, 1983):
69.

Little Egypt

3541. Daily, Bob. *Chicago,* 36 (Dec. 1987): 113-115.
3542. Gold, Sylviane. *Wall Street Journal* (Dec. 2, 1987): 26.

3543. *Variety* (Nov. 4, 1987): 87.

Simo, Ana Maria

Selected Plays

3544. *Alma* (book and lyrics, INTAR, 1988)
3545. *Bayou* (Medusa's Revenge, 1977)
3546. *Exiles* (INTAR, 1982)
3547. *Going To New England* (INTAR, 1990)
3548. *Passion* (South Coast Repertory, Los Angeles, 1987)
3549. *Tea and Edna* (New Dramatists, 1988-1989)
3550. *What Do You See?* (Theater for the New City, 1986)
　　　Playscript: *Third Woman*, 4 (1989): 113-119.

Profiles and Interviews

3551. "Six Writers Named to INTAR Program." *New York Times* (Dec. 29, 1981): C9.
　　　The *Times* reports Simo is one of six Hispanic dramatists to be included in the playwright-in-residence program sponsored by INTAR.

Reviews

3552. Feingold, Michael. *Village Voice* (July 12, 1988): 92.
3553. Hampton, Wilborn. *New York Times* (June 21, 1988): C16.

Exiles

3554. Hoffman, Jan. *Village Voice* (Dec. 28, 1982): 94.

Going To New England

3555. Holden, Stephen. *New York Times* (Mar. 9, 1990): C18.
3556. Solomon, Alisa. *Village Voice* (Mar. 13, 1990): 104.

Passion

3557. Jalon, Allan. *Los Angeles Times* (July 10, 1987), sect. 6: 21.

What Do You See?

3558. Simo, Ana Maria. "What Do You See?" *Third Woman,* 4
       (1989): 113-119.
       The editors include a brief note on the staging
       history of Simo's play *What Do You See?*

Sklar, Roberta

   Selected Plays

   The Daughters Cycle

   See **Coss, Clare**

   Feast or Famine

   See **Segal, Sondra**

   Mutations (with Joseph Chaikin, Open Theatre, 1970-
   1972)

   Profiles

   See item 86 and pages 7, 22.

3559. Brunner, Cornelia. "Roberta Sklar: Toward Creating a
       Women's Theatre." *Drama Review,* 24, ii (June
       1980): 23-40.
       In response to Brunner's penetrating questions,
       Sklar talks candidly and extensively about her dual
       role as director/collaborator and her early
       commitment to experimental theatre at the Cafe
       Cino and the Open Theatre. Sklar regards *The
       Mutation Show,* her final directorial effort at the
       Open Theatre, as the "beginning of [her] feminist
       expression." Part of the reason she left the Open
       Theatre, Sklar explains, was she "had to make a
       change that would articulate my being a woman."
       Since her departure she has worked assiduously
       towards that goal, demonstrating her commitment

through her work with various women's theatre
groups, such as Womanrite Theatre Ensemble and
Women's Experimental Theatre, and collaborations
with Sondra Segal and Clare Coss. Brunner
prefaces the interview with a biographical profile
on Sklar and a discussion of *The Daughters Cycle*.

Reviews

The Daughters Cycle

See **Coss, Clare**

Feast or Famine

see **Segal, Sondra**

Sister/Sister

see **Coss, Clare**

Sloan, Patty

Selected Plays

3560. *Beginnings*
    Playscript: *Beginnings: A Comedy in Two Acts.*
    New York: Samuel French, 1967.
3561. *Man Enough* (Apple Corp. Theater, 1985)
3562. *Night On Bare Mountain* (staged reading, Women's Project,
    1979-1980)

Reviews

Man Enough

3563. Albright, William. *Houston Post* (Mar. 15, 1984), sect. C:
    2.
3564. Shepard, Richard. F. *New York Times* (May 29, 1985),
    sect. 3: C18.
3565. Solomon, Alisa. *Village Voice* (July 23, 1985): 94.

Swados, Elizabeth

Selected Plays

3566. *Agamemnon* (adaptor, New York Shakespeare Festival,
         Vivian Beaumont Theatre, 1977)
3567. *Alice in Concert* (Public Theatre, 1981)
         Playscript: *Alice in Concert*. New York: Samuel
         French, 1987.
3568. *The Beautiful Lady* (with Paul Schmidt, Mark Taper
         Forum, Los Angeles, 1985)
3569. *Dispatches: A Rock-War Musical* (adapted and composed
         by Swados, Public Theatre Cabaret, 1979)
3570. *Doonesbury* (book/lyrics by Garry Trudeau, music by
         Swados, Biltmore Theater, 1983)
         Playscript: *Doonesbury: A Musical Comedy*. New
         York: Holt, Rinehart and Winston, 1984.
3571. *Fragments of a Trilogy* (La Mama ETC, 1975)
3572. *The Haggadah, A Passover Cantata* (Public Theatre, 1980)
         Part of the biblical cantata series: *Esther,*
         Jerusalem, and *Song of Songs.*
         Playscript: *The Haggadah*. New York: Samuel
         French, 1982.
3573. *The Incredible Feeling Show* (adapted from Swados's *The*
         Girl With the Incredible Feeling, First All
         Children's Theatre, 1979)
3574. *Jonah* (adapted from Robert Nathan's *Jonah and the Whale,*
         Public Theatre, 1990)
3575. *Nightclub Cantata* (Top of the Gate, 1977)
         Playscript: *Nightclub Cantata*. New York:
         Dramatists Play Service, 1979.
3576. *Phaedra Britannica* (composer, Swados, CSC Repertory
         Ltd., 1988)
3577. *Rap Master Ronnie* (lyrics by Garry Trudeau, music by
         Elizabeth Swados, Village Gate, 1984)
         Playscript: *Rap Master Ronnie*. New York:
         Broadway Play Publishing, 1985.
3578. *The Red Sneaks* (based on *The Red Shoes,* Theater for a
         New Audience, 1989)
3579. *Runaways* (Public Theatre,1978)
         Playscript: *Runaways*. New York: Samuel French,
         1978.

Profiles and Interviews

See items 743, 1066.

3580. *Contemporary Authors: A Bio-Bibliographical Guide.*
Volumes 97-100. Edited by Frances C. Locher,
522-525. Detroit: Gale Research Company, 1981.
An interview accompanies a biographical sketch as
well as general comments regarding Swados's
theatrical work.

3581. *Contemporary Theatre, Film, and Television.* Volume 1.
Edited by Monica O'Donnell, 484-485. Detroit:
Gale Research Company, 1984.
The entry includes a concise biography and list of
Swados's theatrical productions.

3582. Gussow, Mel. "Lifelong Black Sheep, Age 26, Makes
Good." *New York Times* (Mar. 27, 1978): 16.
Gussow's profile on Swados anticipates the
opening of her play *Runaways* at Joseph Papp's
Public Theatre Cabaret. The article traces Swados's
early years in the theatre to her affiliation with La
Mama where she became one of Ellen Stewart's
"creative children." Swados also talks about the
creation of *Runaways*, the idea of which came from
Swados's "own life and her feeling of
fragmentation."

3583. Swados, Elizabeth. *Listening Out Loud: Becoming a
Composer.* New York: Harper & Row, 1988.
Swados offers practical advice to young composers
on writing music.

Reviews

Agamemnon

3584. *American Theatre Annual* 1976-1977, 58. Detroit: Gale
Research Company, 1978.
3585. Barnes, Clive. *New York Times* (May 19, 1977): C20.

Reprinted in item 3591.
3586. Beaufort, John. *Christian Science Monitor* (May 23, 1977).
Reprinted in item 3591.
3587. Gottfried, Martin. *New York Post* (May 19, 1977): 26.
Reprinted in item 3591.
3588. Kalem, T.E. *Time*, 109 (May 30, 1977): 76.
Reprinted in item 3591.
3589. Kroll, Jack. *Newsweek*, 89 (May 30, 1977): 89.
Reprinted in item 3591.
3590. Munk, Erica. *Village Voice* (May 30, 1977): 87.
3591. *New York Theatre Critics' Reviews*, 38 (May 30, 1977): 234-238.
3592. Oliver, Edith. *The New Yorker*, 53 (May 30, 1977): 84.
3593. Rich, Alan. *New York*, 10 (May 30, 1977): 92.
3594. Watt, Douglas. *New York Daily News* (May 19, 1977).
Reprinted in item 3591.
3595. *Women's Wear Daily* (May 19, 1977).
Reprinted in item 3591.

Alice In Concert

3596. Barnes, Clive. *Times* (London) (Jan. 17, 1981): 10e.
3597. Feingold, Michael. *Village Voice* (Jan. 14-20, 1981): 101.
3598. Oliver, Edith. *The New Yorker*, 54 (Jan. 15, 1979): 89.
3599. Rich, Frank. *New York Times* (Jan. 8, 1981): C17.

The Beautiful Lady

3600. *Variety* (Sep. 4, 1985): 84.

Dispatches

3601. *American Theatre Annual*, 1979-1980, 177. Detroit: Gale Research Company, 1980.
3602. Barnes, Clive. *New York Post* (Apr. 20, 1979).
Reprinted in item 3611.
3603. Beaufort, John. *Christian Science Monitor* (Apr. 25, 1979): 18.
Reprinted in items 3604, 3611.
3604. *Contemporary Literary Criticism: Excerpts from Criticism of the Works of Todays' Novelists, Poets, Playwrights and Other Creative Writers.* Volume

12. Edited by Dedria Bryfonski, 560-561. Detroit: Gale Research Company, 1980.
3605. Eder, Richard. *New York Times* (Apr. 19, 1979): C17. Reprinted in item 3611.
3606. Feingold, Michael. *Village Voice* (Apr. 30, 1979): 89. Reprinted in item 3604.
3607. Kauffmann, Stanley. *Theatre Criticisms*, 88-89. New York: Performing Arts Journal Publications, 1983.
3608. Kroll, Jack. *Newsweek*, 153 (Apr. 30, 1979): 98. Reprinted in item 3611.
3609. Lardner, J. *Washington Post* (Apr. 19, 1979), sect. B: 15.
3610. Munk, Erica. *Village Voice* (Apr. 30, 1979): 88. Reprinted in item 3604.
3611. *New York Theatre Critics' Reviews*, 40 (May 28, 1979): 252-255.
3612. Oliver, Edith. *The New Yorker*, 55 (Apr. 30, 1979): 95.
3613. Simon, John. *New York*, 11 (Mar. 27, 1978): 85. Reprinted in item 3604.
3614. Watt, Douglas. *New York Daily News* (Apr. 19, 1979). Reprinted in item 3611.
3615. Wilson, Edwin. *Wall Street Journal* (Apr. 26, 1979). Reprinted in item 3611.
3616. *Women's Wear Daily* (Apr. 26, 1979): 22. Reprinted in item 3611.

Fragments of a Trilogy

3617. Blumenthal, Eileen. *American Theatre*, 3 (Feb. 1987): 32-33.
3618. Feingold, Michael. *Village Voice* (Jan. 20, 1987): 85.
3619. Gussow, Mel. *New York Times* (Dec. 31, 1975): 17.
3620. _____. *New York Times* (Jan. 6, 1987): C16.

Ghost Sonata

3621. Eder, Richard. *New York Times* (Oct. 10, 1977): 37.
3622. Gussow, Mel. *New York Times* (Oct. 16, 1977), sect. 2: 7.
3623. Munk, Erica. *Village Voice* (Oct. 17, 1977): 89.

The Haggadah

3624. *American Theatre Annual* 1979-1980, 158. Detroit: Gale
Research Company, 1980.
3625. Gussow, Mel. *New York Times* (Apr. 2, 1980): C22.
3626. Kauffmann, Stanley. *Theater Criticisms*, 106-107. New
York: Performing Arts Journal Publications, 1983.

3627. Lawson, Carol. "News of the Theater." *New York Times*
(May 21, 1980): C30.
Lawson reports Joseph Papp will close Swados's
The Haggadah, despite playing to sold out houses.

3628. Simon, John. *New York*, 13 (Apr. 21, 1980): 79.

The Incredible Feeling Show

3629. Kauffmann, Stanley. *New Republic*, 180 (Mar. 24, 1979):
24-25.
Reprinted in item 3604.
3630. Levin, Irene. *AJL Bulletin* (Spring 1977).
Reprinted in item 3604.
3631. Munk, Erica. *Village Voice* (Mar. 12, 1979): 84.
Reprinted in item 3604.

Jonah

3632. Holden, Stephen. *New York Times* (Mar. 23, 1990): C5.
3633. Magruder, James. *Village Voice* (Apr. 3, 1990): 102.

3634. Pall, Ellen. "A Sulky Rock Star Among the Prophets."
New York Times (Mar. 4,1990), sect. 2: 5.
Swados briefly talks about her musical *Jonah*,
based on Robert Nathan's novel of the same title
and the fifth play in her "biblical cycle," which
includes *Haggadah, Jerusalem, Esther*, and *Song of
Songs*. Nathan's Jonah could very well be "a
prophet for the 1980s and 1990s, so narcissistic,
full of complaints, apathetic, unwilling to do
anything for anyone because there wasn't enough in
it for him."

Nightclub Cantata

3635. Barnes, Clive. *New York Times* (Jan. 10, 1977): 29.
    Reprinted in items 3604, 3648.
3636. Beaufort, John. *Christian Science Monitor* (Jan. 14, 1977).
3637. Castellino, M. *San Francisco Chronicle* (May 2, 1982),
    Datebook sect.: 22.
    Castellino briefly discusses *Nightclub Cantata*.
3638. Clurman, Harold. *Nation*, 224 (Jan. 29, 1977): 124-125.
    Reprinted in item 3604.
3639. Coe, Richard L. *Washington Post* (Oct. 13, 1977), sect. B:
    1.8.
3640. Drake, Sylvie. *Los Angeles Times* (Apr. 24, 1980), sect.
    6:1.
3641. *Drama-Logue* (Nov. 20-Dec. 6, 1989): 9.
3642. *Encore*, 6 (Feb. 21, 1977): 41.
3643. Feingold, Michael. *Village Voice* (Jan. 17, 1977): 83.
    Reprinted in item 3604.
3644. Gottfried, Martin. *New York Post* (Jan. 10, 1977): 19.
    Reprinted in item 3648.
3645. Kauffmann, Stanley. *Theater Criticisms*, 39-41. New York:
    Performing Arts Journal Publications, 1983.
3646. Kissel, Howard. *Women's Wear Daily* (Jan. 11, 1977).
    Reprinted in item 3648.
3647. Munk, Erica. *Village Voice* (Jan. 24, 1977): 79.
3648. *New York Theatre Critics' Reviews*, 38 (Mar. 7, 1977):
    359-361.
3649. Oliver, Edith. *The New Yorker*, 53 (Jan. 24, 1977): 64.
    Reprinted in item 3604.
3650. Rich, Alan. *New York*, 10 (Jan. 31, 1977): 68.
    Reprinted in item 3604.
3651. Sharp, Christopher. *Christian Science Monitor* (Jan. 18,
    1977).
    Reprinted in item 3648.
3652. Shirley, Don. *Los Angeles Times* (Nov. 23, 1989), sect. F:
    16.
3653. Thomas, Trevor. *Los Angeles Times* (Apr. 21, 1982), sect.
    6: 1.
3654. Watt, Douglas. *New York Daily News* (Jan. 10, 1977).
    Reprinted in item 3648.
3655. Wetzsteon, Ross. *Village Voice* (June 6, 1977): 91, 93.

3656. Winn, Steven. *San Francisco Chronicle* (May 11, 1982): 39.

Phaedra Britannica

3657. Disch, Thomas M. *Nation*, 248 (Jan. 23, 1989): 100-102.
3658. Gussow, Mel. *New York Times* (Dec. 17, 1988): 15.
3659. Rogoff, Gordon. *Village Voice* (Dec. 27, 1988): 103.

Rap Master Ronnie

3660. Bemrose, John. *Maclean's*, 101 (Jan. 18, 1988): 53.
3661. Christiansen, Richard. *Chicago Tribune* (June 22, 1984), sect. 5: 3.
3662. Kogan, Rick. *Chicago Tribune* (Sep. 13, 1985), sect. 2: 8.
3663. _____. *Chicago Tribune* (Sep. 14, 1985), sect. 12: 1.
3664. _____. *Chicago Tribune* (Nov. 24, 1985), sect. 13: 4.
3665. Lochte, David. *Los Angeles*, 30 (July 1985): 42.
3666. Solomon, Alisa. *Village Voice* (Oct. 16, 1984): 114.
3667. Wardle, Irving. *Times* (London) (Apr. 11, 1985): 15c.

Runaways

3668. *American Theatre Annual* 1978-1979, 83. Detroit: Gale Research Company, 1979.
3669. Barnes, Clive. *New York Post* (May 15, 1978). Reprinted in item 3682.
3670. Beaufort, John. *Christian Science Monitor* (Mar. 15, 1978). Reprinted in item 3682.
3671. Brecher, Kenneth. *Westways*, 70 (Nov. 1978): 58.
3672. Chaillet, Ned. *Times* (London) (June 10, 1981): 9e.
3673. Christiansen, Richard. *Chicago Tribune* (June 22, 1984), sect. 5: 3.
3674. Coe, Richard L. *Washington Post* (May 28, 1978), sect. G: 2.
3675. Drake, Sylvie. *Los Angeles Times* (Dec. 19, 1980), sect. 6: 1, 21.
3676. Eder, Richard. *New York Times* (May 15, 1978): C15. Reprinted in item 3682.
3677. Gussow, Mel. *New York Times* (Mar. 10, 1978): C3. Reprinted in item 3604.
3678. Kalem, T.E. *Time*, 111 (Mar. 20, 1978): 84.

Reprinted in item 3682.
3679. Kauffmann, Stanley. *Theater Criticisms.* 69-71. New York: Performing Arts Journal Publications, 1983.
3680. Kroll, Jack. *Newsweek,* 151 (Mar. 27, 1978): 74-75. Reprinted in items 3604, 3682.
3681. Oliver, Edith. *The New Yorker,* 54 (Mar. 20, 1978): 88-89. Reprinted in item 3604.
3682. *New York Theatre Critics' Reviews,* 39 (May 29, 1978): 278-282.
3683. Novick, Julius. *Village Voice* (Mar. 27, 1978): 73.
3684. Sharp, Christopher. *Women's Wear Daily* (Mar. 13, 1978). Reprinted in item 3682.
3685. Stasio, Marilyn. *Penthouse,* 9 (Aug. 1978): 35-36.
3686. Sherrin, Ned. *Punch,* 272 (Mar. 21, 1979): 502.
3687. Shapiro, Lauro. *Rolling Stone,* 267 (June 15, 1978): 54-56. Reprinted in item 3604.
3688. Simon, John. *New York,* 11 (Mar. 27, 1978): 70. Reprinted in item 3604.
3689. Watt, Douglas. *New York Daily News* (May 15, 1978). Reprinted in item 3682.

Swicord, Robin

Selected Plays

3690. *Captain Daddy's Big Farewell* (staged reading, Actors Studio, 1979-1980)
3691. *Criminal Minds* (Production Company, 1984) Playscript: *Criminal Minds.* New York: Samuel French, 1985.
3692. *Last Days At the Dixie Girl Cafe* (Theater Four, 1979)
3693. *Souvenirs* (staged reading, Actors Studio, 1979)

Reviews

Criminal Minds

3694. Oliver, Edith. *The New Yorker,* 59 (Jan. 23, 1984): 86.
3695. Novick, Julius. *Village Voice* (Jan. 24, 1984): 94.
3696. Rich, Frank. *New York Times* (Jan. 18, 1984): C24.

Last Days At the Dixie Girl Cafe

3697. Fox, Terry Curtis. *Village Voice* (June 4, 1979): 92.
3698. Gussow, Mel. *New York Times* (May 17, 1979): C23.
3699. Kerr, Walter. *New York Times* (June 3, 1979), sect. 2.:
      D5, D24.
3700. Loney, Glenn. *After Dark*, 12 (Aug. 1979): 64.
3701. Oliver, Edith. *The New Yorker*, 55 (May 28, 1979): 93.
3702. *Plays and Players*, 26 (Aug. 1979): 40-41.
3703. Richards, David. *Washington Post* (Apr. 13, 1985): D1,
      D11.
3704. Shirley, Don. *Los Angeles Times* (Nov. 9, 1984), sect. 6:
      6.
3705. Simon, John. *New York*, 12 (June 4, 1979): 73.
3706. Stasio, Marilyn. *New York Post* (May 17, 1979): 43.
3707. Watt, Douglas. *New York Daily News* (May 17, 1979): 85.

Terry, Megan

Selected Plays

3708. *All Them Women* (with Sally Ordway, Westbeth
      Playwrights Feminist Cooperative, 1973-1974)
3709. *American King's English for Queens* (Omaha Magic
      Theatre, Omaha, 1978)
      Playscript: *American King's English for Queens*
      Omaha: Omaha Magic Theatre Press, 1978; *High
      Energy Musicals from the Omaha Magic Theatre*.
      New York: Broadway Play Publishing, 1983.
3710. *American Wedding Ritual* (Omaha Magic Theatre, Omaha,
      1972)
3711. *Amtrak* (Omaha Magic Theatre, Omaha, 1987-1988)
      Playscript: *Studies in American Drama 1945-
      Present*, 4 (1989): 22-81.
      Playscript: *Approaching Simone: A Play*. New
      York: The Feminist Press, 1973; *Women in
      Drama: An Anthology*. Edited by Harriet Kriegel,
      357-408. New York: New American Library, 1975.
3712. *Attempted Rescue on Avenue B: A Beat Fifties Comic
      Opera* (Chicago Theatre Strategy, 1979)
      Playscript: *Attempted Rescue On Avenue B: A
      Beat Fifties Comic Opera*. Omaha, Nebraska:
      Omaha Magic Theatre, 1979.

3713. *Babes in the Bighouse: A Documentary Fantasy Musical About Life in a Women's Prison* (New York Theatre Strategy, 1976)
Playscript: *Babes in the Bighouse: A Documentary Musical Fantasy About Life in a Women's Prison.* Omaha, Nebraska: Omaha Magic Theatre, 1974; *High Energy Musicals from the Omaha Magic Theatre,* 135-211. New York: Broadway Play Publishers, Inc., 1983.

3714. *Babies Unchained* (with Jo Ann Schmidman, Omaha Magic Theatre, Omaha, 1988-1989)

3715. *Body Leaks* (Omaha Magic Theatre, Omaha, 1989)

3716. *Calm Down Mother* (Open Theatre, 1965)
Playscript: *Calm Down Mother: A Transformation for Three Women.* New York: Samuel French, 1966; *Eight Plays from Off-Off Broadway.* Edited by Nick Orze and Michael Smith. Indianapolis: Bobbs-Merrill, 1966. *Plays by and about Women: An Anthology.* Edited by Victoria Sullivan and James Hatch, 274-293. New York Random House, 1973.

3717. *Cancel That Last Thought* (California State University, Humboldt, Arcata, California, 1989)

3718. *Changes* (with Tom O'Horgan, La Mama ETC, 1968)

3719. *Choose a Spot on the Floor* (Omaha Magic Theater, Omaha, 1972)

3720. *Comings and Goings* (La Mama ETC, 1966)
Playscript: see item 3753.

3721. *Couplings and Groupings*
Playscript: *Couplings and Groupings.* New York: Pantheon Books, 1972.

3722. *Eat At Joe's* (Open Theater, 1963)

3723. *Ex-Miss Copper Queen on a Set of Pills* (Cherry Lane Theatre, 1963)
Playscript: *A Century of Plays by American Women.* Edited by Rachel France, 162-173. New York: Richards Rosen Press, 1979; *Plays for Tomorrow.* Volume 1. Edited by Arthur Ballet. Minnesota: University of Minnesota, 1966.

3724. *Family Talk* (with John J. Sheehan, Omaha Magic Theatre, Omaha, 1986)

Playscript: *Family Talk.* Omaha, Nebraska: Omaha Magic Theatre, 1986.

3725. *Fireworks* (Actors Theatre of Louisville, Kentucky,1979)

3726. *The Gloaming/Oh My Darling* (Firehouse Theatre, Minneapolis, 1965)
Playscript: *The Gloaming, Oh My Darling: A Play in One Act.* New York: Samuel French, 1967; see item 3753.

3727. *Goona Goona* (Omaha Magic Theatre, Omaha, 1979)

3728. *Headlights* (Omaha Magic Theatre, Omaha, 1989)

3729. *Hothouse* (Circle Repertory Theatre, 1974)
Playscript: *Hothouse: A Play in Three Acts.* New York: Samuel French, 1974.

3730. *Jack-Jack* (Firehouse Theatre, Minneapolis, 1968)

3731. *Keep Tightly Closed in a Cool, Dry Place* (Open Theatre, 1965)
Playscript: *Four Plays by Megan Terry.* New York: Simon & Schuster, 1967; *Tulane Drama Review,* 10, iv (Summer 1966): 177-213; see item 3753.

3732. *The Key Is At the Bottom* (Mark Taper Forum, Los Angeles, 1967)

3733. *The Magic Realists* (La Mama ETC, 1966)
Playscript: *The Best Short Plays 1968.* Edited by Stanley Richards, 329-359. New York: Chilton Book Company, 1968; *Killing Time; A Guide to Life in the Happy Valley.* Edited by Robert Disch, 328-351. Englewood Cliffs, New Jersey: Prentice-Hall, 197; see item 3739.

3734. *Massachusetts Trust* (Cafe La Mama Troupe, Springold Theatre, Brandeis University, 1968)
Playscript: *The Off- Off Broadway Book.* Edited by Albert Poland, 281-303. Indianapolis: Bobbs-Merrill, 1972.

3735. *Megan Terry's Home, or, Future Soap*
Playscript: *Megan Terry's Home, or, Future Soap.* New York: Samuel French, 1967.

3736. *Mollie Bailey's Family Circus, Featuring Scenes from the Life of Mother Jones* (Mark Taper Forum, Los Angeles, 1975)
Playscript: *Mollie Bailey's Family Circus: Featuring Scenes from the Life of Mother Jones.* New York: Broadway Play Publishers, 1983.

3737. *The Narco Linguine Bust* (Omaha Magic Theatre, Omaha, 1974)
3738. *Nightwalk* (with Sam Shepard and Claude Van Itallie, Open Theater, St. Clement's Church, 1973)
3739. *One More Little Drinkie*
Playscript: *Three One-Act Plays: Sanibel and Captiva. The Magic Realists* and *One More Little Drinkie.* New York: Samuel French, 1970.
3740. *100,001 Horror Stories of the Plains* (with Judith Katz and others, Omaha Magic Theatre, Omaha, 1976.
3741. *The People vs Ranchman* (La Mama ETC, 1967)
Playscript: *People vs Ranchman and Ex-Miss Copper Queen on A Set of Pills: Two Plays.* New York: Samuel French, 1969.
3742. *The Pioneer* (Theater Genesis, 1974)
3743. *Pro Game* (Theatre Genesis, 1974)
Playscript: *Pro Game* and *The Pioneer: Two One-Act Plays.* Holly Springs, Mississippi: Ragnarok Press, 1975.
3744. *Running Gag* (with Jo Ann Schmidman, Omaha Magic Theatre, Omaha, 1979)
Playscript: *Running Gag: A New Musical Performance Event.* Omaha, Nebraska: Omaha Magic Theatre Press, 1980.
3745. *St. Hydro Clemency* (St. Clement's Church, 1973)
3746. *Sanibel and Captiva* (WBGH Radio, Boston, 1968)
Playscript: *Spontaneous Combustion: Eight New American Plays.* Edited by Rochelle Owens, 68-103. New York: Winter House LTD, 1972; see item 3739.
3747. *Sea of Forms* (with Jo Ann Schmidman, Omaha Magic Theatre, Omaha, 1986)
Playscript: *Sea of Forms.* Omaha, Nebraska: Omaha Magic Theatre, 1987.
3748. *Sleazing Toward Athens*
Playscript: *Sleazing Toward Athens: A Transformation Play for Any Number of Players.* Omaha: Omaha Magic Theatre, 1986.
3749. *Susan Peretz at the Manhattan Theatre Club* (Manhattan Theatre Club, 1973)
3750. *Tabula Rasa* (New Dramatists, 1972-1973)

3751. *Thoughts* (with Lamar Alford and Joe Tapia, New Theater of Washington, D.C., 1973-1974)
3752. *The Tommy Allen Show* (Actors Studio, 1971)
    Playscript: *Scripts,* 1 (Dec. 1971): 36-61.
3753. *Viet Rock* (La Mama ETC, 1966)
    Playscript: *Four Plays by Megan Terry.* New York: Simon and Schuster, 1967; *Drama Review* (Summer 1966): 196-228.
3754. *Walking through Walls* (with Jo Ann Schmidman, Omaha Magic Theatre, Omaha, 1987-1988)
3755. *We Can Feed Everybody Here* (Westbeth Feminist's Collective Theatre, 1974)
3756. *Willa-Willie-Bill's Dope Garden* (Griffith Park, Los Angeles, 1976)
    Playscript: *Valhalla.* Edited by Rochelle Holt, 18-21. Birmingham, Alabama: Ragnarok Press, 1977.
3757. *Winners* (Omaha Magic Theatre, Omaha, 1981)

Profiles and Interviews

See items 2, 9, 33, 86, 87, 91 and pages 4-5, 7, 13-14.

3758. Bell-Metereau, Rebecca. "Megan Terry." *Critical Survey of Drama: Supplement.* Edited by Frank Magill, 340-46. Pasadena, California: Salem Press, 1986.
    Bell-Metereau provides a biographical sketch of Terry's life and achievements as well as a cursory analysis of her major plays.

3759. Bennathan, Joss. *Contemporary Dramatists.* Third edition. Edited by James Vinson, 518-20. New York: St. Martin's Press, 1982.
    Bennathan provides a general critique of Terry's work. Includes a list of her plays.

3760. *Contemporary Theatre, Film, and Television.* Volume 5. Edited by Monica O'Donnell, 360-362. Detroit: Gale Research Company, 1988.
    The entry provides a concise biography of Terry's theatrical career and includes a list of her plays, teleplays, and radio scripts.

3761. Daniels, Mary. "Playwright Pens Her Way to the Top."
Chicago Tribune (Aug. 7, 1977), sect. 6: 23.
Daniels writes an informative profile of Megan
Terry shortly before the opening of her play *Babes
in the Bighouse* at the Illinois Theater Center in
Chicago. Terry recalls her theatrical career from its
earliest days at the Seattle Repertory Theater—"I
got all sorts of jobs as an usher, sorting nails,
cleaning johns"— to her current position as
playwright-in-residence at the Omaha Magic
Theater in Nebraska. She moved to Omaha from
New York in order to let go of the "commercial
ambitions" and to get "back in the theater again
where I belong."

3762. Hart, Lynda. "Megan Terry." *American Playwrights Since
1945*. Edited by Philip C. Kolin, 447-456. New
York: Greenwood Press, 1989.
Hart provides an assessment of Terry's critical
reputation, an historical survey of her productions,
a brief analysis of her plays, and suggestions for
future areas of study. Includes a primary and
secondary bibliography of sources.

3763. Hynes, Jo. "Interview: Megan Terry." *Christopher Street*, 2
(June 1978): 33-35.
Hynes's interview, based on a telephone
conversation with Terry, touches briefly on Terry's
early days working in theatre in Seattle, her
association with the Open Theatre and her
subsequent move to the Omaha Magic Theater, her
views on the role of feminism in the theatre and her
mission of "melding . . . feminist/lesbian ideals
into mainstream theater."

3764. Laughlin, Karen L. *Contemporary Authors Bibliographical
Series: American Dramatists*. Volume 3. Edited
by Matthew C. Roudane, 361-378. Detroit: Gale
Research Company, 1989.

A bibliographical essay assessing the critical
reputation of Terry's work. Includes a primary and
secondary bibliography.

3765. Leavitt, Dinah L. "Megan Terry." In *Women In American
Theatre*. Edited by Helen Krich Chinory and Linda
Walsh Jenkins, 285-292. New York: Crown
Publishers, 1981.
In this interview Terry describes herself as "a
feminist . . . a humorist and a humanist." She
writes for and about women because she realizes the
paucity of challenging roles for women. Terry
believes dramatic forms developed in the sixties
allow women to explore their inner beings,
"showing all the possibilities, the ways to go."
When asked about the development of a feminist
aesthetic, Terry retorts, "I'm always fighting
against critics because so many are biased whether
they are feminist critics or male critics. They
always want you to conform to whatever party line
they're putting out. They want to use artists. I
refuse to be used." Leavitt also asks Terry about
her methods of playwriting, her favorite women
writers, and her future in the theatre. Throughout
the interview, Terry refers to several of her plays:
Viet Rock, Couplings and Groupings, and
American King's English for Queens.

3766. Rose, Phyllis J. *Dictionary of Literary Biography.* Volume
7. *Twentieth-Century American Dramatists.* Edited
by John MacNicholas, 277-290. Detroit: Gale
Research Company, 1981.
This introductory article includes an extensive
biographical and critical survey of Terry's theatrical
career. A primary and secondary bibliography of
Terry's works is included.

3767. Terry, Megan. "Anybody Is As Their Land and Air Is."
Studies in American Drama, 4 (1989): 83-90.
Terry describes how the theatre provided her with
the means of pursuing her "love affair" with the
community, from which she had felt alienated and

awkward. Many of the plays Terry has developed at the Omaha Magic Theatre have been born out of her abiding interest in people and their community. For instance, her play *100,001* evolved out of the life stories of the company's grandparents and great-grandparents. And *Goona Goona*, a play about violence in the family, grew out of firsthand interviews with local families as well as with scholars studying the phenomenon. According to Terry, the Magic Theatre continues its commitment to the community by producing at least one show each season that deals with issues confronting the public, "we set to work to make a play to help ourselves, our community, and our young people." Terry also talks about her move to Omaha, which she claims has allowed her to write "five times as much as any place I've lived." See Felicia Hardison Londre's accompanying interview with Megan Terry.

3768. _____. "Two Pages a Day." *Drama Review*, 21, iv (Dec. 1977): 59-64.
Terry reflects upon the art of creating plays, which she says "gives [her] almost as much pleasure as lovemaking." See also her interview in *Performing Arts Journal*, 2 (1977): 17-18.

3769. _____. "Who Says Only Words Make Great Drama?" *New York Times* (Nov. 10, 1968): D1, D3.
Terry admonishes the critics for failing to consider the accomplishments and efforts of the "new theater." Critics, according to Terry, are waiting for the "great major PLAYWRIGHT . . . yearning for the second coming of Christ in the shape of a person who has slugged it out with his typewriter and his psyche in his lonely room and has emerged with 120 pages of 'the word'." Terry argues that playwrights do not necessarily have to create a play in isolation. Many talented writers are using laboratory workshops to "develop a more meaningful and dynamic theater."

General Criticism

See items 18, 22, 38, 47, 49, 54, 67, 68, 78, 102 and pages 5, 7, 22-23.

3770. Banich, Judith and Alex Pinkston. "The Omaha Magic Theatre: An Alternative Theatre for Mid-America." *Theatre Survey*, 30 i & ii (May & Nov. 1989): 127-144.
The authors highlight the major achievements of the Omaha Magic Theater in this survey of its history and development.

3771. Barron, Elizabeth Anne. "A Structural Analysis of Representative Plays of Megan Terry." Ph.D. diss., University of Louisville, 1983.
Barron examines several of Terry's plays produced in New York and Omaha, including the "lesser known" plays which in Barron's opinion deserve critical recognition.

3772. Coppage, Judith Ann. "Megan Terry: The Ideal American Citizen." Ph.D. diss., University of California, Los Angeles, 1968.
Coppage hopes to "call attention" to Terry's innovations in experimental theatre. The dissertation, which is based primarily on Coppage's personal interviews with Terry, is divided into three parts. The first provides a biographical and psychological profile of Terry; the second is an assessment of Terry's plays; and the third includes a discussion of the dramatic techniques and strategies Terry uses in creating her plays.

3773. Diamond, Elin. "(Theoretically) Approaching Megan Terry: Issues of Gender and Identity." *Art and Cinema*, 1 (Fall 1987): 5-7.
Prior to a discussion of Terry's plays, Diamond introduces the reader to some of the problems feminists encounter in studying gender and identity. She raises the question, "Does a female identity carry . . . the onus and constraints of gender?" Or,

Diamond continues, can a woman maintain her
female-ness without retaining the "significations"
that are associated with gender. Drawing upon
semiotics, psychoanalysis, and materialism,
Diamond's provocative essay briefly examines
Terry's use of transformation in several of her plays
to demystify society's attitudes toward gender.

3774. Larson, James Wallace. "Public Dreams: A Critical
Investigation of the Plays of Megan Terry." Ph.D.
diss., University of Kansas, 1988.
Larson attempts to categorize Terry's plays into
three groups: realistic dramas, political and public
service plays and family and role model dramas.
Larson directs his examination from a feminist
vantage point; he sees Terry's plays "infuse theater
with the capacity of presenting the ideology of
feminism as the theatrical experience."

3775. Schechner, Richard. "The Playwright as Wrighter." In *Four
Plays by Megan Terry*, 7-18. New York: Simon
& Schuster, 1967. Reprinted in Schechner's *Public
Domain: Essays on the Theater*, 121-131.
Indianapolis: Bobbs-Merrill, 1969.
Schechner describes Terry's unique collaborative
method, relying heavily on the strategy of
"transformation," to develop her plays. Terry's use
of transformation relies on the actors assisting her
in creating the theatre pieces. Terry's plays evolve,
beginning with "a 'notion', move through a
chrysalis stage of improvisation, become 'solidified'
in a text, and are produced." Schechner concludes
by showing how the strategy of transformation
works in the plays included in the collection.

Reviews and Criticism

American King's English for Queens.

3776. Klein, Kathleen Gregory. "Language and Meaning in Megan
Terry's 1970s Musicals." *Modern Drama*, 27, iv
(Dec. 1984): 574-583.

Klein examines four of Terry's "language" musicals: *American King's English for Queens, Babes in the Bighouse, Brazil Fado,* and *Tommy Allen Show.* In these plays Terry dramatizes the powerful implications of language and its impact on individuals and society. In short, Terry is primarily concerned with how language shapes an individual's thoughts, feelings, and perceptions. As Klein explains "[w]hereas words seldom say what they mean, the reverse (that they mean what they say) is often true." Terry's approach to language, Klein observes, is quite different from the absurdists who manipulated "language to devalue it" or used "meaning to abandon it." Rather, Terry refuses to "allow the idea of meaninglessness to mask the uses made of language, action, and meaning."

3777. Norris, Tim. *Sunday World Herald* (Apr. 9, 1978): 16B.
3778. Taylor, Dan. *Sun Newspapers* (Apr. 13, 1978): 12-c.
Reprinted in *American King's English for Queens* (1978), item 3709.

Approaching Simone

3779. Barnes, Clive. *New York Times* (Mar. 9, 1970): 43.
3780. *Contemporary Literary Criticism: Excerpts from Criticism of the Works of Today's Novelists, Poets, Playwrights, and Other Creative Writers.* Volume 19. Edited by Sharon R. Gunton, 438-440. Detroit: Gale Research Company, 1981.
3781. Hughes, Catherine. *America,* 122 (June 6, 1970): 612.
Reprinted in itme 3780.
3782. _____. *Plays and Players,* 17 (May 1970): 16-17.
3783. Kelly, Kevin. *Boston Globe* (Feb. 28, 1970): 8.
3784. Kroll, Jack. *Newsweek,* 75 (Mar. 16, 1970): 64.

3785. *New York Times* (May 26, 1970): 35
The *Times* announces Terry won an Obie for *Approaching Simone.*

3786. Wagner, Phyllis Jane. "Introduction to *Approaching Simone.*" Wagner's introduction to the text of *Approaching Simone* provides general comments on the play and a profile of Terry's professional life in the theatre. See also Wagner's doctoral dissertation entitled "Megan Terry: Political Playwright" (University of Denver, 1972), which focuses on the plays Terry developed in New York during the 1960s.

Attempted Rescue on Avenue B

3787. Koyama, Christine. *Chicago,* 28 (Mar. 1979): 54.

Babes in the Bighouse

See items 23, 3776.

Brazil Fado

See item 3776.

Calm Down, Mother

3788. Chicken Lady. *Off Our Backs,* 4 (Apr. 1974): 10.
3789. Christon, Lawrence. *Los Angeles Times* (Sep. 17, 1973), sect. 4: 26.
3790. Mahoney, John C. *Los Angeles Times* (Feb. 13, 1981), sect. 6: 19.
3791. *Village Voice* (Mar. 9, 1967): 30.
3792. *Village Voice* (Feb. 14, 1968): 14.

Changes

See item 49.

Comings and Goings

See item 3780.

3793.	Bachrach, Judy. "Of Booze, 'Pills' and Megan Terry."
	Washington Post (Mar. 231, 1974), sect. B: 17.
	Bachrach's profile of Terry anticipates a run of
	Comings and Goings at the Washington Area
	Feminist Theatre. Terry provides plenty of
	comments regarding her career as a dramatist.

3794.	O'Connor, John. *Wall Street Journal* (Mar. 25, 1969): 20.
3795.	*The New Yorker* (Feb. 10, 1973): 114.
	Reprinted in item 3780.
3796.	*Sunday Times* (London) (Nov. 26, 1978): 37.
3797.	*Times* (London) (Apr. 21, 1978): 9.
3798.	*Times* (London) (Oct. 25, 1978): 9e.
3799.	*Times* (London) (Nov. 22, 1978): 14.

The Ex-Miss Copper Queen on a Set of Pills

3800.	Weiner, Bernard. *San Francisco Chronicle* (Mar. 22, 1979):
	51.

Family Talk

3801.	Babnich, Judith. *Theatre Journal*, 39, ii (May 1987): 240-
	241.

The Gloaming, Oh My Darling

3802.	Weiner, Bernard. *San Francisco Chronicle* (June 8, 1977):
	47.
3803.	Sullivan, Dan. *Los Angeles Times* (Jan. 22, 1972), sect. 2:
	9.

Headlights

3804.	Solomon, Alisa. "Turning on *Headlights.*" *American
	Theatre*, 5 (Feb. 1989): 9, 10.
	Solomon describes Terry's play about illiteracy,
	Headlights, opening at the Omaha Magic Theatre in
	February of 1989. Terry explains her play is the
	result of tapes of students and volunteer teachers
	who participated in actual literacy programs, "[t]he
	tapes are heartbreaking . . . but heartbreaking in a

positive way—people talk about how reading changed their lives." The play's "raucous energy, " says Soloman, comes from the play's music and Terry's use of performance art, "[t]o avoid that risk of stasis which comes with the subject matter."

Home

3805. Gent, George. *New York Times* (Jan. 20, 1968): 59.
3806. Gould, Jack. *New York Times* (July 12, 1969): 52.

Hothouse

See item 16.

3807. Barnes, Clive. *New York Times* (Oct. 24, 1974): 49.
3808. Christon, Lawrence. *Los Angeles Times* (Nov. 19, 1981), sect. 6: 1, 4.
3809. Levy, Frances. *Village Voice.* (Aug. 22, 1974): 66. Reprinted in item 3780.
3810. Mahoney, John. C. *Los Angeles Times* (Nov. 23, 1979), sect. 4: 33.
3811. *Saturday/Review World.* (Apr. 6, 1974): 48-49.
3812. Sherbert, Linda. *Atlanta Journal-Constitution* (Oct. 19, 1984, sect. P: 7.
3813. Swisher, Viola H. *After Dark*, 12 (Feb. 1980): 20.
3814. Weiner, Bernard. *San Francisco Chronicle* (Mar. 20, 1979): 43.

Jack-Jack

3815. Altman, Peter. *Minneapolis Star* (May 8, 1968): 20.
3816. Sullivan, Dan. *New York Times* (June 23, 1968): 74.

Keep Tightly Closed in a Cool Dry Place

3817. Bermel, Albert. *New Leader*, 50 (Sep. 11, 1967): 23-24. Reprinted in item 3780.
3818. *Los Angeles Times* (June 18, 1976), sect. 4: 22.
3819. Mahoney, John. C. *Los Angeles Times* (Feb. 13, 1981), sect. 6: 19.

3820. Sullivan, Dan. *Los Angeles Times* (Apr. 27, 1971), sect. 4: 12.

Massachusetts Trust

3821. Hewes, Henry. *Saturday Review*, 51 (Sep. 21, 1968): 28.
3822. Hirsch, Samuel. *Boston Herald-Traveler* (Aug. 23, 1986): 25.
3823. Kelly, Kevin. *Boston Globe* (Aug. 22, 1968): 49.
3824. Kerr, Walter. *New York Times* (Sep. 1, 1968), sect. 2: 1, 3.
Reprinted in Kerr's *God On the Gymnasium Floor and Other Theatrical Adventures*, 45-72. New York: Simon & Schuster, 1971; see item 3780.

Mollie Bailey's Traveling Family Circus

See item 80.

3825. Breslauer, Jan and Helene Keyssar. "Making Magic Public: Megan Terry's Traveling Family Circus." In *Making a Spectacle: Feminist Essays On Contemporary Women's Theatre*. Edited by Lynda Hart, 169-180.
Ann Arbor: University of Michigan Press, 1989. Breslauer and Keyssar's essay focuses on Terry's play *Mollie Bailey's Traveling Family Circus: Featuring Scenes from the Life of Mother Jones*, which she wrote in collaboration with JoAnne Metcalf. In this play as in earlier plays, Terry "pushes boundaries" with the dramatic strategy of transformation and "possibility motifs." The authors observe that Terry's vision holds that not only is it possible for individuals to bring about their own "transfiguratons" but "she also takes the risk of reconfiguring the terrain of women's relations to each other."

Nightwalk

3826. Gussow, Mel. *New York Times* (Sep. 11, 1973): 55.

People vs Ranchman

3827. Barnes, Clive. *New York Times* (Oct. 28, 1968): 56.
3828. Bermel, Albert. *New Leader*, 50 (Sep. 11, 1967): 23-24.
         Reprinted in item 3780.
3829. Frankel, Haskel. *National Observer* (Nov. 11, 1968): 22.
3830. Gussow, Mel. *Newsweek*, 72 (Nov. 11, 1968): 121.
3831. Kerr, Walter. *New York Times* (Nov. 10, 1968), sect. 2:
         D3,D5.

3832. *New York Times* (Nov. 8, 1968): 37.
         The *Times* announces *People vs Ranchman* will
         close on Nov. 17, 1968 at the Fortune Theater after
         22 performances.

3833. Oliver, Edith. *The New Yorker*, 44 (Nov. 9, 1968): 116,
         118.
         Reprinted in item 3780.
3834. Smith, Michael. *Village Voice* (May 18, 1967): 23.
3835. *Time*, 92 (Nov. 8, 1968): 94.

Pro Game/The Pioneer

3836. Feingold, Michael. *Village Voice* (Nov. 7, 1974): 79-81.

Sea of Forms

3837. Bunke, Joan. *Des Moines Sunday Register* (Sep. 14, 1986).
         Reprinted in item 3747.
3838. Millburg, Steve. *Omaha World-Herald* (Sep. 7, 1986), Arts
         sect.: 1.
         Reprinted in item 3747.
3839. Prescher, Dan. *Metropolitan* (Sep. 17, 1986).
         Reprinted in item 3747.

Sleazing Toward Athens

3840. Karloff, Kim. *Daily Nebraskan* (Oct. 10, 1986), Arts sect.:
         1.
3841. Kubert, Larry. *Lincoln Journal* (June 11, 1986).
         Reprinted in item 3748.
3842. Millburg, Steve. *Omaha World-Herald* (June 9, 1986).

Reprinted in item 3748.
3843. Nelson, Karen. *Gateway* (June 13, 1986): 6.
Reprinted in item 3748.

Tommy Allen Show

See item 3776.

Viet Rock

See item 73 and Terry's introduction in *Drama Review*
(item 3753).

3844. Asahina, Robert. "The Basic Training of American
Playwrights: Theater and the Vietnam War."
Theater, 9, ii (1978): 30-37.
In this discourse on the interrelationship of theatre,
television journalism, and the Vietnam War,
Asahina analyzes several experimental and
traditional plays, including Terry's *Viet Rock* and
Adrienne Kennedy's *An Evening With Dead Essex*.
Of *Viet Rock*, for example, Asahina comments that
"what appeared to be radical formal innovations in
Viet Rock. . . . were actually pale imitations of the
technological modes of the rapidly emerging mass
media, especially national televised news."

3845. Berkowitz, Gerald M. *New Broadways: Theatre Across
America, 1950-1980*. Totowa, New Jersey:
Littlefield, 1982.
Berkowitz surveys the forces that influenced the
development of the American professional theatre,
including Broadway, Off and Off Off Broadway, and
major regional theatres, from 1950 through 1980.
Although Berkowitz' survey does not examine
women playwrights or feminist theatre in depth, he
does include a discussion of Megan Terry's
experimentation with collaborative theatre in which
her use of "transformation" created works such as
*Viet Rock, Keep Tightly, and Calm Down,
Mother*. In addition, Berkowitz briefly mentions
Rochelle Owens and her involvement with the

Theatre of Living Arts and Tom O'Horgan, who
directed her play *Futz!*.

3846. Clurman, Harold. *Nation*, 203 (Nov. 28, 1966): 586-587.
      Reprinted in item 3780.
3847. Conlin, Kathleen. *Theatre Southwest*, 6 (Oct. 1980): 13-17.
3848. Gilman, Richard. *Newsweek*, 68 (Nov. 21, 1966): 114.
3849. Gottfried, Martin. *Theater Divided; The Postwar American
      Stage*, 302. Boston: Little, Brown, 1967.
3850. Hughes, Catherine. *America*, 116 (May 20, 1967): 759-
      760.
      Reprinted in item 3780.
3851. _____. *Nation*, 208 (Jan. 20, 1969): 91.
3852. Kazin, Alfred. *Vogue*, 149 (Jan.1967): 52.

3853. Kerr, Walter. *New York Times* (Nov. 11, 1966): 38.
      See also Kerr's review, *New York Times* (Nov.
      27, 1966), sect. 2: 1, 3. For readers' reactions to
      Kerr's reviews see: *New York Times* (Dec. 11,
      1966), sect. 2: 11, 24.

3854. Lester, Eleanor. "At Yale: Joy, Baby, Joy." *New York
      Times* (Oct. 9, 1966), sect. 2: 1, 3.
      Lester's preview article on Terry's *Viet Rock*,
      describes the innovative collaborative style Terry
      employed in developing the play. According to
      Terry, "I wanted to explore certain negative feelings
      I had about the Vietnam war. I wanted to understand
      about aggressiveness and hatred."

3855. Richardson, Jack. *Commentary*, 43 (Mar. 1967): 86-89.
      Reprinted in item 3780.
3856. Simon, John. *Hudson Review*, 20 (Spring 1967): 108-109.
3857. Sullivan, Dan. *Los Angeles Times* (Apr. 27, 1971): 12.
3858. *Time*, 88 (Oct. 21, 1966): 61.

Thuna, Leonora

Selected Plays

3859. *Fugue* (Long Wharf Theatre, New Haven, 1986)

3860. *Let Me Hear You Smile* (with Harry Cauley, Biltmore
           Theatre, 1973)
3861. *The Natural Look* (Longacre Theatre, 1967)
3862. *Show Me Where The Good Times Are* (book by Lee
           Thuna, lyrics by Rhoda Roberts (Edison Theare,
           1970)
           Playscript: *Show Me Where The Good Times Are:
           A Musical.* New York: Samuel French, 1970.

Profiles

3863. *Contemporary Authors: A Bio-Bibliographical Guide.*
           Volume 16. Revised Series. Edited by Linda
           Metzger, 394. Detroit: Gale Research Company,
           1986.
           A biographical sketch is provided, including a list
           of Thuna's theatrical productions.

Reviews

Fugue

3864. Gussow, Mel. *New York Times* (May 1, 1986): C28.

Let Me Hear You Smile

3865. Calta, Louis. *New York Times* (Nov. 16, 1972): 55.
           Calta's item reports that Thuna's play *Let Me Hear
           You Smile* will open at the Biltmore Theater on
           January 17, 1973.

3866. Gottfried, Martin. *Women's Wear Daily* (Jan. 18, 1973)
           Reprinted in item 3869.

3867. Kerr, Walter. *New York Times* (Feb. 11, 1973), sect. 2: 1,
           20.

3868. Leonard, William Torbert. *Once Was Enough*, 105, 135-
           136. Metuchen, New Jersey: Scarecrow, 1986.
           Leonard includes *Let Me Hear You Smile* and *The
           Natural Look* in his discussion of so-called
           Broadway flops. He describes the play's staging

history and plot and includes comments from
various drama critics.

3869. *New York Theatre Critics' Reviews,* 34 (Jan. 15, 1973):
383-385.
3870. Watt, Douglas. *New York Daily News* (Jan. 17, 1973): 42.
Reprinted in item 3869.
3871. Watts, Richard. *New York Post* (Jan. 17, 1973).
Reprinted in item 3869.

The Natural Look

See item 3868.

3872. Cook, Robin. *Wall Street Journal* (Mar. 13, 1967): 12.
3873. Davis, J. *New York Daily News* (Mar. 13, 1967).
3874. Gottfried, Martin. *Women's Wear Daily* (Mar. 13, 1967).
3875. Kerr, Walter. *New York Times* (Mar. 13, 1967): 45
3876. McCarten, John. *The New Yorker,* 43 (Mar. 18, 1967): 121.

3877. *New York Times* (Mar. 14, 1967): 53.
The *Times* announces *The Natural Look* closed at
the Longacre, after 16 previews and one premiere
performance.

3878. Watts, Richard. *New York Post* (Mar. 13, 1967).

Show Me Where the Good Times Are

3879. Barnes, Clive. *New York Times* (Mar. 6, 1970): 32.

3880. *New York Times* (Mar. 31, 1970): 35.
The *Times* announces that Thuna's play *Show Me
Where the Good Times Are* closed at the Edison
Theater after 29 performances.

Tolan, Kathleen

Selected Plays

3881. *Digging In China* (Williamstown Theatre Festival,
Massachusetts, 1983)

3882. *Kate's Diary* (New York Shakespeare Festival, Public
        Theatre, 1989)
        Playscript: *Kate's Diary*. New York: Theatre
        Communications Group, 1990.
3883. *A Weekend Near Madison* (Astor Place Theater, 1983)
        Playscript: *A Weekend Near Madison*. New York:
        Samuel French, 1984; *Out Front: Contemporary
        Gay and Lesbian Plays*. Edited by Don Shewey,
        251-305. New York: Grove Press, 1988.

Profiles

See items 48, 93.

Reviews

Digging In China

3884. Baker, Rob. "Country Calm and Theatrical Flurry." *Theatre
        Communications*, 5 (Nov. 1983): 9-10.
        Baker briefly discusses the production of *Digging
        In China* at the Williamstown Theatre Festival.

Kate's Diary

3885. *American Theatre,* 6 (Mar. 1990): 56.
        The magazine announces *Kate's Diary,* among
        others, has been selected for Theatre
        Communications Group's *Plays in Process* series.

3886. Gussow, Mel. *New York Times* (Nov. 29, 1989): C17.

A Weekend Near Madison

3887. Beaufort, John. *Christian Science Monitor* (Sep. 15, 1983):
        16.
3888. Corliss, Richard. *Time* 121 (Apr. 11, 1983): 99.
3889. DeVries, Hilary. *Christian Science Monitor* (Apr. 11,
        1983): 9.
3890. Drake, Sylvie. *Los Angeles Times* (Sep. 25, 1984), sect. 6:
        5.
3891. Feingold, Michael. *Village Voice* (Sep. 20, 1983): 97.

3892. Field, Bruce. *Drama-Logue* (Sep. 14-20, 1989): 9.
3893. Gussow, Mel. *New York Times* (Mar. 31, 1983): C15.
3894. Kissel, Howard. *Women's Wear Daily* (Sep. 14, 1983).
       Reprinted in item 3897.
3895. Kroll, Jack. *Newsweek*, 101 (Apr. 4, 1983): 81.
3896. McCulloh, T.H. *Los Angeles Times* (Sep. 15, 1989), sect.
       6: 18.
3897. *New York Theatre Critics' Reviews*, 44 (Sep. 5, 1983): 160-
       163.
3898. Oliver, Edith. *The New Yorker*, 59 (Sep. 26, 1983): 127.
3899. Rich, Frank. *New York Times* (Sep. 14, 1983): C22.
3900. Simon, John. *New York*, 16 (Sep. 26, 1983): 102.
3901. Smith, Helen C. *Variety* (Apr. 6, 1983): 81, 83.
3902. Stasio, Marilyn. *New York Post* (Sep. 15, 1983).
       Reprinted in item 3897.
3903. *Variety* (Sep. 21, 1983): 120.
3904. Wardle, Irving. *Times* (London) (Apr. 6, 1983): 10f.
3905. Watt, Douglas. *New York Daily News* (Sep. 14, 1983).
       Reprinted in item 3897.
3906. Wilson, Edwin. *Wall Street Journal* (Apr. 8, 1983): 27.

Trahey, Jane

Selected Plays

3907. *Life with Mother Superior* (with Anna Helen Reuter)
       Playscript: *Life With Mother Superior*. New York:
       Farrar, Straus & Cudahy, 1962.
3908. *Ring Round the Bathtub* (Martin Beck Theater, 1972)
       Playscript: *Ring Round the Bathtub: A Play in
       Three Acts*. New York: Samuel French, 1968.

Profiles

3909. *Contemporary Authors: A Bio-Bibliographical Guide*.
       Volume 17. Edited by Linda Metzger, 458-459.
       Detroit: Gale Research Company, 1986.
       The entry includes a concise biography and a list of
       Trahey's works.

Reviews

Ring Round the Bathtub

3910. Gussow, Mel. *New York Times* (May 1, 1972): 41.

3911. Leonard, William Torbert. *Once Was Enough*. Metuchen,
        New Jersey: Scarecrow, 1986.
        Leonard includes *Ring Round the Bathtub* in his
        discussion of Broadway flops. He describes the
        play's staging history and plot and also provides
        excerpts of reviews from various drama critics.

3912. *The New Yorker*, 48 (May 6, 1972): 56.
3913. *New York Theatre Critics' Reviews*, 33 (May 22, 1972):
        293-294.
3914. Watt, Douglas. *New York Daily News* (May 1, 1972).
        Reprinted in item 3913.
3915. Watts, Richard. *New York Post* (May 1, 1972): 24.
        Reprinted in item 3913.

Trambley, Estela Portillo

See **Portillo-Trambley, Estela**

Walker, Celeste Colson

   Selected Plays

3916. *Camp Logan* (Kuumba House Repertory Theater, Houston,
        1985)
3917. *Once in a Wifetime* (Takoma Theatre, Washington D.C.,
        1984)
3918. *Over Forty* (lyrics and music by Weldon Irvine, Billie
        Holliday Theatre, 1989)
3919. *Reunion in Bartersville* (Billie Holliday Theatre, 1987)
3920. *The Wrecking Ball* (Black Spectrum Theatre, Jamaica, New
        York, 1987)

   Profiles

3921. Peterson, Bernard L. *Contemporary Black American
        Playwrights and Their Plays: A Biographical*

Directory and Dramatic Index, 466-467. New York:
Greenwood Press, 1988.
Peterson provides a biography as well as a staging
history of Walker's plays.

Reviews

Camp Logan

3922. Smith, Sid. *Chicago Tribune* (Feb. 1, 1990), Tempo sect.:
10.

Once in a Wifetime

3923. Brown, Joe. *Washington Post* (Feb. 9, 1984): D13.
3924. Grove, Lloyd. *Washington Post* (Jan. 27, 1984), Weekend
sect.: 10.

Over Forty

3925. Shepard, Richard. *New York Times* (May 16, 1989): C17.
3926. Sommers, Pamela. *Washington Post* (Nov. 27, 1990): C2.

Reunion in Bartersville

3927. Albright, William. *Houston Post* (June 6, 1989): D3.
3928. Bruckner, D.J.R. *New York Times* (Dec. 1, 1987): C20.
3929. Shirley, Don. *Los Angeles Times* (Sep. 4, 1985), sect. 6:
2.

The Wrecking Ball

3930. N.Y. *Amsterdam News* (Mar. 7, 1987): 31.

Walsh, Shela

Selected Plays

3931. *Molly and James*
Playscript: *The Best Short Plays 1988.* Edited by
Ramon Delgado, 175-191. New York: Applause,
1988.

3932. *Tea with Mommy and Jack* (Hudson Guild Theater, 1988)
3933. *Two Sisters At the Beach* (Quaigh Theater, 1988)
3934. *Within the Year* (ATA/Chernuchin Theater, 1983)

Profiles

See profile in item 3931.

Reviews

Tea With Mommy and Jack

3935. *Drama-Logue* (Nov. 24-30, 1988): 25.
3936. Goodman, Walter. *New York Times* (Nov. 2, 1988), sect. 3: C19.
3937. Seibert, Gary. *America*, 159 (Nov. 19, 1988): 416.

Wasserstein, Wendy

Selected Plays

3938. *Any Woman Can't* (Playwrights Horizons, 1973)
3939. *A Girl from Fargo, North Dakota* (with Terrence McNally)
Playscript: "A Girl From Fargo: A Play." *New York Times* (Mar. 18, 1987), sect. 2: 5, 18.
3940. *The Heidi Chronicles* (Playwrights Horizons, 1987)
Playscript: *The Heidi Chronicles and Other Plays.* San Diego: Harcourt Brace Jovanovich, 1990.
3941. *Isn't It Romantic* (Phoenix Theater, 1981)
Playscript: *Isn't It Romantic* New York: Dramatists Play Service, 1985; see item 3940.
3942. *The Man in the Case* (billed with *Orchards*, Lucille Lortel Theater, 1986)
Playscript: *Orchards, Orchards, Orchards: Plays.* New York: Broadway Play Publishing, 1987.
3943. *Maggie/Magalita* (Lamb's Theater Company, 1986)
3944. *Miami* (with Jack Feldman and Bruce Sussman, Playwrights Horizons, 1986)
3945. *Montpelier Pa-Zazz* (Long Wharf Theater, New Haven, 1974)

3946. *Smart Women, Brilliant Choices* (part of the revue *Urban Blight*, Manhattan Theater Club, 1988)
3947. *Uncommon Women and Others* (Phoenix, 1977)
Playscript: *Uncommon Women and Others*. New York: Dramatists Play Service, 1978; see item 3940.
3948. *Tender Offer* (Ensemble Studio Theatre, 1983)
3949. *When Dinah Shore Ruled the Earth* (with Christopher Durang, Yale Cabaret, 1973-1974)

Profiles and Interviews

See items 7, 9, 36, 75, 87, 90, 100, 1554, 3039 and page 23.

3950. Bennetts, Leslie. "An Uncommon Dramatist Prepares Her New Work." *New York Times* (May 24, 1981): D1, D5.
Bennetts profiles Wasserstein prior to the opening of *Isn't It Romantic* at the Marymount Manhattan Theater. Wasserstein dramatizes primarily the experiences of women—"there's so much potential there." Feminism, says Wasserstein, is less a formalized ideology than a set of "possibilities it offers to human beings of either gender."

3951. Cohen, Esther. "Uncommon Woman: An Interview With Wendy Wasserstein." *Women's Studies,* 15, 1-3 (1988): 257-270.
This interview focuses on Wasserstein's manipulation of comedy, which seeks to provide entertainment as well as offering a unique interpretation of life. Many of her women characters, comments Wasserstein, use humor as a diversionary tactic to avoid dealing with their feelings, indicating a fundamental difference in how men and women approach humor. "[M]en sometimes top each other. Women don't do that. Women know how to lay back and have a good time . . . and the gossip is great." And there are differences in how male and female writers are perceived—"When you write plays and you're a

woman writer, you get these questions like, are you
a feminist? She's a dear writer. She's a tough
writer. You don't get this stuff when you're a
man."

3952. *Contemporary Authors: A Bio-Bibliographical Guide to
Current Writers.* Edited by Susan M. Trosky, 452.
Detroit: Gale Research Inc., 1990.
This entry provides general comments concerning
Wasserstein's plays as well as an interview with the
playwright. The entry also includes a biographical
sketch and a list of works.

3953. *Contemporary Theatre, Film, and Televison.* Volume 1.
Edited by Monica O'Donnell, 510. Detroit: Gale
Research Company, 1984.
The entry provides a concise biographical entry as
well as a list of Wasserstein's works.

3954. *Current Biography Yearbook.* Edited by Charles Moritz,
610-613. New York: H.W. Wilson, 1989.
This is a lengthy survey of Wasserstein's life and
theatrical career.

3955. Dodds, Richard. "Comedy Can Be a Serious Business."
Times-Picayune (May 22, 1986), sect. E: 14.
Dodds highlights the career of Wasserstein on the
eve of the opening of *Isn't It Romantic?* at Tulane
University's Center Stage.

3956. Drake, Sylvie. "Will the Real Wendy Please Stand Up?" *Los
Angeles Times* (Oct. 28, 1984), Calendar sect.:
40.
Drake talks with Wasserstein about her life and
theatrical career on the day of the opening of *Isn't It
Romantic* at the L.A. Stage Company West. The
playwright remarks she writes plays to "clarify
things."

3957. Gillespie, Patti. *American Playwrights Since 1945: A
Guide to Scholarship, Criticism, and Performance.*

Edited by Philip C. Kolin, 469-477. New York:
Greenwood Press, 1989.
Gillespie provides an assessment of Wasserstein's
critical reputation, a historical survey of her stage
productions, a brief analysis of her plays, and
suggestions for future areas of study. Includes a
primary and secondary bibliography of sources.

3958.   Gold, Sylviane. "Wendy, The Wayward Wasserstein." *Wall
Street Journal* (Feb. 7, 1984): 30.
Gold briefly profiles Wasserstein, whose play *Isn't
It Romantic* was onstage at Playwrights Horizons.
Wasserstein talks about her family (her father
apparently invented velveteen) as well as her career
in the theatre. She claims writing plays got her
out of gym class and continues to help her "figure
out what [she's] thinking."

3959.   Kaufman, Joanne. "Theater: Wendy and *Heidi.*" *Wall Street
Journal* (Mar.1, 1989): A12.
Kaufman's preview article, written when
Wasserstein's *The Heidi Chronicles* was moving
from Off Broadway to Broadway's Plymouth
Theater, highlights the theatrical career of
Wasserstein. Apparently, the playwright did not
initially consider playwriting as a viable vocation,
"[I] thought [I] would marry a lawyer and move to
Scarsdale and join the Scarsdale players."

3960.   Lombardi, John. "Playwrights on the Horizon." *New York
Times Magazine* (July 17, 1983): 22-23, 30-32.
Wasserstein is included in this article highlighting
the achievements of the Playwrights Horizons
theatre group.

3961.   Rothstein, Mervyn. "Broadway Producers Form Project To
Commission Plays by Americans." *New York
Times* (June 8, 1988): C17.
In an effort to bring new American plays to
Broadway, a group of New York producers have
commissioned six playwrights, including

Wasserstein and Marsha Norman, to write dramatic
pieces for the American Playwrights Project.

3962. Schroeder, Patricia R. *Contemporary Authors
        Bibliographical Series: American Dramatists.*
        Volume 3. Edited by Matthew C. Roudane, 379-
        384. Detroit: Gale Research Inc., 1989.
        A bibliographical essay assessing the critical
        reputation of Wasserstein's work. Includes a
        primary and secondary bibliography.

3963. Shapiro, Walter. "Chronicler of Frayed Feminism: Wendy
        Wasserstein." *Time,* 133 (Mar. 27, 1989): 90-92.
        Shapiro profiles Wasserstein along with discussing
        her hit Broadway play *The Heidi Chronicles.* The
        playwright, observes Shapiro, uses her self-
        deprecating humor as a "defense against both the
        judgment of others and her enveloping Jewish
        family." Yet Wasserstein also uses humor to
        penetrate society, specifically the unhappiness of
        women—"I knew there was this feeling around . . .
        and I thought it should be expressed theatrically."

3964. Swain, Elizabeth. *Contemporary Dramatists.* Fourth
        Edition. Edited by D.L. Kirkpatrick, 1988. 547-
        549. Chicago: St. James Press, 1988.
        Swain briefly assesses the life and work of
        Wasserstein. The entry includes a list of her plays.

3965. "Your 30s: The More Decade." *Harper's Bazaar,* 117 (June
        1984): 146-147, 180.
        Wasserstein is included in this lightweight
        interview of four successful women. The others are
        Diane Sawyer, journalist, Janet Maslin, film critic,
        and Annie Leibovitz, photographer. The questions
        to the interviewees concentrate on their ambitions;
        how they reckon with the emotional stress that is a
        natural consequence of their ambitions; their
        attitudes towards marriage and turning forty; and
        how they handle their finances.

Reviews and Criticism

See items 54, 79.

The Heidi Chronicles

3966. Austin, Gayle. *Theater Journal*, 42, i (Mar. 1990): 107-108.
3967. Barnes, Clive. *New York Post* (Dec. 12, 1988).
     Reprinted in item 3992.
3968. Beaufort, John. *Christian Science Monitor* (Dec. 16, 1988): 24.
     Reprinted in item 3992.
3969. Brustein, Robert. *New Republic*, 200 (Apr. 17, 1989): 32.
3970. Carter, Graydon. *Vogue*, 179 (Mar. 1989): 266B.
3971. *Contemporary Literary Criticism; Excerpts from Criticism of the Work of Today's Novelists, Poets, Playwrights and Other Creative Writers*. Volume 32. Edited by Jean C. Stine, 439-443. Detroit: Gale Research Company, 1985.
3972. Cooke, Richard P. *Wall Street Journal* (June 23, 1989): C16.
3973. Dace, Trish. *Plays International*, 4 (May 1989): 36.

3974. "Drama Desk Awards." *New York Times* (May 23, 1989): C14.
     The item announces *The Heidi Chronicles* received a Drama Desk award for best new play.

3975. *Drama-Logue* (Feb. 23-Mar. 1, 1989): 29.

3976. Egan, Timothy. "He'll Take Seattle (The Rain's Good For Business); Dan Sullivan Has Made the Northwest a Haven for Playwrights Who Are Nurturing New Works." *New York Times* (Jan. 15, 1989): H5, H12.
     Egan highlights the work of Dan Sullivan, artistic director of the Seattle Repertory Theater. According to Egan, Wasserstein's *The Heidi Chronicles* was developed at the Repertory; the play subsequently moved to New York where Sullivan directed the New York production at Playwrights Horizons.

3977. Gold, Sylviane. *Wall Street Journal* (Dec. 16, 1988): 13.

3978. Gussow, Mel. "*Heidi Chronicles* Wins Critics Circle
Prize." *New York Times* (May 16, 1989): C22.
Gussow reports the New York Drama Critics Circle
named Wasserstein's comedy as the best new play
of the 1988-1989 season. See also *Variety* (May
17, 1989): 3.

3979. _____. *New York Times* (Dec. 12, 1988): C13.
Reprinted in item 3992.

3980. "*The Heidi Chronicles* Moving To Broadway." *New York
Times* (Jan. 12, 1989): C24.
This item reports *The Heidi Chronicles* will be
transferring to the Plymouth Theater on Broadway
on March 9, 1989.

3981. "*Heidi Chronicles* Wins Critics' Award." *New York Times*
(May 3, 1989), sect. 3: C25.
The *Times* notes *The Heidi Chronicles* received
the Outer Critics Circle award for the best
Broadway play.

3982. "*Heidi Chronicles* Wins Dramatists Guild Award." *New
York Times* (Apr. 10, 1989): C16.
The Dramatists Guild has announced Wasserstein
has won the 1988 Hull-Warriner Award for *The
Heidi Chronicles.*

3983. Henry, William A. *Time*, 133 (Mar. 20, 1989): 90.
3984. Hodgson, Moira. *Nation*, 248 (May 1, 1989): 604, 606.
3985. Kaufman, Joanne. *Wall Street Journal* (Mar. 1, 1989): A12.
3986. Kissel, Howard. *New York Daily News* (Dec. 12, 1988).
Reprinted in item 3992.
3987. _____. *New York Daily News* (Mar. 10, 1989).
Reprinted in item 3992.
3988. Kramer, Mimi. *The New Yorker*, 64 (Dec. 26, 1988): 81.

3989. Lopate, Phillip. "Christine Lahti Tries to Fashion a Spunky
Heidi." *New York Times* (Sep. 3, 1989): H5, H8-
9.
Lopate's article highlights the career of Lahti, who
stars in the title role of the Broadway production of
the *The Heidi Chronicles.*

3990. Low, Lisa. "Feminism and *The Heidi Chronicles:* Betty
Friedan and Gloria Steinem Reflect." *Christian
Science Monitor* (Oct. 10, 1989): 11.
Friedan and Steinem disagree about the feminist
nature of Wasserstein's Pulitzer Prize winning play
The Heidi Chronicles. Steinem believes the so-
called controversy over the play has been "cooked
up by the media to divide women from one
another." The fact of a play on Broadway dealing
with a woman's life choices, says Steinem, is "a
step forward." Friedan, on the other hand, finds the
play "disturb[ing]." She contends Wasserstein, by
showing Heidi in turmoil about career and family,
"inadvertently fed a media hype, a new feminine
mystique about the either/or choices in a woman's
life."

3991. McGuigan, Cathleen. *Newsweek,* 113 (Mar. 20, 1989): 76-
77.
Reprinted in item 3992.

3992. *New York Theatre Critics' Reviews,* 50 (Feb. 27, 1989):
330-336.

3993. *New York Times* (Feb. 28, 1989): 24.
The *Times* announces Wasserstein has received the
Susan Smith Blackburn Prize for her play *The
Heidi Chronicles.*

3994. Richards, David. *Washington Post* (Mar. 14, 1989), sect.
E: 1.

3995. Robertson, Nan. *New York Times* (July 22, 1988): C2.
Robertson's brief item describes *The Heidi
Chronicles,* opening at the Playwrights Horizons'
Mainstage Theater on November 16, 1988.

3996. Rosenfeld, Megan. *Washington Post* (May 6, 1985), sect. B: 7
Rosenfeld briefly interviews Wasserstein during a run of *Isn't It Romantic* at the Arena Theater.

3997. Rose, Lloyd. *Connoisseur,* 219 (Sep. 1989): 62.

3998. Rothstein, Mervyn. "After the Revolution, What?" *New York Times* (Feb. 1, 1988), sect. 2: 1, 28.
Rothstein profiles Wasserstein and Joan Allen, who appears as Dr. Heidi Holland, in *The Heidi Chronicles* playing at Playwrights Horizons. The play exemplifies, comments Rothstein, the generation of women encountering difficulties of coming of age during the feminist movement. For Wasserstein, that generation "will consist of disappointed women. The ones who open doors usually are."

3999. _____. "'Heidi and 'Jerome Robbins's Broadway' Win the Top Tonys." *New York Times* (June 5, 1989), sect. 3: C13.
Rothstein reports *The Heidi Chronicles* won a Tony award for best new play.

4000. Sander, Michael. *Drama-Logue* (Oct. 26-Nov. 1, 1989): 24.
4001. Simon, John. *New York,* 22 (Jan. 2, 1989): 49.
4002. _____. *New York,* 22 (Mar. 27, 1989): 66-68.
4003. Solomon, Alisa. *Village Voice* (Dec. 20, 1988): 121-122.
4004. Stearns, David Patrick. *USA Today* (Mar. 10, 1989).
Reprinted in item 3992.
4005. Sullivan, Dan. *Los Angeles Times* (Dec. 17, 1988), sect. 5: 3.
4006. _____. *Los Angeles Times* (Jan. 28, 1989), sect. 5: 1, 7.
4007. *Variety* (Oct. 4-10, 1989): 126.

4008. "Wasserstein Wins Award." *New York Times* (Feb. 28, 1989): 24.
The *Times* announces Wasserstein received the Susan Smith Blackburn Prize for her play *The Heidi Chronicles.*

4009. Watt, Douglas. *New York Daily News* (Dec. 23, 1988).
Reprinted in item 3992.
4010. Weales, Gerald. *Commonweal,* 116 (May 5, 1989): 279-80.
4011. Winer, Laurie. *New York Times* (Oct. 9, 1989): C13.
4012. _____. *New York Newsday* (Dec. 12, 1988).
Reprinted in item 3992.

Isn't It Romantic

See items 3950, 3955, 3956, 3958.

4013. Arkatov, Janice. "Director Gutierrez Keeps the Spirit in
Romantic." *Los Angeles Times* (Dec. 25, 1984),
sect. 6: 2.
Arkatov highlights the professional career of Gerald
Gutierrez, director of the New York and West Coast
productions of *Isn't It Romantic*. About
Wasserstein, Gutierrez comments what intrigued
him about her "is her intelligence. She is so damn
smart and funny."

4014. Barnes, Clive. *New York Post* (Dec. 16, 1983).
Reprinted in item 4032.
4015. Beaufort, John. *Christian Science Monitor* (Apr. 25, 1983):
15.
4016. Bolotin, Susan. *Vogue,* 174 (Mar. 1984): 128.
4017. Brown, Joe. *Washington Post* (May 3, 1985), Weekend
sect.: 9.
4018. Cassidy, Claudia. *Chicago,* 34 (Dec. 1985): 28.
4019. Christiansen, Richard. *Chicago Tribune* (Oct. 11, 1985),
sect. 2: 6.
4020. Corliss, Richard. *Time,* 122 (Dec. 26, 1983): 80.
Reprinted in item 4032.
4021. Drake, Sylvie. *Los Angeles Times* (Jan. 31, 1984), sect. 6:
1.
4022. Gussow, Mel. *New York Times* (June 15, 1981): C11.
4023. _____. *New York Times* (Dec. 16, 1983): C3.
Reprinted in items 4971, 4032.
4024. Hoffman, Jan. *Village Voice* (June 17-23, 1981): 77-79.
4025. Hummler, Richard. *Variety* (June 17, 1981): 84.
4026. Kerr, Walter. *New York Times* (June 28, 1981): D3, D10.

4027. _____. *New York Times* (Feb. 26, 1984): H7.
4028. Kissel, Howard. *Women's Wear Daily* (Dec. 16, 1983). Reprinted in item 4032.

4029. Kuchwara, Michael. "Playwright Finds Elusive Success in 'Personal' Comedy." *Houston Post* (Apr. 1, 1985), sect. D: 4.
Wasserstein discusses *Isn't It Romantic,* a comedy, she says, "born in anxiety." She wrote the play to help her understand her anxiety over the marriage of a girlfriend—"I was upset and couldn't understand why."

4030. *Los Angeles,* 29 (Dec. 1984): 54.
4031. Munk, Erica. *Village Voice* (Dec. 27, 1983): 109.
4032. *New York Theatre Critics' Reviews,* 44 (Dec. 12, 1983): 68-71.
4033. Nightingale, Benedict. *New York Times* (Jan. 1, 1984), sect. 2: H2, H14.
Reprinted in item 4971.
4034. Oliver, Edith. *The New Yorker,* 57 (June 22, 1981): 87.
Reprinted in item 4971.
4035. _____. *The New Yorker,* 59 (Dec. 26, 1983): 68.

4036. Richards, David. *Washington Post* (May 3, 1985): C1.
Richards briefly profiles Wasserstein during a run of *Isn't It Romantic* at the Arena Stage.

4037. Simon, John. *New York,* 14 (June 29, 1981): 36-37.
Reprinted in item 4971.
4038. _____. *New York,* 17 (Dec. 26, 1983-Jan. 2, 1984): 106.
4039. Sirkin, Elliot. *Nation,* 238 (Feb. 18, 1984): 200-202.
Reprinted in item 4971.
4040. Sullivan, Dan. *Los Angeles Times* (Oct. 30, 1984), sect. 6: 1.
4041. _____. *Los Angeles Times* (June 5, 1985), sect. 6: 1.
4042. *Village Voice* (June 17, 1981): 77.
4043. Watt, Douglas. *New York Daily News* (Dec. 16, 1983). Reprinted in item 4032.
4044. Wilson, Edwin. *Wall Street Journal* (July 24, 1981): 21.

The Man in the Case

4045. Gold, Sylviane. *Wall Street Journal* (Apr. 28, 1986): 22.
4046. Gussow, Mel. *New York Times* (Apr. 23, 1986): C15.
4047. Pellowe, Susan. *Plays International,* 2 (Aug. 1986): 43.
4048. Rogoff, Gordon. *Village Voice* (May 6, 1986): 96.
4049. Shewey, Don. *New York Times* (Aug. 25, 1985), sect. 2: 4, 26.
4050. _____. *New York Times* (Oct. 9, 1989): C13.

Miami

4051. Nemy, Enid. "Broadway." *New York Times* (June 1, 1984): C2.
Nemy announces Playwrights Horizons will stage *Miami* as a one-night-only performance.

4052. _____. "Broadway." *New York Times* (Jan. 3, 1986): C2.
Nemy briefly discusses the staging of Wasserstein's musical *Miami,* a work in progress.

Smart Women/Brilliant Choices

4053. *Drama-Logue* (July 14-20, 1988): 25.

Tender Offer

4054. Gussow, Mel. *New York Times* (June 1, 1983): C17.
4055. Massa, Robert. *Village Voice* (June 14, 1983): 100.
4056. Oliver, Edith. *The New Yorker,* 59 (June 13, 1983): 98.
Reprinted in item 4971.

Uncommon Women and Others

See item 16.

4057. *American Theatre Annual* 1977-1978, 95. Detroit: Gale Research Company, 1979.
4058. Beaufort, John. *Christian Science Monitor* (Nov. 30, 1977): 26.
Reprinted in item 4071.
4059. _____. *Christian Science Monitor* (Apr. 30, 1986): 24.

4060. Carlson, Susan L. "Comic Textures and Female
Communities 1937 and 1977: Clare Boothe and
Wendy Wasserstein." *Modern Drama,* 27, iv (Dec.
1984): 564-573.
Carlson examines Boothe's *The Women* and
Wasserstein's *Uncommon Women and Others* to
uncover sexist assumptions about comedy,
especially in respect to the depiction of female
characters. Although both plays revolve around
women, they differ in their dramatic effect because
of the playwrights' manipulation of comedy. In
Boothe's work, Carlson argues, the brittleness,
bitterness, and the fragmented female community
results from the playwright's entrapment with
traditional assumptions associated with the
portrayal of women in comedy. Whereas
Wasserstein's drama "shows how a comedy full of
women no longer needs to be a bitter dead end."
Wasserstein breaks through the patriarchal
assumptions of comedy to dramatize a female
community that "nurtures faith, concern, and warm,
easy laughter."

4061. Clurman, Harold. *Nation,* 225 (Dec. 17, 1977): 667-668.
4062. Drake, Sylvie. *Los Angeles Times* (Dec. 20, 1979), sect. 4:
31, 32.
4063. Eder, Richard. *New York Times* (Nov. 22, 1977): 48.
Reprinted in item 4071.
4064. Fox, Terry Curtis. *Village Voice* (Dec. 5, 1977): 85-86.
4065. Kalem, T.E. *Time,* 110 (Dec. 5, 1977): 111.
Reprinted in item 4071.
4066. Kroll, Jack. *Newsweek,* 153 (Mar. 20, 1989): 76-77.
4067. Loney, Glenn. *After Dark,* 10 (Feb. 1978): 25-26.
4068. *Los Angeles,* 12 (Mar. 1980): 21.
4069. Mahoney, John C. *Los Angeles Times* (Feb. 1, 1980),
sect. 5: 14.
4070. Moore, Honor. *Ms.* 6 (Dec. 1977): 37-38.
4071. *New York Theater Critics' Reviews,* 38 (Nov. 28-Dec. 4,
1977): 138-142.

4072. "Pulitzer Prize Winners." *New York Times* (Mar. 31,
1989): B4.

The *Times* reports Wasserstein's *The Heidi Chronicles* won the Pulitzer Prize for drama.

4073. Newton, Edmund. *New York Post* (Nov. 22, 1977): 22.
Reprinted in item 4071.

4074. Oliver, Edith. *The New Yorker*, 53 (Dec. 5, 1977): 115.

4075. "Sex and the Theater: Doing What Comes Naturally."
Dramatists Guild Quarterly, 17, iii (Autumn 1980): 22-33.
Wendy Wasserstein and Eve Merriam join other playwrights in a discussion of sex: how they chose to approach the theme of sexual relations, the problems encountered in production, and how they deal with critics and spectators. Regarding *Uncommon Women and Others*, Wasserstein says critics' assumptions about women talking about sex color their response to her characters— "Inevitably [critics] would say women don't talk this way." Merriam expresses her frustration with actors who refused to recite certain lines from her play *Inner City*.

4076. Sullivan, Dan. *Los Angeles Times* (Aug. 14, 1977), Calendar sect.: 62.

4077. Simon, John. *New York*, 10 (Dec. 12, 1977): 103.

4078. *Variety* (June 17, 1981): 84.

4079. Von Buchou, Stephanie. *San Francisco*, 21 (Jan. 1979): 10.

4080. "Uncommon Play, Uncommonly, Has No Parts For Men."
New York Times (Mar. 12, 1989): 51.
The *Times* announces the Dramatic Society of Stern College for Women will be staging a production of *Uncommon Women and Others*, beginning March 16, 1989.

4081. Watt, Douglas. *New York Daily News* (Nov. 22, 1977): 139.
Reprinted in item 4071.

Watson, Ara

>   **Selected Plays**

4082.   *Bite The Hand* (Ensemble Studio Theatre, 1984)
>   Playscript: *Bite the Hand* and *Mooncastle: Two
>   Short Plays.* New York: Dramatists Play Service,
>   1985.
4083.   *A Different Moon* (WPA Theater, 1983)
>   Playscript: *A Different Moon.* New York:
>   Dramatists Play Service, 1983.
4084.   *The Duck Pond* (Actors Theatre of Louisville, Kentucky,
>   1980-1981)
4085.   *In Between Time* (Actors Theatre of Louisville, Kentucky,
>   1981-1982)
4086.   *Just a Little Hiccup on the Road* (Actors Theatre of
>   Louisville, Kentucky, 1984-1985)
4087.   *Mooncastle*
>   Playscript: see item 4082.
4088.   *Scarecrows* (1986)
4089.   *Treasure Island* (adapted from Robert Louis Stevenson,
>   Cincinnati Playhouse in the Park, 1989)
>   Playscript: *Treasure Island.* New York: Dramatists
>   Play Service.
4090.   *Win/Lose/Draw*
>   See **Gallagher, Mary**

>   **Reviews**

>   *Bite the Hand*

4091.   Arkatov, Janice. "Playwright Returns to One-Act Route."
>   *Los Angeles Times* (June 26, 1988), Calendar
>   sect.: 48.
>   Watson talks about her one-act *Bite the Hand,*
>   which joins one other one-act, Michael Chieffo's
>   *Winning* at the Ensemble Studio Theatre. The
>   playwright enjoys working with the one-act format,
>   "it's a way to tell a story in a precise way that's
>   also very rich." Watson views herself as a writer of
>   women not a "woman's writer." Although she
>   acknowledges her female sensibility, she does not

want "to exclude men." But she feels the
experiences of women are as stageworthy as the
stories men write about, "men need to let us have
our say."

4092. Gussow, Mel. *New York Times* (May 8, 1984): C15.

A Different Moon

4093. Rich, Frank. *New York Times* (Feb. 18, 1983): C3.

Final Placement

See items 1272-1285.

4094. Novick, Julius. *Village Voice* (May 27-June 2, 1981): 90.

Scarecrows

4095. Christiansen, Richard. *Chicago Tribune* (Feb. 19, 1986),
          sect. 2: 8.

Special Family Things

See **Gallager, Mary**

Win/Lose/Draw

See **Gallagher, Mary**

Wendkos, Gina

Selected Plays

4096. *Blue Blood* (P.S. 1, 1982)
4097. *Boys and Girls/Men and Women* (Odyssey Theatre
          Ensemble, 1987)
4098. *Boy's Breath* (La Mama ETC, 1984)
4099. *Dinosaurs* (Cast Theatre, Los Angeles, 1988)
4100. *Four Corners* (with Donna Bond, American Place Theater,
          1985)
4101. *A Gang of Girls* (Cast Theatre, 1988)

4102. *Ginger Ale Afternoon* (Cast Theatre, Hollywood, 1988-
       1989)
4103. *Personality* (with Ellen Ratner, Women's Project, American
       Place Theater, 1986)
       Playscript: *Women Heroes: Six Short Plays from
       the Women's Project,* 25-37. New York: Applause,
       1989.

Profiles and Interviews

4104. Squire, Susan. "Portrait of the Artist as a Young Operator."
       Los Angeles Times Magazine (Dec. 18, 1988): 33-
       36, 48, 54.
       Squire chronicles Wendkos's achievements in
       Hollywood after being "whooshed . . . out of New
       York experimental theater." She claims she left
       New York because its theatrical community fails to
       encourage its playwrights to "flex muscle."
       Although the piece focuses on Wendkos's current
       work in film and television, her early years in New
       York's avant-garde is profiled as well as the genesis
       of her first play *Four Corners.*

Reviews

Blue Blood

4105. Shank, Theodore. *Drama Review,* 27 (Spring 1983): 103-
       105.

Boys and Girls/Men and Women

4106. Arkatov, Janice. *Los Angeles Times* (Oct. 18, 1987),
       Calendar sect.: 59.

4107. _____. "This Playwright Plays Her Personal Cards." *Los
       Angeles Times* (Sep. 21, 1987), sect. 5: 8.
       Wendkos talks about her play *Boys and Girls/Men
       and Women,* playing at the Odyssey, which is
       about a young girl "not being very strong and
       needing a male figure." Following Wendkos's

comments on the play, Arkatov briefly profiles the playwright's professional career.

Boy's Breath

4108. Drake, Sylvie. *Los Angeles Times* (Sep. 4, 1987), sect. 6: 15.
4109. Dunning, Jennifer. *New York Times* (Jan. 22, 1984): 42.
4110. Grubb, Kevin. *Dance Magazine*, 58 (April 1984): 87.
4111. Weiner, Bernard. *San Francisco Chronicle* (Aug. 12, 1983): 66.

Dinosaurs

4112. Arkatov, Janice. "Jealousy Among the Artists in *Dinosaurs.*" *Los Angeles Times* (Feb. 21, 1988), Calendar sect.: 48.
Arkatov announces Wendkos's new play, *Dinosaurs,* will open on Tuesday at the Cast Theatre. As in the past, Wendkos draws from her personal experience in creating this play about artists confronting life once they leave art school.

4113. *Drama-Logue* (Mar. 3-9, 1988): 9.

Four Corners

4114. Ellis, Kirk. *Los Angeles Times* (Aug. 7, 1985), sect. 6 : 5.
4115. Gussow, Mel. *New York Times* (Feb. 11, 1985): C17.
4116. Solomon, Alisa. *Village Voice* (Feb. 19, 1985): 105-106.

A Gang of Girls

4117. Drake, Sylvie. *Los Angeles Times* (May 28, 1988), sect. 6: 9.

Ginger Ale Afternoon

4118. *Drama-Logue* (Apr. 28-May 4, 1988): 22.

Personality

4119.　*Drama-Logue* (Sep. 24-30, 1987): 8.
4120.　Ellis, Kirk. *Los Angeles Times* (Aug. 7, 1985), sect. 6: 5.
4121.　Weiner, Bernard. *San Francisco Chronicle* (Aug. 16, 1986):
　　　　37.

Willis, Jane

Selected Plays

4122.　*Men Without Dates* (Ensemble Studio Theater, 1985)
　　　　Playscript: *Men Without Dates* and *Slam!: Two
　　　　One-Act Plays*. New York: Dramatists Play
　　　　Service, 1985.
4123.　*Slam!* (Ensemble Studio Theater, 1984)
　　　　Playscript: *The Best Short Plays 1986*. Edited by
　　　　Ramon Delgado, 107-121. New York: Applause,
　　　　1986; see item 4122.

Profiles

See item 4123.

Reviews

Men Without Dates

4124.　Feingold, Michael. *Village Voice* (May 28, 1985): 107.
4125.　Oliver, Edith. *The New Yorker*, 61 (June 3, 1985): 114-115.
4126.　Rich, Frank. *New York Times* (May 16, 1985): C23.

Slam!

4127.　Gussow, Mel. *New York Times* (May 5, 1984): 15.
4128.　*Drama-Logue* (Feb. 8, 1989): 9

Wolff, Ruth

Selected Plays

4129.　*The Abdication* (Bristol Old Vic, 1971)
　　　　Playscript: see item 73.
4130.　*Arabic Two* (New Theatre Workshop, 1969)

4131. *Eden Again* (Kennedy Center, Washington D.C., 1976)
4132. *Eleanor of Aquitaine* (staged reading, Playwrights Horizons)
4133. *Empress of China* (Pan Asian Repertory Theatre, 1984)
      Playscript: *Empress of China.* New York:
      Broadway Play Publishing, 1986.
4134. *Folly Cove* (O'Neill Theatre Center National Playwrights'
      Conference, 1968)
4135. *The Golem* (adaptation of H. Leivick's play, St. Mark's
      Playhouse, 1959)
4136. *The Perfect Marriage* (1983)
4137. *Sarah in America* (Kennedy Center, Washington D.C.,
      1981)
4138. *Still Life With Apples* (O'Neill Theatre Center National
      Playwrights' Conference, 1968)

Profiles

See item 73.

4139. *Contemporary Theatre, Film, and Televison.* Volume 2.
      Edited by Monica M. O'Donnell, 346. Detroit:
      Gale Research Inc., 1986.
      This brief biographical sketch includes a list of
      Wolff's works and productions.

Reviews

The Abdication

See 10, 73.

4140. Billington, Michael. *Times* (London) (Jun. 2, 1971): 6g.
4141. Christiansen, Richard. *Chicago Tribune* (Oct. 23, 1981),
      sect. 4: 3.
4142. Von Buchou, Stephanie. *San Francisco*, 21 (Apr. 1979): 10-
      11.
4143. Weiner, Bernard. *San Francisco Chronicle* (Feb. 9, 1979):
      57.

4144. Wolff, Ruth. "We Open In Florence." *New York Times
      Magazine* (Dec. 4, 1977): 50.

Wolff discusses the staging of *The Abdication* in Italy.

Empress of China

4145. Blumenthal, Eileen. *Village Voice* (May 8, 1984): 82.
4146. Gussow, Mel. *New York Times* (Apr. 28, 1984): 12.
4147. *Variety* (Nov. 7, 1984): 102.
4148. Weiner, Bernard. *San Francisco Chronicle* (Feb. 9, 1979): 57.

The Golem

4149. Gelb, Arthur. *New York Times* (Feb. 26, 1959): 38.

Sarah in America

4150. Corry, John. "Broadway." *New York Times* (Feb. 13, 1981), sect. 3: C2.
      Announces *Sarah in America* will not be performed on Broadway because of the negative reviews the play received at the Kennedy Center in Washington D.C.

4151. *Drama-Logue* (June 15-21, 1989): 9.
4152. Sullivan, Dan. *Los Angeles Times* (June 13, 1989), sect. 6: 1.
4153. Wilson, Edwin. *Wall Street Journal* (Feb. 26, 1981): 26.
4154. *Variety* (Feb. 11, 1981): 126.
4155. *Variety* (June 21-27, 1989): 62.

Yamauchi, Wakako

Selected Plays

4156. *And the Soul Shall Dance* (La Mama ETC, 1979)
      Playscript: *West Coast Plays*, 11/12 (Winter/Spring, 1982): 117-163.
4157. *The Chairman's Wife* (East West Players, Los Angeles, 1990)
4158. *The Face Box* (Pan Asian Repertory Theater, 1984)
4159. *Memento* (East West Players, Los Angeles, 1986)

4160. *The Music Lessons* (Public Theatre, 1980)

Profiles and Interviews

See items 1, 8 and page 19.

4161. Arkatov, Janice "The Soul and the Playwright Shall Dance."
Los Angeles Times (Feb. 8, 1986), sect. 5: 3.
Yamauchi talks with Arkatov on the eve of the
opening of her play *Memento* by the East West
Players. Of this play, Yamauchi remarks that it is
"moody" and "deals with love, passion, jealousy."
Although the playwright has been writing short
stories for many years, she began writing plays late
in life. Her first play *And the Soul Shall Dance*,
mounted at East West in 1979, was based on one of
her short stories. Much of her writing recalls her
experiences living in Japanese internment camps
during World War II. "Sure, it's painful to
remember . . . it's part of what made me what I am,
what makes me think the way I do."

4162. Dean, James F. "Interview with Mako: The East West
Players." *West Coast Plays*, 11/12 (Winter/Spring
1982): 186-193.
Mako, artistic director of the East West Players,
talks briefly about Yamauchi's plays.

4163. "9 Playwrights Win Rockefeller Grant." *New York Times*
(Apr. 27, 1980): 70.
The *Times* reports that several playwrights,
including Yamauchi, won Rockefeller Foundation
Playwrights in Residence awards.

4164. Yamauchi, Wakako. "Surviving Wasteland Years." *Christian
Science Monitor* (Nov. 8, 1988): 30.
The playwright recalls her family's experiences
while confined to a Japanese internment camp
during World War II.

Reviews

And The Soul Shall Dance

4165. Corry, John. *New York Times* (June 30, 1979): 8.
4166. Novick, Julius. *Village Voice* (July 9, 1979): 73-74.

The Chairman's Wife

4167. Jonas, Larry. *Drama-Logue* (Feb. 8-14, 1990): 8.
4168. Loynd, Ray. *Los Angeles Times* (Jan. 23, 1990), sect. F: 1.

4169. Shirley, Don. *Los Angeles Times* (July 6, 1989), sect. 6: 5.
       Shirley announces the season for the East West Players. He reports *The Chairman's Wife* will open January 17, 1990.

The Face Box

4170. Gussow, Mel. *New York Times* (Mar. 4, 1984): 49.
4171. Stone, Laurie. *Village Voice* (Mar. 13, 1984): 82.

The Memento

4172. Sullivan, Dan. *Los Angeles Times* (Feb. 17, 1986), sect. 5: 1.

The Music Lessons

4173. Gussow, Mel. *New York Times* (May 16, 1980): C5.
4174. Sullivan, Dan. *Los Angeles Times* (Mar. 16, 1985), sect. 5: 1.

Yankowitz, Susan

Selected Plays

4175. *Alarms* (Monstrous Regiment, Riverside Studios, London, 1987)
4176. *America Piece* (Provisional Theatre, Los Angeles, 1974)

4177. *Baby* (with Sybille Pearson, Ethel Barrymore Theatre, 1983)
4178. *Boxes* (Magic Theater, Berkeley, 1972)
4179. *The Cage* (Omar Khayyam Cafe, 1965)
   Playscript: *Playwrights for Tomorrow*. Volume 11. Edited Arthur H. Ballet, 7-35. Minneapolis: University of Minnesota Press, 1973.
4180. *The Ha-Ha Play* (Cubiculo, 1970)
   Playtext: *Scripts*, 10 (Oct. 1972): 81-105.
4181. *A Knife in the Heart* (Williamstown Theatre Festival, Williamstown, 1984)
4182. *The Lamb* (Academy Theatre, Atlanta, 1973)
4183. *Nightmare* (Yale University, New Haven, 1967)
4184. *The Old Rock-a-Bye* (Cooper Square Arts Theatre, 1968)
4185. *Positions* (Westbeth Playwrights' Feminist Collective, 1972)
4186. *Qui Est Anna Marks* (TEP Theater, Paris, 1979)
4187. *Slaughterhouse Play* (Public Theatre, 1971)
   Playscript: *Yale/Theater*, 2, ii (1969). *New American Plays*. Volume 4. Edited by William Hoffman, 1-70. New York: Hill/Wang, 1971.
4188. *Still Life* (Interart, 1977)
4189. *Terminal* (text by Yankowitz, Open Theater, 1970)
   Playscript: *Scripts*, 1 (Nov. 1971): 17-45; *Three Works by the Open Theater*. Edited by Karen Malpede, 38-91. New York: Drama Book Specialists, 1974; Arthur Sainer. *The Radical Theatre Notebook*, 107-145. New York: Avon, 1975.
4190. *Transplant* (Omaha Magic Theatre, Omaha, 1971)
4191. *True Romances* (Mark Taper Forum, Los Angeles, 1978)
4192. *Who Done It* (Interart, 1982)
4193. *Wicked Women Revue* (collaborator, Westbeth Playwrights' Feminist Collective, 1973)
4194. *Wooden Nickels* (Theater for the New City, 1973)

Profiles

See item 9.

4195. Anderson, Frances. *Contemporary Dramatists*. Third edition.
       Edited by James Vinson, 585-586. New York: St.
       Martin's Press, 1982.
       Anderson provides general critical comments on
       Yankowitz's work as well as a list of her plays.

4196. *Contemporary Authors: A Bio-Bibliographical Guide*.
       Volume 17. New Revised Series. Edited by Linda
       Metzger, 495-96. Detroit: Gale Research Company,
       1986.
       The entry includes a brief biography and a list of
       Yankowitz's plays.

4197. *Contemporary Theatre, Film, and Televison*. Volume 1.
       Edited by Monica M. O'Donnell, 524. Detroit:
       Gale Research Inc., 1984.
       The entry provides a biographical sketch as well as
       a list of the playwright's works.

Reviews

Alarms

4198. Dace, Tish. *Plays International*, 2 (July 1987): 38-39.
4199. _____. *Women & Performance*, 3, iii (1987/1988): 188-
       191.
4200. Kendall. K. *Women's Review of Books*, 4 (July/Aug.1987):
       22-23.
4201. Kingston, Jeremy. *Times* (London) (Feb. 7, 1987): 18f.
4202. Langton, Robert. *Plays and Players*, 403 (Apr. 1987): 23-
       24.
4203. Ray, Robin. *Punch*, 292 (Feb. 18, 1987): 64.

American Piece

4204. Sullivan, Dan. *Los Angeles Times* (Oct. 1, 1974), sect. 4:
       1.

Baby

See **Pearson, Sybille**

A Knife In The Heart

4205. Baker, Rob. "Country Calm & Theatrical Flurry." *Theatre
        Communications* (Nov. 1983): 8-11.
        Baker includes in his discussion of the
        Williamstown Theatre Festival Yankowitz's *A
        Knife in the Heart*, staged at the Festival in 1983.
        Apparently many were surprised, including
        Yankowitz, when Psacharopoulos (aritistic director)
        selected the play for a mainstage production because
        it did not seem "like his kind of play."

4206. Rich, Frank. *New York Times* (Aug. 1, 1982), sect. 2: H1,
        H4.

4207. Stone, Laurie. *Village Voice* (Aug. 30, 1983): 97.

4208. Swan, Christopher. *Christian Science Monitor* (Aug. 8,
        1983): 16.

4209. *Variety* (Sep. 7, 1983): 84.

Terminal

4210. Croyden, Margaret. *New York Times* (Mar. 29, 1970),
        sect. 2: 1.
        This preview article focuses on Joseph Chaikin,
        director of Open Theatre, and his production of
        Terminal.

4211. *Gambit*, 5 (1970): 66-67.

4212. Gussow, Mel. *New York Times* (Apr. 15, 1970): 51.

4213. Kerr, Walter. *New York Times* (May 24, 1970), sect. 2: 3.

4214. Sainer, Arthur. "The Open Theatre." In *Radical Theater
        Notebook*, 147-153. New York: Avon, 1975.
        Sainer interviews Susan Yankowitz, who succeeded
        Marc Kaminsky and Nancy Fales Garrett among
        others in working on *Terminal*. Yankowitz talks
        about how the experience of working with an
        ensemble influenced her as a writer. On the one
        hand, working with a group makes it easier for a
        writer to explore areas that are "too painful"
        because the "fears are shared." However,
        Yankowitz found the collective restrictive because

she lacked total artistic control, "[at] times . . . I felt compromised by leaving in a speech I no longer liked or by eliminating one I thought important." Yankowitz also discusses specific examples of how the theatre group participated in developing the script.

Author Index

The following index lists authors of annotated entries, including authors discussed in the bibliographical essay. Unless specified, the numbers refer to **item** numbers.

Abramson, Doris E., 548
Adler, Thomas, 2831
Alarcon, Norma, 2626
Albright, William, 2182
Alvarez, Lynn, 174
Anderson, Frances, 4195
Anderson, Mary Louise, 587
Arkatov, Janice, 148, 205, 218, 620, 1158, 1966, 2551, 2552, 2569, 2570, 2571, 2832, 2943, 3495, 3516, 4013, 4091, 4112, 4161
Arnold, Stephanie, 1, page 11
Asahina, Robert, 3844
Atchity, Kenneth, 1311
Aucoin, Don, 1932
Austin, Gayle, 3, 4, 549, 1115, 2244
Bachrach, Judy, 3793
Backes, Nancy, 1780
Baker, Rob, 3884, 4204
Banich, Judith, 4670
Barlow, Judith E., 1749, 1750, 1781
Barnes, Clive, 404
Barr, Donald J., 2700
Barranger, Milly, 5
Barron, Elizabeth Anne, 3771
Beauford, Fred, 1191
Bell-Metereau, Rebecca, 115, 3758
Bender, Marilyn, 2153

Bennathan, Joss, 3759
Bennetts, Leslie, 7, 1751, 2327, 2669, 3950
Benston, Kimberly W., 2011
Bent, Ted, 1552
Berg, Beatrice, 738, 3286
Berkowitz, Gerald M., 3845
Berkvist, Robert, 781, 1553
Berson, Misha, 8, 2026, page 11
Betsko, Kathleen, 9, page 10, 13
Bigsby, C.W.E., 2665, page 10
Billman, Carol, 10
Binder, Wolfgang, 1997
Blackwell, Henry, 3308
Blau, Eleanor, 2944, 3041
Blau, Herbert, 2027
Bloom, Lynn Z., 187
Bosworth, Patricia, 3039
Brater, Enoch, 11
Brenson, Michael, 1752
Breslauer, Jan, 2315, 3825
Brockett, Oscar G., page 4
Brown, Janet, 12, pages 6-9
Brown, Patricia Leigh, 1934
Brown-Guillory, Elizabeth, 13, 507, 590, 3309, page 15
Brunner, Cornelia, 3559
Brustein, Robert, 2740
Buckley, Peter, 1554
Buckley, Tom, 3310
Bullins, Ed, page 10
Butruille, Susan G., 2704
Byers-Pevitts, Beverly, 16
Calloway, Earl, 409, 3355
Calta, Louis, 302, 1489, 1958, 3865
Carlson, Susan L., 18, 4060
Carranza, Ruth, 101
Case, Sue-Ellen, 19, 20, pages 8-9, 11-12
Castellano, Olivia, 3087
Catenra, Linda Brandi, 287
Chaudhuri, Una, pages 9, 12-13
Chaillet, Ned, 121
Childress, Alice, 508, 509, 563, 591, pages 4-5, 10, 14
Chinoy, Helen Krich, 21, page 13

Christ, Carol P., 3364
Christiansen, Richard, 753
Christon, Lawrence, 739, 888, 2233
Clayborne, Jon L., 3177
Cody, Gabrielle, pages 11-12
Cohen, Esther, 3951
Cohen, Ron, 2741
Cohn, Ruby, 22
Coleman, Wanda, 334
Considine, Shaun, 3311
Copland, Roger, 139
Coppage, Judith Ann, 3772
Corliss, Richard, 1557
Cornwell, Anita, 3169
Corry, John, 3056, 4150
Coss, Clare, 703, 704
Couch, William, page 10
Crane, Gladys, page 9
Croon, Diana Y. 1724
Crouch, Paula, 818, 819, 2841
Croyden, Margaret, 2635, 4210
Cummings, Scott, 1064, 1065
Curb, Rosemary K., 23, 512, 566, 1203, 2013, 3173, page 6
Dace, Tish, 443
Daniel, Lanelle, 2317
Daniels, Mary, 3761
Dasgupta, Gautam, 67, 1066, 1104
Davis, Tracy C., page 7
Dean, James F., 4162
Demastes, William W., 1598
DeShazer, Mary K., 3365
DeVries, Hilary, 2745
Dewey, Janice, 3088
Di Scipio, Giuseppe Carlo, 304
Diamond, Elin, 24, 2000, 2001, 3773
Dickerson, Glenda, 25
Dillon, John, 567
Dodds, Richard, 3955
Dodson, Owen, 2030
Dolan, Jill, 26-30, pages 8-9, 12-13
Dong, Stella, 3314
Downey, Maureen, 513

Drake, Sylvie, 117, 123, 206, 1068, 1381,1559, 1560, 2593, 2746, 3956
Drexler, Roslyn, 970
Durham, Ayne C., 1561
Dworkin, Susan, 742
Egan, Timothy, 3976
Ellenberger, Harriet, 31
Elliot, Jeffrey, 3373
Erben, Rudolf, 2822
Erstein, Hap, 3115
Escarpenter, Jose, 3102
Eustis, Oskar, 2285
Fabre, Genevieve, 592, page 10
Feral, Josette, 32
Fernandez, Enrique, 3199
Ferris, Lesley, 2513
Fisher, Berenice, 34
Flatley, Guy, 1471
Fletcher, Winona, 2031
Flowers, Gwendolyn, 3394
Flowers, Sandra Hollin, 3375
Forman, Robert J., 2747
Fornes, Maria Irene, 1073
Forte, Jeanie, 35
Frankel, Haskel, 254
Fraser, C. Gerald, 3340
Freedman, Samuel G., 36, 291, 2117, 3043
Freydberg, Elizabeth Hadley, 37, page 15
Fuchs, Elinor, 124, page 12
Funke, Phyllis, 3315
Futterman, Ellen, 3316
Gagen, Jean, 1603
Gagnard, Frank, 2436
Gardner, Sandra, 3266
Garson, Barbara, 1306
Garza, Roberto J., 3083, page 16
Geis, Deborah, 3376
Gerard, Jeremy, 126, 1788
Gillespie, Ann, 3317
Gillespie, Patti, 38, 39, 40, 3957, pages 3-7
Ginsberg, Elaine, 41
Glaze, Linda S., 3102

Goetz, Ruth, 42
Gold, Sylviane, 3958
Goldemberg, Rose Leiman, 1431
Gonzales, Yolanda Broyles, 43
Gonzalez, Gloria, 1457, 1458, 1459
Gonzalez, Laverne, 3089
Goodman, Dean, 44
Gorfinkle, Constance, 2905
Gornick, Vivian, 2156, page 13
Gossett, Hattie, 3127
Gottfried, Martin, 2454
Goulianos, A., 45
Gray, Amlin, 28
Green, Stanley, 743
Greene, Alexis, 47, 728
Griffin, Rita, 416
Gross, Amy, 2850
Grossman, Samuel Larry, 49
Guerra, Jonnie, 1606
Gussow, Mel, 48, 535, 783, 1608, 2172, 2749, 3148, 3336,
         3582, 3978, page 5
Guthmann, Edward, 3496
Haller, Scot, 1562
Hamilton, Camille, 1733
Harbin, Billy J., 1610
Hargrove, Nancy D., 1609
Harmetz, Aljean, 2852
Harriet Kriegel, page 4
Harriot, Esther, 2907
Harris, Jessica B., 1921
Harris, Laurilyn J., 1679
Harris, William, 127
Hart, Lynda, 64, 2093, 3762, page 8
Hay, Samuel A., 553
Hayes, Donald, 3383
Helle, Anita Plath, 1438
Henry, William A., 3198
Herman, Willian, 50
Herrera-Sobek, Maria, 2627
Hewson, David, 761
Hill, Errol, page 10
Hirsch, Foster, 838

Hoffman, Tess, 2750
Holden, Stephen, 470
Honigberg, Nadine, 51
Hubert, Linda L., 839, 2751
Huerta, Jorge A. 3096, page 11
Hunter, Charlayne, 1194
Hurley, Joseph, 1949
Hynes, Jo, 3763
Iko, Momoko, 1858
Isenberg, Barbara, 2856
Jacker, Corinne, 52
Jacobs, Susan, 2488
Jalon, Allan, 3984
Jenkins, Linda Walsh, 21, 53, page 9
Jenner, C. Lee, 3511
Johnston, Laurie, 253
Jones, John, 1563
Jordan, June, 3319
Kalamu ya Salaam, 3170
Kalb, Jonathan, 118
Kane, Leslie, 2858
Kanellos, Nicolas, 3096, page 11
Kaufman, Joanne, 3959
Kennedy, Adrienne, 2003, 2004, 2005
Kevles, Barbara, 3290
Keyssar, Helen, 54, 55, 2589, 3825, 4725, pages 7-9
Killens, John O., 554
Killian, Linda, page 6
King, Anne Mills, 3320
King, Woodie, page 10
Kingsbury, Marty, 56
Kinser, Jerry, 1564
Kleiman, Carol, 744
Kleiman, Dena, 1267
Klein, Alvin, 445, 1401
Klein, Kathleen Gregory, 3776
Klementowski, Nancy, 674
Klemesrud, Judy, 745, 2752
Koehler, Robert, 2788
Koenenn, Joseph C., 3335
Koenig, Rachel, 9
Kolin, Philip C., 2317

Kourilsky, Francoise, page 5
Krebs, Alvin, 3268
Kuchwara, Michael, 4029
Kuftinec, Sonja, 674
Kuhn, John, 1070
Kullman, Colby H., 1565
Kushner, Tony, 1249
La Tempa, Susan, page 4
Lafler, J.W., page 8
Lamb, Margaret, 57, page 3
Lamont, Rosette C., 989, 2310, page 8
Landau, Penny M., 446
Larson, James Wallace, 3774
Latour, Martine, 3321
Lauerman, Connie, 3322
Laughlin, Karen L., 1621, 3764, pages 7-8
Lauretis, Teresa de, page 12
Lauro, Shirley, 3093
Lawson, Carol, 373, 374, 1705, 1979, 2916, 3047, 3627
Leavitt, Dinah L., 58, 3765, pages 7, 13
Lee, Catharine Carr, 3323
Leonard, William Torbert, 2618, 3868, 3911
Lesem, Jeanne, 2418
Lester, Eleanor, 2977
Levin, Toby, 3394
Levine, Jo Ann, 3324
Lewis, Barbara, 59, 3325, 3395
Lewis, Peter, 1338
Lombardi, John, 3960
Lomeli, Francisco A., 2624
Lopate, Phillip, 3989
Lovenheim, Barbara, 863
Low, Lisa, 3990
Lowell, Sondra, 60
Loynd, Ray, 448
Lutenbacher, Cindy, 61
Lyons, Brenda, 3326
McDermott, Kate, page 12
MacDonald, Erik L., 62
Mael, Phyllis, 63, 1497
Malm, Linda, 2455
Malnig, Julie, 66

Malpede, Karen, 65, 3204
Marranca, Bonnie, 67, 1071, 1104, 1154
Maryan, Charles, 3292
Mason, Clifford, 366
Mason, Louise Cheryl, 68
Mason, Susan, 2315
McDonnell, Lisa J.,1566, 1622
McNaughton, Howard, 971
Meserve, Walter J., 69, pages 5-6, 9
Michaelson, Judith, 70
Middlebrook, Diane Wood, 3293
Miles, Julia, 71, page 5
Miller, Jeanne-Marie A. 72, 2016, 3398
Miller, Mary Ellen, 2753
Miner, Madonne, 2798
Mitchell, Carolyn, 3400
Mitchell, Loften, 518
Mitgang, Herbert, 905
Molette, Barbara, 576
Moore, Honor, 73, 74
Morrow, Laura, 1627, 2870
Morrow, Lee Alan, 75
Mullener, Elizabeth, 1568
Munk, Erica, 3451
Murray, James P., 1213
Murray, Timothy, 2801, 2991
Narvaez, Alfonso A., 3403
Natalle, Elizabeth, 76, pages 7-8, 13
Nellhaus, Arlynn, 923
Nemy, Enid, 2318, 4051
Newman, Jill, 3185
Njeri, Itabari, 1725
Nordheimer, Jon, 3107
Norman, Marsha, 2754, 2755
Novoa, Bruce, 3085
O'Malley, Lurana Donnels, 1096
O'Rourke, Joyce Williams, 79
Osborn, Elizabeth, page 11
O'Steen, Kathleen, 621
Olauson, Judith, 78, page 7
Overbeck, Lois More, 2006
Owens, Rochelle, 2978

Pall, Ellen, 3634
Parr, Carmen Salazar, 3092
Patraka, Vivian, 80, 4143, 3243, 3248
Peters, Erskine, 3409
Peterson, Bernard L., 189, 367, 478, 516, 643, 873, 1197, 1366, 1472, 1915, 2007, 2239, 2419, 3076, 3171, 3327, 3921
Pike, Frank, 75
Pinkston, Alex, 3770
Prida, Delores, 3104
Primus, Francesca, 81, 82
Rahman, Aishah, 3128
Ramirez, Arthur, 3093
Ramsey, Priscilla R., 874
Rea, Charlotte, 84
Reich, Howard, 769
Reinhardt, Nancy S., 85, page 6
Reston, James, 2369
Ribowsky, Mark, 3412
Richards, David, 2347, 4036
Richards, Sandra L., 3328, 3414
Roberts, Vera Mowry, 86
Robertson, Nan, 1461, 2200, 3995
Robinson, Alice M., 87
Robinson, Harlow, 2637
Rochlin, Margy, 1569
Rodriguez, Alfonso, 3094
Rose, Phyllis Jane, 88, 3766
Rosenfeld, Megan, 133, 230, 240, 289
Roth, Martha, 89
Rothstein, Mervyn, 90, 1931, 3961, 3998
Rushing, Andrea Benton, 3417
Ryzuk, Mary S., 911, 1897
Sainer, Arthur, 290, 4214
Salinas, Judy, 3095
Sanchez, Sonia, 3172, 3190
Sanchez-Scott, Milcha, 3200
Sanders, Leslie Catharine, page 10
Sandoval, Alberto, 3109
Santiago, Chiori, 2210
Savran, David, 91
Scharine, Richard G., 2808
Schechner, Richard, 3775

Schechter, Joel, 1349
Schiff, Ellen, 2319
Schonberg, Harold C., 1415
Schroeder, Patricia R., 2102, 3962
Segal, Sondra, 703
Sessums, Kevin, 1571
Shange, Ntozake, 3329, 3418, 3419
Shank, Ted, 3519, 3521
Shapiro, Walter, 3963
Sharbutt, Jay, 256, 1572
Shepard, Richard F., 92, 1167, 2240, 2473
Sherbert, Linda, 820, 844
Shewey, Don, 93, 135, 1712, 2352
Shirley, Don, 157, 4169
Shragge, Elaine, 2979
Siegel, June, 94
Simo, Ana Maria, 3558
Simon, John, 1755
Sisley, Emily L., 95, page 12
Sklar, Roberta, 703
Smith, Karen Lynn, 368
Smith, Sid, 1102, 2355
Solomon, Alisa, 3804
Spencer, Jenny S., 2887
Splawn, P. Jane, 2021
Squire, Susan, 4104
Staples, Robert, 3422
Stasio, Marilyn, 2491
Steadman, Susan M. Flierl, 96
Steckling, D. Larry, 2320
Stein, Ruthe, 2052
Stern, Alan, 2727
Sterritt, David, 136
Stinson, Patricia, 2420
Stone, Elizabeth, 2756
Suntree, Susan, 97
Swados, Elizabeth, 3583
Swain, Elizabeth, 2077, 3964
Talbert, Linda Lee, 3427
Tapley, Mel, 3428
Tarbox, Lucia, 1573
Tate, Claudia, 98

Tatum, Charles M., 3097
Taylor, Willene Pulliam, 3175
Temple, Joanne, 99
Tener, Robert L., 2023
Terry, Megan, 3767, 3768, 3769
Thrall, Judy, 100
Thurston, Linda, 2135
Trader, Beverly, 821
Turner, Beth, 2042
Turner, Darwin T., 517, 559, 2042
Turner, S.H. Regina, 101
Umrani, Munir, 3331
Van Dyke, Joyce, pages 8-9
Vowell, Faye Nell, 3086
Wagner, Phyllis Jane, 3786
Waldman, Gloria F., 3103
Walker, Barbara, 3187
Walker, Lou Ann, 1757
Wallach, Allan, 2759
Watson, Kenneth, 3332
Watson-Espener, Maida, page 11
Weales, Gerald, 102
Weiner, Bernard, 1293, 1649, 1862, 2357, 3523, 3528
Westcott, Holly Mims, 2929
Wetzsteon, Ross, 1072, 1758, page 4
White, Miles, 369
Wilkerson, Margaret B., 77, 104, 2043, 2008, page 9
Williams, Mance, 370
Williams, V.A., 560
Wilson, Ann, 3250
Wilson, Edwin, 105, 1574
Winer, Laura, 2208
Winn, Steven, 1025, 1807, 2825
Wolfe, Irmgard H., 2760
Wolff, Ruth, 4144
Worthen, W.B., 1179
Wykoff, Peter C., 3334
Yamauchi, Wakako, 4164
Yarbro-Bejarano, Yvonne, 107, 108, 109, 2630
Zivanovic, Judith, 110
Zolotow, Sam, 1358, 2045

List of Multicultural Playwrights

African-Americans

Angelou, Maya
Carroll, Vinnette
Charles, Martie
Childress, Alice
Collins, Kathleen
DeVeaux, Alexis
Franklin, J.E.
Gibson, P.J.
Grant, Micki
Houston, Velina
Jackson, Elaine
Jones-Meadows, Karen
Kennedy, Adrienne
Lott, Karmyn
Mason, Judi Ann
Morrison, Toni
Perry, Shaunielle
Rahman, Aishah
Sanchez, Sonia
Shange, Ntozake
Walker, Celeste Colson

Asian-Americans

Faigao, Linda
Hagedorn, Jessica
Houston, Velina
Iko, Momoko

Yamauchi, Wakako

Hispanic Americans

Alvarez, Lynn
Chavez, Denise
Cruz, Migdalia
Fornes, Maria Irene
Gonzalez, Gloria
Loomer, Lisa
Moraga, Cherrie
Portillo-Trambley, Estela
Prida, Delores
Sanchez-Scott, Milcha
Simo, Ana Maria

Native American

Houston, Velina

ACS-4427

11/29/94

75-

PS
338
W6
2994
1993